IF ONE WERE TO WRITE A HISTORY...

WRITE A HISTORY...

Selected Writings

IF ONE WERE TO WRITE A HISTORY...

Selected Writings
by
Robert F. Harney

Edited by Pierre Anctil
and Bruno Ramirez

Multicultural History Society of Ontario
1991

The Multicultural History Society of Ontario is a resource centre on the campus of the University of Toronto. It was created in 1976 by a group of academics, civil servants, librarians, and archivists who saw a need for a special effort to preserve materials relevant to the province's immigrant and ethnic history. The Society receives support from the Ministry of Culture and Communications of the Province of Ontario, the Honourable Karen Haslam, Minister.

Canadian Cataloguing in Publication Data

Harney, Robert F., 1939–1989
    If one were to write a history—

(Studies in ethnic and immigration history)
Includes bibliographical references.
ISBN 0–919045-55-3

1. Canada – Emigration and immigration – History.
2. Immigrants – Canada – History. 3. Italy –
Emigration and immigration – History. 4. Italians –
Canada – History. 5. Italian Canadians – History.
6. Ethnicity – Canada.   I. Anctil, Pierre, 1952–
II. Ramirez, Bruno, 1942–   .   III. Multicultural
History Society of Ontario. IV. Title. V. Series.

JV7220.H37 1991   304.8'71   C 91–0985074–1

Published 1991

Design: Steve Eby

Printed and bound in Canada

Previously published essays in this volume are reproduced in the manner in which they originally appeared with the exception of minor factual and typographical errors that have been corrected.

Contents

III THE POLITICS OF ETHNIC RELATIONS

Preface

THE IMMIGRANT AS TEXT

Pierre Anctil

A researcher rarely has occasion for total immersion in the complete works of an author, particularly an academic. Scholarly writings, because of the very conditions under which they are produced, are frequently dispersed in learned journals, and readily take the form of scattered fragments, hardly accessible to the reader in a condensed and definitive form. This was very much the case for Robert F. Harney's *oeuvre*, which this book seeks to collate in a systematic, although not exhaustive manner. In fact, the articles brought together here span almost fifteen years in the career of an author, and cover a seemingly wide range of topics and interests that have little in common other than some connection to the broad field of immigration studies. At least that is the impression that a distracted reader may have *prima facie*, especially if the articles are approached initially as disorderly pieces, perhaps not absorbed in the chronological sequence originally intended, and scanned over several months or years.

If this collection of articles has any merit, it is to elevate Harney's scholarly writings to the level of an *ensemble*, whose cohesion and unity of purpose will become readily apparent, and will alleviate the sense of literary fragmentation that plagued his efforts to the very end. The author, as is well known and often regretted, did not find the energy or could not bring himself to produce a significant *monograph* that would have epitomized his contribution to the development of a historiography of Canadian immigration in this century. He attempted a book on the Italian community in the mid-1980s, but it was left in abeyance with only half the chapters completed. Two of these chapters, "If One Were to Write a History of Postwar Toronto Italia" and "Undoing the Risorgimento,"[1] are included in the present collection.

Apparently, the author conceived of his literary efforts as shards, perhaps later to be reconstituted into a complete theoretical object once

---

[1] A version of "Undoing the Risorgimento" will also appear in a special issue of the *Annali* of the Canadian Academic Centre in Italy (forthcoming).

the circumstances permitted. In the short term, certain institutional obstacles could not be easily surmounted by the author, whose commitment to the field of immigrant studies often had to take the form of intense lobbying vis-à-vis the state and academe. The vast ethnographic task to which Harney had dedicated himself in the seventies, mainly in the Italian *ethnie* of Toronto, soon proved itself to be a herculean endeavour that could not be achieved, or even begun single-handedly. While the vision remained intact, collaborators had to be recruited, a major research and archival institution had to be created from scratch—the Multicultural History Society of Ontario, founded in 1976—and a plan of action prepared. Although Harney remained at heart an ethnohistorian, new requirements and realities arose in the early 1980s that detoured his attention from the historiographic impulse of his earlier works.

One could argue that Harney, in fact, took upon himself the onerous task of becoming a mentor to an entire new generation of researchers, whom he inspired, spurred on, and often dispatched to specific junctures in the field. The eleven pieces of immigrant history contained in this collection of articles should thus, be perceived as many attempts at mapping a methodology and a global approach to the phenomena of Canadian urban ethnicity, each one devoted to a particular aspect or combination of factors, whether it be residential behaviour, the geography of migration, social relations and kinship patterns, cultural identities, and so forth.

Harney excelled, as should become evident from these texts, at defining an area of confluence between several disciplines, which he later enlarged by a systematic and programmatic thrust. To him, the field of ethnicity, because of its centrality in modern Canadian history, superseded considerations of disciplinary self-interest and could only emerge in the eyes of the academic establishments if certain artificial boundaries and limitations were laid aside once and for all. He was an historian in the classic sense of the term, but armed with the tools and presuppositions of a cultural relativist, determined as he was to surmount the cultural barriers and incomprehensions which kept immigrants and Canadian-born citizens worlds apart, though perhaps only separated by a few city blocks. Scaling the walls erected between newcomers and Canadian nativists, or negotiating the huge distances that separated the sojourner from his village or region of origin across oceans, Harney did not shy from learning the lessons of anthropology, oral history, ethnolinguistics, and a variety of other disciplines. Few scholars have understood so clearly that in the field of immigrant studies, data was so wanting and archives so ephemeral that only a concerted effort from several disciplinary angles could arrive at any conclusions which would carry beyond the usual filiopietist platitudes:

One reason historians have shied away from studying the turn of the century in terms of migration disruption is distrust of the sources. We do not have much chance to employ the survey and interviewing techniques used by the anthropologists and sociologists who study contemporary migration. Only bits of oral history material survive, along with risky inferences from migration statistics, to suggest the migrant's real frame of mind.[2]

Such a state of affairs in academe led Harney to leap forward as an historian in espousing the position that the irreplaceable source of data should be the migrant, his perceptions, his dreams, and above all the discourse which he as a toiling human being produced and which served as a vehicle for his internal rationality. In the immigration process, the immigrants and their surrounding culture would become "text," or more precisely, "narration," from which would flow "sense" and "meaning." Asked to contribute, the migrant himself could textualize or, as the Latin etymology suggests, weave the various elements and threads into a tapestry, an account of events and realities beyond the conventional as conceived by various elites and intermediaries. By welcoming as valid archival material the memories of the actors of history themselves, Harney transcended the ethnocentric limitations of the historical method, and gave his object of study the quality of being a subject. Ethnohistory also meant that methods devised in the approach to pre-industrial and pre-literate societies could be transposed effectively in the heart of twentieth century urban Canada. Somewhere at the crossroads of several disciplines the echo of a new voice could be perceived. As he said, the "immigrant often lives in a whirl of conflicting or mutually unintelligible written, spoken and semiotic *texts* which guide him in his choices of loyalty, identification with group, and intensity of ethno-version."[3] This history as it unfolded before him lead Harney to become sensitive to the opacity of metaphors as exemplified in the immigration texts and to the various obstacles tied with translation as he travelled from one language to the other, from one image to the next. If the migrant was text, then perhaps only the subtlety and range of a full literary text could, in turn, truly affect the transposition from his oral discourse to the learned and cultured explanation several semantic levels

---

[2] Robert F. Harney, "Men Without Women: Italian Migrants in Canada, 1885-1930," in Betty Boyd Caroli, Robert F. Harney and Lydio F. Tomasi, eds., *The Italian Immigrant Woman in North America* (Toronto, 1978), p. 84.

[3] Robert F. Harney, "Undoing the Risorgimento: Emigrants from Italy and the Politics of Regionalism" (Unpublished manuscript, see below, pp. 201-226).

above or beyond. Thus, the intellectual became poet and in the process discovered and illustrated the wealth of material collected by ethnohistory. More than a mere compilation or listing of cultural traits, the *oeuvre* would have to convey on an artistic plane the richness and coloration of immigrant testimony. All other methods of writing or expression, even if fully accepted in the academic world, would have fallen short if used in isolation to reveal the ample scope and complexity of the migrant experience.

This systematic, literary *parti-pris*, which so permeates the writings of Harney required that the editors of this book treat his texts first and foremost as pieces of literature. Thus, as ample editing was often required in the case of certain texts, notably unpublished essays, it was decided never to alter the literary thrust of the author or his uniquely complex style of writing. On the other hand, many articles had been handled carelessly at the moment of publication to the point of obscuring the text through inappropriate punctuation or typographical omissions. These unfortunately all too frequent *coquilles* have been rectified, and references have been verified and brought up to date to provide the reader with a text very much in the original form as intended by the author himself. Much of the credit for the literary restoration should be given to Lise Faubert, Administrative Secretary of the French Canada Studies Program, McGill University, who faithfully typed and reviewed the entire manuscript once we had amended it.

PIERRE ANCTIL
Director
French Canada Studies Program
McGill University

Through the Prism of Ethnocultural History

Bruno Ramirez

One of the personal documents I value most dearly is a letter Robert Harney wrote to me in the Fall of 1978. More than two years had passed since we had last seen each other, during which time I had left the University of Toronto, had taught one year at Western, and had moved to Montreal to a permanent teaching position. Those two years must have been quite intense for Bob as well, for that was the time when his dream of an immigration research centre was realized and the Multicultural History Society of Ontario came into being. Although Bob had known all along of my deep commitment to labour history and of my casual interest in immigration history, he had by no means excluded me from his projects. And now in this letter he talked about some of those projects, stressing the urgent need of historical research in the field of Canadian ethnic studies, and asking me to join him in that new and often little appreciated enterprise. With mixed feelings, I responded to Bob's appeal and agreed to prepare a paper on Italian immigration to Montreal for an upcoming conference on "Little Italies" to be held at the MHSO. I did not know at the time that this would be my first step toward a life-long commitment to immigration history. Subsequently, Bob would always be there in one way or another, despite the geographical distance that separated us.

I mention this anecdote because I believe that one key dimension of Bob's contribution to historical studies was his ability to inspire interest among students and friends, both in his immediate circles and as far away as Finland and Australia, and then to nourish that interest through a constant outpouring of ideas, insights, proposals, and papers. Those of us who entered the field through the study of Italian immigration found in Bob's writing, and in his personal concern the essential roadposts that made our travelling more secure and exciting. And I am sure we were not the only ones. Perhaps it is because of this solidarity and dedication to collective scholarship that a great deal of Bob's *oeuvre* is scattered in journals, anthologies, and introductions to conference proceedings, and that he found it almost impossible to carve out the time necessary to bring to fruition those booklength manuscripts he had already mapped out.[1] The

---

[1]   Thanks to the initiative taken by historians Luigi Bruti Liberati and Nicoletta Serio, Italian readers have access to an anthology of Harney's most important early essays: Robert Harney, *Dalla frontiera alle Little Italies: Gli italiani in Canada, 1800-1945* (Rome, 1984).

idea of bringing together in the present volume some of Bob's most in-fluential papers is meant, therefore, not only to pay respect to a life of scholarly dedication, but also to render a service to readers and students, both present and future, who seek in his writings the guidance and un-derstanding that many of us found.

This is not the place to present a complete balance sheet of Bob's writings.[2] A few remarks, however, are in order so as to convey to our readers the influence that those writings exerted on me and other histo-rians and to elucidate the rationale behind the selection and organization of the texts included here.

It is not surprising that Bob's earliest contributions to the field dealt with Italian immigration. As a historian of the country that had become one of Canada's main sources for immigrant populations, he already knew the complex circumstances that had led millions of Italians to cross the Atlantic in order to escape economic hardship and often political oppression as well. He knew how the ruling classes of the newly constituted Italian state had allowed the exodus to erupt and then had sought to regulate it so as to turn it to their economic advantage. So, by the time Bob entered the field of immigration history, he had long known that the Italians who got off the ship in New York, Boston, or Halifax—whether peasants, smallholders, or craftsmen—had little in common with those "uprooted" masses that the then-dominant historiography had so influentially portrayed. Thus, it is through the study of Italian immi-gration that Bob dealt the first blow to those ethnocentric approaches that saw immigrants as primarily candidates for americanization or canadianization. One can already notice in his early analyses of the migration process and of the urban universe Italian immigrants created, Bob's sharp critical eye gradually developing into a style—one that gave much of his writing its particular polemical flavour and that, at the same time, led him straight to what he saw as the "authentic stuff" of immi-gration and ethnic history.

Bob's concern with pushing immigration history out of the historiographical ghetto to which it had long been assigned helped shake the neat divisions that traditionally had marked the historical enterprise.

---

[2] I have provided some initial critical assessments of Harney's work in my following articles: "The Making of an Ethnoculture: Robert Harney's Contri-bution," in Jean Burnet, ed., *Proceedings of the 1989 UNESCO Conference on Migration and the Transformation of Cultures in Canada* (Toronto: Multicultural History Society of Ontario, forthcoming), and "Les études ethniques et le multiculturalisme au Canada," in *Revue internationale d'études canadiennes,* vol. 3 (Ottawa, 1991).

Through his own work and that of several of his students, the Canadian city emerged as a much richer, and more complex universe than the portrayal we had inherited from urban historians. How could one aim at reconstituting the texture of urban daily life without appreciating the marks that ethnocultures have left in our urban space? How could social scientists and politicians boast a Canadian cosmopolitanism without being able to recognize the symbols, the voices, the sounds, the memory culture, and the boundaries that fill out so much of our private and public life?

The questions Bob raised and the answers he tried to offer inevitably led him to tackle some of the most urgent issues of recent Canadian history. In his last writings (some of which are included in this anthology), Bob, better than any immigration historian I know of, was able to endow ethnocultural history with those prismatic qualities that allow us to view in a new light not only much of twentieth-century Canadian history, but also some of the political and constitutional impasses the country is presently facing. What better service could a historian—prompted by a profound sense of human worth and by a dedication to authentic pluralism—render to his fellow researchers and students, and to the country that adopted him?

BRUNO RAMIREZ
Department of History
University of Montreal

I

ITALIAN IMMIGRATION TO NORTH AMERICA

AMBIENTE AND SOCIAL CLASS IN NORTH AMERICAN LITTLE ITALIES*

*I*N THE STUDY OF IMMIGRATION TO NORTH AMERICA, CHAIN MIGRATION AND ETHNIC neighbourhoods have displaced Oscar Handlin's image of the uprooted peasant.[1] But while anthropologists and sociologists have explored the familial and socio-economic life of the newcomers, the historian has tended to write the history of the immigrant and his areas of settlement either in terms of successful assimilation or of the astonishing persistence of ethnicity. In the case of the Italians, for example, there are no systematic accounts of social class and occupational mobility within the ethnic neighbourhood. Class analysis is made more difficult by the use of generic labels such as "Southerner", *contadino*, *cafone*, "construction worker". Hidden behind words like *padroni*, *prominenti*, and even "leader" are the middle and upper classes of the group. This paper discusses some of the trades, attitudes of mind, and senses of rank that existed in an American Little Italy,[2] compares them with those of the emerging Italian ethnic neighbourhood in Toronto, and examines the strength of ethnicity in the face of the "American melting pot" and the "Canadian mosaic".

If we strip the expression "Little Italy" of the prejudice and frivolity of its origins, it becomes a useful way to describe the setting and surrounding atmosphere within which an Italian-American class structure and popular culture emerged in the United States between 1880 and 1930. The ethnic neighbourhood was much more than a geographical fact; it was the *ambiente* of a social and cultural transition that was not at all identical with the process of assimilation. Immigrant neighbourhoods in the United States were neither the fossils of their Old World origins nor imperfect or pathological varieties of the Anglo-conformity. In fact,

---

* This article reprinted with permission from *The Canadian Review of Studies in Nationalism*, no. 2, 1975, pp. 208-224.

Little Italies were always changing. Their distinct neighbourhood history grew from the conjuncture of three variables or parameters: the culture and skills of the incoming people; the opportunity for employment afforded them by the North American economy at the time of their arrival; and the attitude of the receiving society and its government toward the immigrant.

Studies that count the immigrant as a subspecies of the proletariat and the ethnic neighbourhood as just another inner city or working class slum underestimate the variety of the immigrant experience. Historically, a proliferation of roles occurred in the ethnic neighbourhood. Within the *ambiente* the changing relationship between the economic success of the immigrants, their social needs, and the persistence or decline of their Old World cultural values and ties created an entirely new class structure within the ethnic group. In New York, Chicago, and Boston, Little Italies displayed a rich array of occupations and cultural innovations.

Before the massive influx of South Italians, American authorities held stereotyped views of the immigrant communities' social structure. Those groups with the highest visibility outside of the Little Italies – at first ice-cream vendors and street entertainers, then bootblacks and migrant work gangs – formed the basis of the stereotypes. After the Civil War, the Italian neighbourhood in New York City was composed of people who, according to city officials, "were mainly a vagabond but harmless class of organ grinders, rag pickers, bear leaders and the like."[3] So troubled by that stereotype was Mayor Fiorello La Guardia that "it was with a great deal of gusto that…[he] banned the organ grinder from the streets of New York City."[4] Meanwhile, generalizations about the immigrants and their work obscured the variety of social origin, the degree of mobility within Little Italy, and the history of the community itself.

Anti-immigration legislators, distinguishing between the old and welcome North Italian immigration and the new unskilled masses found it convenient to ignore the historical process,[5] but the founding Italian communities, Northern or not, that were to expand into turn-of-the-century Little Italies, had a history. That history was one of social mobility but not clearly of assimilation to American society. A report of the New York Association for Improving the Condition of the Poor described the "North Italian" Little Italy of 1884:

> The courtyard swarms with, in daytime, females in the picturesque attires of Genova and Piedmont, moving between the dirty children. The abundant rags, paper, sacks, barrows, barrels, wash tubs, dogs

and cats are all festooned overhead by clotheslines.... In each yard live 24 families (nominally only, because lodgers here as elsewhere are always welcome).[6]

The Association noted also that boarders often lived in partitioned rooms that measured 5' by 6'. These same families were the Genovese that Caroline Ware found almost a half century later providing, along with the more enterprising of the recent Southern immigrants, "all the prominent men whom the district has produced." Men were *prominenti* in an ethnic neighbourhood. Partially assimilated and city wise, they nonetheless played their role, not within the larger Anglo-conformity but within Little Italy. They were the doctors, undertakers, priests, impressarios, and bankers of the district.[7] Their fathers and grandfathers had formed the embryonic service and cultural community that had attracted greenhorn immigrants. The older group had been among the *padroni*, travel agents, brokers, small importers, and merchants of Italian food staples.

In 1909 the Italian Consul in Boston reported the presence of two groups of *prominenti*: Northern Italians who were successful merchants and in contact with the American business community, and then "the doctors, *avvocati - interpreti, gl'intraprenditore di pompe funebre* (under-takers), priests and presidents of societies who constitute the inevitable appendix of the Southern immigration...."[8] Although the outside community might only see hurdy-gurdy men, fruit peddlers, and ultimately construction workers, Little Italies possessed a great variety of stations, high fluidity of opportunity, and a process that was not so much one of acculturation as one of adjustment and historical change within the ethnic group itself.

The end of free land in North America, prejudice against South Europeans, and the raw manpower demands of capitalism combined to make the new Italian immigrant a man of the cities. Many newcomers saw themselves as sojourners;[9] they needed cash and skill with a *zappa*, the primitive mattock that was the farm tool of the Italian South, prepared them for urban and railroad excavation work more than for the plough farming of the prairies.[10] Historians and sociologists have shown that the South Italian migrants came from rural towns, mainly small nucleated urban areas where living congestion and class differences were present.[11] There was then nothing unnatural in their choice of an urban environment after immigration. R.F. Foerster observed long ago that Italian emigration to the cities of the Americas had clear "affinities...with the phenomenon, universally observed in modern countries, of migration from rural into urban districts...."[12] But the habit of living in towns and the acceptance of a species of urbanism did not mean ability to cope with modernity and industrialization. The Marxist scholar, A. Gramsci, pointed out that South Italian cities were urban but premodern; their social groups were in some way antique relics in the modern world.[13]

To understand the social structures of North American Italian enclaves, we must start with Gramsci's point. *Campanilismo*, jobs, chain migration, contributed to an almost unconscious drive in the immigrant to recreate an *ambiente* of his own, a buffer against the new environment. It was natural that such a plagiarism of a rural town would reproduce the social castes of the *paese*, and a welter of new problems as well. Consciousness of status, distrust of, yet helpless dependence on the literate, and deference to *signori*, followed from the Italian South.[14] Sometimes the people themselves recognized the plagiarism. Constantine Panunzio recounted his shock on first encountering a man called *padrone* in the North End of Boston:

> *Padrone*, said I to myself. Now the word *padrone* in Italy is applied
> to a proprietor, generally a respectable man, at least one whose
> dress and appearance distinguish him as a man of means. This man
> not only showed no signs of good breeding in his face, but he was
> unshaven and dirty and his clothes were sloppy. I could not quite
> understand how he could be called *padrone*.[15]

Even the use in North American dialect of terms such as *bisnissuccio* for *piccolo commercio*[16] contains traces of derision and the self-mockery of a people, uncomfortable living with social mobility, who suspect themselves of parodying their "betters." Still the greenhorns seemed to have a need for a certain *ambiente*, both cultural and socio-economic, where they could measure their pace and their status as they always had.

They were not then ready for the industrial city. Their occupations, sense of self, and definition of notability represented not just their limited choices but a clear preference for a calendar, a sense of daily pace, a social hierarchy that they had brought with them – all in all a liturgy of life fit for the pre-industrial city. Vecoli has shown that Italians in Chicago, though mainly unskilled, were very under-represented in unskilled factory or stockyard work.[17] The choice of outdoor work over factory life is one clear sign of lower class continuity. Even a highly assimilated social worker saw the difference clearly. Writing in *Charities and the Commons* for 1908, Gino Speranza observed that:

> many an Italian who never would have thought of doing any other
> labor than that in the open air, some fine day hears that a neighbor

of his is working in a cigar factory. Ninety-nine chances in one hundred that cigar-maker is a weakling who could not handle pick and shovel and, conscious of his physical deficiency, probably boasts what easy money factory work yields, where a man sits down all day and after work goes home with the factory girls.[18]

The factory, then, was the source of depravity and the corruption of a man's nature, but the city could be lived in as long as the *ambiente* could flourish in the ethnic neighbourhood. The characteristics of that neighbourhood were not just Italian as opposed to American, they were pre-industrial in life style and social structure as well. Many parts of the complex setting that at first may seem to be ethnic resistance may equally be seen as resistance to modernity. For example, willingness to do seasonal construction work, to migrate or travel great distances to work, underemployment, and unemployment were normal conditions of the old country. At the same time, willingness to engage in a large variety of semi-occupations from the gathering of wild greens and mushrooms to weekend ice-cream vending and knife-sharpening fit the pre-modern world view. Legislation in some Massachusetts counties against alien berry pickers reflected the attempt of North American society to protect itself from the almost feudal sense of demesne held by Italian immigrants.[19] The vestigial attempt at family self-sufficiency also appears in the maintenance of a goat or some chickens in the backyard and in the small rented vegetable patches along railway right of ways and on the outskirts of industrial cities. Family endeavours such as rag-picking and scavenging were not only an aspect of this world view but also assumed, in the face of liberal and industrial society, that the family was a single economic unit. Although lesser economic activities might be carried on at a feverish rate, the street corner, saloon, and *bocce* ball court were places for the non-job times and the enforced leisure that was part of the pace of an agricultural year maintained in the heart of the city.

Even subjects that have been studied from a completely different perspective submit to logical patterning within the concept of an *ambiente*. Hostility to unions may reflect the "amoral familism"[20] that Banfield claims is typical of South Italians. More important, it sprang from the assumption that work was a direct relationship between a man and his employer. The immediacy and personal nature of employment stuck with the peasant even though as a senator back in Italy complained, "once it was enough to make an oral contract with our peasant and one was sure of his word; today instead the American siren makes one forget such duties...."[21] Education, while clearly a problem of generations and assimilation, can be understood in the context of the pre-industrial family.[22] When a mother begged "please don't send my children to an American school, for as soon as they learn English they will not be my children anymore,"[23] she meant more than a language gap would divide her from her children. Such children, who should be part of the working family unit and contributors to its well-being, would no longer understand their role in the home or the family economy. They would embrace the liberal self-interest of American family members. In the words of the Italian Vice-Consul in San Francisco, they would "call their fathers dagos and...[be] ...no less veteran in the battle for life than their Anglo-Saxon companions."[24]

This picture of the lower orders of Little Italy suggests that while discrimination, lack of skills, and resistance to assimilation played their part, attitudes of mind, carried over from the Italian setting, fostered certain work habits and life styles. Within this complex of attitudes, although many seemed based on resignation, others encouraged social mobility. Circumstance favoured these other elements. The difficulties of finding a position in one's craft in North America made the immigrant more aware of social and job mobility than he had ever been. For example, only 5% of the Italians who worked in the mines of Pennsylvania had been miners in the old country. By way of contrast 49% of the Germans and 84% of the Scots had been miners before.[25]

Another circumstance of importance was the background of many immigrants. Although they worked with pick and shovel for day wages in America, they were not *giornalieri*, *salariati*, and *braccianti* of Italy. For the most part, they came from the small holding class,[26] men who held tenaciously to tiny patrimonies, or who sought in the new world the mortgage and dowry money that would stabilize or improve their status. Many were by disposition petty capitalists who, like Verga's fishing family, the Malavoglia, in the novel *House by the Medlar Tree* constantly probed at nature to see if one of their semi-occupations, such as hauling and selling a cargo of *lupini*, would change the family fortunes. In the slang of another ethnic neighbourhood, some sought a hustle. Such a hustle based on a good sense of *bisnissuccio* might free the family from the bondage of heavy manual labour, from being *bestie*. They were like the Sicilian in Cusumano's account of the Cinisi colony in New York who began by importing a few figs and lemons from his relatives and selling to his neighbours,[27] and perhaps ended up like Ciro Terranova, the artichoke king who got a penny on every artichoke to enter the city of New York.[28] Many other men rose simply through back-breaking labour in the construction trade. The point is this – the *ambiente* of Little Italy, despite the loiterers in its streets, did not discourage upward mobility. Occupational and social mobility in turn were not in tandem with assimilation or industrialization.[29]

When we speak of the role of the middle and upper classes in the district, Little Italy appears as both a natural formation and a contrivance. Almost every Little Italy of any importance had an older group of immigrants, often from the North. Many members of that older community and some of the newcomers formed a group composed of "small *commercianti* who import the specialities of their *paese* for a *paesano* clientele; bankers, travel agents, and notaries public."[30] Middle class status or prominence depended on fulfilling the needs of the immigrant clientele. One man labeled *padrone* had a career that spanned at least nine occupations; they were foreman, saloon keeper, banker, interpreter, grocer, notary, travel agent, contractor, politician. In all he served as intermediary and exploiter or patron.[31] The Dillingham Commission noted that most of the immigrant bankers in New York were also travel agents, many were also realtors, notaries, or *padroni*/labour bureaux.[32]

A glance at the services rendered reinforces the images of a non-modern society, of self-containment, and of Old World traits. Beyond the new essentials of "immigrant banking," arranging ships passage, food supply and lodging, the intermediaries served in three major capacities. They were the dispensors of employment, the contractors, or *padroni*; they replaced the *signori* and *mercanti di campagna* of the old country. The lawyers and notaries (often the same people as the bankers/travel agents) also protected the lower orders from the evil intent of their neighbours and the outside world. One bought their literacy as protection from North American prejudice and from *truffatori* (scoundrels). Finally there were those who helped in the rites of passage from the priest to the funeral directors and caterers. Thus the middle class that came into existence reflected broadly the post-feudal but pre-industrial setting: small merchants, literate mediators with the larger world, and brokers in land or employment. These were the middle classes of the Italian South; and just as in the South, many of them had come from humble origins. Now under new titles, they dominated Little Italy. Some of them would have to become notables in order to give the community its own *signori*. Luigi Villari expressed the urban and cultured Italian's scorn for this new world plagiarism:

> We have therefore an amorphous and incomplete society, lacking
> many of the elements that constitute a perfect social organism; it is an
> army without officers, commanded by corporals and sergeants....

This was so, he felt, because "the Italians…now form the proletariat of America and work at the pleasure of American capitalists and industrialists…"[33] Villari's view mistakenly assumed industrialism as necessary to a full urban social structure. The ethnic neighbourhood not only contained an elaborate class structure, it also evolved a language and culture that reflected and reinforced that structure.

From the beginning, there had been an uneasy relationship with the mother culture. If the social structure looked askew to Villari because it lacked an industrial upper class, what was even more noticeably missing was an intelligentsia from school teacher to cafe idler, that had existed at home. The report of the Industrial Commission of 1901 dwelt on this point:

> Still another element of the Italian population is made up of persons of a high social grade at home – young men of the upper and lower middle classes who have been either fully or in part prepared to enter some profession or government office and who cannot find opportunity to do so…. This class, however, is the most difficult to provide for in the city, if they insist upon having the work which they have regarded as corresponding to their social standing.[34]

Needless to say, there were few such people in the migration and both their return rate and their acculturation rate were paradoxically high. Their absence left a living language and a popular culture in the hands of the immigrant and the intermediaries. The result was a world of neologisms and cultural variants that, although it may have appeared as acculturation to outsiders, increased cohesion.[35]

Early Italian travellers to New York's Little Italy had been perturbed by large pictures of the King or Garibaldi or the *tricolore* hanging from the shops of immigrant bankers.[36] The exploitation of patriotic symbols as shared culture was obvious. Later travellers and consular reports were more apt to remark derisively on the *gergo*, the language of *iesse* and *oraitte*, a "language Italian in appearance but American in derivation."[37] Gino Speranza saw urban congestion as the very condition of life for the banker and the *padrone*: "In exact ratio with the topographical nearness of his clients and *paesani* does he control them for good or bad,"[38] he said of the *padroni*. But he missed the point a bit, since now *ambiente* held the classes momentarily in a caste relationship. The creation of the *gergo* required that the illiterate have an intermediary who was a *paesano* but who could speak English and the emerging dialect. In the United States new words were found both for new realities and new ideas. *Fruttistendo* and *salone* are obvious. *Bordi* or *bordanti* for roomers, also reflected new conditions. The introduction of *bisinisse* for *piccoli affari* was even more telltale.

This community was not the bastard society that educated Italians and Americanized early immigrants assailed with scorn as a place where "the misfits of Italian society...were *i prominenti*" or a place of a "thousand trifling, provincial and local animosities...a conglomeration of folks [which] would have been as much an anomaly in Italy as it was in America."[39] It was also not the happy halfway house depicted by a recent historian of Chicago Italians:

> The migrant colony and its institutions fulfilled their functions not of prolonging old world traits and patterns but of providing important first steps in assimilation and they did so effectively.... Over the years newcomers and their children moved up the economic ladder progressing from unskilled labour into commercial, trade, and professional lines.[40]

In this idyll, progress and assimilation are identical and the flow from the bottom of Little Italy to the top occupational status groups in America is seen as a continuum. Beyond questioning such a sanguine view of social mobility for ethnics, it is important to distinguish the career possibilities within the *ambiente* of the ethnic group – that social mobility, particularly if it did not entail geographical mobility, had little relation to assimilation or acculturation. In practice, it may have meant a classical liberal winnowing up for the children of *i prominenti* and of the middle classes. But the *ambiente* itself was reinforced and partly created by those middle classes who had a positive stake in maintaining it.[41] An analogy may be found in the victory of Columbus Day over the feast days of many local saints. Not assimilation but rather a consolidation of Little Italy's culture resulted.

If the expression Little Italy seemed inadequate when speaking of the variety of Italian settlement areas in turn of the century America, it is downright perverse so to describe Italo-Toronto. Only errant police investigators and "ethnic leaders" could assert that 1/4 to 1/2 million Italians form a cohesive community. The expression "Little Italy" sounded either archaic or "like an expression outsiders would use" to most Italo-Canadians interviewed. Ninety percent of the eighth grade school children Italian-born or first generation in a West End Toronto separate school had never been to the two intersections most often characterized by non-Italians as Little Italies.[42] A study of leadership in Italo-Toronto has shown, too, the essential disunity reflected in the lack of consensus about the meaning of "leader".[43] Still the concept of an *ambiente* seems valid. A typical answer, though confused about location, usually referred to an atmosphere and to a life style that was neither Italian nor Canadian.

At first glance, the history and future of Italo-Toronto seem rich in contrasts with the Italo-American experience. The Italy of the 1950s, from which so many came, was an industrialized society. Literacy, sense of nationality, and mass consumption with its ancillaries of popular advertising and service industries, set it apart from the impoverished culture and society of Southern Italy at the turn of the century. And although Calabrese and Friulan may congregate in different parts of Italo-Toronto, some of the crippling localism of American Little Italy is gone. Moreover, the Canadian government speaks, though sometimes haltingly, of a mosaic and not of a melting pot.

One can apply some of the ideas from the discussion of American Little Italies to Italo-Toronto from 1946 to the 1970s. We ought to consider the role of the Italo-Canadian receiving community; the occupational skills, predispositions, and mobility of the postwar immigrants; the development of a class structure in Toronto; and some evidence that occupational mobility in terms of status change could create a full social structure within the ethnic group.

Although there exist sociological studies about Italians in Toronto, there is very little material on their history.[44] Yet it is clear that an older community (in this case one dating from the 1900s and thereafter), did provide some neighbourhood framework for the newcomers. A certain number of professionals, merchants, and those with lesser skills, rediscovered their *italianità* in the face of the mass migration of the 1950s. No studies dealing adequately with the older community's own history or its response to the newcomers exist, but some hint of the difficulty between the receiving group's role as mediators and the arriving immigrants' view of the older Italo-Canadians as *umbertini* (Victorian) can be found in O. Bressan's *Non Dateci Lenticchie*.[45] The relationship always hovers between patronage and exploitation.

What of the newcomers to Canada? Were they really more ready for industrial society than their Italo-American predecessors? Did they re-create their own hierarchies and social classes in Toronto? The question is not an easy one to answer. Like the immigrants in America before them, they were accustomed to a species of urban life and their sense of status embraced a number of sophisticated categories. Many had experienced some mobility during World War II, all had been subjected to an intense, if sometimes ineffectual, socialization process by the Fascist government. Thanks to the *Annuario Statistico Italiano* and to the

Annual Reports of the Immigration department, we can study the newcomers' occupational backgrounds and their intended trades in Canada. Fleshing out their history once in Canada will be more arduous.[46]

It has been estimated that of the 160,000 Italian migrants who joined the Canadian labour force between 1946-1963, semi-skilled or unskilled workers numbered about 125,000. There is nothing to suggest that these migrants were more prepared for factory work than their Italo-American predecessors. Of nineteen trade unions listed in the Italo-Canadian directory, only four – clothing, shoe manufacturing, bakery, and hotel – are not connected with the building trades. If we survey the peak years of Italian immigration to Italo-Toronto, it becomes clear that although general labourers outnumber the semi-skilled workers almost two to one, even the semi-skilled are engaged in trades more likely to be the victims of industrialization than to be its beneficiaries. Theirs are indeed the small trades that interpose between the lower and middle classes of South Italian towns. For many, immigration meant the end of *mestiere* (their trade). If we look just at the semi-skilled crafts, we see that 425 blacksmiths entered Canada from Italy in the peak years. With them came over 1,600 cobblers, 2,000 tailors, 800 bakers, 4,000 carpenters and 2,000 brick and stone masons. One can almost picture the depopulated main streets of the small towns they left behind.

In general, Italian immigrants have recreated their old world in Canada, as they did in the United States. Construction work has replaced the *latifundia* (large estates) as the ultimate source of wealth, however, so that developers and contractors, along with some professionals and businessmen, have become the new *signori*. Some may have hands a little too calloused to be other than *cafoni arrichiti*, yet they merit the same kind of deference. The role of intermediaries also remains the same. A simple man must be protected from litigation, the government and unemployment. He must save money, maintain or sponsor his family, and buy property. The brokers necessary to perform the functions were and still are the same in Naples, New York, or Toronto. They are lawyers, notaries, bankers/*strozzini*, *padroni*/labour bureaux, travel agents and realtors, and occasionally social workers or honest civil servants. For lack of adequate information, we can only assume that this middle class is an amalgam of the older receiving community of Italo-Canadians, immigrant professionals and semi-professionals, and a number of upwardly mobile aspirants from among the less-skilled immigrants.

Below these professional middle classes, Italo-Canada, it appears, is different. Even if the Italian immigrant of the 1950s was not an industrial man, he came from an industrialized nation. The simpler needs of the *contadini* have been replaced by an array of consumer demands that go beyond imported oil, cheeses and meats. The Italo-Canadian may seek clothing, phonograph records, household wares and ultimately Fiats, as part of his identity. As Amy Bernardy said of the Italian colony of Boston years before, culture and business are inextricably tied together. The Italo-Canadian press, the intermediaries, the merchants and shopkeepers – all of whom might have represented the assimilating and upwardly mobile Italian elements – have had every reason to maintain the *ambiente* of a Little Italy instead. In their effort, they have been powerfully abetted by the prevailing Canadian idea of the ethnic mosaic.

So, while many Italian immigrants choose the path of acculturation, a full social structure can and does exist within the Italian ethnic neighbourhoods. This is reflected in the development of Italian surburbs; some of the differences between a downtown, a Downsview or a Weston address in greater Toronto will shortly be as subtle and yet as forceful as older distinctions about *paese*. Since the Canadian government is not committed to rapid assimilation, Toronto's immigrants may not face any concerted onslaught against their *ambiente*. Attempts to introduce Italian into the schools, Italian Language and Literature departments in Canadian universities, and a healthy ethnic press and radio suggest that an Italian intelligentsia, either missing or uncoordinated in the American setting, will play an important role in the history of Toronto's Italian community.

It is far too soon to tell, however, how much a benign government attitude toward "otherness" will affect the class structure, culture and ethnicity of Italian neighbourhoods. Will such an attitude do more to foster a separate identity than the defensive reactions to assimilationist prejudice and the disregard of the capitalists did in the United States a century ago? Government policy is, after all, only one of the variables that shape the history of a Little Italy. It is possible that an ideological commitment to national survival in the New World may be less persistent than the natural life span of an ethnic *ambiente*. For example, the teaching of the Italian language in Toronto schools may in fact cause a decline in the use of dialect and *gergo*. To the extent that dialect is a natural, familial and evolving heritage, it is surely more resilient than an artificially taught language in the schools. Multicultural programmes always run the risk of confusing primordial ethnicity with ideological nationalism. In the face of the complex interplay of factors that create ethnic neighbourhood history, premature statements about the differences between the American melting pot and the Canadian mosaic remain nothing but shibboleths masquerading as explanations. More historical study of the immigrant areas and their formation in both the United States and Canada is in order.

Notes

1. See R. Vecoli, "Contadini in Chicago: A Critique of the Uprooted," *Journal of American History*, 51 (1964); and J.S. McDonald, "Chain Migration, Ethnic Neighbourhood Formation and Social Network," *Millbank Memorial Fund Quarterly*, 13 (1964).

2. I am aware of the problems with the expression "Little Italy" but it does convey a sense of *ambiente* and not community. Community, as social scientists use the term, is not applicable to a world of factionalism and *campanilismo*. "Italian colony," the preferred phrasing of consular officials and literate Italian travelers is also inappropriate. The generalizations in this paper are based on a number of little Italies, but chiefly those of New York, Boston, and Chicago.

3. U.S. Government, *Report of the Industrial Commission, 1901: Immigration and Education* (Washington, 1901), XV, 472.

4. F. LaGuardia, *An Autobiography: The Making of An Insurgent* (New York, 1961), pp. 27-28.

5. See O. Handlin, "Old Immigrants and New," in *Race and Nationality in American Life* (New York, 1957).

6. Report of the Association for Improving the Condition of the Poor (New York, 1884), quoted in *Industrial Commission, 1901*, XV, 427.

7. C. Ware, *Greenwich Village, 1920-1930* (New York, 1965), pp. 153-154. Ware duly notes that those South Italians who came as early as the Genovese and Piedmontese had also produced service professionals in later generations.

8. Report of Cav. Gustavo Tosti, r. console in Boston in Commissariato dell'Emigrazione, *Emigrazione e Colonie. Raccolta di rapporti dei R.R. Agenti diplomatici e consolari* (Rome, 1909), III, 164. See also S. Thernstrom, "Immigrants and Wasps. Ethnic Differences in Occupational Mobility in Boston, 1890-1940," in S. Thernstrom and R. Sennett, *Nineteenth Century Cities: Essays in the New Urban History* (New Haven, 1969), p. 156. Despite the author's claim that ethnics were not as upwardly mobile as others, his charts show a rapid rise into white collar employment for the Italian immigrant cohort of 1880-1890. This seems to have occurred just about at the time of the influx of large numbers of Italian newcomers.

9. It should be recalled that both the street entertainers and tinkers of the early migration were transients. They were followed by equally migratory labour gangs. See L. Iorizzo, "The Padrone and Immigrant Distribution," in S. M. Tomasi and M. H. Engel, eds., *The Italian Experience in the United States* (New York, 1970); and L. Villari, "L'Emigrazione italiana negli stati uniti d'America," *Nuova Antologia*, 143 (1906), 296. The small merchants who provided for the migrants' needs were the first stable elements in Little Italy and prospered. C. Ware, *Greenwich Village*, p. 153, shows that some of the *prominenti* were children of men who had run the first two "immigrant hotels" in the area.

10. See Palma Castiglione, quoted in G. Abbott, *The Immigrant and the Community* (New York, 1921), pp. 96-97; and C. Panunzio, *The Soul of an Immigrant* (New York, 1921), pp. 76-77.

11. R. Vecoli, "Contadini in Chicago," 404-405; and J. Lopreato, *Italian Americans* (New York, 1970), p. 41.

12. R. F. Foerster, *The Italian Emigration of our Times* (Cambridge, 1919), p. 418.

13. A. Gramsci, *Sul Risorgimento* (Rome, 1967), p. 100.

14. See F. Cancian, "The Southern Italian Peasant: World View and Political Behaviour," in *Anthropological Quarterly*, 34 (1961), 10.

15. C. Panunzio, *Soul of an Immigrant*, p. 78.

16. See Amy Bernardy, *Italia randagia attraverso gli Stati Uniti* (Turin, 1914), p. 91. The term "businessman" is still used in New York and Toronto dialect for a *uomo d'affari*.

17. R. Vecoli, "Contadini in Chicago," 410. Lopreato, *Italian Americans*, is more confused on the difference between urbanism and industrialism, see pp. 41, 46, and 78. Women from the neighbourhood were often involved in factory work. However, this did not initially affect the *ambiente*. Women had done piece work, food processing, and seasonal work in the Italian South. Since the family, until it fell under the influence of the Jewish example (see R. Glanz, *Jew and Italian Historic Group Relations and the New Immigration* [New York, 1971], felt little reason to educate daughters but had less home and farm labour for them to do, it was natural that they would go into factories - first in the needle trades, but also in cigarette and macaroni factories. (See *Industrial Commission*. XV, 474)

18. G. Speranza, "Italians in Congested Districts," in *Charities and the Commons*, 20 (1908), 55.

19. The Massachusetts legislation is cited in J. Higham, *Strangers in the Land: Patterns of American Nativism, 1860-1925* (New Brunswick, 1955), p. 162. On the importance of simple food gathering, see D. Dolci, *Poverty in Sicily* (London, 1966). Foraging for greens, snails, frogs, and mushrooms was seen as the peasants' right.

20. E. Banfield, *The Moral Basis of a Backward Society* (New York, 1958), especially Chapter 7. Harry Golden, in his introduction to H. Hapgood's *The Spirit of the Ghetto* (New York, 1972), p. 12, observed that on the Lower East Side, "many of these people [garment workers] wept when the industry, in 1912-1914, became unionized. They were afraid they would lose their livelihood."

21. V. Di Somma, "L'Emigrazione nel Mezzogiorno," *Nuova Antologia*, 140 (1907), 513.

22. Many North Italians with skills were union activists. When Italian locals were created that reinforced the *ambiente*, unions were often supported. See E. Fenton, "Italians in the Labor Movement," *Pennsylvania History*, 26 (1959).

23. C. Panunzio, *Soul of An Immigrant*, p. 254.

24. Report of the r. vice console G. Ricciardi in San Francisco, in *Raccolta di Rapporti* (1909), III, 248.

25. U.S. Government, *Reports of the Immigration Commission* (Dillingham Commission), Document #747, 61st Congress (Washington, 1911), VL 273.

26. See J.S. McDonald, "Italy's Rural Social Structure and Emigration," *Occidente*, 12 (1956).

27. R.E. Park and J. Miller, *Old World Traits Transplanted* (New York, 1921), p. 149.

28. Joe Cipolla, *The Mafia Cookbook* (New York, 1970), p. 32.

29. A. Bernardy, *America Vissuta* (Turin, 1911), p. 308, wrongly, I think, contrasts the American "mechanical ability and opportunist and businesslike spirit" with "the rudimentary business spirit" of the immigrant. Yet she does see that "a contrary and tenacious spirit" grips Little Italy. That spirit is not anti-commercial but anti-industrial. Problems of measuring mobility and status in such circumstances are explained in M. Katz, "Occupational Classification in History," *Journal of Interdisciplinary History*, 3 (1972).

30. A. Pecorino, *Gli Americani nella vita moderna osservati da un italiano* (1909), quoted in G. Prezzolini, *I Trapiantati* (Milan, 1963), pp. 239-240.

31. L. Iorizzo and S. Mondello, *The Italian-Americans* (New York, 1971), p. 143.

32. *Dillingham Commission*, IV, 145.

33. L. Villari, "L'Emigrazione italiana negli Stati Uniti," CXLIII, 298.

34. U. S. Government, *Industrial Commission*, 1901, XV, 474.

35. A. Bernardy, *America Vissuta*, p. 324. In Italo-America she noticed "culture and finance fuse in a unique civilizing trust."

36. G. Giacosa, "Gli Italiani a New York ed a Chicago," *Nuova Antologia*, 124 (1892), 635.

37. A. Bernardy, *Italia randagia*, pp. 88-122, and G. Prezzolini, *I Trapiantati*, pp. 282-288 and 319-329. The Italian Consul arriving in Buenos Aires asked what language stevedores were speaking and was told that it was Italian. R.F. Foerster, *The Italian Emigration*, p. 431.

38. G. Speranza, "Italians in Congested Districts," p. 56.

39. C. Panunzio, *Soul of An Immigrant*, p. 232.

40. H. Nelli, *Italians in Chicago, 1880-1930: A Study in Ethnic Mobility* (Oxford, 1970), p. 20.

41. On the difference between individual and community assimilation see M. Livolsi, "Integrazione dell'immigrato e integrazione communitari", *Studi emigrazione*, 2, No. 5, 123-149.

42. Students and former students have done much of the informal interviewing for me. The school children were polled by Paul Vella of St. Wilfred's School. Palmacchio Di Iulio, Immigration Counsellor at Toronto airport,

interviewed large numbers of first and second generation Italians and offered much good advice.

43. C. Jansen, "Leadership in the Toronto Italian Ethnic Group," *International Migration Review*, 4 (1969).

44. The most important studies are by S. Sidlofsky, *Post-War Immigrants in the Changing Metropolis with Special Reference to Toronto's Italian Population* (Ph.D. thesis, Univ. of Toronto, 1969); and A. Richmond, *Immigrants and Ethnic Groups in Metropolitan Toronto* (Toronto, 1967).

45. O. Bressan, *Non Dateci Lenticchie. Esperienze, Commenti, Prospettive di Vita Italo-Canadese* (Toronto, 1958), pp. 106-110.

46. *Annuario Statistico Italiano* and Dept. of Citizenship and Immigration, *Annual Report* for the 1950s. (Ottawa, 1950s).

THE
COMMERCE
OF MIGRATION*

———— ❧ ————

*B*ETWEEN NATIONAL UNIFICATION IN *1870* AND *W*ORLD *W*AR *I*, MILLIONS OF Italians migrated to the Americas. In Italy that emigration became part of a national polemic on the need for colonies and the problem of the South. As immigration, the migration became a sub-theme in American urban and ethnic historiography. The differences in perspective and concern of those who view the migration as emigration and those who see it as immigration obscure the continuities in the migrant society. This paper is about an aspect of that continuum, the mediating and exploiting role of the middle classes in Italy and America.

American observers saw misery and hunger driving South Italians overseas. J.F. Carr wrote in *Outlook* that: "through whole districts in this overcrowded land Italians have to choose between emigration and starvation."[1] Some Italian advocates of emigration like Senator Nobili-Vitelleschi felt that without mass migration: "the land would strangle in its own excess population (soffocare nella sua pletora), and everyone would have to eat one another to survive...."[2] On both sides of the Atlantic, stereotypes and self-images colluded to make Italian emigration seem natural. The South of Italy was poor, over-populated, and mis-governed. America was a land rich and underpopulated, ergo migration. In such a natural human flood, differentiation of classes and roles, dis-tinctions between natural and artificial uprooting appeared insignificant. It was assumed that misery drove men from Italy and *La Miserià* was so total that the perils of migration, the hostility of "AngloSaxons", and the difficult struggles ahead could not deter the peasant.[3] The prefects of Southern Italy, overwhelmingly attributed migration to misery.[4]

* This article reprinted with permission from *Canadian Ethnic Studies/Etudes ethniques au Canada*, vol. 9, no. 1, 1977, pp. 42-53.

Unfortunately, misery was exactly what North American historians saw as Europe's peasant condition, the misery of potato famine and the hungry 1840s, the misery of the Russian Pale and pogroms. The plight of Southern Italy seemed to be of the same order. In *The Uprooted*, Oscar Handlin confidently generalized about the European situation: "Year by year, there were fewer alternatives until the critical day when only a single choice remained – to emigrate or to die."[5] But misery in Italy did not really mean to "emigrate or to die." In 1906, about 435,000 left Italy for America; in the same year, 158,000 returned to Italy. Some came back for good, others, like the *rondini* (swallows), were simply commuting from harvest to harvest, from Autumn in Piedmont to Spring in Argentina.[6] There is no way to compare return rate with that of the Irish and Germans of the hungry 1840s or the Jews of the Pale, but the answer, even accepting changes in transport, is self-evident. R.F. Foerster observed of the Italian emigrants in 1919 that though "the notion of flight is rudimentary.... Rarely if ever does it alone govern the man's conduct." Most Southerners, had a "notion, however vague, of a tangible positive gain to be secured, a notion that generally depends upon the evidence of other's success."[7]

Interpretations of Italian emigration stressing the volition of the migrants and the role of a secondary group of caretakers, exploiters and agents have taken a number of forms. Emphasis on agents and sub-agents has often been a conservative device in Italy used to deny or obscure the real plight of the South or to justify the policing of emigration in the interest of the land owning classes.[8] South Italian radicals condemned the legislation of the 1880s that sought to regulate the activity of South American state recruiters, control steamship companies and reduce the numbers of official subagents. Since such critics of the government saw the roots of the problem in the backwardness and suppression of the South, analogies to the negro slave trade, phrases such as *commercio di carne umana* (trade in human flesh) or *i negrieri* (slave traders) and *merce/uomo* (men as goods) came easily to their tongues. Legislation against agents, they felt, was either a conservative ruse or the product of a naive devil theory.[9] Grazia Dore, in her *La Democrazia italiana e l'emigrazione in America*, (1964) remarked that the term *agenti* was employed by the government both as a pejorative and to imply the artificial nature of emigration. She added that some of the Southern bourgeoisie, seeing easy profit in the emigation trade, served as subagents for steamship compagnies, labour contractors and South America "white settler agents."[10] Unfortunately, Dore's concern was political history; she ignored the natural role of the middle classes as mediators between the literate and illiterate, between countryside and city, between the individual migrant and alien government.

In North America, following the lead of the Congressional Commission of 1911 (referred to henceforth as the Dillingham Commission), historians have uncovered two "unnatural" stimuli in Italian migration, the steamship agents and the *padroni*, or contract labour boss. In its most pernicious form – peasants seduced by a labour contract from their European villages and virtually in thrall to a boss in North America – the *padrone* system had a brief if lurid career. With the growth of Little Italy communities, exploitation began to take more subtle forms.[11] In 1888, the Italian vice-consul reported that there were no longer *padroni* in New York City.[12] A recent historian of the Chicago Italians even claims that the bulk of prepaid passages were probably paid for by relatives rather than labour contractors.[13] However, the Dillingham Commission, sensing the limits of its definitions and investigation, was not naive enough to count the *padroni* out completely. The Commission noted that immigrant bankers' offices (often travel agencies as well) had a way of serving as hiring halls and labour bureaux.[14]

Other villains in the piece were obviously the big steamship companies who encouraged uprooting, winked at the illegal practices of their subagents, and were pleased when the emigrant failed because it assured them of an eastbound cargo in the lucrative Mediterranean trade.[15] One line, the Inman Steamship Company, in 1892, was reputed to have 3,500 agents in Europe. Drumming up steerage trade was "a business which can be almost indefinitely expanded by vigorous pushing. A skillful agent can induce any number of simple and credulous peasants of a backward European country to emigrate, who had scarcely had such an idea in their heads before."[16] The Fagin-like qualities of men who ran strings of bootblacks from the Basilicata, the *padrone* as *negriere*, and the callous approach of the steamship companies in filling their steerage quotas were all real but they turned a socio-economic situation into a morality play. The study of the role of intermediaries remains too political in Italy and too moral and too fragmentary in North America.

The new interpretation of Italian emigration, identifying the role of chain migration, ethnic receiving neighbourhoods and continuity of kinship ties from Italy to the receiving country improves upon the devil theories about *padroni* and agents. The Australian demographer, J.S. Macdonald, presents a model for emigration "in which prospective migrants learn of opportunities, are provided with transportation, and have initial accommodation and employment arranged by means of primary social relationships with previous migrants."[17] The "chain migration" interpretation has an easy answer to the charge that South Italians are "amoral familists" who distrust everyone beyond their nuclear family. Emigration itself brought more extended kinship and friendship systems out of desuetude because they were needed. This is the contention of an excellent study of Buffalo Italians by V. Y McLaughlin. Stress on family ties and the anthropological approach have advantages but one obvious drawback is the tendency to observe the strength of the immigrant family and to see ethnic neighbourhoods as primitive idylls, where money, class and terror – all realities of the Italian countryside – do not penetrate. McLaughlin, for example, discusses the number of boarding houses in Buffalo and remarks that many boarders were *paesani* of the homeowners. There is no mention of the possibility of their paying rent, let alone of their being gouged or exploited.[18]

The process of migration was not as familial and *paesano* as "chain migration" theory implies nor as episodic and rapacious as the literature about *padroni* would suggest. Often ignored is the impact of class structure in Southern Italy, in the migration itself, and in the Little Italy receiving depots. "Middle class brokers" served and preyed upon their countrymen from Calabrian village, along the railways, to Naples, and finally in New York, Buenos Aires, and Toronto. Neither in Italy nor in America was this so-called *borghesia mediatrice* (middle class go-between) class a caste. Just as people known as *generetti* (little big people) or *mercanti di campagna* (merchants of the countryside) emerged in the South of Italy after unity, so too the business of emigration made other emigrants rich or richer in America. In that world of preindustrial social groups, petty transactions and literacy as "white magic," the role of the middle classes is ill-defined. If one accepts the view of Antonio Gramsci that "the South was reduced to a semi-colonized market of the North",[19] it is possible to see that a natural product of such an economy is men. The "slavetraders" may have been a few *padroni* in America or the subagents and agents of large steamship companies in the Italian South but all the middle classes gained from the commerce of migration.[20]

Money and socio-economic structure were at the heart of emigration. To understand the role of middle-class intermediaries, we must enlarge our definition of agents, and look for all the parts of the process of migration where services were rendered and money exchanged. The agents were all those who stood between the parochial, rural lower classes and the large society, those who mediated between feudalism and modernity.

The steamship, as the intrusion of modern technology into the South, allowed the middle classes a role in migration to North America and in the process of urbanization itself. They responded to the enlarged economy with their only product, men. When, for example, the government in the 1900s, tried to reduce the number of official subagents to one for each district with more for those areas recognized as remote, almost 2,000 communes petitioned to be classified as remote areas.[21] Men obviously encouraged emigration for the *senseria* (steamship company bounty) alone, and in towns like those that petitioned, most of the non-peasant structure saw profit in emigration. Prime Minister Crispi defined agents inclusively in his 1888 legislation.[22] Article 6 of Crispi's Law promised jail and a fine for any unlicensed person "who, for financial gain, counselled or excited the peasants of the nation to emigrate, who furnished and procured ships passage for the emigrants, intervened as mediators between the emigrant and the steamship lines, or who transported them to the port of embarkation, or to the place of destination, or in any way, personally, or by means of others, with verbal, written or printed information set out to promote emigration."

Sensing perhaps, the blurred line between cash transactions, favour and patronage in such a setting, Article 7 added a fine of 1,000 lire for clergy, mayors, and communal officials who, using written or verbal exhortation promoted emigration "anche senza fine di lucre," (even without a profit motive). In fact, the problem faced was a simple one and endemic in the South. The government intended to use the wolves as shepherds for the flock. In the various legislative efforts to regulate emigration and to mitigate the harsh conditions of emigration, the people made responsible were those for whom migration had become a lucrative trade. An Italian Senator, supporting legislation that made local committees of notables responsible for the emigrant's well-being saw the problem: "And when one speaks of local authority, we mean to speak of all; from mayor to pharmacist, from tax collector and doctor to field guard – all must treat the peasant differently." Yet any addition to the rules increased the power of go-betweens.[23] Bureaucrat or businessman, the middle-class brokers stood between the less literate and the newly enlarged state and economy.

A case in point is the Royal Decree of 1901 requiring the prospective emigrant to apply in writing or orally to the mayor of the commune for a passport.[24] The latter would investigate and, if he approved, forward a *nulla osta* (no obstacle) to the prefect who would judge the case. To receive the *nulla osta*, the emigrant had to guarantee that he was leaving no dependents; that he was not under age; that he was not an ex-convict, and that he was not enmeshed in Italy's military conscription and reserve system. If all went well, the emigrant would receive his passport for 2 or

3 lire. With the problem of illiteracy and the peasant's assumptions about government corruption in mind, let us examine the possibilities of this minor and well-intentioned piece of legislation.

It is here one should question the concept of "amoral familialism" and "chain migration" in the *Mezzogiorno*. How will the emigrant move through the maze of unknown regulations; can he do it through emigration-wise relatives? Perhaps. The "war of all against all" has in the South of Italy as in any capitalist society a logical extension. What cannot be done through the family, can be done with money. Money insures that services rendered are in the self-interest of both parties. A little *bustarella* (a small envelope full of lire) for the mayor, even if he is an honest man, some votive candles bought for the Church when the priest writes a letter to a brother in Boston. Social and economic interaction in a South Italian village does not end at the borders of the family. Somewhere near those borders money could produce truces and allies in the war of all against all, and it made one man's family interest another man's family interest. In fact, what is pathetic about the South Italian conversion to a money nexus is that the peasant's understanding of it causes him to force money on those honest brokers, "caretakers" and state officials whom he need not pay. "Chain migration" and travel-wise veterans could only provide the map of whom to pay and how much to pay. If, as Macdonald claims, familialism and patronage were "the motor driving the chains which took so many emigrants from this part of Italy..." then money was the grease on the chains, and the migrants knew it.[25]

Our emigrant, then assuming that government is a thing of "foreign thieves" must take the first steps toward the American shore through a maze of papers, extortion and hostility. Let us see how many ways he can spend his money. He might perhaps hire a notary to write up the petition to the mayor for a *nulla osta*; his own illiteracy, the fact that the notary is the mayor's cousin, and the tendency of the genteel classes to treat him as a beast of burden make that a wise precaution. Now what if he had dependents or had been convicted of a felony, might he not pass the line of legality and, *bustarella* in hand, sally forth to buy the necessary approval. If he were too young, he could pay a notary or lawyer for signed statements that he was of age, and if there were complications in his military status, he could expect to spend both legal and illegal money. Then he waited for his passport, fearing, as only the illiterate can, the places he had marked his name, and the papers he had seen passed. In the very act of leaving, he may have tied himself down: "The sale of his cottage or farm hut, the mortgaging of a few goods to procure money for the trip" or the outright deal with a loan shark were not things that freed him from his *paese* but tied him to the local "middle class brokers."[26] The man called a *mercante di campagna* in one source may simply be a loan shark in another, and if a Verga novel can be trusted, he may often be an uncle as well. Money borrowed against property ran as high as 60%. Tribute to the middle class and its full scale commitment to profit as intermediaries is the fact that by 1913 interest on mortgages and loans was down from 50% to 3 or 4%, and the day was gone, according to one source, when "a single agent in a single year in not too big a town, could make 25,000 lire."[27] The ship's bounty, even at 50 lire, was but the beginning; it was only the most obvious transfer of money in the migrant process. The *via dolorosa* of Oscar Handlin's uprooted peasant of the 1840s was by the 1890s an organized and mechanized *via commerciale* for South Italians.

"The inevitable decorations at every train station [were] the placards of sailing and steamship companies," and in the harbour area of Naples more banners, agencies with confusing names, and men with as much chance of being fleeced as of embarking. "The region around the harbour [was] thronged with steamship ticket offices, often flying the American flag and with emigration agencies, and the line between the two [was] frequently very difficult to draw."[28] The importance of "chain migration" lay in the fact that they "had folk knowledge of the obstacles and pitfalls ahead." For example, peasants from a certain village in Basilicata could resist the gaudy advertising for Lloyd Sabaudo or the German steamships because they had been told by a veteran migrant that "on English ships, one always eats more civilly".[29] Even though forewarned, the migrants travelling from village to town to Naples were subject, before they reached the port, to such a camorra of *sensali, incettatore, viaticali, grande, piccoli, minuti, commercianti*, – all names for go-betweens – that one can describe the trade as having primary and secondary benefits. Naples, a somnolent port, grew rapidly and that growth was based on the trade in men. In 1900, the port of Naples represented only 8% of the total port activity of Italy but was first in third class passengers.[30] The port too was embarkation point for wine, olive oil, garlic, cheese, macaroni and other products for growing Italian colonies overseas. Returning migrants – the successful *Americani* travelling first class, the failed *cafoni* in steerage – remittances, ship provisioning, kept the port expanding. After humans, the coal for the new railways was the most important cargo coming in. Narrow gauge track networks spread out from Naples.[31] No one has studied their development and relationship to emigration, but the small coaches and the routes chosen suggest that they were an integral part of the commercial network of migration.

Only local area studies will fully explain the ramifications of emigration. For every account of fields left fallow and gentry left without peasants, references exist about refurbished villages along the railway right-of-way. A Sicilian mayor claimed that only American remittances kept most small holders from losing their property for non-payment of taxes.[32] Still, it is clear that bureaucrat, notary, lawyer, innkeeper, loan shark, *mercante di campagna*, runners in the harbour city, agents, even train conductors depended on the emigration trade. On the other side of the ocean the scale of remittances, uninterrupted traffic of emigrant and repatriate, all the auxiliary food trades, seasonal migrants and the network of financial and commercial exchange justify treating Southern Italy and Italy overseas as one society and one informal economy, and parallels to the rural/urban migration become more trenchant. No Italian city, least of all Naples, provided enough urban employment for the Southern masses, but when New York, Chicago and Pittsburgh are treated as part of a whole, then a useful picture emerges. Replace agents in Italy, *padroni* in America, not just with "chain migration and ethnic neighbourhood," but with the thought that the same social relations and class structures (allowing ecological variants) existed on both sides of the Atlantic. The expansion of employment for peasants in the industrial world outside of Italy meant expanding opportunity for the pre-industrial middle class in Southern Italy. According to Isaacs, "at all times a relatively large number of capitalist immigrants has soon joined the ranks of the destitute while others, after starting without any means, become highly successful within a relatively short time." As one old emigrant put it: "The big fish always follow the minnows that they feed on."[33]

Paeans to American opportunity such as one finds in Nelli's study of Italians in Chicago – "Over the years newcomers and their children moved up the economic ladder, progressing from unskilled labour into commercial, trade, and professional lines, " – obscure the social structure and economy of emigration. In an earlier riposte to *The Uprooted*, Vecoli observed that most immigrants came from or near a "rural city" not "simple communities of agriculturists...their social structure included the gentry and middle class as well as the peasants."[34] Even if more new men were apparent in a Little Italy's elite, they had "arrived" in the same way as the middle-class *generetti* in Southern Italy. The trade that made them successful was a trade in men and in handling the problems of less literate country-men. Let me give, before I go on, some impression of the magnitude and the intercontinental nature of that trade.[35]

Most contemporaries noted the steamship companies' preference for the South European passenger trade because of the high rate of returnees.[36]

The flow of people in a peak year like 1907 – about 250,000 returnees and 300,000 outward bound – provides a sense of the scale and the unity of the immigrant business. Money went and came with the migrants. The Dillingham Commission estimated that 85 million dollars was sent to Italy in 1907; $52 million of that was processed by immigrant bankers. The Cashiers Office at Ellis Island as a depository of alien funds held as much as $500,000 monthly. An "Immigrant Clearing House" of the Trunk Line Railroad Association on Ellis Island often handled $40,000 a day in cash ticket sales.[37]

Remittances were made to relatives for the support of the young or the old, for sisters' dowries, as bride prices, or as passage money in cash or in the form of prepaid tickets. Money was also sent home to pay mortgages contracted to make the original trip or to invest in new land.[38] All such transactions passed through the sticky hands of brokers on both sides of the ocean. Profit ranged from the staid and honest 2 or 3% on every transaction taken in by the subagents of the Banca di Napoli to that of "shrewd speculators acquiring vacant land parcels at low prices, in anticipation of the return of emigrants, then breaking them into cultivable units, and selling them in advance."[39] The process of departing and the process of remitting served the long-range purposes of those who since the *Risorgimento* had seen the land as a commodity and not a patrimony. The mortgaging and selling and the rebuying of small-holds, the consolidation of arable property, beyond providing endless opportunity for notary, lawyer, banker, pawnbroker and local bureaucrat, continued a process begun against the impecunious nobility by the *mercante di campagna*. In Italy overseas, ethnic realtor, "immigrant banker," broker, and travel agent waited to perform similar functions. The continuum was noticed by an Italian Senator writing in 1905.[40] He observed that, though the crops and employment situation in the South were no better or worse in 1904 than other years, there was a decline in migration, new mortgages, and land sales. He reasoned that the decline had to be the result of a crisis of confidence, engendered by the presidential campaign in the U.S. and the bloody strikes with Italian involvement in Colorado and Pennsylvania. One economic pulse beat for the Italian South and for Italo-America.

Earlier, the short life of the real *padrone* structure was mentioned. The term itself, conjuring up both too much *padrone* and too much ward healer, has not died. Although disinclined to see the role of brokers and the money economy in the "family" process of emigration, "chain migration" theorists have not completely given up the *padrone*. Macdonald, for example, includes under that heading "employment agents, sweatshops, subcontractors, bankers, landlords, foremen, scribes, interpreters, legal advisers or ward bosses."[41] Two American historians have provided an interesting study of a man whom they label a *padrone*.[42] His career included the following occupational sequence: 1888 – foreman, saloon owner, 1890 – emigrant banker and court interpreter, 1891 – grocery business, notary public, and steamship agency, 1893 – general contractor and ultimately political notable. The progression in this *padrone's* career suggests that he was a general go-between, a *mediatore*, that he began as a labour boss simply reflected the mediation needs of the first migrants. His later career grew from serving as broker in the variety of encounters that immigrants had with the Old and New World governments and economies. In other words, he provided the same services as his middle class counterparts in the Italian South. In the same way, his pretensions to power in the Republican Party ran parallel to the *generetti's* attempt to join the older *signori* of the South.[43] All in all, it would be better to drop the attenuated term *padrone* and recognize the ethnic middle classes.

Using the less equivocal term "immigrant banker", the Dillingham Commission tried to explain the intermediary role of the immigrant middle-class in turn-of-the-century New York. The need for intermediaries in North America was as great or greater than in Italy. Instead of a Tuscan bureaucrat or Piedmontese *carabiniere*, one might have to face an Irish "cop" or Yankee customs officer. High illiteracy rates created an equally high dependence on scribes, notaries, and interpreters. Now the neologisms that bred in the strange new world of migration increased dependence upon the "middle class" *paesano* who spoke English, Italian, dialect and the new Italo-American language of *setaiola* (city-hall) and *grosseria* (store).[44] The handling of money, bureaucratic problems, and minor legal questions, some loan sharking and problems of transport were the main business of the go-between on both sides of the ocean. On both sides, dependence on a literate *paesano* was the lesser evil in the face of officials assumed to be thieves and known to be outsiders. Familialism and patronage in simple anthropological terms are just not compatible with the number of notaries and quasi-lawyers in the South Italian global village.

Of 47 Italian immigrant bankers investigated by Dillingham's Commission, all served as agents or subagents for steamship companies: 34 carried on other business as well.[45] 20 were notaries; 6 realtors; 8 employment agents; 9 postal substations and 7 grocery stores.

Imagine the immigrant broker's storefront and look at a contemporary Toronto ethnic travel agency; "all available space is filled with steamship posters, money-changing notices and many coloured placards, alluring always in the inducements they present." There above the door, it says *Banco Italiano-Notario-publico - agente marittimo*. The affairs that go on inside the door affect the economy of two continents. The notarized papers, prepaid tickets and mortgage agreements have their counterpart in Avellino, Benevento, Campobasso, all the cities of the South. The banker takes 3% on your remittance, but he speaks your dialect. He buys your lire at 5% discount and sells at 3%, but even the *Banco di Napoli* agent cannot understand your problem, fails to stay open in the evening and he does not know where your home town is. Your remittance may change the cadastral structure of your village, make your sister marriageable, or fix your mother's cottage roof, but a percentage of it at both ends falls in myriad and wonderful ways to the middle-class brokers. Why should the ethnic neighbourhood be different from the home town, and why not continue to accept the evil one knows over the unknown evils of American or Piedmontese bureaucracy?

Although there are obvious changes in the *ambiente* and ecology of migration, the idea of a "commerce of migration" and of a *borghesia mediatrice* can be pursued in contemporary Toronto.[46] The most important changes are probably, 1/ the aeroplane, 2/ the increased consciousness of Italian nationality and increased literacy in the post-Fascist period, and 3/ the presence in the Canadian-Italian migration of more Northern Italians and more urban people. Despite these changes, the "commerce of migration" in Canada, it seems to me, provides better comparisons for research with the old migration than does the contemporary United States where two generations of nostalgia have softened the image of exploiters, relatives and *paesani*. Most groups of Italo-Americans now unconsciously or pridefully overemphasize the extended family and its patriarchal strength. Healthy family structure is, after all, one of the criterions that they use to distinguish themselves from more recent Latin and Black migrants.[47]

The Italian community of greater Toronto numbers almost half a million people. The continuity between this Italo-Canada and Italy is less tentative than in the earlier migration. The technical acceleration of communications; the competition between CP and Alitalia for the airborne version of steerage, is obvious. The new immigrant, more literate and attuned to a mass consumption economy, is followed to Canada by more than the cheese, oil and occasional musical *maestri* that came after the Umbertine peasants who migrated to the United States. Phonograph records, clothing styles, packaged foods, Fiats, follow and create or bring a merchant class to profit from and distribute them. Even a construction worker who winters on unemployment cheques among the mandarin oranges and prickly pears of his *paese* does his part for the social and economic continuity.

Despite higher literacy and the benign welfare state, the emigrant still seems to need a "middle class go-between." Mistakes at airports, before government agents, and in banks can be just as costly as they were in Naples in 1895 or New York in 1910. Signing the wrong papers can bring anything from unwanted aluminum siding to deportation. It was estimated in 1961 that 25% of the Italians in Toronto spoke no English at all. Many others were surely functionally illiterate in English; most are more comfortable in dialect than in Italian itself. In his book, *Non Dateci Lenticchie*, O. Bressan, a "leader" in Italo-Toronto, notes that his countrymen have "a pessimistic concept of public officials in general and of state and parastatal officials in particular."[48] The same structure of illiteracy and distrust of government agencies that characterized life in the south of Italy exists in contemporary Toronto. Naturally then, intermediaries emerge or follow the migration. "Caretakers" and "intellectuals" dedicated to serving the migrants also proliferate. Toronto has political groups, religious and educational institutions, and philanthropic organizations for the immigrant community.[49] To the extent that the middle classes – those who are *civile e gentile* in the eyes of the migrant – dominate these institutions, they are little different from commercial intermediaries like banks and travel agencies: "The claim of any person or institution to be inspired by zeal for public rather than private advantage will be regarded as a fraud."[50] In observing this, Banfield mistakenly considered peasant distrust of the middle class as an aspect of amoral familialism's "war of all against all." However, distrust is the heritage of how expensive dependence on one's "betters" in Italy has been, especially since the advent of the cash economy. Can you really trust a man who offers to translate for you at an immigration hearing, or to make out your tax returns without charge? What is his game? Since the end of feudalism, or at least of the *Risorgimento*, the common people have paid in cash and deference for their inferior social and educational status, and they are used to it.

There is in Italo-Toronto, dependence on middle-class "brokers" ranging from ethnic driver education schools and realtors to consulting only doctors from one's *paese*. The most typical broker in the community is probably the travel agent. The Italo-Canadian Commercial Directory for 1971 lists about fifty travel agents in Toronto, although the number would be far greater if it included formal and informal subagents.[51] Toronto agencies often have business or familial ties with subagents in

Italy, and some also tend to serve a specific *paese*: e.g., the Trinacria agency for Sicilians, the Venezia agency for people from the northeast of Italy. The pattern follows that of the "immigrant banks" of New York in the 1900s. The agent serves as go-between for his immigrant client in almost all conceivable encounters with the outside world.

A travel agency advertisement in the *Italo-Canadian Commercial Directory* almost duplicates the immigrant banker's advertisements addended to the Dillingham Commission reports of 1911. After mentioning the travel part of the business, the agency offers *"servizio Contabilita,* Bookkeeping service, Income Tax, *procure* [proxies], *atti notarili, cambio valuto, servizio per il publico [sic] fino alle ore 9:00 pm."* Another travel agent offers *"prenotazioni e biglietti ogni destinazione"* but also *"pratiche di ogni genere, rimesse di denaro...."*[52] The following in order of frequency are the services that first generation Toronto Italians expected a travel agent to render: 1/ Tickets, prepaid tickets for relatives in Italy and other travel arrangements, 2/ Arrangement of passports, 3/ "going to Immigration," 4/ Remittances, 5/ Helping with unemployment insurance, 6/ Making out Income Tax forms, 7/ Dealing with the Workmen's Compensation Board, OHSIP, Old Age Pensions, and 8/ Dissolving partnerships and other notarial work.[53]

After doctors and lawyers, travel agents ranked highest among Italo-Canadian professionals and semi-professionals in the minds of those interviewed. Some people, in fact, expected to pay a fee for visiting a travel agent just as they would for visiting a doctor or lawyer. The most common remark about these agents was that they "know the right people." Although the phrase smacks of mystery and criminality, it is simpler than that. According to one immigrant, his travel agent was his "voice to the outside." That is what the intermediaries always were. Because of their assimilation to *italianità*, the money economy, and the Piedmontese conquest, the South Italian middle classes stood between local society and the larger polity. The "immigrant bankers" of the American East Coast dominated their countrymen because they were already bourgeois or Italo-American while the newcomers were still greenhorns and peasants. In Toronto, the intermediaries are also men between cultures. They may support ethnic radio stations and Italo-Canadian newspapers; they promote local Italian culture, but their role in the community comes as much from their assimilation to Canadian life as from their higher levels of literacy and sophistication.

Their humbler countrymen pay the intermediaries for the use of their literacy and assimilation. For example, it is estimated that, before the introduction of the current points system, 80% of the migrants to

Toronto from Italy were "sponsored." Sponsorship constitutes the most obvious form of chain migration. Yet 60% of the people interviewed had consulted travel agents about sponsoring relatives, and some had depended upon agents to find them sponsors. All had paid for the services rendered over and above the price of prepaid tickets. When asked why he had consulted an agent about sponsorship, a veteran migrant showed the resignation and skepticism of those who depend upon intermediaries. "You may not need a travel agent to get to Canada;" he said, "then again, you may not need a priest to get to heaven."

All this is not intended to suggest the existence of a criminal bourgeoisie or to justify the "waspish" response of those who have always dismissed immigrant problems as the exploitation of one "dirty foreigner" by another. It does maintain that coherent class analysis can cross oceans in a way that the random and episodic study of separate kinds of exploitation cannot. And, now that it is not fashionable to see the immigrant as an uprooted and disoriented countryman, the alternative view should not simply be an anthropological idyll where smiling people use their sense of kinship to cope with modernity. Modernity existed in migration in the form of *lire*, *denari*, *soldi*, and dollar bills. A semi-professional, commercial, and bureaucratic bourgeoisie was and is as much a part of an Italian ethnic neighbourhood or of a Neapolitan village as are religious festivals, grandmothers in black and godfathers.

Notes

1. John Foster Carr, "The Coming of the Italian," *Outlook,* LXXXII (1906), p. 421.

2. Sen. F. Nobili-Vitelleschi. "Espansione coloniale de emigrazione" *Nuova Antologia* (May 1902) 183:107.

3. F. S. Nitti "L'Emigrazione italiana e suoi avversari" (1888) *Scritti sulla questione meriodionale* (Bari, 1959) II:327.

4. F.S. Nitti. "L'Emigrazione." II:333-334 for a breakdown of the prefectoral reports. G. Dore. *La Democrazia italiana e l'emigrazione in America.* (Brescia, 1964) p. 45 suggests that the phrasing of the questionnaire sent to the prefects encouraged *miserià* as an answer.

5. O. Handlin. *The Uprooted.* (New York, 1951) p. 37.

6. F. Thistlethwaite. "Migration from Overseas in the Nineteenth and Twentieth Centuries" in H. Moller. *Population Movements in Modern European History* (New York, 1964) p. 77. *La golondrina* left Italy in November and went to Latin America for the summer there. In 1904, 10% of Italian migrants entering the United States had been there before. The aeroplane has made such seasonal migration from Italy to the Americas even more common.

7. Robert F. Foerster. *The Italian Emmigration of Our Times.* (Cambridge, Harvard, 1919) p. 416.

8. The best account of the politics and legislation of emigration is F. Manzotti, *La Polemica sull'emigrazione nell'Italia unita.* (Milano, 1969).

9. F.S. Nitti. "L'Emigrazione." pp. 305-307; F. Manzotti. *La Polemica*, pp. 69-76.

10. G. Dore. *La Democrazia italiana*, pp. 38-42.

11. *Reports and Abstracts of the Immigration Commission*, 41 volumes, Document No. 747, 61st Congress: 3rd Session (Washington, 1911). Cited henceforth as the *Dillingham Commission*. The *padrone* system and the legislation directed against it are discussed in Volume II of the *Abstracts*, pp. 375-408. The Commission apparently felt that the system was so moribund by 1910 that it did not deserve a separate report. For a warning against the uncritical use of the Commission's Reports see O. Handlin. *Race and Nationality in American Life*, N.Y. 1957.

12. C. Erickson. *American Industry and the European Immigrant, 1860-1885.* (Cambridge, Harvard, 1957) pp. 85-86.

13. H. Nelli, *Italians in Chicago, 1880-1930. A study in Ethnic Mobility.* (New York, 1970) pp. 55-87.

14. *Dillingham Commission.* II: 419.

15. *Dillingham Commission.* I:26.

16. H.P. Fairchild. *Immigration*. (New York, 1913) pp. 148-149.

17. J. S. Macdonald. "Chain Migration. Ethnic Neighbourhood Formation and Social Network." *Millbank Memorial Fund Quarterly*. XLII (Jan. 1964) p. 82.

18. E. Banfield. *The Moral Bases of a Backward Society*. (New York, 1958). V. Y. McLaughlin. "Working Class Immigrant Families: First Generation Italians in Buffalo, New York". Paper delivered at the Organization of American Historians (April, 1971) pp. 6-7 and 11-13.

19. A. Gramsci. *Sul Risorgimento*. (Roma, 1967) p. 103.

20. The term *negriero* (slave trader) was used by F.S. Nitti. "La Nuova Fase della emigrazione d'Italia" (1896) in *Scritti sulla questione meridionale* II:387. A. Mosso. *Vita moderna degli italiani*. (Milan 1906) uses the phrase "commercio di carne umana" p. 76.

21. A. Mosso. *Vita moderna*, pp. 77-78.

22. Quoted in F.S. Nitti. "L'Emigrazione" pp. 304-305.

23. See V. di Somma. "L'Emigrazione nel Mezzogiorno" *Nuova Antologia* (1 June 1907) CXXIX: 517.

24. Royal Decree of 1901 in *Dillingham Commission*, IV: 211. On illiteracy rates see *Annuario Statistico* analysed in *Dillingham Commission*, IV: 186-187. The chief migrating areas of the Italian South (Abruzzi, Apulia, Basilicata and Calabria) had about 60% male illiteracy and 80% female illiteracy. Illiteracy in Sicily was probably higher. Since emigrants came usually from the more rural parts of these areas, the rate of illiteracy among them was probably even higher. V. di Somma. "L'Emigrazione" p. 514. "In 1905, in a commune of about 2,000 people, of 22 inscribed for military service, only 2 presented themselves, all the others had emigrated."

25. J. S. Macdonald and L. Macdonald, "Italian Migration to Australia. Manifest Function of Bureaucracy versus Latent Function of Informal Networks." *Journal of Social History* (Spring 1967) p. 254.

26. A. di San Giuliano. "L'Emigrazione italiana negli Stati Uniti d'America" *Nuova Antologia* (July, 195?) CXVIII: 89-91. See G. Verga. *I Malavoglia*.

27. Amy Bernardy. *Italia Randagia attraverso gli Stati Uniti*. (Torino, 1913) p. 313. However, H.P. Fairchild, *Greek Immigration in the United States* (New Haven, 1911) p. 222 suggests that the weight of remittances lowers the mortgage rate. In either case, the middle class receives its share.

28. A. Bernardy. *Italia Randagia*, p. 311; H.P. Fairchild. *Immigration,* p. 151.

29. A. Bernardy. *Italia Randagia*, p. 312.

30. G. Aliberti. *Profilo del Economia napoletana dall' Unità al Fascismo, Storia di Napoli*, (1975) X. L. Fontana Russo, "La Marina mercantile e l'emigrazione" *Rivista coloniale* (May-June, 1908). R.F. Foerster. *Italian Immigration*, pp. 467-468.

31. F. Benedetti. "Le Strade ferrate della Basilicata e della Calabria" *Nuova Antologia* (June 1902) 183:500-512. This article describes the railroad development but sees no connection with migration.

32. A. Mosso. *Vita moderna*, p. 114 and L. Bodio. "Dell' emigrazione italiana e della legge 31 gennaio 1901 per la tutela degli emigranti" *Nuova Antologia* (June, 1902) 183-533.

33. J. Isaac. *Economics of Migration* (London, 1947). p. 232.

34. H. Nelli. *Italians in Chicago.* p. 20. R. Vecoli. "Contadini in Chicago: A critique of the Uprooted" *Journal of American History* (Dec. 1964) LI: 3, pp. 408-409.

35. R.F. Foerster. *Italian Immigration*, p. 15 on emigrants; pp. 19-20 on repatriation. J. Isaac. *Economics of Migration*, p. 63 estimates a 40% return rate. Foerster points out the limits of the statistics which were based on passports issued and emigration from Italian ports plus Le Havre. Since passports were good for three years, three seasonal migrations as well as any illegal (draft-dodging) migration could go undetected. See also F. P. Cerase. "Nostalgia or Disenchantment: Considerations on Return Migration" in S. Tomasi and M. Engel (eds.) *The Italian Experience in the United States.* (Staten Island, 1970). See Ph.D. thesis on Italian repatriation and remittances written for NYU by Betty Boyd Caroli.

36. A. Mosso. *Vita moderna.* pp. 72-74; *Dillingham Commission*, I: 26.

37. *Dillingham Commission.* II: 427. Vol. 37, Chapter V of the Commission reports had a detailed analysis of Italian remittances and the practices of immigrant bankers. See esp. pp. 271-285. For Ellis Island statistics, the memoirs of the Commissioner E. Corsi. *In The Shadow of Liberty. The Chronicle of Ellis Island.* (New York, 1935), pp. 123-126.

38. J. Isaac. *Economics of Migration*, pp. 244-245; A. Bernardy. *Italia Randagia.* p. 314, and A. Mosso. *Vita moderna*, p. 114.

39. R.F. Foerster. *Italian Immigration*, p. 451.

40. A. di San Giuliano. "L'Emigrazione italiana", p. 91.

41. J. S. Macdonald and L. Macdonald. "Italian Migration to Australia, p. 257.

42. L. Iorizzo and S. Mondello. *The Italian Americans.* (New York, 1971) p. 143. The career is that of Thomas Marnell of Syracuse. The authors describe him as "a classic example of the small Italian businessman's struggle for economic and political power for himself and his people."

43. The mayor in G. di Lampedusa *The Leopard* is an excellent example of a Sicilian *generetto.*

44. A. Bernardy. *Italia Randagia*, pp. 89-93, on new dialects.

45. *Dillingham Commission*, 37: 211 and 311; on immigrant banks generally pp. 197-350.

46. The impressions of Toronto's Italian community in this part of the paper are drawn mainly from two sources. For eight years, students in my Italian history course at the University of Toronto have written one of their two term papers on "anonymous immigrant history" subjects. Palmacchio Di Iulio, pre-Law Student and Immigration Receiving Counselor at the Malton Airport and Joseph Cornacchia, Law Student, helped in the interviewing of over a hundred first generation Toronto Italians.

47. For a scholarly example of this emphasis see L. Tomasi. *The Italian American Family* (New York), 1972, p. 8.

48. O. Bressan. *Non Dateci Lenticchie. Esperienze, Commenti, Prospettive di Vita Italo-Canadase.* (Toronto, 1958) p. 26.

49. For the use of the term "caretakers" as do-gooders see H. Gans. *The Urban Villagers. Group and Class in the Life of Italian-Americans.* (New York, 1962) pp. 142-162. There is a list of Associazioni assistenziali e culturali in *Italo-Canadian Commercial Directory, 1971 (Metro Toronto)* (Toronto, 1971) p. 8.

50. Banfield. *The Moral Bases of a Backward Society*, p. 98.

51. *Italo-Canadian Commercial Directory*, pp. 50-51.

52. *Italo-Canadian Commercial Directory*, pp. 51 and 52: Compare these advertisements with the examples in *Dillingham Commission.* 37:340. Appendix VI.

53. Of a hundred people interviewed, 90% expected services 2 and 3 from a travel agent; about 70% expected service 4, and 40% to 60% expected the other services. To the migrant, the phrase "going to immigration" meant that the agent solved a problem or "arranged" a difficult case. The agents seemed to protect their role as mediators by affecting an air of mystery about the nature of such transactions.

TORONTO'S
LITTLE ITALY
1885-1945*

—————— ❧ ——————

*I*TALIAN COLONIES IN CANADA, UNLIKE THOSE IN THE UNITED STATES, HAVE burgeoned rather than withered since World War Two. Differences in immigration policies between the two countries, revived family or village chain migration, and information about job opportunities in Canada brought thousands of new Italian immigrants to southern Ontario after 1947. Toronto is now a metropolitan area with upwards of half a million Italian immigrants and their descendants. It is also a city with visible and massive Italian neighbourhoods and with healthy ethnocultural institutions that afford an Italian Canadian the opportunity to live and die within an immigrant Italian *ambiente*.

This paper, however, deals not with the contemporary immigrant city but with the more threatened history and vanished world of the pre-World War Two Italian Canadian: a world which formed part of the classic turn-of-the-century Italian diaspora throughout the Americas, a space which was neither fully Canadian nor Italian.

Only a few immigrants from the Italian peninsula had reached Toronto by the middle of the nineteenth century; the city did not emerge as a significant location on the cognitive map of Italy overseas until the 1900s. Even then, although the Toronto settlement served as port of entry and base camp for Italian sojourners who worked in the mining, timber and railway towns of the north or along the Welland Canal to the southwest, the city was not generally well known in Italy. As late as 1914, the Società Umanitaria's *Calendario per Gli Emigranti*, an influential guidebook for immigrants, included a map of Canada that pinpointed the

* First published in *Little Italies in North America*, edited by Robert F. Harney and J. Vincenza Scarpaci (Toronto: Multicultural History Society of Ontario, 1981), pp. 41-62.

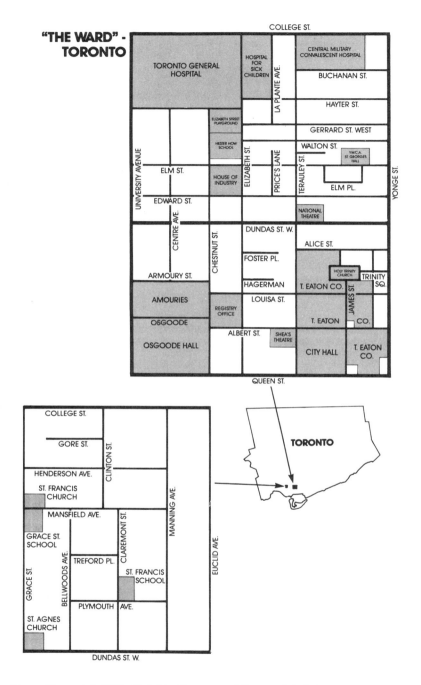

From "Toronto's Little Italy" in Harney and Scarpaci (eds.)

cataracts at Niagara and the city of Montreal but not Toronto.[1] It was as if the migrant labourers sent into the Ontario bush by *padroni* in Montreal and storekeeper/labour bureaus in Buffalo fell off the face of the known earth.

However, there were by the 1890s some places in Italy, ironically enough in rural and isolated areas, in which Toronto as a target of migration was much discussed. For potential migrants from Laurenzana and Pisticci in Basilicata, Pachino, Vita, and Termini Imerese in Sicily and later, Modugno and Monteleone in the Puglia, from areas around Chieti in Abruzzi, Cosenza in Calabria, Udine in Friuli, Caserta near Naples, Toronto was a familiar destination. Information about transportation to and job opportunities in Ontario, about Anglo-Canadian mores, was commonplace among the populace of those areas.[2]

In a sense, Toronto's Italian settlement can be understood best not as a Little Italy but rather as the terminal or way station for a variety of colonies serving the transatlantic networks of many small towns in Italy. The immigrant quarter in Toronto was St. John's Ward, known simply as "The Ward", stretching up from the train station and west of Yonge Street. By the turn of the century it had become a cluster of *colonie*, little outposts of Europe's rural towns, each trying to cope in their own way with the intrusion of a cash economy, over-population, rising levels of expectations and all the other disruptions unleashed by modernity.

If we understand the so-called Little Italy in these terms rather than assuming its Italian national identity, the attitudes and behaviour of its people become more comprehensible, and the occupational pattern of the early settlers emerges as an aspect of the venturesomeness and initiative of each small-town chain of migration. For example, Laurenzana in Basilicata provided a disproportionate number of the city's bandsmen and musicians. Laurenzanese youth, migrating to Toronto, were slotted into specific orchestra and band positions by those who came before them.[3] In that town, prospective immigrants were pre-trained for insertion into the Canadian occupational structure. Such a flexible approach to occupation gives a sophistication and specification to the idea of all migration as a flow of labour to capital and opportunity; it also shows the limitations of studies which use only North American census information to understand *mestiere* (occupation) and status. Migrants depended on relatives, *paesani* and ethnic brokers for intelligence about job opportunities, but, in a sense, each small town in Italy and its *colonia* in Toronto mediated the occupational as well as the family flow. Monteleonesi dominated the shoeshine business. Sicilians moved easily from railway work to banana peddling to domination of fruit and greengrocer enterprise in the city. A Canadian-English grammar for adult foreign students contained a lesson about Mr. Conti, the Italian fruit dealer, but the banana men themselves knew that they were Sicilians from Termini Imerese or Vita and fraternized little with Italians.[4]

It would be wise then for the historian to approach the immigrant settlement, before World War Two, without either the nationalist prejudice of Italian officials and intelligentsia, or the prejudice of the host society, which in its acceptance of stereotypes ignored sub-ethnic or regional differences. The people of Toronto's Ward before 1914 were not Italians *manqué*, torn asunder by *campanilismo*, regional rivalries and local factionalism. That view of them is only possible if one ignores their self-identity and their true ethnoculture. Thirty or so years of political unity in Italy had produced a litany of rhetoric, misgovernment, disappointment and official *Italianità* but not an Italian nationality. The newcomers to Toronto in 1900 were first of all men of their *paese*, and the larger immigrant neighbourhood was not initially a warmly ascriptive urban village of people who had known one another for generations.

Those in the colony who emphasized *Italianità* rather than *paese* loyalty – the newspaper editor, the Methodist preacher, the court translator, a little group of immigrants with more education than the rest – were atypical in both their literacy and influence. Plain folks may have applauded anyone who started a speech with "Noi italiani", as the newspaper editor did, or "connazionali" as the apostolic delegate did, but such an Italian national view of themselves grew slowly in Toronto. The exigencies of life in the new world, the advantage of widening ethnic contact for enterprise, the surge of patriotic feeling for endangered Italy that came with World War One, did help a larger Italian or Italian-Canadian identity to evolve, but that was a North American historical process, not a fact of immigration and it never fully replaced the ascriptive world of the *paese* and its *colonia*.

In the first decade of settlement, the newcomers' networks were not Italian, but specific to their *paese*. For example, Toronto's Pachinesi knew more about events in their hometown and that hometown's other major *colonie* in Lawrence, Massachusetts, and Caracas, Venezuela, than about "other Italians" in Toronto. Until World War One, only a few institutions in Little Italy contained the word "Italian" in their title, and prominent among them were a Methodist mission and a market run by a man with no *paesani* in Toronto.

Italian identity and inter-*paese* contact grew slowly as a result of proximity and shared experience in Canada, and the formation of a single national parish in 1908, Our Lady of Mt. Carmel, did force consolidation of identity (although two communities continued to war over possession of San Rocco as patron). So there was an Italian National Club and the city's first three mutual aid societies bore national or monarchist names: the Umberto Primo, the Vittorio Emanuele and the Operaia Italiana, and by their statutes were open to all Italians. However, when those societies reacting to the decline in membership and the patriotic fervour of the war effort, merged in 1919, to form the Societa di Mutuo Soccorso Italo-Canadese, their records show that the majority of the fraternal members came, in fact, from several towns in Basilicata and Calabria. Nor was there any inevitable urge to create a single Italian or Italian-Canadian identity. When the *colonia* of a given *paese* in the city reached a critical density, sub-ethnic institutions revived or emerged. When the Trinacria (Sicilian), the Famee Furlane (Friulian), Stella Alpina (Piedmontese) societies were formed, even when the Lucchese walked out of the Circolo Colombo because it was dominated by Modugnese, the men involved were not betraying *Italianità* or demonstrating the debilitating effects of *campanilismo* and of factiousness – they were being who they were.

So even though we use Toronto's Little Italy as our frame, in some sense we are describing neither Italians nor Toronto. We are talking about immigrants with loyalties to specific places in Italy and to different segments of the Italian group in Canada. Each *paesano* network inclined its members to a specific view of Toronto's possibilities, of other Italians there, and of other ethnic groups in the city. A street name, a factory location, evoked different images in different Italian villages.

The fate of separate *paese* chains in Little Italy's later history is analogous to that of a stream that goes underground. That seems a sufficient paraphrase of the sociologist's "ethnic-ascriptive solidarities criss-crossing the lonely differentiations of the urban non-kinship Gesellschaften."[5] Sophisticated use of quantification – city directories, parish records and fraternal membership cards – in coordination with the collective memory are producing a complex of typologies within Little Italy in which home-town networks run like veins – the choice of neighbourhood (on the block scale), of occupations, of solidarity, of mutual aid society, of stores and businesses to patronize, of the timing of the transition from a sojourner's to a settler's point of view – all show telltale traces of paesanism. The number of fellow townsmen in Toronto affected a man's ability to be an entrepreneur, his ascriptive status in the community (his political potential), and one can only assume also had impact on everything from his attitude toward Fascism to his pace of acculturation.

The first role of this *colonia* as *paesano* collectivity (or *u paesanu*, as Amy Bernardy has called the sub-ethnic labour broker), was to assure that Toronto remained a profitable target of migration for the *paese's* people.[8] From the earliest music teachers and hurdy-gurdy men to the banana peddlers and day labourers, the newcomers could only survive, as sojourners or settlers, if their skill or willingness to work could be matched quickly to a need of a Canadian employer or a Toronto clientele.

Chain migration meshed with the fate of goods and services in the modern city itself. The transition from the immigration of artists and intellectuals to the immigration of artisans to the immigration of semi-skilled workers simply followed the industrialization of the North American city – the development of factory-made goods and a mass consumption in which the immigrant was both producer and consumer. Italian migration to Toronto reflected changes in the city as much as realities in Italy, and the pre-selection of those who could survive in Toronto was made by families and towns in the old country where Toronto's potential as a target in terms of jobs and of friends and relatives was fully understood.

In effect, as Toronto's Little Italy grew, its versatility as a migration target and its importance to certain towns in Italy also grew. It is clear that newcomers, often the first generation as well, shared a common mental landscape with those from their hometown wherever they were. In 1906, about one-third of Toronto's Italians went back to their hometowns for the winter.[7] Canadian authorities saw that as a slightly pathological sign of transience; think instead of the transactions – familial, economic, and of knowledge – that return from the *colonie* to the *paeselli* probably entailed.

Italian settlements in cities like Toronto grew for another reason. Toronto's Little Italy could be compared to a coastal enclave on a foreign shore. Most railway work gangs and most small Italian outposts in the mining or railroad towns of the Ontario hinterland fell back on Toronto or Montreal for protection against the hostile countryside. The Little Italy that grew up first around the train yards and the wholesale market and then in the Ward in downtown Toronto was the metropolis, along with Montreal, for small huddled *colonie* throughout the interior of the province.

If one sees Toronto's Little Italy in this light, questions about magnitude and permanence – transience arise. The government census and *Might's City Directory* help only a little; the migrant and non-propertied were always under-enumerated. That was inevitable since the census-taker thought of Toronto as a self-contained entity while the migrant worker treated it only as a base camp. Before 1911, the census was taken in April, after that in June, but many men had already left for the north or the Niagara peninsula by the first thaw. Consequently, the number of Italians in the city was underestimated; also, under-enumeration of navvies produced an impression of permanence and middle-class prosperity among the Italians that was only partially true. Men came and went, unrecorded by the larger society:

> As a rule, a good percentage of them are absent from the city during some months in the year. A number have been employed in the new bridge being built near Brockville, by the Ottawa and New York railroad; others have recently gone to work on the railways near Hull, Muskoka, and Niagara Falls, and a good many others have been employed on the Peterborough canal.[8]

This 1897 description of the Toronto Italian workforce affords a proper perspective on the city's role. The city was a place from which to sally forth, or to fall on when unemployed and unable to return to Italy. It was the address to which relatives sent mail. It was the location of the importer of pasta and tomato paste; it was the location of the immigrant banker who transmitted savings to loved ones. In fact, it was where one was, even if one were in the bush several hundred miles away.

Although Toronto and Montreal served many thousands of Italian migrants yearly, the stable communities grew more slowly, and the statistics suggest that migrants still outnumbered permanent settlers. The 1911 census of Italian-born in Toronto counted more than 2,200 males to 800 women in Little Italy. The imbalance between males and females was probably even greater than that, and it suggests a world of boarding-houses, where *paesani* or others lived as boarders with established families.[9]

By tracking through city directories and assessment rolls, one can map the development of a settled Italian community in Toronto, a community that was varied and rich in its occupational structure. Seeing what happened is not, however, understanding how it happened. Who were the new class of shopkeepers and professionals who emerged after 1910? Were they all the offspring of that earliest middle-class immigration? Did young migrants begin as navvies, work as peddlers and succeed as businessmen, or did a different type of immigrant come with sufficient capital to enter directly into the middle classes? The percentage of those who travelled to North America as steerage passengers would seem to suggest otherwise. In other words, we do not know the origins of the bourgeoisie in the first Little Italies.

The emergence of an Italian *ambiente* in Toronto's Ward depended on three circumstances.[10] First, in spite of facile use of the adjective "unskilled," most of the migrants who settled in the city did have a trade, if only at apprentice level. They worked as navvies but they knew how to make shoes, tailor clothes, barber and work as stonemasons. Italians in Toronto, like other small-town and village people, brought a number of precise skills to the city's economy. Here are some occupations the Italian peasant newcomers practised: cooper, grinder, cutter, mirror maker, corset-maker, bell hanger, carriage and coat maker, coal and wood dealer, banana peddler, music teacher, tobacco and cigar retailer, boot-black and boot maker, figurine and model maker, chair canist, plasterer, weaver, confectioner, tailor, image maker, carter, blacksmith, barber, restaurateur, huckster, artist, artificial flower maker, butcher, gun maker, hairdresser, hat manufacturer, boardinghouse keeper, instrument maker, leather and oil dealer, importer of dye and importer of fancy goods, liqueurs and wines, looking glass and picture framer. And oral testimony refines even further status and occupational variety. At one time the man who sold whirligigs and balloons at parades was the richest money-lender in the Ward; many occupations, from informal boardinghouse keeper to translator and document arranger, of course, never appeared in the records of the host society, although income from them served to launch successful real estate and insurance careers.

The second influence on the Italian character of the Ward was the seasonal nature of outdoor labour in Canada. The natural entrepreneurship of many migrants led to a constant probing of economic possibilities in the city during periods of unemployment. The heritage of chronic seasonal underemployment in rural Italy made it natural to accept a multiplicity of jobs as one's lot. Finally, and most important, the demand for unskilled labour almost imperceptibly passed from the countryside to the city. Not doubletracking the transcontinental railways through remote bush areas but rather digging sewers and laying street railway lines in Toronto became the chief source of work for navvies. After 1905 – a great fire the year before had prompted much demolition and building work – more and more navvies became permanent residents of the city, and Toronto's Little Italy achieved the critical mass necessary to support and encourage a kaleidoscope of enterprises and occupations.

The new Italian immigrant workforce was intimately and complexly bound up with the city's growth. Immigrant labour, whether in the form of peddlers, sewer workers or streetcar-track gangs enabled the middle classes of the city to live away from the commercial core of Toronto. It enabled them to live in a style that scant years before had been the preserve of only the wealthy. (It enabled them to live away from the undesirable newcomers as well.) The Sicilian banana men or the Calabrians and

Abruzzians who created a sewer system where there had only been out-houses and cesspools were, through backbreaking labour, supplying amenities to the middle classes. Other Italians who found work in the needle trades in the Spadina area or who rolled cigars and cigarettes all day were also making middle-class life *gentile e civile*, while creating mass production and mass consumption without rapid industrialization.

The relationship of the Italian labourer to the city's economic boom sometimes appears downright providential, if not actually causative. For example, the technological shift, beginning in the 1900s, from wooden boardwalks and dirt roads to cement sidewalks and paved roads corre-sponds so closely to the arrival of Italians in the urban workforce that it defies coincidence. Italian navvies, through bitter experience in the Ontario North or on rocky farms in Italy, knew about excavating, grad-ing and shoring up ground. Large numbers of them, from a land where wood was too scarce to be a building material, had apprenticed as stone-masons. (Few were trained as carpenters.) After the great fire of 1904, Toronto emerged as a city of brick, cement and cobblestone, from its sewers to the large new hospitals in the Ward. It is almost inconceivable that the city could have been so transformed without Italian workers.

Beyond the enlarged payroll that the navvies, now an urban workforce, began to bring home to the Ward, the Italian community had several other major sources of income from the receiving society. Ironi-cally, many of those minor trades that had languished in the restricted market of Italian agrotowns flourished in the no-man's land between con-sumer demand and the slow industrialization of Toronto. Barbers, cob-blers, tailors, victuallers could depend on the middle-class desire for service and new luxuries to provide employment. In these trades, too, Canadian stereotyping – the idea that "this is what those people do and are good at" – seems to have aided these enterprises. So much so that entrepreneurship was sometimes more important than apprentice skills. One of the first successful Italian barbershops (ten chairs) on Toronto's main street was started by a man who had apprenticed as a shoemaker in Pisticci.

Nowhere did stereotype and talent interweave more than in the perishable foods trade. From the earliest days of settlement, there had been Italian fruit stores, and after 1900 the navvy-turned-fruit-peddler was ubiquitous. By 1912 at least half of the fruit stores in Toronto were Italian-owned. Contrast that with only about a hundred out of 1,500 grocery stores, and with less than 10 per cent of the barbershops in Italian hands. Syrians, Macedonians and Greeks provided sharp competition in shoe-shine work, diners and the sale of confectioneries.

Two points emerge. By 1905 the Italians in Toronto earned their primary income by performing their stereotyped roles. In other words, they did the jobs that Canadian society expected of them. On the other hand, that money – from navvies, peddlers, and so forth – was spent within the *ambiente* of the Ward on a myriad of goods and services that gave the lie to the stereotypes. A typical intersection of little Italy might have a steamship agency that doubled as "immigrant banker" or post office, several boardinghouses or inns, a notary and interpreter. These enterprises obviously served as conduits for money, goods and people from Toronto to Italy and to the work sites in the interior. Bakeries and confectioneries, a shoemaker's shop and a newspaper office, along with many little stores selling Italian-style cheese, canned fish, vegetables, and pasta also lined the street. The Ward had few multi-storey buildings, and proprietors tended to live in back or over their shops. The presence of kosher poulterers and fish markets retarded Italian enterprise in those trades. Restaurants, a saloon, the headquarters of several mutual aid organizations were prominent as well. Barbershop steps and the fronts of clubs served as public squares in the evening. The Little Flower Methodist mission was in the heart of Little Italy, while the first Italian parish, Our Lady of Mt. Carmel, was on the fringes of the community.

While the locations of the first clusters of Italian immigrants near the train yards and then in the Ward behind the business district could be explained simply enough, the history of secondary Italian colonies in the city is more complex. Churches, the proximity of work, new public transit routes and cheap housing drew people to new areas, but so did accident and, of course, chain or family migration patterns within the city itself. First we must record the courage and enterprise of men who spoke little English and yet chose to live outside the Ward among their clientele. A high percentage of barbers, tailors, peddlers commuted back to the Ward every evening, but other men dared to move out.

As we have already seen, fruit vendors in particular resided in non-immigrant neighbourhoods. Many such merchants remained isolated. In a number of cases, however, their shops became the nuclei of new Italian residential areas. Men who began in the fruit business became grocers and provisioners. This often meant a change from a Canadian to an immigrant clientele. Sewer or street work near their stores turned them into subcontractors, steamships agents and boarding-house keepers as well. Remarkably, all this activity could go on from the same corner store and upstairs flats that had passed into the hands of a fruit merchant at the beginning of the century.

One sort of distribution that may have been as important as the fruit vendors was that promoted by the street railway development and by the construction of railway sheds in greater Toronto. Just as the railroads played a key role in the settlement of various ethnic groups across the continent, so the substations and junctions created little groups of foreign labourers and later of their dependants in various outlying parts of the city. Track maintenance in the severe winters further attenuated the pattern of settlement. In the city itself the street railway and the radial trolleys served to disperse the original Italian community. Track workers, motormen, and ultimately drivers who worked the long and often split twelve-hour shifts on the street railways found it logical to reside at different turns and junctions on the line.

New settlements patently represented geographical mobility, but it is not clear that any upward mobility was involved. Sample street studies of two of the new areas demonstrate no real difference of occupation or income from the Ward. The housing in the new areas was better than in the Ward, and initially there was less commercial life mixed in with residences. There is, however, some evidence that the new neighbourhoods relied more heavily on one or another *paesello's* network in attracting new settlers.

World War One marked the decline of the Ward as Toronto's main Little Italy. The exhilaration of sharing a patriotic and monarchist war effort with fellow Canadians and with compatriots in Europe gave way to difficult times and fatherless households. Some migrant males in the reserve never returned to Canada. The immigrant housing in the Ward, or the commercial and institutional frontiers of the expanding downtown, had long been a target for reformers and speculators, and the expansion of institutions like the Toronto General Hospital destroyed much of the type of housing that newcomers had depended on. Although many of the Italian communities' central institutions – the parish of Our Lady of Mt. Carmel, the two social clubs, Italian National Club and the Circolo Colombo – remained in the Ward, the younger population and the newcomers of the immediate postwar period were, by 1920, moving west to St. Agnes parish (around College and Grace streets) and to St. Clement's (St. Mary's of the Angels), the new Italian parish being built in the Dufferin area.

Toronto Italia, which had begun as a patchwork of changing or multiple identities, networks and neighbourhoods, at once sub-ethnic and Italian, became a distinct Italian-Canadian entity during the years between the initial consolidation of the settlement before World War One and the total consular and Fascist effort to define the entity in the 1930s. Perhaps by mentioning some research strategies and by profiling some of the communities' institutions, we can recreate some of the ethno-cultural *ambiente* of those years.

One could draw a picture of happy industrious immigrants and their children, playing *bocce*, organizing processions and prospering. In the corner, a small, dark cloud threatens. Slowly and insidiously the settle-ment is corrupted and seized by the Italian consulate, the bourgeois *notabili*, lay and clerical, and the Fascio all'Estero. Anti-Fascist apologists draw such a portrait. In fact, the interwar Little Italies were complex and tension-filled societal entities; they were beset by contradictions in their own class structure, and by regional distrust – the dark side of sub-eth-nic networks in the Depression. The Italian immigrants had been sub-jected to the structural violence of a culturally and bureaucratically homogeneous Anglo-Celtic city. From British-born constables to Scottish health nurses to Irish priests, demons to turn one inward on the safety of the neighbourhood outnumbered multicultural "caretakers."

After 1921 immigration restrictions that seemed anti-Italian were also introduced. The growth of ethnic identity and the later sympathy for Fas-cism, where it did exist, sprang from the same sources – a combination of struggling against discrimination, wounded ethnic *amour propre*, and World War One patriotism. The amalgam showed itself in every aspect of the *ambiente*. Even the Church, dominated by unsympathetic Irish and German prelates, added to the pain.

The provincial superior of the Redemptorists had written at the turn of the century warning Toronto's archbishop that "we know that the spiri-tual betterment of these southern Italians is an almost impossible task."[11] Later, the Italian pastor of St. Clement's showed some of the scars that characterized the assaulted immigrant in the Little Italies and prepared the way for the Lateran Pact and Fascism to influence the community later. In his 1920 parish bulletin, he wrote:

> In the war, we have shown that we are not degenerate Latins as some wished to believe. In Peace we must also show our true col-ors in the matter of Religion. "...Italians We will build our new church in this city and remove the blemish from the good name of Italians."[12]

John Diggins has characterized American Italians as being "ripe for Fascism" because of a "nascent inferiority complex, nostalgic national-ism, and a fear for family solidarity and community."[13] It should come as no surprise that each of those same feelings was also present among Toronto's Italians, and in Canada each had an immediate cutting edge. For example, the introduction of immigration quotas and restrictionism directed specifically at South Europeans in the 1920s led to "a nascent inferiority complex". The heroic memory of the 1915 return of Italian reservists and volunteers from across Canada back to Europe to participate in the war against the Hapsburgs, gave a precise Italian-Canadian content to the "nostalgic nationalism." And the statistics of exogamy and of conversion to Protestantism gave grounds for disquiet about the Italian immigrant family and its traditions. Perhaps the only weakness in Diggins' analysis is that it fails to mention how even before the Fascist formulas of *valorizzazione Italiani* emerged, those three feelings entwined to suggest either renewed *Italianità* or full accultur-ation as the only solution for the *colonia*.

By the 1920s, Toronto's Italians numbered somewhere between then and fifteen thousand people concentrated in crowded neighbourhoods; the winter population, with sojourners filling the boardinghouses, was much higher than that of the summer when labourers dispersed to job sites in the North or along the Welland Canal. As late as 1940, over nine thousand people of Italian descent, about two-thirds of them in the city, resided in three wards. The centres of the three neighbourhoods were the three parishes, Our Lady of Mt. Carmel, St. Agnes (later St. Francis) and St. Clement's (later St. Mary's of the Angels). In these neighbour-hoods the Italian-Canadian residential and commercial density was such that a visible, if not always definable, *ambiente* existed. The steamship agencies, informal banks, newspaper offices, bookstores, restaurants and clubs of the community were there. (There were subtle differences among the three neighbourhoods that had less to do with class and pros-perity and more with the degree to which the two newer parishes in the west had a slightly younger age pyramid, a higher ratio of first-generation Italians to immigrants and clearer patterns of subethnic block settlement resulting from chain migration.)

Although other Italians lived and worked outside the Little Italies, these three neighbourhoods served as reference points. It was to the neighbourhood that they came to replenish their ethnic food supply, see relatives, hear news of work or news from home, and find leisure and social activity. The neighbourhood was the portal back through *colonia* gossip or steamship agent to the hometown in Italy, and to its diaspora through the chief port of disembarkation, New York. Thus it is not at all strange that the *Guida per gli Italiani nel Canada* of 1929 listed the ad-dress of the Italian consul in New York first, of the American consul in Toronto second, and only then, that of the Italian consul in Toronto.[14]

The discussion of the social economy of the neighbourhood and of cultural/political activities which follows, skews the history of Italians in

Canada somewhat. It reflects the world and world view of the articulate immigrants who used the ethnoculture as the medium of their business universe – from grocers and steamship agents ("Ai Connazionali raccomandiamo la loro cooperazione patrocinando le Ditta registrate in questa Guida perché è chiaro che essi sono desiderose di fare affari cogli italiani" – "To our fellow Italians we recommend they patronize the businesses that advertise in this guide because it is obvious that they wish to serve the Italian community") to those who wrote the constitutions of the mutual aid societies urging members to preach and practice *fratellanza fra la colonia*, to the Fascist consular officials and their allies, the club and organization *notabili*, who wished through "energetic tutelage" to teach the community "to think and act *italian-amente*." All of these leaders advocated an ethnic collectivity and community which was not a reality.[15]

This was true of the democratic anti-Fascists who reminded the local Fascio in the pages of *L'Emigrato* that the *colonia* had organized itself during World War One without "either Fascism or instructions from Rome but simply in response to its own conscience."[16] In other words, those whose records and remarks come to the historian from traditional sources leave a picture of Little Italy as a cultural and political entity ignoring the ragged edges of slippage (acculturation) or the underlying, and ofter controlling, role of sub-ethnic (regional) identity and network.

Permit me a note of caution here. This paper is not about Italian ethnicity in Toronto, but only about Little Italy. The census of 1941, as we have noted, shows at least one-third of the Italian population was not in the ethnically defined geographical cluster. By that time, over 80 per cent of Italians were naturalized Canadians; only British stock had a higher rate of intermarriage with other groups than the Italians did. And while 90 per cent of those over forty gave Italian as their mother tongue, the figure dropped to half for those under fifteen and only 2 per cent of the Italian-descent group spoke only Italian. So a Little Italy reflected not an Italian enclave but rather an ethnoculture in flux, and no study of the neighbourhood can ever yield up a truthful measure of the confused spectrum of loyalty – to *paese*, to Italy, to Italo-Canada, to English Canada – along which members of the group ranged.

The interwar *colonia* contained a variety of associations and organizations which influenced its attitudes. Periodically efforts were made to coordinate those associations into an umbrella organization, a *comitato intersociale* by the Italian consular officials, but such efforts rarely succeeded. That lack of success had deeper causes than fractiousness or jealousy among leaders. If one looks at the officers of different organizations in the 1920s, one is immediately struck by the diversity and relative equality of the elite. Although the stereotype of Italian settlements usually contains *prominenti, notabili, grossi personaggi, padroni* who are seen as controlling sentiment and often business as well, Toronto Little Italies simply were not like that.[17] No Italian consul, no Franciscan or Salesian priest, no president of a benevolent society or head of a Friulan, Sicilian, Lucchese, or Basilicata *paese* club or clan group, no immigrant banker effectively dominated or controlled anyone but his own clientele. Even the notables who gravitated to the local Fascio had, in the 1920s, little influence beyond it. It was rare for a man to be an officer of more than one organization and ascriptive status based on having many *paesani* or a good reputation clearly mattered more than business success or general political clout in being elected to organizational positions. Some men and families from Pisticci and Laurenzana clearly enjoyed great informal reputations. The president of the Societa di Mutuo Soccorso Italo-Canadese could stare down the stray Black Hander in the community with impunity, threaten to punch the Fascist consul, force the clergy to keep a youth athletic club from being infiltrated by the *Avanguardisti*, (a Fascist youth group), condone the publishing of an anti-Fascist newspaper from the society's offices and yet be willing to extend his influence beyond the early settlers from his *paese*.

A well-known doctor, one of only four of Italian descent, himself a veteran of the war and of the earliest Fascist street fighting in Italy, could not carry large numbers of patients into Fascism with him even though he appeared on the executive of the Fascio, the Ex-Combattants Association, and the Comitato Intersociale, and even though he was respected for his education and as a healer. Power was not transferable because, in a sense, despite the wishful thinking of the intelligentsia, there was no *colonia*. A list of the so-called *associazioni coloniali* – from the Giuseppe Garibaldi Orange Lodge (led by a Protestant Italian evangelist), through mutual aid societies, drama groups, lodges of the Sons of Italy, sodalities, *paese* clubs, to leisure clubs – reflects the remarkably diffuse activity and leadership in the colony.

Cross-referencing the lists of officers of associations with one another does not yield interlocking directorates or a single colonial elite. A published list of Italian businessmen and professionals in Toronto from the 1930s offers a chance to study the class base of the organizational leadership. It becomes clear that class or occupational status influenced organizational life far less than paesanism and ascriptive reputation did. Even the contrived societies steered by the consulate and the Fascio involved volatile alliances of professionals and businessmen with local fanatics, veterans and *fascisti di prima ora*, representing a local parallel to the Italian reality of the 1920s.

While all these opportunists insisted on the need for the *colonia* to be a single entity and viewed its inhabitants as compatriots or as a community of Italian families, the common people of the neighbourhoods had their habits of defensiveness about dialect-speaking, about humble origins, about the familialism and paesanism reinforced. They were made constantly to see themselves as failed Italians by their own intelligentsia.

In fact, they were simply who they were – immigrants and migrants in North America caught between their own startling mobility and their search for security, moving through socio-economic networks and cultural settings at once regional, Italian and Canadian.

For example, the bankruptcy files of Ontario contain proceedings that deal with two of the more devastating immigrant bank/steamship agent defaults in the city in the 1930s. From those records, the historian can build a detailed picture of a Little Italy entrepreneurial career in its relationship to family, *paese* group and the whole *colonia*. From the extant guides and almanacs of the community, one can find the number and variety of Italian professionals and businesses, and the memory culture provides information about their clientele and regional background. This sort of detail when compared with other Little Italies leads to very interesting historical differences.

The consolidation of the *colonia* into a single Italian-Canadian ethnicity never fully replaced the more natural local and familial values of the immigrants. It did however give the appearance of heightened Italian patriotism and of less factionalism. So it served as both cause and effect, and occasionally justification, for the interventionism that the Italian consular service was to practise. Lamenting the fractiousness of Little Italies – "a place of a thousand trifling, provincial, and local animosities"…"an army without officers, commanded by corporals and sergeants" – had been a favourite pastime of the Italian consuls and upper-class visitors from Italy long before the Fascist rise to power. The slogan of the Fascists and their plan to provide the moral impetus, ("lo spirito propulsore") to the Italianizing of the Little Italies was merely the culmination of such thought.[18]

The Italian consular officials, immigrant bankers and colony intelligentsia had a virtual monopoly of contact with the homeland. When the former became agents of Fascism, the impact on the local community was inevitable. Probably a little over one-third of Toronto's Italian community were Italian-born, but most families had more precise ties with the homeland than nostalgia or a vague sense of kin. The continuous volume of flow of remittances is a better way of measuring that than pointing to the drying up of new immigration that came with restrictions in 1924.

So although Toronto had its own *fascisti di prima ora*, who were veterans of the Italian war effort, and then immigrated, and although the *colonia* had certainly been prepared by the patriotic gore of World War One and the Revisionist rhetoric of the postwar years for the coming of Fascism, when it came, it came as an intervention of the Italian government into the affairs of a Canadian ethnic group.

In return for "energetic tutelage," the protection promised "under the tricolore," North American Italians and their communities would, Mussolini hoped, be subject to a "penetrazione duraturo ed efficace" of Fascist values. They would be shaped into a powerful lobby that could put pressure on the American and Canadian governments in favour of the political interests of the Italian homeland. In fact, Bastianini, the head of the Fascio all'Estero, compared the political clout of a "few million Irish Americans" and the Jugoslav committees in the United States during World War One to the political disorganization and impotence of "Little Italies". He saw in the new Fascio a means of creating "un anima sola" in the colonies, a means of overcoming that sense of Italy pervasive among the immigrants, as "una somma di ricordi tristi e lieti o un cumulo di rancori repressi." The new effort would lead to an increased Italianization by every means in every field.[19] Italianizing of the *colonie*, of course, meant not just making the ethnic group prouder of itself and more consequential in North American politics, it also implied that with Fascist leadership, localisms and fractiousness which characterized Little Italies would be broken down and replaced with high (national) Italian politics and culture.

So through the consular service, Fascist Italy intended to "guide the lives, co-ordinate and encourage the activities, encourage initiation of our people in foreign lands." The immigrant would no longer be abandoned to his new proprietors; the regime hoped to keep him as much an Italian – with the rights and duties of the citizen – as it could. Between 1925 and 1940, the Italian consular service in Canada succeeded in some of its goals. Certainly they compounded the confusion of immigrants between the party and the homeland, and the bureaucracy; they also managed to leave the impression with the larger Anglo-Canadian society that most Italian-Canadians were involved with Fascism. Although that was not other than a respectable activity until after 1935, the later reaction to it cost the community dearly. For those who found themselves rounded up as dangerous subversives in 1940 simply because their names appeared on the guest list of the Casa d'Italia (consular offices as well), there was terrible irony in the metaphor of Mussolini's earliest speeches on the new "energetic tutelage." In 1923, the Duce had described the new cable being laid to the Americas as "un braccio gigantesco che la patria distende sui suoi figli lontani per attrarli a se e per renderli sempre più partecipi dei sui dolori delle sue gioie, del suo lavoro, della sua grandezza e della sua gloria" – ("a giant arm which the nation extends to its sons far away in order to attract them to itself and to let them share in its sorrows, joys, its work, its greatness and its glory.")[20] Contact with the "giant arm" had given many Canadians of Italian descent a real taste of the old country's sorrows.

However, as late as 1934, those in the Italian community who protested against Fascist influence in Toronto were seen as a cranky leftist minority and those who supported Mussolini's regime were viewed, not incorrectly, as simply doing honour to their heritage. It was only when Great Britain herself turned against Mussolini, during the Ethiopian conflict, that the more powerful agencies of Anglo-Canadian public opinion began to attack foreign influence in Toronto. Until then Mussolini, the champion of the middle classes against Bolshevism, seemed to be winning respect and approval for Italy in the world. His solution to the problem of the "red flaggers" and later the Depression found support from part of the press in Canada, from many businessmen, academics and veterans. Respectable Italian-Canadians, full of the patriotism of World War One, could, between 1922 and 1935, support Fascism with the full approval of their fellow Canadians. At last for the Anglo-Saxons, who, many Italians felt, had never understood the importance of Dante or Verdi, there was an Italian and an Italy to obliterate the image of ragged street musicians and migrant track labourers. That Italian and his way of running a country was praised by everyone from the American ambassador to leading British politicians. In a debate at McGill, Knights of Columbus debaters had outpointed a visiting Oxford team which had tried to defend the proposition that Fascism was not good for Italy. A Canadian senator, not of Italian descent, had contributed the money to paint Mussolini's picture on the apse of Madonna della Difesa parish in Montreal's Mile End. At the Central Neighbourhood House in Toronto, long a centre of the Anglo-Celtic "caretakers" efforts to acculturate Italians, a little bit of Fascism was an accepted part of the Italian Ladies Club ritual:

> At tables gay with the national colours are served homemade maca-
> roni, force-meat and salad, all the traditional dishes – the whole

thing prepared by club members. Following the feast comes the dance when young and old join in the Tarantella – accompanied by the tambourine, and the evening is brought to a close with the Fascisti "national anthem."[21]

So the singing of "Giovinezza" was as cute, as Italian, as normal to Anglo-Canadians as was the tarantella. Obviously there was no conflict between admiration for Fascism and acceptance in Canadian society before 1935. That fact alone probably led many Italian-Canadians into closer contact with the regime than they might otherwise have deemed wise. And criticism of Fascism was turned aside by "respectable" Anglo-Canadians who continued to see the critics as reds and malcontents or to see the problem as one of factions within Little Italy. For example, protest to the Separate School Board that children were being inculcated with Fascism in the Italian heritage (after hours) classes, was turned aside by the Italian priest the board consulted. He said that the protest came from a well-known CCF club member who, worse yet, was a member of the Giuseppe Garibaldi Orange Lodge. A leader of the local Fascio, defending the classes, wrote that they avoided "the teaching of any political doctrine or of any other subject other than religion, Italian languages, and elementary notions of Italian history and geography."[22]

In general, the host society took the view, encouraged by the Fascist editor of *Il Bollettino*, the dominant paper in Toronto, that the enthusiasm for Fascism was a matter for the *colonia* not Canada to concern itself with, and that while some Toronto Italians "might admire fascism as it operates in Italy, they had no desire to impose such a doctrine on Canadians."[23] In effect this meant that the community was left to itself to resist the Fascist and consular initiatives.

The logic of serving as a moral impetus perhaps made the vice-consuls see their role more as vice-duce occasionally. It is certain that they, as much as many of the residents of the *colonia*, confused Fascism with their bureaucratic duties and confused the centralization of the daily liturgy of the community with the cause of Italian culture in Canada. A note from the consul in Montreal about the Italian press there (and much the same would have been said of *Il Bollettino* in Toronto) showed this conflation: "Both periodicals are Fascist – and serve the interests of Italy and of the Italian community, following with discipline the direction of this Consulate."[24] Organizing and controlling the *colonia* and using its *ambiente* in the interest of the regime and Rome seemed, then, a possibility by the early 1930s. The major institutions and the *prominenti* were ready. What remained was some effort to reach out to the whole *colonia* to cement them to the regime and to confirm the absolute identification of government, Fascism and Italians abroad or more simply of the vice-consul and his colony.

The resistance to the consular/Fascist plan can be seen on two levels. On the one hand, there was organized ideological resistance from badly split leftist groups – socialist, communist and anarchist. Toronto had its Matteotti club and an anti-Fascist Mazzini club (auxiliary to the CCF club). By the 1930s these groups, with some intervention and help from New York and international elements, had created three short-lived anti-Fascist newspapers in the city: *La Voce Operaia, Il Lavoratore*, and finally *La Voce Degli Italo-Canadesi*. Through front organizations like the League Against War and Fascism, they fought back against Fascist influence. This latter's greatest moment came in 1937, when they disrupted a Fascist rally in favour of Italy's intervention in Ethiopia at the Odd Fellows Hall on College Street. At the rally, one of the more articulate local Fascists, later interned, in his oration had said, one assumes by way of justifying Italian imperialism, that "Garibaldi did more to raise the negro to the level of the white man than any other man in the world's history." [25]

The organized international anti-Fascist resistance was loud and rowdy but ineffective. Much more admirable was the proud common-sensical, Italian-Canadian resistance to the consulate and to the more pompous Fascist notables. That resistance grew up around the social clubs and mutual aid societies like the Fratellanza and the Societa Italo-Canadese. Labour leaders like Lou Palermo and the societies generally resisted the various campaigns and devices of the consul and his allies. From the headquarters of the Societa Italo-Canadese appeared *L'Emigrato*, the single most effective and Toronto-based statement of anti-Fascism. *L'Emigrato* didn't lack grim humour, for when it heard that each lodge of the Fascio would be named after "quello di un morto per la causa fascista" ("one of those who has died for the Fascist cause"), it suggested the first one should be named Giacomo Matteotti. The paper insisted throughout on two simple points. First that one could be a 100 per cent Italian while not being a Fascist, and second, that "not aversion to Mussolini, not anti-fascism alone but simply the need for dignity and feeling for their land of adoption was turning the Italian colony against the Fascio and the consulate." [26]

Although overbearing, Fascist officials in Canada were generally neither fanatics nor fools. The Consul General in Ottawa, for example, continually warned Rome against becoming involved with either French-Canadian right wing manifestations or native anti-semitic and pro-Nazi groups such as the Anglo-Celtic Toronto Swastika Club, later called the Beaches Protection Associations. He also hesitated to give a list of Fascio members to his German consular colleague, and often the consuls seemed to find the loyal notables on the one hand and the excombattants on the other a burden rather than a help in reaching the whole community. The better among them recognized and tolerated the umbertine (Victorian) and conservative quality of Italian-Canadian fascism; a quality expressed by Harry Corti, the aging editor of *La Tribuna*, who told a meeting of the Stella Alpina "that one mustn't forget that in Italy beside the government and the Duce, there is also the King and that is a good thing."[27]

From 1930 on, then, there was a natural Fascist logic to the idea of creating a viceregal palace for the consul in Toronto that would be the centre for the maintenance of the cultural and ethnic life of the community. Such a cultural centre would shelter all the organizations of the colony. In the short time allowed them between the consolidation of influence in the late 1920s and the reversal of Canadian opinion toward Fascism brought on by the Ethiopian War, the Fascio and the consul undertook a number of efforts to increase the community's *Italianità*. Some devices were inspired from Rome, and some reflected the real ethnic cultural needs of the *colonia*, either in the form of the *prominenti's* dream for status and hierarchy or the more demotic need for "fellow-feeling," a taste of high culture and ethnic pride. Through Dopolavoro, the Fascists organized sport activities and free trips to Italy for children to study the mother tongue. This program was often free of politics: and was truly popular with Italian-Canadians.

The year in which most of the effort to centralize ethnicity came to a head was 1934. In that year the campaigns for the creation of a Casa d'Italia in Toronto began. A simultaneous effort to have the Italian John Cabot recognized as official discoverer of Canada rather than Jacques Cartier, began as artifice, but inspired popular enthusiasm. The decision to create or build a Casa d'Italia was, of course, part of an effort that went on throughout Italian communities overseas, and a mark of the colonial mentality of the Toronto community then and of many of the students of it now is that they tend to see the issue as generated by local Toronto events and the machinations of vice-consuls and Fascists here.

When the decision to buy one of Toronto's more stately downtown properties, "Chudleigh", in the heart of the city at Dundas and Beverley, was made, it was a public assertion of the respectability of Fascism and the substance, taste and probity of the *colonia*. Even though the campaign to raise funds from Toronto Italians to buy the property included the usual rumours of corruption, fraud and personal gain. So despite the fact that the Casa d'Italia was to be the focus of the struggle between 1938 and 1941 and of the denouement of consular power and fascism in the *ambiente*, to understand it properly we need to assert that the colony and Anglo-Canadians found it an absolutely acceptable and patriotic idea in 1934. This description of the announcement of the plans for an Italian cultural centre from the *Globe* of 5 November, 1934 (Italian Armistice Day) shows all the themes of respectability and compatibility between the loyal allies of World War One, the veterans of each nationality in between Fascism and Canada:

> The platform was a colourful spectacle, being decorated with the Union Jack and the Italian colours, in the midst of which were set pictures of King George V, King Victor Emanuele III and Mussolini. Interspersed among the chairs were numerous banners of various Italian organizations and as the Vice-Consul entered, the York Township Boys' Brass Band played the British National Anthem, and at various points during the speeches when Il Duce's name was mentioned the audience rose and gave the Fascist salute while the band played "Giovinezza", the Fascist hymn. On the platform were Professor E. Goggio of the University of Toronto and Dr. P. Fontanella. All speeches were in Italian, and at the conclusion a march to the Cenotaph took place, where the Vice-Consul laid a wreath in honour of Italy's dead.[28]

It took several years for the Casa d'Italia at Beverley and Dundas to emerge. During that period *Il Bollettino*, the clergy, and most of the *prominenti* supported all of the moves of the consul even though the *colonia* itself was raising the money. As a Fascist editorial put it, "intanto il Cav. Tiberi è soddisfatto. La sua soddisfazione é la migliore assicurazione per noi" ("In the meantime Cavaliere Tiberi [the consul] is fulfilling his duties and that assures all is well"). The Casa d'Italia established at "Chudleigh" became the centre of government, Fascist and community activities. Italian-language classes, Dopolavoro, and many other community clubs and cultural groups met there. Government consular activities also went on there.

As Fascist foreign policy became aggression, Canadian public opinion, following that of Great Britain, grew hostile to Italy and to the overt political activity in the Toronto and Montreal Italian communities. At a time when Toronto's Italian women were sending their wedding rings to be melted down to pay for Italy's new imperialism, the Canadian press denounced Mussolini's aggression in Ethiopia. Between 1936 and 1940 Italians recognized the possibility of conflict between their primary loyalty to Canada and sympathy for the mother country and its politics. When Italy declared war against Great Britain and her allies, Italian-Canadians were confused and apprehensive. One old Italian, interned as a dangerous enemy alien at Petawawa, had to ask a fellow prisoner whether Italy had declared war on France or Germany.[29]

Non-Italians who had flirted with the varieties of Fascism overcame their indiscretions by loyalty and sacrifice during the war. It was not so easy for Toronto Italians. On 13 June, 1940, the Minister of Justice announced to the House of Commons the government's policy toward known Fascists and all those of "Italian racial origins who have become naturalized British subjects since September 1, 1929." Mr. Lapointe explained that "the very minute that news was received that Italy had declared war on Great Britain and France I signed an order for the internment of many hundreds of men whose names were on the list of the RCMP as suspects. I cannot give the House the number; I have been asked by the head of the Mounted Police not to do this because it might hamper his work."[30]

One can imagine the terror and upset among the city's people of Italian descent. The RCMP raids were directed only against potential fifth columnists but they appeared inclusive and retrospective in their definition of Fascists. The rumour persisted in Toronto that the RCMP confiscated the guest book of the Casa d'Italia and rounded up everyone on it. More frightening was the violence and vigilantism of the Toronto public. It was reported in the House and in the press that at least sixteen Italian storefronts in the city were vandalized when war broke out. Instances of harassment and estrangement occurred with painful frequency in the first days of the war. Then, too, while members of Parliament assured the government that various German groups were loyal Canadian citizens, no Toronto voices there were raised on behalf of the Italians. Far from it. The member from Broadview warned that "During the Spanish trouble, Italian submarines found shelter on the southeast coast of that country, and Italy has modern submarines that can cross the Atlantic Ocean and return without refueling." Continued American neutrality and the ties of kinship and commerce between Toronto and New York Italians also troubled the legislators.

> This writer goes on to say that we must watch out when Italy enters the war, because of the number of foreigners in the United States, and the German-Italian-Russian spy propaganda. He also says that

there are more coloured people in that country than there are in Africa and urges that some organization in the Dominion should cope with these questions before it is too late.[31]

The member for York West congratulated the government on the absence of sabotage in his riding which was "an industrial constituency, one in which we have a large number of foreigners." Thus the disloyalty of the Italian population was thwarted and assumed at the same time.

The impact of internment on Toronto Italians is hard to assess. It cannot be compared with the removal of the Japanese. No one's property was confiscated. More political and random than racial, the cost to the community was nonetheless terrible. Men who one day held government contracts to produce war material, the next day found themselves shipped to Camp Petawawa where they languished or wasted their talent on road gangs. A Montreal Italian, Mario Duliani, has written a moving account of the life at Petawawa, *La Ville sans femmes*. Fascists and Italian-Canadian leaders were interned at the camp, but the real hardship fell upon their dependants. Families were left with no livelihood during the difficult first months of the war. The Church and other organizations reacted carefully lest their efforts be interpreted as support for Fascist sympathizers.

The Fascist years and the difficult sifting out of loyalties and prejudice during the war years were the final writing on the palimpsest that Toronto's prewar Little Italies provided for the post-World War Two Italian settlements here. A new and vaster immigration of Italians began in the 1950s. In any single year in the decade of the 1950s, more Italian immigrants came to Toronto than the total of the city's prewar Italian-Canadian population. But the Italian-Canadians shaped the new neighbourhoods. Their locations in the city, the chains of migration that drew newcomers from certain *paesi*, and the leadership, all reflected the early settlers' influence and their own historical experience.

Notes

1. Società Umanitaria, *Calendario per Gli Emigranti* (Milan, 1914).

2. Much of the reconstruction of historical detail about the early Italian community is drawn from the tape-recorded reminiscences of older immigrants to the city. An extensive bank of this oral testimony is held by the Multicultural History Society of Ontario.

3. On the Laurenzanesi, see the unpublished University of Toronto, M.A. thesis by J. Zucchi, "Paesani in a Toronto Neighbourhood: Italian Immigrants in the Ward, 1870-1940" (1979).

4. A. Fitzpatrick, *Handbook for New Canadians: A Reader* (Toronto, 1919), p. 49.

5. J.M. Cuddihy, *The Ordeal of Civility, Freud, Marx, Levi-Strauss and the Jewish Struggle with Modernity* (New York: Delta, 1976), p. 179.

6. A. Bernardy, *America Vissuta* (Turin, 1911), p. 323.

7. *The Globe and Mail* (Toronto), 21 December 1906, p. 10.

8. Robert F. Harney, "Chiaroscuro: Italians in Toronto, 1885-1915" in *Italian Americana* (Spring 1975), pp.143-167.

9. Robert F. Harney, "Boarding and Belonging" in *Urban History Review* (October 1978), pp. 8-37.

10. Robert F. Harney, "Ambiente and Social Class in North American Little Italies" in *Canadian Review of Studies in Nationalism*, 2(1975), pp. 208-224.

11. Correspondance of Archbishop McEvay, McEvay Papers, Toronto Diocesan Archives.

12. Parrochia di San Clemente, *Annuario 1920*.

13. John Diggins, *Mussolini and Fascism. The View from America* (Princeton, 1972), p. 80.

14. *Guida per gli Italiani nel Canada 1929* (Toronto, 1929). Only a study of steamship passenger lists can show the true magnitude of the Italian flow through New York and Boston to Toronto.

15. Constitutions of Fratellanza and of the Societa Italo-Canadese mutual aid societies in the collection of the Multicultural History Society of Ontario. The Fascist consular view can be found in G. Bastianini, "I Fasci italiani all'estero," *Gerarchia* LV: 10 (October 1925), p. 635.

16. *L'Emigrato* (Toronto) March 30, 1932, anno 11:5, p. 1. Copy in Multicultural History Society collection.

17. The following discussion of the *notabili* and Fascism depends upon extensive oral testimony as well as analysis of the leadership of the Italian community's organization as reported in various guides and the *Ente sociale* sections of *Il Bollettino Italo-Canadese* and other newspapers.

18. L. Villari, "L'Emigrazione italiana negli Stati Uniti," *Nuova Antologia* CXLIII, p. 298.

19. Bastianini, "I Fasci italiani all estero," p. 636.

20. *Opera Omnia di Benito Mussolini*, XXIII, p. 88; for the "braccio gigantesco" speech, see *Opera Omnia* XIX, p. 408.

21. Central Neighourhood House, 1930, a pamphlet in the CNH collection of City of Toronto Archives.

22. Meeting of the Committee of Supervision, 5 May 1939, *Minutes*. Separate School Board of Toronto Archives.

23. Tommaso Mari quoted in *The Telegram*, "Italians Here Linked with Fascists." 21 October 1936, p. 7.

24. Archivio Storico Diplomatico of the Italian Ministero degli Affari Esteri in the Serie Affari Politici, 29 July 1936, Canada 3/4 telepresso #12905-283 (microfilm of these consular reports held by the Multicultural History Society of Ontario.) *Il Bollettino* of Toronto received a $60 a month subsidy.

25. The Public Archives of Canada and the Multicultural History Society of Ontario have microfilmed runs of *La Voce Operaia*, *Il Lavoratore*, and *La Voce degli Italo-Canadesi*. An account of the meeting at the Odd Fellows Hall can be found in the *Toronto Star*, "Toronto Italians fight in Streets Over War Issue," August 13, 1935.

26. *L'Emigrato*, March 30, 1932 ll: 5, pp. 3 and 1. Multicultural History Society of Ontario collection.

27. *La Favilla*, 1926.

28. *The Globe and Mail*, 20 September 1937.

29. M. Duliani, *La Ville sans femmes* (Montréal, 1945) p. 54.

30. Speeches of the Minister of Justice, 11 and 13 June, 1940, House of Commons (Canada) *Debates* (1940) 1: p. 637, 744-45.

31. *Manchester Guardian* article read into the parliamentary record by Tommy Church, M.P. for Broadview, House of Commons *Debates* (1940) 1: p. 717 and speech of A.R. Adamson, M.P. for York West, *Debates*, 13 June 1940, 1: p. 757.

IF ONE WERE TO WRITE
A HISTORY OF POSTWAR
TORONTO ITALIA *

❦

METROPOLITAN TORONTO RANKS WITH SÃO PAOLO, NEW YORK, CHICAGO AND Buenos Aires as one of the largest Italian settlement areas outside Italy. Estimates of the number of those Italian descent among Toronto's two and half million inhabitants vary from a quarter of a million to half a million. That is, up to one-quarter of the city's population.[1]

The remarkable feature of Toronto Italia is not its size but the immediacy of its ties with Italy, an immediacy born of the fact that the vast majority of Italians in the city are post-World War Two immigrants or their children. Toronto Italia then is an immigrant collectivity and that fact, more than the serendipity of residing in a country which professes, through its multicultural policies, a belief in pluralism and the right of immigrants to maintain their language and ways, accounts for the vivacity and the kaleidoscopic permutations of ethnic identity and ethnoculture which characterize the city's Italian neighbourhoods.

When the noted English Risorgimentalist, Denis Mack Smith, was asked why he had confined most of his scholarship to the nineteenth century and had never tried to write about post-World War Two Italy, he responded by observing that the postwar period was too much of a muddle for the kind of history he liked to write. He found contemporary Italy "immensely complicated and lacking in form and shape."[2] His reaction may mirror that of all historians asked to deal with a looming recent past in which trends seem inchoate, and random facts defiant of encodation in an interpretative narrative.

It is time for the postwar Toronto Italia experience to be organized in more than demographic and sociological frames. The tendency of historians of the earlier mass migration to accept unquestioningly a

---

* Published in *Atti di Conferenza Centro Italiano di Formazione Europea*, 1987.

synchronic view of the postwar era as if the forty-year history of the *ethnie* were a single anthropological or sociological moment, a long present tense, should end. We have followed too readily the historicist American scholarship which tends to study immigrant settlement, and ethno-cultures from a third-generation perspective lying beyond assimilation or ethnicism (the "new ethnicity" of the 1960s). This approach is pre-occupied with the study of the ethnic group in terms of boundaries– measuring social, economic, and geographical data for those tell-tale signs of acculturation, success, "startling" ethnic persistence, prejudice or "ethnically blocked mobility." Its practitioners seem to assume that no interior political, cultural, or social history of the *ethnie* itself, worthy of study, exists. Their approach has the advantage of making study of the group diachronic rather than simply synchronic, but it remains about boundaries rather than content and seems inadequate to the recent Canadian situation.

I have found myself then in search of what Hayden White has called an emplotment,[3] a particular and appropriate story form in which to fit the facts of postwar Toronto Italia so that they offer more than merely a chronicle and transform themselves into "a comprehensible drama of development," which I shall refer to as a narrative. The reader will recog-nize the allusion to Italo Calvino's *If on a Winter's Night a Traveller (Se una notte d'inverno un viaggiatore)* in the style of the title of this essay. From the title, he or she should gather either that I believe that I have failed to find an emplotment that works, or that I am content to suggest some of the many narratives that seem possible, or that I have found for myself a deeper narrative in my encounter with the chaotic mass of source material, memory culture, and folk wisdom which exists.

Preliminary work of an archival and monographic kind will be neces-sary before a full-fledged history of Toronto Italia, 1945-85, is possible. Despite the existence since 1953 of an Italian-language newspaper and, fitfully, of competitors to it,[4] no analysis has been done of editorial poli-cies, publishers' attitudes, advertising, or readership. No effort to trace changing immigrant concern about *paese*, Italy, their *paesani* in diaspora, Toronto or Canada, by sampling and measuring press coverage over an extended period, has been undertaken. Although much analysis of cen-sus material goes on, it is rarely made congruent with data arising from the community such as parish records and association membership lists, data which could be used to correlate immigrant cohort (year of arrival), age, occupation, region of origin, residential history and what I will call degree of ethnoversion – intensity and frequency of involvement with Ital-ian networks, institutions and emblems.

For this last measure of course, the adjective *Italian* is inadequate. Distinctions must be made among *paese*, regional, Italian, and Italian Canadian – the latter, the hybrid result of a Toronto ethnogenesis in the late 1960s and the 1970s. Over forty years one can, for example, observe the decline or loss of meaning of *paese* and regional emblematics in commerce. Regional names for firms such as Gran Sasso plumbing, Sila trucking, La Ciociara food slowly, perhaps generationally, give way as signs to Italian this or Italian that. This process of ethnicization takes its own path, which is neither in the service of acculturation nor of the maintenance of primordial ethnicity. For example, neither a regional sports hero such as the boxer Primo Carnera once was for the city's Friulani,[5] nor Italian-Canadian sports heroes of prewar stock such as the NHL's Esposito brothers, appear able to compete for a share of the adulation that the World Cup winning Squadra Azzura, Italian soccer team, receives. In the heart of the *ethnie*, soccer, not hockey or other "North American" games, has been reasserted as the sport seen as most appropriate for the immigrants' children.

A sensitive study of such variations in emblems of identity over time, as well as one which would deal with the continuum of identification and association from *paese* to region, from Italian to Italian Canadian or new Canadian, that could distinguish between immigrant family ethnoculture and the North American ethnicization process, also would seem to be a prerequisite for giving form to a history of Toronto Italia.

Despite the lack of "interior history orientation" I have referred to in statistical studies,[6] I would like to stop here and offer a brief demographic profile of the postwar Italian Torontonians – who they are in terms of time of arrival, education, occupations, regions of origin, ethnoculture and their position in the life of the city. Between 1951 and 1981, the population of Toronto doubled from a little over a million people to its present two and a half million people. The source of that growth is made obvious by the fact that in the 1981 census 43 per cent of the city's population was listed as born outside the country and that after immigrants from the United Kingdom, the largest group of newcomers were from Italy. While the city's population doubled in those thirty years, the Italian descent group grew eight- to tenfold, from under 30,000 to upwards of 300,000. This new concentration of Italians, generally in one broad corridor of settlement throughout the west end of the city – there is an outrigger community made up heavily of Sicilians and people from southeastern Italy in the east end as well – plays a central role in public perceptions of change and development in Metropolitan Toronto. Despite large, new, urban concentrations of Chinese, Portuguese, Greeks and displaced east

Europeans, it is the Italians who are seen as the immigrants whose arrival coincided with the rapid growth and economic development of the city and its hinterland.

If the Italians of Toronto play a central role in the city, they also dominate – increasingly at the expense of Montreal's beleaguered "Little Italy" – *Italianità* in Canada. As many as six out of every ten Canadians of Italian descent live in southern Ontario, four out of ten in Metropolitan Toronto. During the period of mass Italian migration in the late 1950s and 1960s, almost 40 per cent of the Italians entering Canada gave Toronto as their destination.

The Italians of Toronto, according to the 1971 Census, were 54 per cent immigrant and 28 per cent the children of immigrants. Only 17 per cent of the group were the children of Canadian-born. In an earlier study of the census, the impact of immigrants on the collectivity was even more apparent. Anthony Richmond showed that only 3 per cent of the ethnic group were prewar immigrants, and that over 50 per cent had come to Toronto between 1951 and 1961. In 1971 only 6 per cent of the group had both parents in North America, and in the latest census the Italian-born continue to make up more than half of the population of the *ethnie*. That figure, however, includes a very large number of young adults, born in Italy but educated in Toronto. (They are the Italian children who made up 45 per cent of the non-English-speaking students in the school system in the 1961 census.)

Beyond the boon they provided for the separate (parochial) school system, these young adults in their behaviour now, quintessentially represent the choice between living within the *ethnie* or assimilation. From their ranks come the bureaucrats and "organic intelligentsia" of Italian-Canadian institutions, the small businessmen and heritage language teachers as well as the *ethnie's* increasing number of young professionals, but I have found no reliable way of measuring how many from those same ranks simply move on into the larger English-speaking city.

Almost 10 per cent of Toronto's people list Italian as their mother tongue. It is difficult though to determine what that means in terms of tendencies toward language retention or loss since the mother-tongue group and the Italian-born group are roughly the same size. (A figure which shows only 4 per cent mother-tongue retention in the third generation in the 1971 census is skewed since the vast majority of third-generation Italian Canadians in 1971 were descendents of those prewar immigrants who underwent rapid assimilation in the 1930s and 1940s to escape from the *braccia gigantesca of consolarfascismo* and the subsequent Canadian Italophobia.)[7] The rate of endogamy – marriage within the group – in 1971 was 74 per cent for males and 84 per cent for females in contrast to a pre-World War Two rate of only 55 per cent for Italian-Canadian males.[8] The increased percentage suggests the large pool of potential mates within the new *ethnie*, the thousands of hopeful young immigrant couples who arrived in the period, as well as some of the tribalizing thoughts that may accompany both official multiculturalism and efforts by immigrant or ethnocultural leadership to hold the collectivity together.

Typically none of the important statistics on marriage between immigrants from different regions of Italy, or marriage between descendants of pre- and postwar immigrants are readily arrived at. Those last figures would be quite useful, for despite the nasty habit of referring to prewar immigrants and their children as *mangia-cakes* – presumably because of their high levels of acculturation or fossilized Umbertine peasant ways – the postwar immigrants initially depended a great deal on those Italian Canadians. (For a while it was voguish for the immigrant intelligentsia to refer to themselves as Canadian Italians and the *mangia-cakes* as Italian Canadians.)

Statistics on schooling and occupational skills do not lend credence to the view of those Canadian Italians that they came with more sophistication rather than just more *Italianità* than their predecessors. Of the 28,000 Italian immigrants listed as entering Canada with skilled trades between 1945 and 1965 – presumably the remainder were peasants and labourers with a sprinkling of urban white-collar workers and professionals – 20,000 practised the following traditional trades in rank order: stonemasons/bricklayers, carpenters, tailors, seamstresses, barbers, mechanics and shoemakers. (Of course, these Canadian government categories do not reflect real skills or artisan pride.) The census for the same period shows that roughly 65 per cent of Italian household heads in the city had less than eight grades of elementary education, and there are indications that female formal education levels were even lower. As with the earlier Italian mass immigration, it is difficult to chart the rise of, or arrival of *prominenti* – middle-class leaders and intelligentsia – among the newcomers. Perhaps it takes fewer *trombetti* than one thinks to make a loud noise.

Much is made of regionalism among Italian immigrants to Toronto. In popular narrative, regionalism, or more narrow paesanism, is accorded explanatory power in shaping alliances which inform socio-economic and political activity in the *ethnie*. In terms of reliable facts and numbers, or of a means for measuring their profundity of significance, regionalism and paesanism remain among the most illusive subjects in the search for a way to encode and interpret behaviour in the *ethnie*. While I was preparing this paper, a call came to me from the office of the CIBPA (Canadian Italian Business and Professional Association) where a heated argument had broken out over which regional group, Calabrese or Abruzzese and Molisani, was a majority in Toronto. I called them back for the answer, but we could only agree on the fact that it didn't matter really because the Friulani and Siciliani, though fewer in number, were just as important in the collectivity. I should add that there was a humour to the exchange which implied that some of the sharper edges of *campanilismo* (parochialism) have been blunted, perhaps by the general success of the immigrants or the fact that no statistics, which might show the rate of success to be invidious by region of origin, are available.

Although no separate figures on regions of origin for Toronto Italians exist, statistics from 1957 (a typical year of high Italian migration to Canada) seem to correspond to current folk wisdom about origins. In that year 5,000 each of Abruzzesi-Molisani and of Calabresi came to Canada. Two thousand each arrived from Friuli, from other parts of the Veneto and from Lazio, and a little over a thousand each from Sicilia, Puglia and the Campania.[9] The fact of regional origin is not the same as regionalism.[10] The narrative will have to look more closely at the power of regionalism, at its relationship to factionalism, and to the image of factionalism.

The complicated relationship between regional pride and inter-regional suspicion and rivalry is one of the many reasons I have chosen to use the word *ethnie* to describe the collectivity of Italians in Toronto since the war. I have chosen it also in order to avoid a misleading use of community, which carries with it concepts claiming too much in this instance. "Little Italy" seems a demeaning and ultimately meaningless archaism, and *colonia* has always been less a description than an organizing slogan for rascals (*truffatori*) from Italy or from within the *ethnie*. The adjective or ethnonym *Italian* also, upon closer examination, has little power of valid description. It is a census artifact which becomes a tool for enabling the bigoted or aspirant to deny the variety of views, identities, and conditions which exist in the *ethnie*. One of the results of a well-wrought history of the *ethnie* might be discovering a valid usage for Italian, or Italian Canadian and a subtlety in the use of *ethnie* which could distinguish sub-communities in the collectivity, as well as occasions such as the World Cup victory, or responses to earthquakes in Friuli or Calabria when the collectivity acted also as a community.

Two final points about material life and attitudes before I turn to the emplotment of the narrative. The first deals with the issue of intensity of participation and ethnoversion. In 1977 the new National Congress of

Italian Canadians carried out a survey which proved embarrassing (not least because it was so unscientifically done).[11] The survey showed that 68 per cent of the respondents had never heard of the NCIC, and that if one ignored parishes, 69 per cent belonged to no Italian-Canadian organization. Of the ethnic clubs or associations in which 30 per cent did participate, less than half carried on their business in Italian. The rest used either English or a mix of English and Italian. The findings were based on nation-wide statistics and certainly both participation and Italian language use in Toronto would be higher, but it should also be noted that the survey was done in the mid-1970s, at the height of both "ethnicizing" campaigns led by the National Congress of Italian Canadians and government attempts to encourage ethnocultural maintenance through official multiculturalism. The figures simply reinforce the point that the census category *Italian* is not a measure of sentiment or commitment.

Study of occupational, social, geographical and economic mobility, as it exists in Toronto now, seems unable to penetrate to the reality of socio-economic status and the sensibilities of the immigrants and their children about class, paesanism and, camaraderies. In the memory culture,[12] there is a very common tendency among older postwar immigrants to recall the lost days of the 1950s and 1960s when all were *paesani* or *fratelli*, when there were few class differences within the group or within regional subgroups, when men helped one another, giving freely of their trades and skills, and all were exploited by a variety of *stranieri* – Irish union bosses, Anglo-Celtic officialdom, Jewish developers, and *mangia-cake* contractors. It would be ungracious or ignoble to deny them this "founding myth," but it, like the obtuse nature of mobility analyses of the collectivity, obstructs the effort at a true history which must deal with efforts to organize the Italian labour force, the rise of a class of successful contractors, and the emergence of some truly rich developers and land speculators.

In the most recent Statistics Canada extrapolations on the *ethnie* by Kalbach and Richmond,[13] some of the limits of the method emerge to perplex the practitioners. For although the immigrant generation shows almost "ethnically blocked mobility" in terms of listing the same occupations, neighbourhoods, and taxable incomes in 1981 as in 1961, any observer can see that the development of the city, which has largely depended on Italian construction workers since the 1950s, produced, along with a surfeit of injured workmen and *ritornati*, miles of Italian family-owned housing. (According to the 1971 census, 77 per cent of the ethnic group owned their own home. One should also include in the analysis all the homes paid for or built with the immigrants' money back in the Italian sending *paesi*.) This development also produced well-off contractors, a "brokering" commercial middle class (*borghesia mediatrice e commerciale*), and an elite of developers and industrialists. More to the point, the analysis of the latest census demonstrates that the children of these "immobile" immigrants are statistically over-represented in the city's universities, professional schools and by age cohort, in the professions. Moreover, this second generation of postwar Toronto Italia already has achieved the average income of the British and French charter groups.

The answer to this paradox suggested by Franc Sturino and others lies in the lack of subtlety of the census or of those who use it, and the *furbezza* or wisdom of the immigrants.[14] Public university education in Canada is relatively cheap; much work goes on in residential construction as part of an untraceable and untaxable sub-economy, immigrants of mainly rural origin know how to maximize their family well-being by seasonal food processing, and extended family and *paesani* cooperation which makes Italians prosper materially beyond the ken of their non-Italian neighbours and enumerators.

A heuristic device much favoured by post-Risorgimento historians was that of writing *pagine della storia* as telling examples. For now all the various possible narratives for the years 1945-85 can only be such "pages." Narrative could exist given the proper research base for the following: 1) changes in the geographical enclave and its *ambiente*; 2) the internal politics and institutional development of the *ethnie*; 3) the labour history of the Italian immigrants, men and women; 4) the rise of a business and professional middle class; 5) the ecclesiastical and folk religious history of the group; and 6) an intellectual history of changing perceptions of identity and destination, e.g. attenuated ethnicity, full assimilation, return to the *madrepatria*. Study of prejudice which the group encountered from the circumambient society, as well as the prejudice of some Italians towards the *pesci*, their Portuguese neighbours; the Jews, their competitors in business; the *neri*, the West Indians and East Indians moving into the neighbourhood; the Irish, with whom they compete for control of the separate school board, and *sistemazione* as teachers, would also be necessary for a complete picture of the *ethnie* to emerge.

For the founding years, 1945-60, it seems possible to combine the many narratives into one story. That story centres on attempts to regain control of the so-called Casa d'Italia,[15] the downtown mansion that had been bought in the mid-1930s by community subscription, and given as a consulate to the fascist government. The attempt to regain the Casa was one of the first concerted efforts to overcome the fear, shame and *atimia* which fascism and the war years had produced in the community. From a period of intense fascist tutelage and official ethno-nationalism, a period when most community-based institutions had been undermined or sub-jected to fascistization in the guise of Italianization, the Italians of Toronto had passed to a time of recrimination, "lying low", internments, suspicion, and hostility from the non-Italians around them – a period of discredited leadership.

A few organizations had been less compromised; they had kept their headquarters (*sede*) outside the Casa, and that fact alone gave them some anti-fascist reputation. Two benevolent societies, the Fratellanza and the Società Italo-Canadese, joined by the Italian Immigrant Aid Society, pro-vided a core of organization for the postwar years. On the other hand, the Sons of Italy (Figli d'Italia) and their anti-fascist breakaway rivals, the Order of Italian Canadians, had limited influence in the postwar period.

The campaign to regain the Casa was fraught with ironies since most of those involved, as well as the Canadian officials they consulted with, agreed that eventually the building should be returned, not to the com-munity but to the Italian government. (In fact, the matter was more complex than that since the Canadian wartime custodian had sold the building to the Canadian government; the Mounties, who used the building were loathe to move out, and the Italian community found itself lobbying through influential friends like the local member of Parliament, who would later become senator, David Croll, to retrieve the building for the Italian government, which at that time seemed to express no interest in the matter.) By 1958 when the Canadian government agreed to give up the Casa, the geographical focus of the *ethnie* had moved considerably northward from the building's location, and the emotional focus of the ethnic group was about to settle on the issue of exploitation of Italian labour in the city. The site of the Casa, an old mansion – once elegant but by then decrepit – in an area which has since become Toronto's China-town, no longer recommended it as a symbolic centre of the Italian *ethnie*. In fact, when the Italian government did decide after almost two decades of hesitation, to use the site as a consulate again, one of those Italian-Canadian leaders who had earlier fought to retrieve the building described it to the *Corriere Canadese* as an unacceptable place to repre-sent the "più vasta communità etnica di Toronto."[16]

For such men, the building later of Villa Colombo and the Italian Canadian Cultural Centre – eight miles or more north in the heart of the newer Italian settlement area – would serve as a symbol of the ethnic group's success. I cannot ascertain whether the Italian government's decision to accept the old Casa site far from the current community had any symbolic weight – a consul's work goes beyond his *colonia* after all –

or simply represents a decision to take advantage of the opportunity to be housed in what is again an elegant and centrally-located, downtown mansion.

The campaign to retrieve the Casa had two important results. The first came as an almost accidental solution to the question of what use the Casa would be put to until its future was decided. The building was occupied in 1962 by COSTI (Centro Organizzativo Scuole Tecniche Italiane), a new skills and language training centre for immigrants, which for many years represented all that was best in the *ethnie's* and the Italian government's sense of responsibility to Italian immigrants and to the larger city.[17]

Sometime in the mid-1950s mainly as a result of the campaign to reclaim the Casa, an umbrella organization was created to represent the *ethnie's* interests. (An effort to organize around the postwar Aid for Italy movement had begun as early as 1947.) The organization took the form of a federation of associations known as FACI (Federation of Canadian Italian Associations). Member associations included benevolent societies such as the Fratellanza and the Società Italo-Canadese; regional clubs such as the Famee Furlane, Circolo Calabrese, Società Trinacria, and a Marchegiano club, as well as *paese* clubs for Vitese and Pachinese from Sicily and Monteleonesi and Modugnesi from Puglia. The Italian local of the Amalgamated Clothing Workers, the Italian Immigrant Aid Society, the Italian Canadian Recreation Club, and several Holy Name societies were also members. The Figli d'Italia lodges and those of the Order of Italo-Canadians seemed to have had associate status.

By 1956 the presence of the new Italian migrants with their different ways and different agenda could be felt in the federation. The *Corriere Canadese* reported a 1956 meeting at which one prewar patriot, a steamship agent, gave an impassioned speech about the return of the Casa. He was followed by a new member representing a recently formed *paese* sports club who rose to complain that he could not follow the issues being raised about the Casa because the federation's meetings were being carried on in English! He and other newcomers felt excluded.[18] In 1957 the federation, realizing that some bridge between old and new associations was necessary if it were to retain any representative quality as an umbrella organization, put out a call to "all newly formed Italian Societies at present in existence in Toronto" to join. The organization was still healthy enough in 1960 to be at the centre of the controversy over the disposition of the Casa. Then with the labour troubles of the 1960s and the shift of settlement northward, this first federation, if not its constituent associations, vanished from the record.

In 1969 when a new FACI (the acronym this time significantly in Italian, Federazione delle Associazioni e dei Clubs Italo-Canadese) with fifty-eight member associations was born; no mention was made of the first FACI even though the president of the first FACI, now among the few prewar leaders active in the *ethnie*, was involved. The lack of acknowledgement by the newcomers of that first attempt, made mainly by Italian Canadians of prewar immigrant origin to create a united front for the *ethnie*, in effect to begin the process of ethnicization, seems to confirm Gramsci's observation that *gruppi subalterni* – for what else are ethnic groups in North America – are condemned to seeing their history episodically and to having it so written.

A May 1960 headline in the *Corriere Canadese* asked "Perche La Casa d'Italia Mantiene Le Porte Chiuse."[19] The newspaper then sought counsel as to whether the building should become a cultural, a social services, or a recreational centre. The newspaper's editor called on the following people to answer the questions posed: club officers, the clergy, and leaders of associations (*dirigenti delle FACI, il Clero, esponenti delle Associazione, Clubs, Confraternita, Societa italo-canadese*). If he had included consular officials, the editor's list would have perfectly defined the cultural and political elite of Toronto Italia.

Something about the apparently unabashed elitism of his request caused me to step back from the narrative and gave me a chance to notice a jarring distance of tone and preoccupation between headlines about an *Inchiesta Sulla Casa,* and a small item two pages farther into the paper which recorded donations, often of only a few dollars by workers and contractors to a fund for the families of six Italian labourers killed in a tunnel cave-in while digging the Toronto subway line.

I had been drawn along by one group's view of what comprised the significant chronicle of events in Toronto Italia. There were underway other serious narratives such as that of the struggle of migrant workers for safer conditions and better pay – which I had slighted. Obviously I needed to think more carefully about the elite the *Corriere Canadese* had inadvertently defined, and its role in creating the record I was relying on.

This elite and the nascent organic intelligentsia around it divides, I believe, into four groups, each with a view of, or definition of the *ethnie*, the meaning of the ethnonym Italian, and an attitude toward the "ethnic project" of Italians in Canada in terms of the meaning of the passage from the old country, the processes of change, and the final destiny of the group and its members in the New World. Each group fosters its own sense of the true and significant narrative of Toronto Italia, 1945-85, and the contours of each account differs markedly. The differences begin with the various ways each group views the people of the *ethnie*. For one group, the immigrants were workers, and the children of workers emigrated abroad (lavoratori e figli dei lavoratori emigrati all estero); for the second, they were new Canadians; for the third, they were Italian Canadians or Canadian Italians; and for the fourth, they were an immigrant cohort at any given time responding or acting upon family, fellow townsmen (*paesani*) and mixed national loyalties and perhaps even nascent class ones.

Of the elements mentioned by the editor, the clergy, perhaps because of their own diversity of origin, did not hold as a collectivity to any single view. Some priests, such as the Italian-American Franciscans active in Toronto, saw the immigrants as Italian Canadians. Other clergy, however, especially those directly from Italy and from various forms of non-parish activism, viewed the immigrants as essentially *lavoratori* abroad, migrants or guest workers like those in western Europe.

This latter view seems to have been held – with varying degrees of mitigating good sense – by Italian government officials and the organic intelligentsia around them, from FILEF, ACLI and Fernando Santi representatives to those immigrants who remained absorbed with, and in allegiance to Italian political parties. Such a view of the newcomers has among its consequences, the corollary that the *ethnie* is best understood as a colonia and that leadership should come naturally from the consulate. Of the four or five standard types of emplotment for narrative – romance, tragedy, comedy, epic, and farce or satire – the one most appropriate to this view is tragedy. The story of the *ethnie* becomes the story of a culture lost, or rather a people lost to their culture, of an Italian government opportunity to influence fumbled, of the fear of being accorded low status in the eyes of the Anglo-Saxon hosts, of a world in which, to quote a famous earlier consul in the United States, Luigi Villari, there were "a thousand trifling, provincial, and local animosities" and an "army without officers commanded by corporals and sergeants."[20] There are also among the organic intelligentsia of the Left who serve "workers abroad," some who see the narrative as centred on the exploitation of workers, and the essence of the tragedy lying in the failure of the *patronato* to protect adequately. But more often than not, they too measure the situation in terms of partisan politics. The more traditional Italian representatives seem to favour a narrative which emphasizes events and facts which redound to the national honour of Italy, reflect her unique cultural status in Europe, or the innate skills of her *oriundi* (descendants).

The second view of the immigrants as new Canadians derives ultimately from Canadian authorities, though its agents were, and are often the children of the immigrants themselves turned into cultural bureaucrats and school teachers. In this view, the real story of the Italian immigrants, of all immigrants, lies in their contribution to Canada, and the aptitude with which they adjust to Canadian ways. The proper literary form for this view is romance, a tale of men and women in a new land which they help to build. Ethnoculture and ethnic identity are here treated as transient values, worthwhile devices by which to ease one's way into full-fledged participation in Canadian life, or as quaint "cultural baggage" to be celebrated in the mosaic.

The third group of the elite corresponds roughly to those who lead or man the larger ethnocultural organizations, who are themselves ethnoverted and believe that the hybrid identity, Italian Canadian or Canadian Italian, represents a reality, and a collective value which may persist in the New World indefinitely. It is this group that now dominates what little history – in the sense of controlling the record of events and the writing of the narrative – exists in the *ethnie*. This is so not least of all because this elite disposes of the funds or the political access routes to Canadian government funds, upon which much of the immigrant or ethnoverted organic intelligentsia survives. In its least guarded moments, a narrative they encourage becomes a collective biography of those who have achieved prominence since immigrating, "uomini di successo Italo-Canadesi." Their approach shares the church view that it is nice to have saints so that lesser men can have models of comportment to admire and emulate. On that one point, their understanding of the "ethnic project," and that of Italian officialdom converge. Respectability for the ethnic group, for the homeland (*madrepatria*), and for the parvenu (*cafone arricchito*) are reinforced by the sort of filio-pietist research which finds a pantheon of great Italians such as Caboto, Bressani, and Marconi in the Canadian national past.[21] Modern social scientific history is seen as either mean-minded, or as thinly veiled Marxist hostility to those who succeed in capitalist society. The preferred narrative form here is also romance with traces of the mock epic when the notables dare or good taste fails.

Some of the younger leadership educated in North America, are embarrassed by the lack of sophistication in this approach. They have moved toward an incorporation of the fourth interpretation of community, the folk view common to those in *paese* and regional clubs, and to those who find cultural satisfaction in sub-national associations, dialect, and the living vagaries of *Italiese* and change in the collectivity. This narrative about the *ethnie* verges on a shared folk memory and is a mixture of comedy and popular epic. Stories usually involve using peasant cunning to outwit naive or officious *Inglesi* (Anglo-Celts), to humble *trombetti* (self-important leaders), to avoid ideological conflict. They cherish paesanism and regionalism at the same time as they assert the fundamental *fratellanza* of all Italians in the *ethnie*. Such immigrants are the most susceptible to the new tentatives being made by regional governments in Italy, especially Friuli, Molise, and Calabria, to have influence among those overseas. In fact immigrants' lives in this narrative are seen as the small-folk epics they are, with emphasis put on the courage to migrate, years of austerity, overwork and exploitation, as well as satisfactions and cultural uncertainties which come with time in the land and advancing years. In this narrative, the personal sense of time and accounts of work history, as well as recollections of changing attitudes about ethnoculture coincide, for the most part with the real sequence of migration, building of the Toronto infrastructure and prosperity and show little awareness of the political and organizational dramas which are part of the ethnicization process and other elite narratives.

Each of the four groups emphasize different moments and different clusters of emblematics which rally the ethnic group, which turn, or try to turn the collectivity into a community. Such moments can revolve around public issues or be simply celebratory. A careful analysis of them may provide a chance to describe the different ways of being Italian Canadian. In other words such an analysis may make it possible to use the ethnonym with sufficient subtlety to be able to see when and why some segments of the group mobilize for communal activity while others do not.

Several recurring categories of rallying situations and emblems exist. They are Italian national tragedies, e.g., earthquakes, floods, the death of Aldo Moro; celebrations, e.g., the World Cup victory, the opening of Villa Colombo, or other facilities, the appointment of Italian Canadians to high office; the coming to town of popular figures, e.g., Pavarotti, Gina Lollabrigida, or a professional soccer club such as Juventus. These rallying points can release a pent-up sense of the need for community, but none of them bring unanimity. What healthy human entity would wish to have unanimity? A careful eye can discern one or the other elite definitions of the *ethnie* at work in a preference for Pavarotti over Loren or Lollabrigida as visitor, or disdain for all of them as vaguely *mangia-cake,* and preference for visits by the likes of Dolci, Calvino or Bassano. Of course, acquiring a show of Da Vinci drawings for the Italian cultural centre transcends such cultural bickering.

Sometimes differences over emblematics arise between immigration cohorts rather than elites. The postwar immigrants are not inclined to support the prewar impresario Johnny Lombardi's annual "Italian Day" at

Toronto's Center Island, which features spaghetti-eating and bathing beauty contests. The question of whether the Dante Alighieri Society should watch contemporary Italian films or hear lectures on Leopardi has elements of elite competition. Even the toponymy of the newly ethnicized core can be a bone of contention. One of the first Canadianizing elements is sharing anti-Americanism, and so many Italian Canadians view the Columbus cult as too Italian American. The new Italian apartment building for the elderly in Toronto is named Caboto Terrace and that is seen, by those who care about it, as proper repatriation of a process which had previously created "Villa Colombo" rest home, Columbus Centre, and Columbus Day week. Even the communal sense that arises with the effort to help regions of Italy after major earthquakes, precisely because they occur in only one region at a time, has its frayed edges. Several other more contrived forms of rally have some success in making the collectivity momentarily a community. Slurs upon the reputation and good name of the Italian-Canadian community such as imputations of widespread organized crime – especially when made by national agencies like the Canadian Broadcasting Corporation or by Toronto police officials – stir some general demand for a B'nai B'rith style anti-defamation organization. (For some reason, much of the filiopietist historiography which searches for "respectable" Italian descent heroes in the Canadian past or indulges in the celebration of immigrant achievers has as its first impulse, a response to myths of organized crime.)

More precise issues can, on occasion, mobilize large numbers of people, often from different segments of the *ethnie*. For example, the struggle for the right to learn Italian as a heritage language in the public schools has replaced the struggle against the "streaming" or "tracking" of Italian immigrant children into vocational and commercial rather than university preparatory courses, and it draws support from the same substantial cross-section of the community as the earlier battle. Another form of rally – against unfair labour practices, to improve the workers quality of life, and to deal justly with the problems of injured workmen – can mobilize, with the help of newspapers such as the *Corriere Canadese* and, more consistently, the *Forze Nuove*,[22] as well as Italian and non-Italian trade union officials and politicians, some in the *ethnie*, into a continuing and chastening counter-point to the emphasis which exists at the core on capitalist success and on cultural problems at the expense of social issues. In the changing of emblematic heroes – from Columbus to Caboto to Marconi – in the fact that almost as much to-do could be aroused in the 1970s over the need for the University of Toronto to create a separate Italian Studies Department (Italian had been taught previously in an Hispanic and Italian Department) as over responding to the Green Paper, and other government initiatives to make immigration more difficult, one may choose to see either the transition from the pre-occupations of an immigrant settlement to those of an ethnic group competing for status in North America, or the victory of the bourgeois hegemony, through uses of its "organic intelligentsia," over the *ethnie's* real daily life and project, improving the quality of life.

It is remarkable, given the fact that the mass of migrants arriving after 1951 joined the construction industry work-force and played such a central role in the city's development, that a serious historiography has not emerged in or outside the *ethnie* about Italians, the economy, the labour movement, and the parts of the political spectrum dependent on labour support. In those decades of rapid development and economic expansion – the 1950s and the 1960s – the unbridled capitalism of devel-opers and contractors (among the latter, some of the new immigrants) was matched by the willingness of immigrant labour to work hard, long and unsafely in order to maximize their *gruzzolo* – nest-egg – either to return to Italy or to bring over family. Men died, were exploited, persevered and succeeded. That was the beginning of the socio-economic history of the *ethnie* – a time in which neither ethnicization nor acculturation had much meaning – and detailed study of that period would be the necessary underpinning of any valid history of postwar Toronto Italia.[23]

As some emerged as *contrattori*, others returned to Italy as casualties or men with savings. At the same time, wives joined the work-force, often for the first time, as *sartini* – cleaning ladies and factory hands. Their absence from the home, particularly in the years before older dependent relatives arrived to help with children and household tasks, undercut both the *Italianità* and the sense of well-being of the home. The rate of differentiation of wealth, if not always of status, in those years among men who had begun as equals must have been astonishing. Since petty capitalist success was as often based on entrepreneurship and cunning as it was on varying levels of willingness to work hard and differences in skills, the changes must also have been troubling. It is likely that the folk memory's assertions of camaraderie and insistence on the primary non-class based *paesani* groupings by those first labourers, represents an attempt to avoid looking too closely at those times. That this labour and socio-economic history has barely begun reflects the inadequacy of Canadian labour history, especially in settings where proletarian status is not accompanied by proletarian sensibilities.[24] It also reflects a conscious or unconscious suppression of the "mean" labour history of the group by those who do not find it an acceptable potential narrative for a respectable *ethnie*.

In a brief commendable attempt in 1975 to suggest the need for such a history of the Italian labour movement, the former director of COSTI provided a frame for future study.[25] He saw the period, 1945-60, as one when non-Italian union representatives made sporadic attempts to organize the new work-force, and when various branches of government enamoured with rapid development, were not inclined to step in to protect the work-force. Then from 1960-75 there was a period of labour violence, union organizing in the heart of the Italian community, rapid enrolment of Italians, proliferation of locals, and the emergence of Italian-Canadian union officials, as well as the appearance of powerful, heavily Italian, umbrella organizations such as the Labourers Local 183. (By 1971 the *Italo-Canadian Directory of Toronto* listed about twenty unions, mainly in construction, service and food trades – all of which had Italian officials.)

The central moment of this labour history arrived in 1960 and 1961. Since bad or pop history seems always to flow to places where serious history is overdue, the critical events of 1960-61 have been described in a book entitled *Sweethearts: the Builders, the Mob and the Men.*[26] In an account which makes a confused story incomprehensible, but carries its readers with innuendoes about organized crime and political corruption, the author describes the attempt in 1961 by Bruno Zanini and others to organize the Italian immigrant workers to protect themselves from falling wages, which their own competition partially caused, and to change inadequate safety conditions at residential construction sites in Toronto. The rising death rate from industrial accidents, a *Toronto Telegram* campaign against the callousness and corruption of contractors and developers, combined with the recalcitrant bigotry or inability of traditional union leaders in the face of the Italian work-force, led to the events of 1961 which included a summer of strikes and labour violence. At the outset of the trouble over 2,000 workers gathered in Brandon Hall – the site of the Italian Canadian Recreation Club and also an informal centre for Italian contractors – to follow Zanini into battle.

The results of that season of violence were: 1) the emergence of clearer lines between organized labourers, some skilled trades and contractors, as well as between commercial and residential construction work; 2) the intervention of the Government of Ontario to end the worst excesses in employment practices and enforce work site safety; 3) an eventual Royal Commission on Violence in the Construction Industry which sought to exonerate capitalism by rediscovering the Mafia. The leader of the movement, Zanini, who had shown charismatic quality in his ability to read and control the workers but inconsistency of character, disappeared from prominence; no one like him has since arisen. Nonetheless, 2,000 Italian workers, without tutelage from either the consulate or the respectable elites, had met and found common cause, and through a concerted effort had begun to change for the better the very bases of their material life in Canada. Someday, one hopes, it will be possible to write this narrative of Italian-Canadian labour in the rich detail it deserves.

By the beginning of the 1970s, the outlines of a new attempt to organize the collectivity into a community were emerging. Some men who had prospered in the 1950s and 1960s now turned inward to the *ethnie* out of a sense of gratitude and service, or as their critics saw it, a need to legitimize their status as *prominenti*. They encountered two pools of ethnoverted organic intelligentsia ready to serve and anxious to find a sinecure (*posizione*). The first were drawn from that inevitable trickle of white-collar immigrants that comes with the mass flow. This group included a number still tied to one strand or another of Italian politics, a number of former priests with political beliefs ranging from the radical to Demo-Christian conservatism. As sometime journalists, students, editors, "researchers" (*ricercatori*), etc., this migrant intelligentsia found a leadership often unsure of its culture, always unsure of its Italian language, ready to encourage the growth of an organic intelligentsia as long as it occasionally served as flack for their virtue, and made justification for the elite's wealth and power, and in fact, created a hegemony. Young Italian-born graduates of Canadian universities, many of them thwarted by lack of access to professional schools or buoyed by the emergent bureaucracy of multiculturalism and recognizing the difficulties, even illogic, of pursuing the study of Italian language and literature as a career in Canada, provided a natural pool of talent for the new positions opening up in umbrella Italian-Canadian institutions. This leadership responded to, and husbanded the process of ethnicization, conforming to multiculturalism, and asserting the growing group and individual respectability of Toronto Italia.

As before there were emergency issues such as earthquakes to draw the collectivity together, but there was also emerging a central "ethnic project," of the sort that affects all immigrant groups undergoing ethnogenesis. That project can be seen in its concrete and in its more notional way as: 1) the building of "institutional completeness" with Italian-Canadian organizations and sites which can serve the *ethnie* from the cradle to the grave; 2) the aura of respectability and status as an ethnic group within the larger civic competition of ethnic groups, which comes with accomplishing such institutional completeness and which, as corollary or result, ends a perceived "bad" reputation in terms of organized crime or humble origins. This is not to suggest that the ethnic group's accomplishments are less remarkable because they are done with an eye to their effect on the image of Italians in Canada, nor are they less valuable because a capitalist host society requires men of wealth and influence to accomplish, if not necessarily reign over, such communal goals. The idea that such efforts do not spring from the interior history of the group alone but have to do with a heightened sense of being watched by others may, however, help one trying to read a narrative into events such as the creation of the second FACI in 1969, and then of the National Congress of Italian Canadians in 1977, or the building of Villa Colombo and Columbus Centre. It may also help one to understand that groups in the elite hope, without either much manipulation or reflectivity, to impose a pattern for narrative on the future historian.

The new FACI of 1969 took much the same form as the first umbrella organization of the 1950s.[27] There were initially fifty-eight member associations ranging from the small in size, a radical association like the Risorgimento Club, or intent, the Puglia Sports Club to the CIBPA (Canadian Italian Businessmen and Professionals Association). Most of the constituent organizations were by this time clearly representative of the postwar migration, but a few prominent prewar leaders were also present. Although welcomed into existence by the Ontario government, which was by its own admission anxious to "obtain a responsible, responsive and representative viewpoint of the Italian community in Metro Toronto," FACI's affairs did not prosper. There were deep divisions in the leadership, accusations of favouritism based on regionalism, and an apparent tendency to look with great intensity to the emblematics such as organizing Columbus Day week rather than to issues such as a community response to the new immigration policies emerging in the Green Paper, or the new policy on ethnic groups emerging from Vol. IV of the great Royal Commission on Bilingualism and Biculturalism.[28]

A fair history of FACI would have to include an analysis of the variety of Toronto's Italian collectivity – as large as Florence and drawn from much more disparate parts of Italy – which the new umbrella organization had to represent. It is unfortunate that with one eye always cocked to the boundary to see how others perceive them, spokesmen, leaders, and organic intelligentsia have always mistaken variety for factionalism, and debate for a sign of an unseemly lack of shared ethnic project.[29] That differences between one leader of Sicilian descent, Protestant faith, small business origins and Conservative politics with another leader of Milanese origin, technical education and Liberal politics should be seen as divisive or shameful rather than as a healthy starting point for debate and dialogue may speak to a deeper problem both in organizing the *ethnie* and its history. Things should not be expected of a people in migration that are not expected of them in their homeland.

While FACI appeared to flounder in search of a purpose, a growing interest in creating a rest home, Villa Colombo, for the Italian-Canadian elderly rekindled energy. In the mid-1970s the effort to raise funds for the building of Villa Colombo, like the earlier Casa d'Italia campaign, had the side effect of drawing the collectivity toward community. The fact that some of the ideological Left claimed to see in the Villa, a device by which the rich earned merit in the *ethnie* while providing for their parents and those of very few others, seems to have had the effect – now that the Villa, Columbus Centre, and Caboto Terrace are the heart of community culture and social service agencies – of neutralizing elements critical of the mainstream leadership structure. The ethnicization process and the building of the physical plant were meant to reflect what that leadership believes to be the success, and respectability of the ethnic group, and they have.[30] Some tactic beyond petulance and litigation would be necessary to demonstrate that these good communal results are both too limited and an artifice.

One side of the *ethnie's* story which could be told with more consistency is that which deals with the role and attitude of the Italian government toward Toronto Italia. Until more documentation and research is available, this narrative too remains episodic. Rumour and gossip thrive where there is no history. There are, in Toronto, myths of good and evil consuls, a memory of one which verges on the hagiographic, a newspaper literature about another which is scurrilous. The historian has little possibility of knowing how much truth such folk views have or whether they merely represent ideological conflicts. What is true is that the relation between the consulate and the community can arouse passion. A *stornello,* a type of Neapolitan broadside song, written for one consul, included the verse, "ci ha l'allergia, per tutto quello ch'é democrazia" [he has an allergy to everything that is democracy].[31] Another newspaper expressed the hope that "il prossimo Console arriva senza etichette politiche" [that the next consul arrives without political party affiliations].[32] The consulate has not been good at telling its side of things. At the same time, and regardless of the obvious ideological or personal venom of some of the attacks on Italian representatives, there is a consistency of theme in the polemic which suggests that the *ethnie* chafes under too direct an influence from Rome. Enough nasty jokes about education experts who did their training in Eritrea being sent to Toronto circulate that the Italian government would be wise to encourage a non-ideological, social scientific history of the consular service, its recruitment, attitudes, decision-making, etc.

It is interesting, for example, to see how difficult it is to measure the significance of Toronto Italian participation in the great Rome Congress of Emigration sponsored in February 1975 by the Comitato Consultivo Italiano all'Estero. Although many entities with their *sede* in Rome sent delegates, and at least one Toronto intellectual went as representative of an Italian political party, those who attended were for the most part a strangely distinct part of the elite, men who were seen by the rest of the community, perhaps clearly for the first time, as more Italian than Italian Canadian.

One of those who attended came back – possibly for ideological reasons that had to do with which political currents were likely to have most influence on the consulate and *patronato* – to carry on a vigorous campaign against efforts to increase the influence of the *madrepatria* (homeland) on the *ethnie*.[33] "We Italo-Canadians live in a climate of multi-cultural tolerance and to us the Italy of political party factions constantly in conflict with one another seems a bit far away." He went on to write that Toronto Italia welcomed help but preferred the concept of "co-ordination" to that of "tutelage," and he expressed the hope that Italian representatives would "respect the history and personality of our Italian-Canadian community." These remarks appeared in a magazine published by individuals who were representative of the new leadership in the Italian Canadian Benevolent Corporation, and the later National Congress of Italian Canadians (NCIC). The negative reports in *Canadian Mosaico* were less a declaration of hostilities than an assertion that Toronto Italia had passed a critical point from immigrant *colonia* to North American ethnic group in the progression of its reality and attitudes; a new relationship to Italy would have to evolve. *La Gazzetta* of Windsor described an ideal new relationship between Italian and Italian-Canadian institutions in a 1978 editorial. All those entities with *sede* abroad which affect the collectivity "from FILEF to the Dante Alighieri Society" will have "to be convinced that they must recognize Il Congresso and col-laborate with it in various sectors; schools, culture, the press, social welfare, youth, accident, etc."[34]

I believe that a detailed study of events and attitudes in the mid-1970s would show a true revolution of sentiment and identity, only dimly perceived at the time, which brought the ethno-community to maturity. Ironically but typically, this very North American process of ethno-genesis coincided as well with high levels of personal slippage (assimilation) and still higher levels of acculturation. The period is characterized by: 1) rapid institutional expansion – Villa Colombo, the expansion of FACI into the NCIC; 2) political success – the appointment of Peter Bosa as a senator, the role of Charles Caccia in the federal Liberal government, the presence of three NDP members of the provincial Parliament – all of these politicians, postwar immigrants; 3) the emergence to "middle management" and professional status in the *ethnie* of Canadian-educated children of immigrants; and 4) a rallying around an ethnic identity as Italian Canadians at the expense of excessive region-alism, Italianness, and Canadianness, *sans épithète*, and even, in the instance of the squabbling over whether Caboto or Colombo deserved to be honoured as the group's Adam at the expense of Italian Americans.

The discrete events of the period, so diverse in nature, all seem to serve this process of ethnogenesis, which was all the more quickly propelled by latent ethnic self-disesteem (*atimia*) and civic competitive-ness, i.e., concern for the good name and reputation of the Italian group among their Canadian neighbours. Accounts of the accomplishments of those years always carry with them this sense of artifice and of per-forming, even competing on a multicultural stage. Thus, at the fund-raising dinner for Villa Colombo while the Catholic archbishop spoke of goodwill and the minister of State for Multiculturalism emphasized the importance of giving "old folks the opportunity to continue to live as a group," a different theme emerged among the Italian-Canadian cele-brants. Charles Caccia, MP, described the Villa as "an example of love, tenacity, and organization which was able to be given to Canada." Madonia, the president of FACI, described the Villa as "the way in which the community is able to demonstrate that it is capable of excellence." The final speech by Joseph Carrier, who had been president of that first FACI which fought to acquire the Case d'Italia, described the "importance of this project to the Italian community." [35] The *Corriere Canadese*, covering these events, noted that "also communities numer-ically much smaller than the Italian, such as the Chinese and Japanese, have their own old age homes. Why not us?" [36]

In 1971 the Italian Canadian Recreation Club found it advantageous to advertise its lack of *campanilismo* (regionalist spirit) and its com-mitment to a new Italian-Canadian *comunità*: "All'Italo Canadian Recreation Club siamo innanzitutto italiani…[there followed the names of all regional groups from Abruzzesi to Veneti]…le nostre porte sono aperte a tutti."[37] This sort of self-conscious assertion appears over and over again throughout the 1970s. In the midst of the magnificent response to the plight of Friuli after the devastating 1976 earthquake there, Toronto Italia spokesmen/intelligentsia celebrated less the humanity of the moment and more its imposition of community on the collectivity. The *Canadian Mosaico* reported that for the first time in Canada, "tutti gli italiani si sentono fratelli." A newspaper editorial by Sergio Tagliavini identified the Friuli tragedy and the subsequent decision to send all the money gathered (almost $700,000) from the annual Mother's Day fund-raising telethon for Villa Colombo to Friuli, as the moment when the Italians of Toronto found a new dimension; when they became and felt "veramente tutti italiani di fuori di ogni barriera regionale."[38] A year later the flyer announcing the establishment of the NCIC, *Cosa é il Congresso Nazionale degli Italo Canadesi?*, included eighteen principles, the first and last of which, as well as many in between, referred to safeguarding the interests of Italian Canadians and upholding the prestige, dignity, and good name of the Italians. The process of ethnicization seemed to be leading Toronto Italians into the sort of concern with ethnic identity, inter-ethnic standing, boundaries which, especially in the United States, often seem to outstrip interest in the ethnocultural stuff supposedly being nurtured.

In fact then, Toronto Italia, still the most immigrant of North American Italian settlements, has ripened, perhaps under the hothouse influence of multiculturalism into a North American *ethnie* in less than two generations. The people of the *ethnie*, for the most part, have achieved a quality of life which could only have been a dream when they arrived in the 1950s. At the heart of the collectivity lie institutions which, in their physical size, their relative architectural grace, and their "institutional completeness," shelter, should still even the slightest flutter of the heart of those who suffer from *atimia*, fear bogey-men such as factionalism, criminality, and familism.

If all that is a triumph of a sort – and it certainly is for the humble labourers who flooded into Toronto in the 1950s, and their children – it is not an answer to questions posed about the "collective project" and the destiny of those who have left Italy for good. The Italian-Canadian identity and ethnoculture continue to be best studied as a process – a progression neither moving necessarily farther away from Italy nor toward full acculturation. It is also important for the historian not to succumb to the "naturalness" of ethnic persistence even in a multicultural society. There are constantly moments of cultural uncertainty within the *ethnie* which reflect choices of identity, and a species of *ethnie* or "nation building" under way. Such moments remind us that the *ethnie* is both a construct, and a process. When the cultural centre acquired its original Da Vinci drawing, it hired a local security agency to guard it. During the day a middle-aged sirdar, a former Sikh soldier in a uniform which was a rumpled and pathetic parody of a police uniform, guarded the drawing. At night during the cultural ceremonies, two former *carabinieri*, decked out in the melodramatic garb of the Italian federal police, flanked the drawing. In the morning the sirdar would return for he, and not the *carabinieri*, reflected the daily life of Toronto Italia.

Notes

1. Unless otherwise noted, all statistics are taken from C.J. Jansen and L. LaCavera, *Fact Book on Italian Canadians* (Toronto, 1981).

2. Interview in the *New York Times, Sunday Literary Magazine*, 1 September 1985, p. 9.

3. H. White, "Historical Text as Literary Artifact," in *Topics of Discourse: Essays in Cultural Criticism* (Baltimore, 1978), pp. 83-86 & 67.

4. For a list and discussion of the postwar Toronto Italian press, see G. Grohovaz, "Toronto's Italian Press after the Second World War," in *Polyphony: The Bulletin of the Multicultural History Society of Ontario*, IV, 1 (Toronto, 1982).

5. G. Grohovaz, ed., *1932-1985, the First Half Century/Il Primo Mezzo Secolo* (Toronto, 1982).

6. Beyond the Jansen and LaCavera, *Fact Book*, the following contain useful demographic data: W.G. Marston, "Social Class Segregation within Ethnic Groups in Toronto," in *Canadian Review of Sociology and Anthropology*, VI, 2 (Montreal, 1969), pp. 45-79; A. Richmond, *Immigrants and Ethnic Groups in Metropolitan Toronto* (Toronto, 1967); and L. Tomasi, "The Italian Community in Toronto: a Demographic Profile," in *International Migration Review*, XI, 4, (New York, 1977).

7. See R.F. Harney, "Toronto's Little Italy, 1885-1945," in R.F. Harney and J.V. Scarpaci, eds., *Little Italies in North America* (Toronto, 1981), pp. 41-62.

8. Analysis of Italian Canadians in the 1941 census can be found in *Immigration Branch,* Government of Canada 1949-50, *Historical Background*, RG 76, CXXXI, File 28885.

9. *Annuario Statistico Italiano* (Rome, 1960), Tavole. Espatri di emigrati per via marittime, 1951-59.

10. Although regional origin is not the same as regional sentiment, the existence of a coherent regional or sub-national group such as the Friulani – with their early presence in the city (the Famee Furlane was founded in 1932), numbers, separate *sede*, distinctive language, visible economic success, good political connections (including one of the two Italians in the Canadian Senate and close ties, in fact honorary rights at the Fogolar for the only federal minister of Italian origin – a northerner if not a Friulian), their Canadian children at once culturally dutiful in terms of language retention, Furlan and Italian, and often regional endogamy, yet possessed of high levels of education and assimilation – creates a situation in which a species of intra-*ethnie* civic competition arises. Certainly efforts by the Calabrese, both in Toronto, and in the regional government are premised on a sense of the advantages of asserting sub-national networks and cultures.

11. *Italian Canadians: a Cross Section. A National Survey of Italian Canadian Communities* (Ottawa, 1978).

12. The Multicultural History Society of Ontario holds several hundred hours of taped interviews with postwar Italian immigrants in its sound archives. The interviews are structured generally in the manner suggested in R.F. Harney, *Oral Testimony and Ethnic Studies* (Toronto, 1978).

13. W. Kalbach and A. Richmond, *Factors in the Adjustment of Immigrants and Their Descendants* (Ottawa, 1981).

14. Franc Sturino, "Outside and Inside Views of Upward Mobility: the Case of Canada's Italians," paper delivered at the Canadian Ethnic Association Conference in Thunder Bay, October 1983.

15. A *busta* of letters between officials of the first FACI and Canadian government officials; legal documents, and newspaper clippings referring to the Casa d'Italia can be found in the Donato Di Giulio Papers at the Multicultural History Society of Ontario.

16. *Corriere Canadese*, 14 April (Toronto, 1975), p. 4.

17. About thirty archival feet of COSTI papers have been deposited with the Multicultural History Society of Ontario, and are now housed in the Archives of Ontario. Those who founded the institution, especially Charles Caccia, MP, and Joseph Carraro, should be interviewed, and a serious history of COSTI begun.

18. *Corriere Canadese*, 26 October 1956, p. 14.

19. *Corriere Canadese*, 10 May 1960, p. 3. One reason an elite was recognizable may have been willingness to pay for the privilege to lead. The vice-president of FACI wrote back to the editor that, "persons who wish to elevate the state of the Italian community must be ready and willing to pay for the privilege ...to give to the less fortunate what the public wishes but is denied the luxury of having."

20. L. Villari, "L'Emigrazione italiana negli Stati Uniti," in *Nuova Antologia* CXLIII, 190- (Rome) p. 298.

21. R. F. Harney, *Dalla Frontiera alle Little Italies: Gli Italiani in Canada 1800-1945* (Rome, 1984), p. 313, for a discussion of *atimia* and filiopietism.

22. *Forze Nuove* has been for some years the voice of a number of Italian-Canadian radical and socialist intellectuals. It provides an important counterpoint to mainstream thinking and news coverage. It is difficult to measure its impact or readership, but it has been more successful, and of higher quality than the short-lived communist paper, *Nuovo Mondo*.

23. There does exist one useful scholarly study of those years. It is the doctoral dissertation by S. Sidlofsky, *Postwar Immigrants in the Changing Metropolis with Special Reference to Toronto's Italian Population* (Ph.D. dissertation, University of Toronto, 1969).

24. One younger historian who has begun to do excellent work on this topic is Franca Iacovetta. See for example "From *Contadina* to Worker: Southern Italian Immigrant Working Women in Toronto, 1947-62," in Jean Burnet, ed., *Looking into My Sister's Eyes: an Exploration in Women's History* (Toronto, 1986).

25. Joseph Carraro, "Le unioni e la comunità italiana," in *Canadian Mosaico, II, 2* (Toronto, 1975), pp. 30-31.

26. C. Wismer, *Sweethearts: the Builders, the Mob and the Men* (Toronto, 1980).

27. Papers relating to FACI on deposit at the Multicultural History Society of Ontario.

28. *The Cultural Contribution of the Other Ethnic Groups*, Vol. IV of the Royal Commission on Bilingualism and Biculturalism (Ottawa, 1969).

29. For an excellent discussion of how an ethnic group perceives internal dissent, see Raymond Breton, "La Communauté ethnique, communauté politique," in *Sociologie et Sociétés*, XV, 2 (Montreal, 1985), pp. 23-37.

30. There is an extensive debate on the appropriateness of Villa Colombo, Columbus Centre, and the Italian Canadian Businessmen's Corporation – the organization created to raise funds and control the development of the *ethnie's* core – in *Corriere Canadese, Il Giornale di Toronto* and *Forze Nuove*. There is also unseemly litigation over statements made in that coverage.

31. *Communita Viva,* IX, 8-9 August (Toronto, 1980), pp. 5-9.

32. *Forze Nuove*, June (Toronto, 1980).

33. L. Pautasso, "Il Punto di Vista di un Italo-Canadese," in *Canadian Mosaico,* II, 4 (1975). The same author published the periodical *Quaderni Canadesi*, which ran a number of articles comparing the Italian government in the 1970s with the *consolarfascismo* of the 1930s.

34. *La Gazzetta,* June (Windsor, 1978), editorial by Professor W. Temelini.

35. V. Ariemma, "Update on Villa Colombo," in *Facts and Opinions*, XI (Toronto, 1974).

36. *Corriere Canadese*, 1 June, 1974. One can be forgiven, I hope, for seeing some of the same *atimia* in this matter as that expressed by the pastor of St. Clement's Church in Toronto in 1920, whose fund-raising speech ended with, " ...we have shown we are not degenerate Latins ...We will build our new church in this city and remove the blemish from the good name of Italians," Parrochia di San Clemente (Toronto) *Annuario 1920*.

37. See the advertisement for Italian Canadian Recreation Club in *Italo-Canadian Commercial Directory* (Toronto, 1971), p. 55.

38. Sergio Tagliavini editorial in *Corriere Canadese*, 11-12 May 1976, p. 1.

II

IMMIGRATION AND URBAN LIFE

ETHNICITY
AND
NEIGHBOURHOODS*

❦

THE SESQUICENTENNIAL ANNIVERSARY OF TORONTO HAS INSPIRED THE PUBLICATION of a number of books on its history as a city. None, except this volume, deal with what has become the most salient feature of Toronto in its one hundred and fiftieth year, its role as a preferred target of migration for people from every corner of the globe, its polyethnic character and its reputation for tolerance of human variety.

At a time when public relations campaigns make much of the city's ethnic mosaic in order to encourage tourism and investment, and politicians seem almost to credit themselves for the growth of a civic ethos of multiculturalism, it seems useful to learn more about Toronto's ethnic and immigrant past, to examine the city's actual record, in terms of inter-ethnic encounter, tolerance and attitudes toward pluralism. The essays on ethnic enclaves and ethnocultures in the city before World War Two that have been brought together in *Gathering Place* are a first attempt to contribute to that learning.

The current celebratory mood of the city and the remarkable flowering of immigrant cultures here since the Second World War lead to a false retrospect about the history of ethnic groups in the city, one in which the past and the present are conflated into a single, oversimplified story. In his superb pseudo-geography, *Invisible Cities*, Italo Calvino writes: "Beware of saying to them that sometimes different cities follow one another on the same site with the same name, born and dying without knowing one another, without communication among themselves."[1] The lack of comprehension to which Calvino refers is not just among ethnic groups,

---

* This article published in *Gathering Place: Peoples and Neighbourhoods of Toronto, 1934-1945*, edited by Robert F. Harney (Toronto: Multicultural History Society of Ontario, 1985), pp. 1-24.

but occurs as well among the various generations or migration cohorts within each ethnic group. History as slogans and stereotypes flourishes when serious history has not been attempted, and little or no serious history of Toronto's different peoples and their lives in the city has been written until very recently. We have been abandoned to labels such as "Toronto the Good", which conjure up images of a totally homogeneous colonial city with all its immigrants from the British Isles. The inadequacy of that view of the past has spawned a newer view which sees the city through the eyes of its post-World War Two polyethnicity and assumes a Toronto past in which great numbers of non-British immigrants were forced to hide their ethnocultures, were oppressed or shunted aside or quickly harried into Canadianness. Both views, of course, are rhetoric masquerading as history.

For Toronto, then, the past, in Marc Bloch's words, "is a given quantity that nothing can change", but "knowledge of the past is a thing in process". If that process is left to public relations officers and partisans to impose upon, in an anachronistic way, it becomes more useful as a text for reading the current struggle between pluralists and traditionalists in the city than as a picture of the city's past. One would think that study of the census and city directories would answer the two basic questions: was Toronto a mere extension of Great Britain into the mid-section of the American continent, or had it, like equivalent American cities, received large-scale foreign immigration? If the latter were so, was it also so that, by what is now seen as a failure of civic virtue, the Anglo-Celtic host society and elite chose to suppress all manifestations of other ethnocultures in the city? Behind the last question lurks the assumption that newcomers generally wished to maintain old-world ways and ethnic group coherence rather than seek well-being and integration through rapid acculturation.

Both forms of retrospective falsification confuse an overwhelming statistical predominance of immigrants from the British Isles with ethnic homogeneity. English, Scots, Irish Catholics, Irish Protestants and Welsh did display separate ethnic identities in terms of associational life, sometimes language, religion, culture and settlement patterns. To test the truth of this assertion, ask any Irish Catholic who tried to break the Orange Lodge monopoly on the better positions in city government or the police, or ask any English artisan who encountered Canadian nativism whether discrimination affected them in nineteenth century Toronto. Along with the 10 per cent of the population that did come from "foreign lands", these ethnic differences among immigrants from Great Britain created patterns of separateness which foreshadowed the post-First and Second World War ethnocultures and ethnic enclaves in the city.

One can then scan the census figures for the city in the pre-World War Two period either for evidence of the overwhelming British presence, or for a glimpse of the presence of other peoples. If it is valid to ask whether Toronto the Good was a uniquely British city in North America or an incipient polyglot one like New York or Chicago, a fitting predecessor to the cosmopolitan giant of today, in absolute numerical terms the answer is unequivocal. Even in 1911, after twenty years of mass migration and countless warnings by social gospellers, nativist union leaders and frightened racists about the impending inundation of the city by foreigners, the figures still show Toronto with 80 per cent of its population of British descent. About 4 per cent of the population was Jewish. Perhaps 2 per cent was of German origin, many of them long in the city and acculturated. Only the 4, 000 Italians, the 1,000 Chinese and various Slavic groups – Macedonians, Ukrainians, Poles – and the Finns lived in visible concentrations of population like the Jews.

Even by 1941 the percentage of the city claiming British descent had not declined much. Then in a city of almost 700,000, there was no non-British ethnic group, which made up more than 5 per cent of the population, other than the Jews. Nonetheless, more than 14,000 Italians, 11,000 Poles, 10,000 Ukrainians, several thousand each of Finns, Chinese, Greeks and Macedonians, along with almost 50,000 Jews, did live in Toronto. They were made highly visible by their proximity to city hall and the commercial downtown or their concentration in certain industrial areas. Toronto, before 1945, had ethnic enclaves and was in certain areas a polyglot city, far more cosmopolitan than Wyndham Lewis's "mournful Scottish version of a North American city". On the other hand, it remained overwhelmingly British in terms of the origins of its people, its attitudes and, of course, the place of the English language.

While the census cannot tell us much about the sensibilities, identities and *mentalités* of ethnic groups, or about inter-ethnic encounters, it can do more than simply show us that 10 per cent of the population was non-British. Patterns of settlement record what sociologists call the residential segregation index and enable us to sense the degree of each group's dependence on immigrant ethnoculture, their "clannishness", or their exclusion from the mainstream. For instance, although immigrants from Scotland as well as those who gave German as their ancestry were almost equally distributed throughout the city's four census areas in 1911, Jews, Italians, Chinese, Ukrainians and Macedonians showed no such even dispersal through the city. Rather they were heavily concentrated in those neighbourhoods such as the St. John's Ward, the Kensington Market area, the Toronto Junction and the East End, which form the backdrop of many of the essays in this volume.

William Lyon Mackenzie King, the future prime minister, in a series of *Daily Mail and Empire* articles in 1897, made the first serious attempt to understand and study the ethnic enclaves of Toronto. King wrote:

> The presence of large numbers of foreigners in Toronto makes an inquiry into these conditions a subject as interesting as it is timely. Does their presence here portend an evil for this city such as the above statistics which have just come upon the cities of the United States, or is the class of foreigners in this city here cast in a better mould and are they likely to prove at once good citizens and a strength to the community? These are questions of more than vital moment to the city, and answers can only be found in examination of the present condition of the people, a comparative study of their numbers, occupations and methods of living, their relations to the civic, religious and industrial life, together with a retrospective glance into the past as to the causes which brought them here and a speculative forecast as to the probable increase in their numbers which may be affected in the future?[2]

King went on to write about Germans, French, Jews, Syrians and Italians among others and did so in what was a remarkably informed and fair manner for his time. He did, however, confirm a false dichotomy that remains a problem in migration studies. "The Irish, Scots, English, Americans and Newfoundlanders", he wrote, were "so nearly akin in thought, customs, and manners to the Canadians themselves... that in speaking of a foreign population, they have generally been disregarded altogether. For with the exception of maintaining a few national societies, their foreign connection is in no way distinctively marked in civic life."

In the more democratic and pluralistic language of our time, we would be unlikely to frame questions about immigration and ethnicity in the manner King did. Nonetheless, his agenda of study is not that far from the preliminary one necessary for a retrospective ethnography of the city now. Most of those who have followed him in commenting on "foreigners" in Toronto did so in a context in which they clearly took the presence of immigrant neighbourhoods, or "foreign quarters", to be a form of urban blight. *Missionary Outlook* in 1910 observed:

> Every large city on this continent has its fourfold problem of the slum, the saloons, the foreign colonies and the districts of vice. The

foreign colony may not be properly called a slum, but it represents a community that is about to become an important factor in our social life and will become a menace in our civilization unless it learns to assimilate the moral and religious ideals and the standards of citizenship.[3]

Any useful studies of the mores and folkways of immigrants and their children were not likely to prosper within the perimeters of the social gospel camp. From 1897 until the last half dozen years, no one, except a few evangelists and immigration restrictionists who brought a special anxiety to their work, has followed King in the effort to study the ethnic minorities and the ethnic neighbourhoods of the city of Toronto.

James Scobie observes in the introduction to this study of the city of Buenos Aires that reams of research, "on urban services, such as paving, parks, sewage, police, lighting and garbage disposal, on the location, regulation and expanse of industry, on education, public health, morality and amusements",[4] have been produced on cities, but little is written about the people of a city. Rather than try to understand the non-British of the city, most scholars writing about Toronto have naturally enough concentrated on those whom they see as affecting power relations and the economic development of the city or as significant in the city's mainstream cultural and political life.[5]

In fact, though evangelists, city nurses, police officials, academics and teachers turned attention to the immigrant neighbourhoods of the city between 1900 and 1940, they did so without any clear understanding of what those neighbourhoods were, nor did they ask the relevant questions. Were the immigrant quarters simply stepping-stones towards acculturation, breathing spaces for immigrants and their children until they could become Canadians? Were they working-class neighbourhoods, or were they, as they were believed to be by much of their own ethnic intelligentsia, self-apppointed elites and officials from the lands of emigration, stratified sub-societies and colonies within a larger diaspora? Were they new communities created by people in need of creating local ascriptive worlds within the larger, colder space of a Canadian industrial city? Did the European and Asian immigrants who gathered in ethnic enclaves do so willingly in order to preserve their old-world cultural baggage intact, or would they have been willing to embrace Anglo-Canadian ways if made welcome? Were such neighbourhoods fossils of the old world, or places of regeneration where a new ethnicity and new set of emblems, new networks of acquaintanceship and new eclectic North American ideas and values could grow up?

The terms used then and now – immigrant quarters, working-class neighbourhoods, ethnic enclaves, ghettos, Little Italies, Chinatowns, ethnocultural community – create a problem. They do not so much describe the social system and cultural life of particular groups of people in the city as they delineate the categories which such groups are supposed to inhabit. If the validity of these categories is assumed, the observer is relieved from any attempt to learn about and understand these groups. For example, all immigrants in a working-class neighbourhood may not be in the working-class, and those who are may not be so in terms of their class of origin, class of destination, or *mentalités*. Moreover, ethnic enclaves are rarely made up uniformly of one ethnic group. Nor does consensus within the group necessarily follow from shared ethnicity. A sense of the variety of individual approaches to acculturation, personal and familial migration projects, senses of sojourning and settling, adjustment to the new world within the ethnic community, the persistence of sub-ethnicities, and so on, is lost when the usual nomenclature is imposed on migration and ethnicity in process.

Study of ethnicity in Canada as a North American process is best understood when integrated into a spatial, in this case an urban, frame. The obverse would seem to have equal merit. No great North American city can be understood without being studied as a city of immigrants, of newcomers and their children, as a destination of myriad group and individual migration projects. Describing city government or municipal politics, the building of an urban economy and the evolution of the city as polity obviously has value. To do so without understanding ethnicity in the city seems a bit like analysing the captain and crew of an ocean liner but not noticing the passengers, what they expect of the vessel and why they are travelling. Without knowing the networks, folkways and values of the city's immigrants, whether from the United Kingdom or not, studying the encounter between city officials and the people of the city is at best one-sided, at worst vacuous.

Since the possibility for a more deeply textured history of the city and its people exists, we must pursue it beyond the limited historiographical inheritance we have been given for the study of Toronto. The absence of traditional urban studies has spared Toronto some of the misdirection which came from the behaviouralists' emphasis on using the census, on rates of economic, social and geographical mobility as codes to measure acculturation and integration, a methodological tide which first buoyed and then set adrift urban studies in the United States.[6] Toronto's ethnic and social historians, by their late start, know that such an approach based on the host society's sources is particularly unfit as full explanation of immigrant and ethnic communities. For the most part, they would agree with Mr. Dooley, Finley Peter Dunne's fictitious Irish American bartender, who remarked on academic history in his time to a friend: "I know history isn't true Hinnissy cause it ain't like what I see ivry day in Halsted Street. If anyone comes along with a histhry iv Greece and Rome that will show me the people fightin', gettin' dhrunk, makin' love, gettin' married, owin' the grocery man, and bein' without hard coal, I'll believe there was a Greece and Rome, but not before."[7]

Mr. Dooley had it right. If we fail to plumb the depths of attitudes toward Canada, toward the old country, to understand ethnic identity and ethnocultures, to understand the immigrant's reactions to rebuffs or his attitudes towards his culture and those he identified as his fellows, then immigrants to Toronto – once dismissed as migrant navvies, "sheenies", "bohunks", "wops", or just unskilled workers – will again be dismissed, this time by a generation of social, labour and urban historians who reduce them to statistics. The broad categories of social history, like the broad categories of prejudice, are conveniences for those too lazy to comprehend the complicated nature of man in the city and of individual migration projects or separate ethnocultures.

To call for an interior history of immigrant and ethnic communities in Toronto before the Second World War is not to suggest some autonomous substructure, which allows us to ignore the reality of the circumambient city. Quite the reverse; it requires that we find ways to understand all the actors in the city's history, to understand the trauma of encounter at the boundaries of identity in the classroom, the corner restaurant, the factory or at leisure on street corners.

Migration routes, projects and destinations are always in flux. The immigrant adjusts to new situations in new places, changing or resisting. With our current state of scholarship we can only wonder now why old-world styles and ideas were discarded or defiantly maintained after some calculation of the cost, or after repeated approval or disapproval by the Canadian host society. Obviously we have to know the significance of those ways and ideas for the immigrant before we can understand, not just the immigrant group itself, but the processes of acculturation and the nature of daily life in the city. If we remember that the immigrants were conscious participants in all intercultural encounters, then the study of ethnic boundaries can begin to yield up answers about identity and *mentalités* themselves – what Fredrik Barth dismissively calls "the stuff" inside the ethnic boundary.[8] For ethnic boundaries turn out to be penumbras of opinion, choice and situation, not just hardedged perimeters between the immigrants and the old stock.

When, under the influence of the Irish national revival, W.B. Yeats set out to discover the common people of Ireland, he was startled to realize that their history was virtually unknown. "Ancient map makers wrote across unexplored regions, 'Here are lions'. Across the villages of fishermen and turners of the earth, so different are these from us, we can but write one line that is certain, 'Here are ghosts'."[9] Anyone who sets out in the 1980s to understand the ethnic neighbourhoods of Toronto before the Second World War may well believe, like Yeats, that Toronto's ethnic enclaves are uncharted, unexplored and little comprehended empty spaces on the map.

Separate settlement in this city, the creation of urban spaces that were somehow different from the Toronto mainstream and yet produced an ambience different from that of the country of origin, happened for a number of reasons. The sense of fellow-feeling, the in-gathering for reasons of language, both out of pride of language and out of pain produced by *diglossia*,* the need to maintain folkways and mores, the location of work, the price of housing and transportation, the need for coherence in the face of outside hostility – all these contributed to neighbourhood creation. In Toronto, the city that developed after the pioneer period increasingly took the form of a grid. Such a regular plan lent itself only grudgingly to the creation of ethnic nooks and crannies. For example, the history of the St. John's Ward, in the heart of the city, as an underdeveloped area and immigrant quarter to the west of Yonge Street and behind the city hall, was in fact very short lived. The completion of the grid with Bay Street and Dundas Street in the early twentieth century, along with the introduction of sewers, ended what had been essentially an encapsulated immigrant world. The development of commercial and public institutions followed and drove immigrants farther west into the back alleys that later produced Kensington Market and farther yet, in the case of the Italians, to the short, non-gridded streets around St. Agnes Church. At the same time, Poles, Macedonians,

---

* *Diglossia* is bilingualism in two languages of uneven status in society. Typically the family language, or immigrant language, is the more comfortable medium but the one valued less in the city. For immigrants from rural backgrounds, *triglossia* existed. Dialect, ethnic language and English were viewed in ascending order of value in terms of the host society, but descending order of affection by the immigrant.

Finns and others settled in the small cross streets of the industrial sectors of the East End, the Niagara region, and later the Junction in the West End.

One remarkable feature of all of these neighbourhoods for the city explorer or urban archaeologist is the degree to which the sites do not now correspond to the general grid layout of the city but, if not extirpated by freeways or housing projects, have still the quality of an enclosed space conducive to close and familiar street life. Whether in Kensington Place, near Little Trinity Church in the East End, or around the Clinton Street area of the second Little Italy, there still clings a feeling that these were neighbourhoods in a very immediate and face-to-face sense.

Historical sources on immigrants in Toronto can be divided into three groups. First there are municipal records, statistical and circumstantial, ranging from assessment roles and city directories to pedlars' licence lists, arrest logs, police books and student cards in the various inner-city grammar schools. Such materials can be used to recreate the setting of encounter and much of the factual surroundings of immigrant life. Then there is the literature of the urban actors themselves. On the one side is the writing of those already in the land, ranging from evangelical pamphlets of the social gospel missions, reports of settlement houses, royal commissions, medical officers' reports, boards of education papers and the English-speaking press. Such sources obviously can provide a valuable picture of the interplay between perception and reality in urban history. However, to pass through ethnic boundaries to ethnic identities, the immigrant's own account of his urban experience is also necessary. For that there is oral testimony, the fragile memory of the immigrants themselves, to be used with the same caution one would apply to any kind of subjective written biography, reminiscence or memoir. There are church almanacs, jubilee volumes, the minutes of fraternal and mutual aid organizations, letters and guides to letter writing in English and in the old-country language. There are also the reports of officials, foreign consuls and intellectuals travelling from the countries of origin passing through Toronto.

The numbers of those immigrants who came to Canada before World War Two are thinning dangerously. The city's history will pay dearly if we neglect the systematic gathering of oral testimony and other ethnocultural materials which could enrich our knowledge of people in the city. As it was for Yeats, so for us the most important source of information will be the people who, as immigrants and the children of immigrants, lived in ethnic neighbourhoods and who possess in their collective memory, personal papers, or as guardians of the records of now defunct ethnic associations, the history of those places.

Immigrants need no longer be depicted either as proto-Torontonians or proto-Canadians, as people on the threshold of acculturation, or as potential fossils, living in colonies of an old country, maintaining cultural baggage which changed little until it fell away like scales from the eyes in a healing Canadian environment. Instead, scholars may begin to see the immigrant colony itself as having a history, a process of development. Improved ways of observing group ethnicity may lead to more comprehension of the nature of personal ethnicity so that immigrants may come to be seen neither as simply the pre-articulate masses of Toronto, nor as Italians, Finns, Poles, etc., but as specific kinds of Torontonians – Italian, Finnish, Polish Torontonians – who underwent individually and as groups a variety of urban experiences, met a variety of receptions which affected their strategies for living here and contributed in a variety of ways to the city's growth.

The new emphasis on history from the "bottom up",[10] along with ethnohistory's interest in analysis of culture and society, invites us to move beyond the study of the external and quantifiable to the more deeply textured and nuanced study of *mentalités*, perceptions in encounter and conflict, strategies for adjustment or persistence in relation to the changing real condition of being immigrant and for coping with a changing personal or group sense of ethnos. The task of ethnohistory should be the difficult one suggested in the phrase of Jacobo Timmerman, "to penetrate the affective world of the other". To do that, we need to look at the immigrant and ethnic neighbourhoods of the city without assuming we comprehend the intent of each person's migration project, the intensity of their ethnic networks or of their loyalties to ethnoculture.

To understand the linkage among identity, cognitive maps, psychic worlds,[11] commitment to family and friends, and then to understand how these individual commitments paralleled a continuum of place, family, work site, church, association, street-corner life, we need also to comprehend the immigrants' sense of space. We can do this by simply changing our frame of reference. The great anthropologist Oscar Lewis once lamented that anthropologists who became ethnohistorians spent most of their time talking to old Amerindians and practising a methodology they called participant observation, but rarely bothered to look at the sources of the United States Bureau of Indian Affairs or the Canadian government, since they believed that the written word represented only the view of an arrogant and ignorant conqueror of the indigenous people.[12] Historians of the city have tended to the opposite sin by thinking that they can reconstruct the reality of urban immigrant life from the writings and documents of the caretakers of the host society. Such sources leave the historian on the edge of the city's ethnocultural reality. Recreating the past from them is a bit like writing the history of British Africa or of French Indo-China from the memoirs of soldiers and missionaries alone.

Few of Toronto's ethnic neighbourhoods could qualify in the Marxist sense as "internal colonies", societies "within a society based on racial, linguistic and marked cultural differences of social class", and subject to control by "the dominant classes and institutions of the metropolis."[13] Yet the concept of internal colonies is at least as useful a model for prewar Toronto as images of homogeneity or rapid assimilation. It reminds us to look at the ethnic community as a separate place, to think of its interior life and not just its boundaries. It reminds us of what Walter Firey observed studying Boston's neighbourhoods many years ago: a neighbourhood is at one and the same time part of the city hierarchy and system and a "little homeland", a spatial corollary to a set of values, of networks, of ways of thinking and being, of ethos.[14] In Toronto some groups obviously required a "little homeland" more than others, and the result was immigrant neighbourhoods. English, Scots and Irish, except for concentrations in Cabbagetown, were not confined in enclaves. Despite tell-tale accents, they did not encounter systematic discrimination. They did, as Mackenzie King noted, form associations, from the St. George Society to the Dewi Sant and the Orange Lodge, and they did encounter enough hostility that some concepts of ethnic neighbourhood or enclave apply to them as well. Peoples' ways were shaped by living in neighbourhoods, around them, among a majority group, or indeed even by escaping from them and practising that most common third- or fourth-generation phenomenon, "weekend ethnicity": returning to the immigrant areas for religious services, food supply, haircut, or family visits only on the weekend.

Ethnic neighbourhoods can be studied as concentrated universes in two quite different ways. One is accessible to plotting by analysing factual sources, especially written city records, and by forms of social scientific measurement. Another is more notional. It is about the *mentalités* of immigrants and about the psychic worlds they inhabit.

This more complex and notional sense of the neighbourhood then as an ambience, a psychic world for the immigrants and their children and perhaps their children's children, with its moving mix of ethnocultures, part-cultures and pressures to change the mores and folkways, produced by encounter with the North American situation, is a world we must come to know. If we allow ourselves just for a moment "to surrender", in Vladimir Nabokov's words, "to a sort of retrospective imagination which feeds analytical faculty with boundless alternatives", every usage and event in the enclave becomes an intricate key for studying attitudes and identities.

Borrowing from social anthropology, we can begin to understand the value of extending and deepening our moment of observation of the immigrants and their children in their neighbourhoods.[15] Freed of the retrospective falsification that comes from fervent but anachronistic multiculturalism, and equally free from an historicism that sees all immigrants pausing only momentarily on the threshold to the house of Canadian ways, we have an opportunity to fill in the blank spots on our map of the city. We can find ways to comprehend the group's sense of group, not just the intensity and frequency of the use of neighbourhood or ethnic networks, but the changing significance, for the immigrant and each succeeding generation, of various community institutions, such as a home town club, a nationalist association, or a parish.

By learning more about the role of mutual aid societies, the ethnic press, church, drama and leisure clubs, the importance of islands of acquaintanceship within the community and the ethnolinguistic psychology which made people choose one language over another, as well as about changing symbols and emblematics of the group, we may arrive at a demotic intellectual history, a history of how the people think. If we can begin to know their attitudes about settling, or merely sojourning, about upward mobility, about social class, about other ethnic groups in Toronto, if we can learn more of the dreams they held for their children, the strategies they chose either to persist in their own culture or acculturate in Canada, we will be on the verge of being able to write a whole social and cultural history of the city.

Information and insight into all these ideas are accessible to us if we combine the little used sources generated from inside the community, such as club and church records and ethnic newspapers and print ephemera, with a more extensive and systematic use of oral testimony. The city might then have the sort of history Lawrence Levine describes as "the attempt to present and understand the thought of people who though quite articulate in their own lifetimes have been rendered inarticulate by scholars who devoted too much of their attention to less recalcitrant subjects."[16] Levine's thought parallels almost exactly that of the social anthropologist Clifford Geertz who writes, "at base, thinking is a public activity. Its natural habitat is the house yard, the market place and the town square." [17]

The convergence of the two disciplines holds special possibilities for urban and immigrant studies. Although declining and increasingly fragile, the necessary sources for the study of Italians, Jews, Chinese, Greeks, Macedonians and the many peoples and neighbourhoods of Toronto in the late nineteenth and twentieth century are still available. The equivalent of Geertz's house yard, marketplace and town square existed in each one of Toronto's ethnic neighbourhoods. Throughout Toronto there were such house yards, behind boardinghouses or rough-caste cottages in the alleys of the Ward, Kensington or the East End. They were places where kin, friends from home towns in the old country and neighbours gathered. They were also places where small-scale agriculture, commerce, industry and a bit of animal husbandry went on. There people foregathered for seasonal food processing – pickling, butchering, sausage-making and wine-making – for impromptu picnics and communal meals. They gathered to exchange collective wisdom about important decisions – sending for relatives from the old country, following work opportunities out of the city, moving out of the neighbour-hood, improving a house or selling it, allowing a child to continue his or her education. The house yard was a place where hundreds of the small human decisions, which affected the city's economy, appearance and culture, were made.

The equivalent of the marketplace in Geertz's analysis were the corner stores, the factories and life on the work gangs. For the children, it was the schoolyards, playgrounds and settlement houses. Each was in a different spatial and psychic relationship to the "little homeland", the ethnic neighbourhood and the ethnic group. They were places where men and women had to negotiate their ethnicity, make those constant adjust-ments of style and thinking which were the milestones in the process of learning to live within the larger North American urban setting. They learned when one could trust someone from outside the ethnic group. They learned the more difficult lesson of not trusting some even within their own regional group. They had opportunity to study what was threat-ening and what was useful about municipal politics and city government. In this way, Toronto's ethnic groups thought, reacted and became actors in the city's history.

In the little corner stores, cafés and social clubs, animated and informed debate took place on the politics of the old country and the problems of the new. A participant observer might have seen something of ethnicity as process if he could have recorded the changing ratio of old-world talk to Toronto talk, as well as the levels of intensity accompanying each subject. Surrogate for that field work which was not done is the local ethnic press. Concordances on topics covered and on their placement in the paper give some sense of the changing concerns of the ethnic communities. In the work gangs and factories immigrants had opportunities to understand the advantages and disadvantages of ethnic cohesion in the face of an exploitive capitalist system or other ethnic groups. Encountering workers of other ethnic origins in the factories, they discovered their commonalities and differences. All of these "marketplaces" were the scenes of public discourse and decision-making which affected the city itself.

Finally and central to the neighbourhood was what Geertz refers to as the "town square". In many of the city's ethnic neighbourhoods one could reconstruct the neighbourhood outward from the church or *shul*. For usually a religious building, occasionally a secular hall, just as in the villages of origin, defined the geographic and psychic core of the immigrant neighbourhoods. That core affected even those within the ethnic group who chose to go their own way towards secularism, or who joined one of the North American evangelical faiths beckoning them toward rapid acculturation. Whether seen as friend or enemy, the church or the local hall was a part of an immigrant's map and a gathering place. It was in front of the church on Sundays, in the associational halls or home town clubs, or waiting for an ethnic newspaper to appear on a corner stand, in the streets watching children play, or shopping that the ethnic nodal point – no matter what its spatial contours – took on the context of a "town square". Corners in the Ward, in the Italian neighbourhoods to the west, in front of *shuls* or Orthodox churches, on Maria Street in the Junction, served as forums for the evolution of ethnic group thought. It was there that the reinforcing sense of the neighbourhood as ethnic enclave, as well as a sometimes irritating sense of its role as a *villagio pettegolo*, a gossipy village, emerged. Since most such neighbourhoods served as base camp for those of the immigrant groups who dared to go outside to work in the Ontario north on construction sites, to peddle, or to run fruit stores, confectioneries, dry good shops and restaurants, the "town square", especially on the weekend, had a special role in both spreading news and reaffirming the coherence of the ethnic group.

We can come much closer to understanding how currents of thought within the ethnic group affected the enclave, its culture and identity. Not understanding these things, it seems unlikely that an urban historian can paint a fair or accurate picture of the immigrant as participant in the larger city. For if we do not know, for example, whether a Catholic priest in a certain parish supported a strike action in a nearby factory, or whether immigrants from a small Balkan country were more preoccupied with the nationalist struggle at home than with their social struggle on a work site, while other immigrants from eastern Europe wrote and performed plays with titles like *Unemployed on Spadina* in order to denounce the Canadian system, we can hardly measure the impact of immigrants on the city's workforce, life and politics, or the impact of the city upon them.

Being part of an immigrant group and living in an ethnic enclave meant hearing and reading both more and less information on various subjects than those in the larger host society did. It meant receiving news with a different emphasis on almost every matter of politics and culture. What was transmitted once in the "town square" and through the ethnic press now reaches people via cable television. Toronto is a city whose populace has always been fractured, in its receipt of information, into ethnocultural groups. To take an example from outside our period, the front page of a Hungarian Marxist newspaper printed in the city in 1950 contained a picture of Ho Chi Minh and a discussion of the Vietnamese problem at a time when Ho Chi Minh was largely unknown to English-speaking Toronto and the tragedy of Indochina remote. It is remarkable that no historian of the city has studied how this multiplicity of overlapping "communication systems" in Toronto affects our political life and intergroup understanding.

In the same way that the fracturing of information is a consequence of being a polyethnic city, so too each ethnic group or immigrant cohort had a different spatial definition of the city itself. Both in the geographical sense of an enclave and in the more notional sense of ambience, the neighbourhood as a combination of individual cognitive maps and psychic worlds for immigrants and their children provided their focus and anchor in the city.

Each sojourner or settler possessed, as well as a detailed cognitive map of his world, a sense of where his fellows were in Toronto and of what parts of the city mattered to him. The immigrant's alternative atlas, of course, could not be confined to Toronto. It included key points such as his town of origin, the routes and stops on his crossing, as well as locations where his extended kin were throughout the world. The historian who tries to fit the ethnic group too neatly, geographically and psychically, into the city does damage both to urban history and to the study of migration and ethnicity itself. For example, Toronto's Ward in the 1900s served both Italians and Jews throughout the province. From it men who went to work seasonally on the labour intensive northern frontiers of Ontario, or peddled through the lonely countryside, drew supplies and cultural sustenance. Through the neighbourhood they kept in touch with other colonies of their own kind, their home town and fellow-townsmen throughout the diaspora. Through the neighbourhood passed cash remittances, ethnic goods – from tomato paste to *taleysim* – brides, returnees and intelligence reports about travel routes, work, housing and the reception newcomers could expect in other parts of the country. In this manner the neighbourhood as an ambience was always larger than the actual enclave. On the other hand, many of the immigrants who settled or sojourned in the Ward had very little knowledge or contact with other nearby Toronto neighbourhoods. Toronto was then an urban space which, in semiotic terms, spoke to each immigrant group differently and spoke to all of them. Since their settled British and acculturated neighbours saw the city differently, they misunderstood the newcomers' behavior.

Foreign immigrants and their children rarely developed a balanced map of the whole city. An understanding of its other people, of the use of its other spaces, or its history developed slowly. The first *Bulgaro-English Dictionary* included phrases on how to take the streetcar to King Street East "where the Macedonians live", side by side with how to find the Wabash ticket agent for trains to other Macedonian settlements near Chicago or St. Louis. It had no phrases about the Ward or Rosedale.[18] A place of work, or housing, or leisure for one group was a place seen as an unfriendly environment or simply unknown to another group. Thus Macedonians knew there was no work for them at Gooderham's even though that distillery was in the middle of their settlement. Italians knew that one needed to change one's name and hide one's origin to clerk in the big department stores, and all foreigners knew that the Hydro Commission hired only workers of British descent under the pretext, or on the grounds, that communication in English was necessary. Lithuanian men on their way from boardinghouses on Queen Street West to factories in the East End picked up box lunches paid for on a weekly basis from Chinese lunch grills near their boardinghouses. Yet they never ventured into Chinatown for a Chinese meal even though that neighbourhood lay between them and work.

For most groups, picnics and outings, even a visit to the graves of loved ones in Mount Hope Cemetery, required a trek across unfamiliar and threatening space. Leisure itself was a segregated activity for the immigrant generation, and the pattern followed them out of the city. Property owned by members of the ethnic group, by benevolent associations or parishes, usually on the outskirts of Toronto, were safe sites for planned leisure, picnics, or ethnic outings. Pontypool, east of the city, and Belle Ewart, near Lake Simcoe, were such locations for the Jews. Nearby farms served Italians, Macedonians, Chinese and Poles in the same way. In the neighbourhood, men and women built systems and networks that enabled them to survive as Torontonians and, in most instances, made it possible for their children to sally forth into the larger city to work, and to share public leisure places such as the CNE and Sunnyside. Many of the immigrants probably understood their neighbourhood and the city much in the way that Italo Calvino suggests in *Invisible Cities*. There he describes the mythical city of Vasilia – Toronto's real Junction, Cabbagetown, Ward, or Kensington Market would do just as well:

> In a city, to establish the relations to sustain the city's life, the inhabitants stretched strings from the corners of the houses, white or black or grey, or black and white, according to whether they mark a relationship of blood or trade, authority, agency. When the strings become so numerous that you can no longer pass among them, the inhabitants leave, the houses are dismantled. Only their strings and their supports remain.[19]

Good urban historians will learn how to read a narrative in those strings and their supports. It will not be easy, for few locations in the city were the exclusive neighbourhood of a single ethnic group. Kensington Market, once called the *mercato giudeo* by Italian immigrants, had by the twenties and thirties lost its exclusively Jewish character and become polyethnic. The Junction, the city's premier candidate as an ethnic industrial working-class neighbourhood, now boasts a Polish hall, an Albanian hall, a Maltese parish, a little synagogue on Maria Street, a Croatian club, an Irish club and had at one time an Italian pasta factory. The neighbourhood seems always to have been truly polyethnic.

Stores in the Junction that served Canadian Pacific Railway workers in the daytime became Macedonian hangouts at night. Separate and public schools brought children of many backgrounds together. In the battle for control of the young, it was in the playgrounds and schoolyards throughout the city where the guardians of the host society effectively took children away from the streets and from their parents' culture. In fact, if studied closely enough, the surface of neighbourhoods like the Junction give way to deeper patterns of sub-neighbourhoods. In the Junction, some streets served the workers in the stockyards, mainly Macedonians, while nearby streets housed artisans, mainly German and Jewish, from the Heinzmann piano factory, once the largest employer in the neighbourhood. Yet other streets housed mostly families which worked for the CPR, mainly Anglo-Celtic. So the ethno-histories of Maria, Mulock and Glendenan streets in the Junction diverge over time almost as much as the histories of the Junction and Kensington Market. In the East End, Cabbagetown, Corktown and the Macedonian's cognitive map of their East-End neighbourhood blurred and shared much the same space. In the same manner the Ward itself, the city's chief Jewish ghetto at the turn of the century, was also the city's Chinatown and its chief Little Italy.

If nothing else, this intimate sharing of areas by immigrant groups suggests that the usual frame of study – immigrants *vis-à-vis* a WASP or Anglo-Celtic dominant society – misses the real dynamic of encounter, exchange and competition among newcomers from many lands. The polyethnic reality reconfirms the view that the history of a great North American city can rarely be properly written unless it is also ethnic and immigration history. Unfortunately for Toronto, the history of the Junction area, the history of the Ward and the history of Kensington Market, just as the history of several ethnic groups not dealt with in this volume, who lived with high levels of residential segregation in the city before the Second World War – Lithuanians, Maltese and Hungarians, for example – have yet to be done.

Many of Toronto's newcomers had been cultural or religious minorities in their land of origin. Jews, Macedonians, Galicians, even the Catholic Irish and south Italians had had some experience in having to create and sustain their own ethnocultural institutions against regimes that were hostile or remote. Few, however, had experienced the uprooting or, conversely, the freedom to speculate about and alter identity. Although concern about a homeland or about the diaspora of one's people throughout the world persisted, such concerns themselves became elements in the forging of a new sense of group for which the neighbourhood was the territorial base. Karl Deutsch has observed that, "an isolated minority in a strange new country might increase its efforts to recall its past and to standardize its behaviour so as to erase again and again the eroding effects of the new environment on its traditional culture."[20]   In such circumstances, the role of leaders and the nature of their status and appeal obviously calls for analysis. Reflective and ideological efforts at maintaining folkways, values and language, although themselves a long step away from primordial ethnicity, especially for those groups from the tsarist borderlands, came in logical sequence for the immigrant in North America. Each ethnoculture seemed to hold differing attitudes on the importance of group coherence. Ethnic leaders and intelligentsia encouraged different strategies for group survival, which posited roles for church, language and nationalist political party in group life.

Some of the political left in each group looked beyond ethnic persistence to a world of contact with the working class of other ethnic groups. As with those who joined North American evangelical churches, the rates of acculturation of those on the left were often more rapid, either because they came to know the larger city more quickly or found the ethnic enclave less nurturing and its leaders – priests, businessmen, foreign consuls – less acceptable. Historians have not reconstructed the degree to which, over two or three generations, ethnicity was the continuing organizer of existence in the city for many people. Some immigrants may have seen their ethnicity as simply an epiphenomenon of immigration – something of value for themselves but not their children or their children's children. Some tried to keep their ethnoculture in the form in which they brought it from the old country; others negotiated their ethnicity, altering its content or displaying ethnocultural ways selectively where they were acceptable to the host society, or when they brought them comfort or seemed right. Ethnic identity, even national feeling for the homeland, remained for most of the first two Canadian generations of any immigrant group a latent value which arose in times of crisis – such as an earthquake in the old country, an encounter with prejudice in the new, a measurement for choosing a certain politician in the city for whom to vote.

Whether experience with maintaining minority institutions in a hostile environment was long and deep, as with the Jews, or a relatively new phenomenon of national revival, as with the Galicians and Macedonians, none of the immigrant groups had faced the need to create entirely new institutions. The need to do so, in fact, was a central aspect of ethnicity as North American process. For example, when Macedonians in Toronto decided to organize their own church in 1911, it lead them into what most Torontonians saw as visibly Macedonian national politics. On the other hand, what they did was almost entirely neoteric for them as Macedonians. People, accustomed to a village church, used to a community of elders who were just that, older and wiser, used to a priest leading them, found themselves gathering in private homes in Macedonian neighbourhoods of the city. They created a slate of immigrant delegates from thirty-one different villages of origin for the purpose of tithing one another to build a single church, not a number of village churches. Reflecting the youth of the immigrant population, only four out of the twenty elected as village elders in Toronto were over thirty years old.[21] The condition of being Macedonian in Toronto, of being ethnic in a

Canadian city, did not then replicate the old country any more than it was simply a stage towards acculturation and an Anglo-Canadian lifestyle.

This same irony existed in the creation of an Italian parish or a Polish parish. Although such parishes might appear ethnic to the larger Toronto society, or to the Irish Catholic hierarchy, they were not the "old-world transplanted". At Our Lady of Mt. Carmel, Barese, Sicilian and Venetian patron saints rubbed shoulders in a way that they would not have done in Italy. The "very Italian" feast of San Rocco seemed a melange of Canadianisms to the immigrants. The mass had an Irish celebrant, a Jewish boy from the Ward was the solo instrumentalist and "God Save the King" was played.[22] In fact, such churches were a totally new phenomenon for the people in the parish on several levels. Worshipping with co-nationals not from their home town, they encountered identities, accents and folkways they did not know. Often they developed Polish or Italian national identity together in the new world almost coincident with becoming Polish or Italian Torontonians. Moreover, Roman Catholic immigrants had to question, often for the first time, the authority and power of the church in order to gain their separate parish. Though usually viewed by the host society as an import from the old country, the national clubs, parishes and benevolent associations, which transcended home town and *landslayt* loyalties, were essentially a Toronto phenomenon and seen as such by the immigrants.

Ethnoculture is not a thing apart, merely something to which "social events, behaviour, institutions, or processes can be constantly attributed", but is rather a context within which such things can be intelligibly described. Once we see the immigrants as serious actors in the city's history, then the need to know more about their associational life, the intensity and variety of networks of acquaintanceship, the sub-economies which they created in various neighbourhoods and throughout the city, their emblems, folkways and ethnicism (ethnonationalism) becomes obvious. One of the best ways to do this is to learn how to apply the ethnographer's technique of reading "a narrative into cultural artifacts". The goal is not the rediscovery of Toronto's ethnic past, but the discovery of ways to read the significance of ethnicity in the lives of individuals, ethnic groups and the city itself.

To practise such retrospective ethnography on immigrant groups in Toronto before 1940, we need to find those "artifacts" such as cultural events through which we can read such a narrative. In special issues of *Polyphony* on the study of the immigrant press, ethnocultural theatre and religious institutions, I have suggested some ways in which sources, related to those institutions interior to the ethnocommunities, could be used to develop a more richly textured history of groups in the city.[23] Oral testimony, used more systematically, could help make the authentic voice of the immigrant in the city heard. If certain sub-groups or generational cohorts were interviewed in conjunction with a larger effort to use the census, city directories or church and school records to build a prosopographic base, then oral history would take on new value and reliability as a source. For example, one could attempt to interview and follow the lives of a single prewar class from St. Agnes school in the heart of Little Italy, or trace the careers and networks of sets of godparents from one year in the church records, or trustees from an orthodox church, or the executive from an ethnocultural association. Done well, such studies would move beyond impression and biography to become the basis of a social history, more intricate and truer than that based on quantifying gross numerical patterns in the census.

Picnics, dances, strikes, sermons, events in an association or benevolent hall, church organizations and enterprises, evenings in a café, saloon or political club are settings which provide a chance to move away from the "thin description" of mobility studies toward the "thick description" possible about the changing mores, emblems and folkways and the constant decision-making which is the process of ethnicity in a North American city and the route to understanding the many paths to being a Torontonian. A picnic organized by a *paese* club from Italy or a Macedonian village association, a dance sponsored by a socialist club among Finns or Lithuanians in the city was surrounded by emblems, organizations and sub-events susceptible to analysis. Moreover, such events had different symbolic meaning for different participants. For the immigrant generation such affairs, with their intensity of fellow-feeling, often took priority over all other social activities in their lives. For their children and perhaps even for the immigrants as they grew longer in the land, the annual associational dance or picnic had to compete with a minor league baseball game at Stanley Park or a hockey match at Maple Leaf Gardens. Analysis of the celebration of a saint's feast day, a Ward political outing, or an ethnic pamphlet brings us closer to the real sentiments and real networks of each group in the city at any given time.

For example, the organizing of an annual picnic, beyond being simply a festive event, provided a ceremonial occasion for the playing out and affirming of various obligations, networks and commitments. It was a chance to affirm membership in the ethnoculture and loyalty to group language, traditions, or liturgy. It was the occasion for the healing or confirmation of political or parochial schisms within an ethnic community. It provides us, through its changing emblems, with data which can be finely calibrated for observing ethnoculture as process. In the decision about whether the main motifs of a spring pageant will be drawn from old-country sources or highlight the new Canadian tradition of a group, of how themes of homeland and of new country are mixed, can be read the history of identity. Through such descriptions we might discover real rather than stereotyped differences in predisposition among groups. For example, one benevolent society might respond to labour problems by raising money for strike funds, another might censor members for speaking back to a foreman in a factory and thus threatening the reputation and well-being of the whole ethnic group.

Materials as apparently neutral as those about the running of a credit union can be used to reconstruct the associative, coercive and moral commitments which held an ethnic group together. For example, by studying patterns of those granted loans in a Slavic credit union, dominated by a clergyman, we might discover subtle efforts to impose endogamy on the group by denying loans to those who marry out. Such credit unions could use the need to enforce political orthodoxy, denying, as they did in some instances, credit to those who did not either pay lip service to ethnic associations or practise the predominant religion of the ethnic group; or denying it to those who were too far to the political left in the eyes of the mainstream ethnic leadership. Institutions continually redefined the boundaries and values of the group, yet they have not been the subject of serious socioeconomic or political analysis.

Recently the good urban historian's task has been likened to that of a traffic cop standing at a busy intersection where two main avenues, one the history of the nation and the other the history of migration processes and of the various groups entering the city, meet.[24] There are also side streets into the intersection which carry the traffic of labour history, women's history, ecclesiastical history. In Toronto not just the streets of the grid, but even more the sidewalks, the blind alleys and the side streets were crowded, before World War Two, with people of many backgrounds about to become actors, or launch their children as actors, in the drama of the city.

Each of the eleven studies of ethnic groups in this volume shows a sense of urban space, understands that there was an intricate relationship between the reasons why people migrated to Toronto, where and how they settled in the city and how they were received. In turn, some of the studies show that the patterns of ethnic settlement reflect not just ethnicity but also the reality of the ethnic neighbourhoods as "little homelands", ambiences which were neither simply fossils of the old country nor fully of the new. Such little homelands were the settings for evolving identities, for sub-economies and ethnocultures constantly in process. No one who reads the pages which follow should ever again be content with monochromatic histories of city politics and politicians or class analyses of our urban past that lack comprehension of the city's ethnocultural variety.

Notes

1. Italo Calvino, *Invisible Cities* (New York, 1972), p. 30.

2. W.L. Mackenzie King, "Foreigners Who Live in Toronto", in *The Daily Mail and Empire*, 25 September 1897.

3. *Missionary Outlook* (Toronto), XXX, no. 12 (December 1910), p. 267, a special issue on the Fred Victor and other city missions. For secular views of the immigrant quarter as an urban pathology, see *What Is the 'Ward' Going to Do with Toronto* (Toronto: Bureau of Municipal Research, 1918) and Margaret Bell, "Toronto's Melting Pot", *Canadian Magazine*, XXXVII, no. 8 (July 1913), pp. 234-42.

4. James Scobie, *Buenos Aires. Plaza to Suburb, 1870-1910* (New York, 1974), p. viii.

5. J.M.S. Careless, *Toronto to 1918. An Illustrated History* (Toronto, 1984), effectively incorporates the lives of the Anglo-Celtic common people in his history of the city. On the non-British, see R.F. Harney and H. Troper, *Immigrants: A Portrait of the Urban Experience 1890-1930* (Toronto, 1976) and S. Speisman, *The Jews of Toronto. A History until 1937* (Toronto, 1979).

6. An attempt to apply behaviouralist and mobility measurements to a Canadian city is M. Katz, *The People of Hamilton, Canada West. Family and Class in a Mid-Nineteenth Century City* (Cambridge, Mass., 1975). Studies which use mobility rates analysis specifically to understand ethnic differences are Stephan Thernstrom, "Immigrants and Wasps: Ethnic Differences in Occupational Mobility in Boston, 1880-1940", in S. Thernstrom and R. Sennett, eds., *Nineteenth Century Cities: Essays in the New Urban History* (New Haven, 1969) and T. Kessner, *The Golden Door. Italian and Jewish Immigrant Mobility in New York City, 1880-1915* (New York, 1977). A good critique of the methodology is James Henretta, "Study of Social Mobility – Ideological Assumptions and Conceptual Bias", in *Labour History* 18, no. 2(1977), pp. 165-78.

7. Finley Peter Dunne, *Mr. Dooley on Ivrything and Ivrybody* (New York, 1963), p. 207.

8. See Fredrik Barth, *Ethnic Groups and Boundaries* (Boston, 1969).

9. William Butler Yeats, "Village Ghosts", in *Mythologies* (New York, 1978) p. 15.

10. The first historian to develop the idea of "history from the bottom up" is Jesse Lemisch. See his "The American Revolution Seen from the Bottom Up", in B.J. Bernstein, ed., *Towards A New Past: Dissenting Essays in American History* (New York, 1968), pp. 3-45. The idea is attributed to B.A. Botkin's *Lay My Burden Down. A Folk History of Slavery* (Chicago, 1945), C. Joyner, "Oral History as Communicative Event: A Folkloristic Perspective", *The Oral History Review* (1979), pp. 47-52.

11. For the concept of cognitive maps, see Kevin Lynch, *The Image of the City* (Cambridge, Mass. 1960).

12. Oscar Lewis, "The Effects of White Contact on Blackfoot Culture", in *Anthropological Essays* (New York, 1970), pp. 138-39.

13. M. LaGuerre, "Internal Dependency: The Structural Position of the Black Ghetto in American Society", *Journal of Ethnic Studies* 6, no. 4, pp. 29-44.

14. Walter Firey, "Sentiment and Symbolism as Ecological Variable", *American Sociological Review* 10 (1945), reprinted in Scott and Ann Greer, eds., *Neighbourhood and Ghetto. The Local Area in Large-Scale Society* (New York, 1974).

15. A good sample of this literature can be found in James L. Watson, ed., *Between Two Cultures. Migrants and Minorities in Britain* (Oxford, 1977).

16. Lawrence Levine, *Black Culture and Black Consciousness. Afro-American Folkthought from Slavery to Freedom* (New York, 1977) p. ix.

17. C. Geertz, "Thick Description: Toward an Interpretive Theory of Culture", and for specific reference to the "social nature of thought", see "Person, Time and Conduct in Bali", in C. Geertz, *The Interpretation of Cultures. Selected Essays* (New York, 1973), pp. 3-32 and pp. 360-61:

    A cultural artifact – whether suttee among Balinese or baseball in America – is analogous to a dream or Freudian slip. While it may have material cause and practical ends, the artifact is ultimately a nexus of significance, a potential narrative which the anthropologist is called on to decipher. If properly addressed, it will tell an important story about the collective mental life of the people among whom it is found.

    With the appropriate changes of detail this description of Geertz's idea of a cultural artifact can be applied to ethnohistory or retrospective ethnography in a city like Toronto. The description appears in P. Robinson's review of C. Geertz, *Local Knowledge. Further Essays in Interpretive Anthropology* (New York, 1983), in the *New York Times Book Review* (25 September 1983), p. 11.

18. D. Malincheff and J. Theophilact, *The First Bulgarian-English Pocket Dictionary* (Toronto, 1913).

19. I. Calvino, *Invisible Cities*, p. 76.

20. K. Deutsch, *Nationalism and Social Communication. An Inquiry into the Foundation of Nationality* (Cambridge, Mass., 1966), p. 121.

21. *50th Anniversary SS. Cyril and Methody Macedonian-Bulgarian Orthodox Cathedral, 1910-1960* (Toronto, 1960).

22. *The Ward Graphic* (Toronto, n.d.), p. 14. An occasional publication of Central Neighbourhood House, copy in the Multicultural History Society of Ontario collection.

23. *Polyphony: The Bulletin of the Multicultural History Society of Ontario*, vol. 1, no. 2 (Summer 1978), religion and ethnocultural communities; *Polyphony*, vol. 2, no. 2 (Winter 1979), benevolent and mutual aid societies in Ontario;

Polyphony, vol. 4, no. 1 (Spring/Summer 1982), the ethnic press in Ontario; and *Polyphony*, vol. 5, no. 2 (Fall/Winter 1983), immigrant theatre.

24. The image is borrowed from Arthur Goren's appreciation of Moses Rischin's study of New York's Lower East Side. See A. Goren, "The Promise of the Promised City: Moses Rischin, American History and the Jews", in *American Jewish History*, LXXIII, no. 2 (December 1983), p. 173.

BOARDING
AND
BELONGING*

———— ❦ ————

*T*HE GAP BETWEEN THE SUBJECT MATTER OF MIGRATION STUDIES AND THAT OF
North American urban and ethnic history has narrowed in recent years.
Historians of migration now study in detail the precise local causes of the
movement from old world locations and the pattern of the consequent
diaspora. At the same time, those who study major American cities and
small industrial towns have begun to show some appreciation of the
relationship between migration causes and settlement. In most studies,
however, there remains a lacuna between accounts and explanations of
the crossing and the history of ethnic institutional and neighbourhood
life on the North American side. Although we have moved from Oscar
Handlin's compelling, if often incorrect, metaphors of "uprootedness"
and "in fellow-felling" to explain the processes of migrating, ghettoizing,
and acculturating, we continue to depend too much on mono-causal
agents of settlement such as family chain migration or the padrone
system.[1] Using these ideas to carry them over the rough spots in narration, historians lose sight of the important mental transition from
sojourner to settler among newcomers, and of the formative period in
ethnic settlement when male sojourners predominated. Even if it is a
proper reflection of the sojourner's ambivalence as a man neither in his
home place nor reconciled to his new place, this lack of study destroys
our chance to discover the stages of cultural and institutional transition
from migration to sojourning and settlement.

Abrupt transition from the locus of migration to full-fledged ethnic
settlement and the use of padronism or extended family as *deus ex machina*
to turn migrants into urban North Americans can be found in even the best
recent studies of immigrants in cities as, for example, in H. Nelli's *Italians*

---

* This article reprinted with permission from *Urban History Review*, no. 2, 1978,
  pp. 8-37.

in Chicago and J. Barton's *Peasants and Strangers: Italians, Rumanians and Slovaks in an American City.*[2] Nelli, building a model of padronism and an indistinguishable mass of the exploited for whom the generic "southerner" provides both a class and ethnic identity, must wait until the newcomers have broken the sojourning thrall enough to be on Chicago's registered voter rolls or in commercial directories before he is able to study geographical and occupational mobility. For the sojourning period, he offers nothing but the stock characters, padrone and southerner, and a few biographies of exceptional immigrants. There is, in his account, neither a history and analysis of sojourner institutions nor a guide to the changing sentiments, intentions and ethnic identity of the newcomers.

Barton makes more effort to explain the pattern of settlement in North America in terms of old world causes such as family and *paese* loyalties and the larger push factors that existed in specific European areas. There is, however, no "interior" history of the migrants. We do not know their frame of mind, their levels of expectation, nor how long they intended to stay. Nor is any thought given to whether knowing these things would enable us to understand better the pace of acculturation or the intensity of ethnic persistence in Cleveland. So, although Barton implements the best ideas of Handlin about the migrant as a villager and of Vecoli about family and *paese* reconstitution in the city, his chapters on the Old World remain strangely disjoined from those which deal with the new ethnic institutions of the city such as benevolent societies, visible ethnic business enterprises, and parishes. By failing to appreciate and study the informal, often amoebic, institutions of the sojourning period and by maintaining stock characters like the padrone and the southerner, the historian fails the immigrant in his continuous, if tortuous, journey from migrant to "ethnic" and retrospectively confirms the stereotyping of male sojourners as Wops, Bohunks, birds of passage, *cafoni* – the faceless guestworkers of North America at the turn of the century.[3]

It is my belief that a chrysalis of the ethnic settlement of the North American ethnic group itself, its boundaries and its content, can be found in those first years of urban migrant life, now shrouded in creation myths and filio-pieties. Careful study of the sojourner, his frame of mind, his needs, his amoebic institutions, and the impact of the sojourn on his identity will demonstrate this. Such study will require the use of oral testimony as well as a change in approach. In fact, North American historians have ceased to view immigration, the ethnic colony and acculturation as an obvious continuum, and, in the face of startling ethnic persistence, more time has been spent rethinking the relationship between the last two pictures in the triptych than between the first two. The distinctions between migrants and immigrants, sojourners and settlers[4] is not always made and the result is that family settlement is very often seen as the first stage of ethnic neighbourhood life.

Now, when so many excellent local studies of specific ethnic groups and their settlement are appearing, it seems the right time to reassert the need for thorough comparative studies of the migration, sojourning, and settlement patterns of each ethnic group. Stock characters such as steamship agents, immigrant bankers, foraging foremen sent to Europe to recruit and labour brokers, need to be studied as part of an economic structure rather than simply appearing on the stage in the immigrant drama. Households with boarders, extended families, boarding-houses, *padrone*-run bunkhouses and commissaries, informal *paese* clubs, mutual aid and burial societies – all elements in the sojourner's world – require analysis as institutions,[5] if we are to understand the transition from sojourning to settling to ethnicity in terms worthy of historians rather than those of latter day restrictionists or settlement house workers.[6]

I will look at the institution of boarding from the perspective of the sojourner and the settler. We must first remove some of the confusion that surrounds the practice of boarding among newcomers, and then we can see it as a form of entrepreneurship for some settlers, as a social institution fulfilling most needs for sojourners, and finally as a frame within which aspects of North American ethnicity were defined. Two points need to be made at the outset. In attempting to show the entrepreneurial and institutional nature of boarding, I am not denying the important contribution made to the subject from the perspective of household and family studies. For example, Modell and Hareven's excellent study, "Urbanization and the Malleable Household: An Examination of Boarding and Lodging in American Families", although it does not pay attention to sojourning as a concept, informs most of my thinking on the places of households in the study of boarding.[7] Also, I am aware that much damage is done to separate ethnic traditions and patterns of boarding by my cross-cultural approach. I wish only to show in this paper that the condition of being a sojourner, which was shared by most male migrants of the so-called "new immigration" of the 20th century, encouraged similar institutions among all groups.[8]

Questions of morality and definition linger from then, and before we can discuss the role of boarding in the sojourner economy and society, some confusions need to be sorted out. The Dillingham Commission, despite its misuse of the statistics on boarding, offered in 1911 a sensible classification of varieties of the boarding phenomenon among newcomers. The three general categories listed were: households consisting of two or more families living together; households consisting of one or more families with boarders and lodgers; and "scattering households" in which no family is present and called for this reason "group households". This last category divides into "either…a group of men who share all expenses or…a 'boarding house' usually [run by] a man without a family, and boarders and lodgers."[9]

Two subspecies of the first and last classifications have received most attention from historians. The household of an extended family has been the focus of chain migration studies, and the boarding house/inn as an adjunct of padronism has interested those who view migration as a strict relationship of labour, flowing through brokers, to capitalist demand. The phenomenon of several families, related or from the same old country locale, living as a single household was not uncommon, especially for short periods of time while people inserted themselves into the North American economy. However, one or more families living with relatives or fellow countrymen as boarders was far more than a "malleable household"; it was also a complex network of informal trust, written contract and cash exchange. Oral testimony shows that there was almost always exchange of money, precision about services rendered and terms of *modus vivendi*, as well as careful accounting of food and other costs. Analysis of boarding among sojourners then as simply family or household history does fall short of the cash nexus that existed and animated the institution at least as much as "in fellow-felling" did. The other subspecies, which skews our understanding of boarding much more than a too simple view of family and paesanism, is the extreme form of exploitation found in *padroni* inns and isolated work camps.

Confusing the traits of remote work camps with boarding itself is the same as identifying private enterprise with monopoly capitalism. Indeed, it was monopoly – through cultural or geographical isolation – of lodging, transport, job opportunity and food supply which produced the extreme forms of exploitation. In both Canada and the United States, work camps on the railways, shanties near coal patches, isolated barge canal camp sites and lumber camps led to virtual enslavement…a condition which was luridly detailed by social reformers and immigration, industrial, and royal commissions. This spectre of the *padrone*-run commissary and bunkhouse or of the overcrowded inn near train stations and harbours created the aura of depravity and criminality which surrounds all of the Dillingham Commission's third category, "group households".[10]

In the case of Sicilians in the southern United States and the Chinese along the entire west coast of the Americas, insertion into the North American economy, often to replace black slave labour, was so reminiscent of negro servitude that the housing of the newcomers was naturally compared to slave quarters.[11] In 1930, an exposé of *padrone* and company-run camps in West Virginia showed that Italian migrant labour was often shanghaied, threatened with physical violence, and that camp security was maintained by armed guards and, in one case, a gatling gun.[12] Thus, the housing of foreign sojourners and the image of slavery ran together in the public mind. In the cities, immigrant entrepreneurs sometimes kept their employees in crowded lodgings near their shops. Especially in cases when those employees were immigrant minors, such as Greek or Basilicatan bootblacks or Syrian and Lebanese confectioners and pedlars, boarding became associated with white slavery and child abuse.[13]

Boarding in the city was rarely seen as the product of rapid population growth and poor urban planning or, conversely, as the sojourner's choice. For Nelli's Chicago, it was the *padrone* control of lodging itself which served as the mechanism by which target migrants were trapped and sojourners transformed into settlers.

> Unemployed workers who remained in Chicago had no problems in obtaining food or lodgings, for *padroni* and Italian bankers saved and operated tenement houses where they encouraged guests to indulge in extravagance in order to place them more completely in debt.[14]

Turn-of-the-century eyewitnesses noted the geographical proximity of "employment agencies, saloons, cheap lodging houses, lunchrooms and cheap or second-hand clothing stores."[15] Amy Bernardy saw the same link between boarding and labour exploitation in Boston's North End:

> The problem of capital and labour shines through between the lines in the notice outside the *banchista's* office: 'need 300 men for work on the railroad.' The horror of the unsanitary and degrading accommodations shows itself beneath the laconic sign: 'bordo' or 'we take in boarders'.[16]

In Toronto, a cluster of bankers, travel agencies and hotels existed in the heart of the first 'Little Italy' in the St. John's Ward; the Venezia Hotel, a steamship agency, an "immigrant bank" and a working class hotel dominated the main intersection of the second neighbourhood around St. Francis (St. Agnes) Parish. The Royal Commission which dealt with fraudulent labour practices surrounding the importation of Italian labour to Montreal demonstrated the close ties between the Canadian Pacific's recruiters, the *padrone*, Antonio Cordasco, and a number of boarding houses.[17]   Inevitably the boarding of alien migrant males became almost synonymous in Canadian cities, as it already was in the rural work camps, with exploitation and monopoly of services. In fact, any sense that sojourners might prefer such a boarding system was lost in a haze of moral outrage. The very place of boarding as an aspect of the commerce of migration rather than an exploitative end in itself became lost. The United States Industrial Commission of 1901 heard this testimony: "However, I have called the attention of the commission to many cases of Italian hotel keepers who have tried to get hold of the Italian immigrants in order to speculate upon them." And boarding was identified with outright violent crime as well. "Others have told me", wrote the director of Ellis Island, "how they were led to boarding houses where they were beaten and robbed or shanghaied to some far off mine, quarry or construction site."[18]

If boarding came into the cities from the remote work camps with a criminal record, in the city, the sojourners and their lodging system were immediately caught in yet another vortex of moral and sociological confusion. Boarding was associated with overcrowding, tenement conditions and the dangers of the "lodger evil". All of those masks of social disintegration intensified when the "pipeline to the cesspools of Europe" was attached. The lodger evil itself, of course, had emerged as a moral issue only when the majority of boarders in the city ceased to be middle class and were replaced by rural, lower class migrants and foreigners.[19]   In that sense, ethnic and cultural disparities were merely a convenient rallying cry for the city reformers and social gospellers, but reform, inspired by the social gospel or not, and prejudice fed on each other. J.S. Woodsworth, describing immigrants in Winnipeg and Toronto, could not comprehend why Galicians would live "twenty-four in one room where only seven should have been. Fancy such conditions", he added, "with illimitable prairies stretching to the north and west."[20] Thus, someone like Woodsworth could see boarding as an aspect of clannishness, a failure to acculturate, and a judgmental category which served to portray the sojourners (not incorrectly, only maliciously) as being like Emily Dickinson's rats, "the concisest tenants of the Earth", providing unfair competition for native stock. By living and surviving in the bestial nests of the boarding house, sojourners not only lowered standards, but also threatened to succeed. In Toronto, the muckraking newspaper *Jack Canuck* clearly expressed the danger that the sojourner might prove to be the fittest breed in the industrial city: "Not so the Italian. He is content to 'pig-in' with a crowd of others and live under conditions which an Anglo-Saxon would be ashamed of."[21]

The Report of the Toronto Medical Health Officer Dealing with the Recent Investigation of Slum Conditions in Toronto, Embodying Recommendations for the Amelioration of the Same, prepared for the city by Dr. Hastings in 1911, contained a typical interplay of hostility toward boarding, foreigners and the burgeoning industrial city itself. Charts of overcrowded rooms, dark rooms, rear houses, tenement houses, common lodging houses, cellar dwellings and one-roomed dwellings – all obviously employed as indices of squalor and social disintegration – were juxtaposed page on page with lists of ethnic households in the neighbourhoods studied in the report.[22] Boarding then, rather than being approached as a possible variation on the "malleable household", a sign of the resilience and initiative of migrant networks, was treated as urban pathology.[23]

If we can pass from the moralizing and emotion that surrounds turn-of-the-century boarding to its social reality, a different set of questions can be asked about the institution itself: questions about the uses of family and household to cope with a new North American situation, about boarding as a form of ethnic entrepreneurship and proprietorship – one of the earliest such forms – and as a community institution and a force shaping the boundaries of ethnicity itself. Further questions about the role of boarding in establishing the *ambiente* and density necessary for an ethnic settlement, and indeed, in moving the sojourner into the position and attitudes of a settler need answering as well. A new perspective, informed by much oral testimony and by the concept of sojourning, when combined with an understanding of different ethnic household traditions, should enable us to see boarding as one of those key institutions now lost in the mists between migration and permanent settlement.

Whether we are dealing with a family with boarders or a "group household", no amount of rhetoric about paesanism and kinship ties should draw us away from the economic matrix of the institution as it was understood and used by both the boarder and the keeper of boarders. For the boarders, the nature of the arrangement satisfied the needs of their sojourning frame of mind. That frame of mind (*mentalità*) called for maximizing savings, minimizing potentially costly encounters with the host society, and, as much as circumstances permitted, recreating or remaining in the *ambiente* of the home country.[24] Considered in these terms, one can see that the family-run boarding system was not so much a different institution from the "group household" as it was a felicitous and highly efficient form of it. Enterprise, a labour intensive and administrative organization around a working wife and serving children, was not only a traditional aspect of the European rural family but was also an efficient adaptation of that tradition to the city. The study of boarding benefits enormously from recent interpretations of the role of women in the work force and reassertions of older ones about the family as a single economic unit.[25]

Boarding then was a practical use of family and village ties as well as of certain qualities within the pre-industrial family itself. Historians have rarely felt that they could penetrate the complex nucleus of fellow-feeling and entrepreneurship in the relationship of relatives and fellow villagers who lodged together in North America.[26] In 1941, Oscar Handlin's eloquence could not hide the fact that he had thrown in the towel with the remark that, among the Boston Irish, "no matter how cramped the quarters of those already settled, there was always room *for the sake of rent, charity or kinship*."[27] Even in Vecoli's articulate critique of Handlin's *Uprooted*, the sojourner's family and "belongingness with his fellow townsmen" are contrasted with padronism, as if the former had no cash nexus.[28] Since then, perhaps because of the heritage of padronism or the image of sex roles, the study of boarding among Italian migrants remains too dichotomized. Certainly Slavic and Hungarian studies have no trouble in dealing with the family with boarders and the "missus" of the establishment as both a household and a well-organized business enterprise.[29]

Thomas Kessner's recent study of Jewish and Italian social mobility in New York City concludes that "lodgers represented the closest of neighbours and immigrants were careful to choose those of similar ethnic origin and religious background. These boarders became part of the immigrant household." Kessner notes in passing that in 1880 most Italian *bordanti* in the city were unrelated to the family with whom they formed a household, and that even by 1905, by which time chain migration could presumably have done its work, over 62% of *bordanti* were unrelated to the household in which they lived.[30] All this suggests more family enterprise than chain migration and kinship.

Among Italian lodgers, words like *bossa* for the keeper of the house, *bordo* for their arrangement, and *bordante* to describe themselves were borrowed and the Italian expression *convivenza* was rarely used. Perhaps an ethno-linguist could explain what qualities in the Italian North American household were sufficiently alien to require such borrowing. That boarding confused the newcomers themselves can also be seen in the attempt to force an ascriptive setting. Older boarders were called uncle by the young women who, after marriage to a boarding-boss, found themselves wives and keepers of boarders. Younger lodgers called the lady of the house auntie or *nonna* (grandmother), and *la padrona* when they referred to her with third parties. Hungarians usually referred to the boarding-boss's wife as the miszisz.[31] Many of these terms were obviously used to impose vigorous sexual controls on the boarding house, but they also reflect the attempt to make the institution fit either household or family situations which could be understood from the old world experience.

The use of terms of respect or of familial designations between boarder and the boarding-boss's wife cannot obscure either the menial labour status of the woman who ran the boarding establishment, or the precise business arrangements which existed between boarder and keeper. Although oral testimony invariably emphasizes the atmosphere of trust, family values and sense of shared fate in early Italian Canadian boarding, further questioning always brings out descriptions of highly structured arrangements about services rendered, payment for services, controls on boarder behaviour and on the organization of boarding itself. These latter aspects are clearer in the "group household" than in the family with boarders or the boarding-boss variations, but they are present in all forms of immigrant boarding.

A Methodist colporteur in Toronto complained that Sicilian women in the 1900s were so busy tending to boarders that they could not come to church gatherings; he did not understand that caring for a group of *bordanti*, or a boardinghouse, was an occupation for the whole family and a profession for the wife of the household: "Thus the rooming house is lucrative because it utilizes almost completely the family spare time labour. Similar is the case with lunch bars, grocery stores, etc." [32] Whether we can find sufficient material in traditional sources, such as assessment rolls, income statistics and city directories, to measure how lucrative keeping boarders was as an ethnic enterprise, the psychic saving involved in keeping the mother and wife at home to work and in maintaining the family as a single economic unit was clearly supplemented by much real profit from taking in sojourners.[33]

Fortunate the settler who could turn his household and his dependents into a source of income while still working outside the home himself. He was like the rich *contadino* of the old country who owned a draft animal which could be rented out for extra income. A wife as a beast of burden in the boarding business was certainly the equivalent of a mule in southern Italy or Macedonia, and small children were as valuable an asset as healthy sons had been on the land.[34] The profit margin for the family with boarders was potentially great, limited only by the energy of the family, the size of the house, the satisfaction of the clientele and, very occasionally, public inspection and intervention. For example, in Toronto in 1911, at a time when an Italian unskilled sojourner could earn about $2 a day as a labourer, a Toronto Italian family collected $3 a month from each of thirty boarders. The house they used rented for $28 a month. Depending on food arrangements, clear profit as well as free shelter accrued to the entrepreneurial family, and the husband was able to work full time outside of the home. In other instances, men paid $1.25 a week or the equivalent of a day's wages on board. The Hastings Report remarked darkly that there was "some evidence that certain small hotels and old rooming houses are about to undergo the dangerous trans-formation into foreign lodging houses".[35] If the Report saw such changes as heralding the spread of slum conditions, we should see it as proof of a successful entrepreneurial form and evidence of the existence of a satisfied clientele. Egisto Rossi, a special commissioner for the Italian government, calculated the sojourner's reasons for supporting a boarding system:

> Accepting my conclusions about the second and third points, it should be noted that the cost of food and lodging in Canada does not differ much from that of the United States. With 3 or 4 dollars a week, a manual labourer can live well enough in both countries. Certainly, our labourers do not spend on average more than 15 dol-lars a month, and that when you consider that they earn usually about $1.25 to $1.75 a day, enables them to save and to return to Italy at the end of a season with some *gruzzolo di denaro* (nest-egg).

Thus, there is every reason to believe that groups of sojourners would have created boarding institutions if entrepreneurial families and board-ing-bosses had not done so.[36] That is, after all, what the existence of so many "group" or "scattering households", as described by the Dilling-ham Commission and many other contemporaries, signifies.

Despite the camaraderie and intra-ethnic warmth that emerges from much of the oral testimony, boarding was a business. In an oral history of Pennsylvania immigrants, the authors describe a boarder in a South Slav establishment who found his "plate [turned] upside down at the boarding house when he did not have work." Moreover, the definitions of services to be rendered between keeper and boarder, regardless of kinship or paesanism, were so precise and so quickly surrounded by local custom that it very soon did not depend on the ritual of affecting kinship described earlier. Whether the mistress of such a "malleable household" was called *la padrona*, auntie, or the missus, if she took money for bed and board, she accepted a more rigorous set of commitments for service than any boarding house boss.[37] The woman was responsible for serving the boarders in a way that closely resembled the duties of a peasant wife to her husband. (Perhaps that is why, in the Hungarian case, the "missus" was assumed by many boarders also to share sexual favours with them, and why Italian feminists like Amy Bernardy railed against boarding as a source of adultery.)[38]

Giovanni Verga, in one of his short stories about Sicilian life, describes the obligations of a good peasant wife thus: "She made sure that he found a fresh sheet on the bed, the macaroni made and the bread for the following week already leavening." [39] The female boarding house keeper, and this varied considerably from ethnic group to ethnic group, washed the workers' soiled work clothes, bedding and dirty underclothes, and sometimes even the back and legs of the boarders themselves when they came in from mines and factories. The services rendered require much more study, for the status of women and the sexual mores of each country of emigration must have affected services offered in North American boarding arrangements.

Contractual arrangements revolved around the food supply, clothing and bedding, but it was the first of these that seems almost to have been a preoccupation. A Roumanian account indicates that groups of boarders sometimes moved in search of better food.[40] For historians and social scientists who fear that contemporary emphasis on varieties of ethnic cuisine may trivialize ethnicity, the study of the place of food in boarding is instructive. The food supply was the most flexible of the sojourner's costs, and its preparation, along with language and daily contact with boarders of the same origin, was the most salient aspect of the sojourner's struggle to insulate himself from cultural change. The boarder balanced his concern to maximize savings with his need for ample and hearty food in labour intensive job situations. He refused usually to sacrifice fully his *ambiente* and culture by eating food prepared in an "English" or North American style every day of the week.

The boarding-boss of the housewife with boarders wished to maximize profits while not alienating clientele. Again, it is obvious that excesses occurred where isolation and company indifference gave the commissary or those in charge of the food supply a virtual monopoly. For example, since most foremen and section bosses of Italian work gangs on the Canadian Pacific Railroad depended on Montreal *padroni* for their supply of Italian food, the railroad navvies in isolated camps paid as much as five times the going city rate for mouldy bread and tainted sardines (anchovies). In the city, competition between forms of lodging and perhaps greater "fellow-feeling" caused more balance between the profit motive and the workers' tastes and requirements. On the other hand, taste in food did maintain ethnic boundaries. Certainly sojourners saw it as an important difference between themselves and other groups, and it was used as a reason for maintaining ethnically homogeneous bunkhouses at many work sites. "All Japanese stay in same bunkhouse. The Canadians live in a separate bunkhouse and of course didn't like to eat Japanese food from our Japanese cook." What was true of isolated camp sites was equally true of the city, and *Jack Canuck*, lamenting the clannishness of Italians and the fact that they received work from the city through subcontracts, remarked: "It is said that the Italians employed by the city of Toronto refuse to buy any other than Italian macaroni. That they live in gangs of from 6 to 9 in one room...."[41] The newspaper's bitter comment tells us something about the place of boarding in the creation of ethnic density, of making other ethnic enterprises such as food importation possible, and the importance of food in defining ethnic boundaries and choice of housing.

Although carefully arrived at agreements between a boarding-boss and his boarders or in a "group household" might be expected, the degree of organization in the arrangement of meals in the household with boarders is a bit startling. Even in warm, family-based and *paesani* (fellow townsmen) boarding circumstances, the question of food supply was matter for careful accounting and individual, if usually unwritten, contracts. In one household, a hurdy gurdy man and his wife kept three or four younger boarders, often men from their *paese*. In the kitchen was a great black stove with separate pots of food prepared by each lodger for himself. An affluent or prodigal man might be preparing veal while a boarder more concerned about the cost of prepaid steamship tickets limited himself to the same meatless *minestra* or pasta every day. Yet another had made a full board arrangement with the family and ate their prepared meal with them. Everyone took his food from the stove and sat down to eat at the kitchen table together.[42]

A Slovak migrant in the Niagara peninsula described his boarding arrangement thus:

> The rooming house...see we paid the lady a dollar a month for cooking. You paid a dollar and we paid the room extra. And every week she bought what she need in the grocery store. She was purchaser. She chose – sometimes she says well tomorrow we're going to have real meat or something like that – or breaded veal or pork chops. Okay everybody agree. And then, end of the week – Sunday usually – they calculate everything – how much she spent – and then she spread the expenses amongst all of us. We pay a dollar and she had a free board. And her husband had to pay same as we do.[43]

The ethos of this arrangement hovers between family, trust and good business, and the possible mutations of the boarding arrangement seem endless. Without a much larger sample, and some attempt at controlling that sample by time, place and ethnic group, it is difficult to tell how much old world traditions affected the nature of the arrangement, but it should be clear that the simple line between family and enterprise is quite useless. For example, a Donau-Schwaben (German from Hungary) boarding house in Welland, Ontario had only lodgers who were related to one another and the owner. The lady of the household cooked for all the men, but

> We paid so much a week and she cooked. She cooked for us and we could buy our own food and take it to her and she cooks it or sometimes – the butcher came to the house. Butcher send young fellow and he notes down what you want and the next day they delivered it.[44]

The boarding system was further complicated by whether the household was responsible for preparing the lunch pail for each worker/boarder as well. In that instance, the matter could range from a commitment to so many sandwiches or cold sausage per day to no agreement. (In Toronto, for example, many Polish and Lithuanian boarders in the Niagara-Queen Street factory district found it easier to save by buying monthly lunch tickets from local Chinese and Macedonian restaurants who had packed lunches waiting for them each morning as they passed by.)

The sojourners' preoccupation with their meal arrangements grew from two different sources. First, as the most variable of their expenses, it bore constant and close scrutiny by men committed to saving. However, we must not deny the centrality of familiar cuisine to their maintenance of popular culture while away from the homeland. Moreover, it seems likely that boarding as an important and pioneering form of enterprise in immigrant neighbourhoods would not have existed if those who maintained boarders could not meet their dietary and culinary demands. Those Roumanian boarders in Cleveland expected a Sunday noon meal of noodle soup, pork meat and dumplings. They demanded sauerkraut, sausage, and pureed white beans a certain number of times a week.[45] Like the Italian labourers who would only eat imported pasta, the Roumanians were practicing a primitive but determined consumer power. Their existence made possible small entrepreneurial successes for those who imported pasta and tomatoes or made sauerkraut to some old country formula. Storefronts, *ambiente* and ethnic settlement followed.

Concern over the cost, quality and ethnicity of food existed in the "group households" as much as in the family with boarders, where instead of agreements with *la padrona* the boarders had to evolve a regime as a group. The organization of a cooking roster, rent payments, a budget of shared costs for food and drink, and even the laying out of rules for behaviour between boarders took time and consensus. Sometimes one would be hard put to tell the difference between a commercial boarding-boss and the sort of authoritarian leader who emerged to dominate such households. Usually the latter was an older member of an extended family of males involved in the boarding establishment, or a village man whose reputation had been great in the old country as well. He might differ from a boarding-boss only in so far that his power lay in his influence rather than in proprietorship over the location.[46] In other cases, remarkable democracy prevailed. More oral testimony, especially about weekly budget meetings and arrangement of a roster, will certainly show that "group boarding" nurtured the more formal institutions of the later community, such as burial societies, mutual aid organizations and *paese* clubs. Some boarding establishments sounded more like settlement houses or fraternal organizations than households anyway. Peter Roberts described what he, as a social gospel-ler, had found to be an ideal "group household" of Japanese in Omaha:

> One of the best samples of housekeeping I have ever seen was done by the 140 Japanese who lived in the House of the Good Shepherd in South Omaha. A board of managers had charge of the affairs of the group. The secretary of the board kept all records, accounts, and transacted all business with outsiders; the commmissary had charge of the feeding of the group; the cooking, washing, and scrub-bing were systematized, and each member was bound by a set of rules that secured peace and order.[47]

As we turn to the role of boarding in the dynamic of changing ethnic identities in North America, we should observe that for the true sojourner, the boarding place, whether under a *padrone* system, with a family, or in a "group household", provided a means of living with one's own on a scale larger than the family, and yet, smaller than the host society or even of that North American invention, the ethnic group. The lodging place served as the focus of "fellow-feeling", of gossip about townsmen and countrymen who were mavericks, philanderers or drunks, of the news' network coming from the home village, of intelligence about job opportunities, of the arranging of marriages and the travel of other family members and finally, of who were reliable merchants, money-lenders and go-betweens. It was the place to play old world card games and spend leisure time. In that sense, the boarding house, especially if one includes the saloons and ancillary enterprises often in its immediate environs, had for the sojourner a variety of the ethnic "completeness of institutions"[48] that Raymond Breton has described as necessary to a later stage of ethnic development.

In its informal and amoebic way, boarding provided for all the needs of the sojourners. If we could keep that in mind, the early period of ethnic settlement, dominated by male migrants and boarding arrangements, could be understood not in terms of the failure of acculturation or the pathology of marginality, but as a period when the sojourners' needs were met and when those entrepreneurs who drew their income from serving and exploiting the sojourners began the formation of permanent settlement and, indeed, of an ethnic bourgeoisie. One need only think of the sojourner's agenda to predict those institutions which would grow up in his presence and those which would be retarded.[49] Institutions of acculturation or culture mattered little. There were no children to educate in the new ways or to make steadfast in the old. For most of the groups involved, the presence of women was required to make ethnic parishes necessary. On the other hand, the sojourners did require ethnic food, rough leisure in the form of saloons, coffee-houses and billiard rooms, steamship agencies, banks, employment bureaux and some form of mutual aid or burial insurance. Just as oral testimony can show the presence of successful immigrant enterprise before city directory or tax roll evidence existed,[50] interviews also confirm that early community business notables and leaders of *paese* clubs or benevolent societies began as heads of group households or as boarding house bosses. Dr. Juliana Puskas of the Hungarian Academy of Sciences has pointed out that in those groups, such as the South Slav and the Hungarian, where the *miszisz* had a special role in running the boarding establishment, many such women were the moving spirits and first officers of parish and benevolent society committees.[51]

One suspects that the study of boarding and especially of the "group household" could bring us to the very heart of the relationship between ethnic identity and socio-economic reality, as well as providing a means of understanding the shifting boundaries of that identity. At a simple level, boarding often provided a neighbourhood with the density and concentration of people necessary to attract or create institutions which more overtly nurtured a separate ethnic existence. At a more important level, boarding as a form of clustering people from the same homeland began the process of breaking down extreme localism, even when each house-hold seemed to represent only one local origin and thus, led to what Helen Lopata has described as the "gradually emerging fabric" of North American ethnicity.[52]

If we look closely at the place and scale of "fellow-feeling" in board-ing, we can begin to grasp the way in which localism and ethnicity among the sojourners existed as both a continuum of identities and as conflict-ing loyalties or, at least, loyalties of different intensities. For example, when in Upton Sinclair's *The Jungle*, Jurgis Rudkus and his Lithuanian group reach the Chicago stockyard area, they find housing that seems to reflect both their Lithuanian ethnicity and the melting pot:

> There were four such flats in each building, and each of the four was a "boarding house" for the occupancy of foreigners – the Lithu-anians, Poles, Slovaks or Bohemians. Some of these places were kept by private persons, some were co-operatives.[53]

Rudkus, however, did not end up in that boarding-house because he was a Lithuanian, he was led to it by a man from his own village: "The two families literally fell upon each others' necks – *for it had been years since Jokubas Szedvilas had met a man from his part of Lithuania*." In almost every account of boarding, what appears to be camaraderie based on large ethnic definitions recedes upon closer examination, and one finds people from one village, town or district clustering together. Optimum size for "group households" and families with boarders tended to stay within such parochial definitions of their group. In such instances, at least within the boarding establishment, ethnicity did not extend beyond the *paese* or local area of emigration. Yet boarding was an expedient and a functional institution for sojourners, allowing them to adapt their sense of "fellow-feeling" to the scale of ethnicity imposed upon them by the nature of their migration, their jobs or their lodgings.

A look at a single sojourner's experience can demonstrate this point. Paul Bertoia, an immigrant from near Udine in Friuli, the northeast of Italy, arrived alone in Toronto after World War I. In search of work and relatives, he went on to Edmonton. There he stayed in a boarding house/inn known to its residents as the Roma Hotel. One floor was occupied completely by Friulan sojourners, and the next floor by Trevisans from a neighbouring region of Italy. Each floor had its own cooking, dialect, card games and camaraderie, even though the inn was named for Italy's capital and the native Edmontonians considered everyone in the building an Italian migrant. When Mr. Bertoia boarded with kinfolk in

Drumheller, he associated chiefly with people from his home town near Udine and later, when he came to Toronto, became involved in benevolent organizations like the Fratellanza which took in members from all over the Italian peninsula.[54] His ethnic reference group changed according to his setting.

Men who found themselves in more remote work situations with few *paesani* with them, seem to have developed a sense of belonging to a larger Italian or Italian Canadian ethnic group more quickly than those who were able to lodge with *paesani*:

Question: Were there a lot of people working on that job from your home town in Calabria?

Answer: No. They were mostly from other provinces. Was mixed you know. Mostly from southern Italy. In this gang we passed the winter in this converted horse stable – we were all Italian.[55]

Mr. Carnovale, the man who answered the above query, had three possible reference groups other than acculturation to Canadian ways: his *paese*, his region defined either as Calabria or the Italian south (*Mezzo giorno*), or the nation state of Italy. It is impossible to doubt that the background of the men with whom he sojourned and boarded did not affect his commitment to one identity or another, or at least his place along a continuum from *campanilismo* to an Italian Canadian ethnic sense. In that way, detailed study of the social setting of the migrants might begin to yield answers about the historical process of ethnicity.

In an account of a Macedonian "group household" in Toronto in 1920, we can see how the smallest details of the boarding organization could cement village ties or break them down either in favour of a larger Macedonian identity or of acculturation. A father defends his son who has burnt the daily stew prepared for other boarders. There is an angry exchange of words and, despite the fact that they are all fellow villagers, no turning back. Some moved and found new households; they passed either into the so-called "English" boarding houses or found another Macedonian "group household". In either case, the real conditions of their sojourn caused them to move away from their village loyalties and identity.[56]

If a burnt stew could threaten "fellow-feeling", it should also show that boarding in a "group household", even of fellow townsmen, was no idyll. All the tensions of inter-family jealousies and of life without womenfolk existed. For those families who left after such a contretemps, the "group household" and the village or *paese* that it served in the diaspora lost meaning in that sense which Harold Isaacs, quoting Robert Frost, felt was at the core of ethnicity: as "the place where, when you've got to go there, they've got to take you in."[57] For the many ethnic identities in flux at the turn of the century, boundaries moved, not just because of the broad categories of prejudice used by the North American host society, but also because of the vicissitudes of the sojourning community.[58] Boarding situations, length of sojourn and neighbourhood density meant that local identities brought from the Old World gave way, although never for various ascriptive purposes disappearing, in favour of North American ethnicity. Toronto's Italians appeared out of a skein of earlier relationships in which Calabrese generally boarded with Calabrese, and Abruzzese with Abruzzese. (Sicilians and Friulians did not mix at all with the mainland Southern Italians.) Even people from regions living together represented a change from localism. At the turn of the century people from the original towns of settlement like Laurenzana and Pisticci had formed their own boarding households and institutions. The Dillingham Commission had counted Brava (Cape Verdean coloured Portuguese) as a separate ethnic group and had listed their boarding houses separately. Ruthenes, Galicians and Bukovinians found their larger identity as Ukrainian only slowly.

In a sense, not only were ethnic institutions born in the sojourning years, so was North American ethnicity itself. Historians who wish to understand the relationship between the social and geographical processes of migration and the growth of ethnic identity would do well to look more closely at those first years of sojourning and at the institutions adapted to cope with North America. The sojourners themselves knew that it was an important social and cultural formative period. The Appalachian saying of our time sums it up nicely: "We ain't what we want to be and we ain't what we're going to be, but we ain't what we were."[59]

Notes

1. O. Handlin, *The Uprooted* (Boston, 1951); R. Vecoli, "Contadini in Chicago: A Critique of the Uprooted", *Journal of American History*, Vol. LI (December 1964), pp. 404-417.

2. H. Nelli, *Italians in Chicago, 1880-1930: A Study in Ethnic Mobility* (Oxford, 1970), offers a detailed chapter on geographical settlement with no analysis of institutions before 1920. A later chapter uses the padrone system to explain occupational patterns. See also, J. Barton, *Peasants and Strangers: Italians, Rumanians and Slovaks in an American City, 1890-1950* (Harvard, 1975). Chapter II uses chain migration to make the leap from a statistical analysis of old world emigration to a skimpy and anecdotal knowledge of sojourning communities. Moreover, there is some disjuncture between emigration locations and origins of Cleveland migrants.

3. R. Juliani, "American Voices, Italian Accents: The Perception of Social Conditions and Personal Motives by Immigrants", *Italian Americana*, Vol. 1, No. 1 (Autumn 1974), pp. 1-25; and "The Origin and Development of the Italian Community in Philadelphia", in J. Bodnar, ed., *The Ethnic Experience in Pennsylvania* (Lewisburg, 1973), pp. 233-261. Juliani's use of oral testimony and background in sociology allow him to say more about the mind set of first arrivals, their institutions and *paesani* services.

4. P. Siu, "The Sojourner", *American Journal of Sociology*, Vol. 58 (July 1952), pp. 34-44. Siu describes the sojourner as not a "marginal man", but one committed to maintaining himself in a manner which will enable him to re-insert himself easily in his country of origin.

5. Of the institutions mentioned, probably the *padrone* system has received most systematic attention from historians. See L. Iorizzo, "The Padrone and Immigrant Distribution", in S.M. Tomasi and M.H. Engel, eds., *The Italian Experience in the United States* (Staten Island, 1970), pp. 43-75; R.F. Harney, "The Padrone and the Immigrant", *The Canadian Review of American Studies*, Vol. 5 (Fall 1974), pp. 101-118; H.B. Nelli, "The Italian Padrone System in the United States", *Labor History*, Vol. 5, No. 2 (Spring 1964), pp. 153-167.

6. There were of course many excellent studies of specific institutions by contemporary social scientists. Two which deal with the sojourners well are G. Abbott, "The Chicago Employment Agency and the Immigrant Worker", *American Journal of Sociology*, Vol. XIV, No. 3 (November 1908); and E. Bradwin, *The Bunkhouse Man* (New York, 1928). I am using institution in the simplest sense – a relationship or behavioural pattern of importance in the life of a community or society.

7. John Modell and Tamara Hareven, "Urbanization and the Malleable Household: An Examination of Boarding and Lodging in American Families", *Journal of Marriage and Family*, Vol. 35 (August 1973), pp. 467-78.

8. The only detailed study of an ethnic boarding house that I am aware of is A. Vazsonyi, "The Star Boarder: Traces of Cicisbeism in an Immigrant Community", in *Tractata Altaica* (Wiesbaden, 1976), pp. 695-713. This is an ethnological romp through the mores and arrangements of mid-American Hungarian boarders.

9. *U.S. Immigration Commission, 1907-1910 Reports* (henceforth cited as *Dillingham Commission*), Vol. I, *Abstracts*, pp. 422-438. For agreement with Modell and Hareven that the semantic distinction between boarding and lodging was irrelevant, see *Dillingham Commission*, Vol. 26, pp. 79-80. Although padronism and so-called immigrant hotels fall under the last classification, group household, it is clear that many inns and hotels that ran in traditional commercial terms also were essentially ethnic institutions. See D. Esslinger, *Immigrants and the City: Ethnicity and Mobility in a 19th Century Midwestern Community* (Port Washington, 1975), p. 45, has an interesting account of German hotels in downtown South Bend but does not seem to see the phenomenon as an aspect of ethnic enterprise or of the changing Polish and German ethnic boundaries of the roomers.

10. See *Reports of the Industrial Commission* (Washington, 1910) Vol. XV, pp. x-xii; and *Royal Commission appointed to inquire into the Immigration of Italian Labourers to Montreal and the Alleged Fraudulent Practices of Employment Agencies* (Ottawa, 1905). *Dillingham Commission*, II, p. 427.

11. J. Scarpaci, "Immigrants in the New South: Italians in Louisiana's Sugar Parishes, 1880-1910", in F. Assante, *Il Movimento migratorio italiano dall' unita nazionale ai giorni nostri* (Naples, 1976), pp. 206-209. In the Chinese case, the steamship agents' "holding pens" for migrants at Macao bound for America were called barracoons, the word for slave quarters in most of the Iberian world. See John Foster, *American Diplomacy in the Orient* (Boston, 1903), p. 280.

12. "Forced Labor in West Virginia", *The Outlook*, June 13, 1903.

13. T. Saloutos, *The Greeks in the United States* (Cambridge, 1964), pp. 52-53; *Dillingham Commission*, Vol. 2, pp. 401 & 405.

14. H. Nelli, *Italians in Chicago*, p. 60; for the concept of the target migrant, see J.M. Nelson, *Temporary versus Permanent Cityward Migration: Causes and Consequences* (MIT, 1976).

15. G. Abbott, "The Chicago Employment Agency", p. 294.

16. A. Bernardy, *America Vissuta* (Torino, 1911), p. 316.

17. See *Royal Commission (Italians)*; and R.F. Harney, "Chiaroscuro: Italians in Toronto, 1885-1915", *Italian Americana*, Vol. 1, No. 2 (Spring 1975), pp. 143-167.

18. *Industrial Commission*, Vol. XV, p. 157; B. Brandenburg, *Imported Americans* (New York, 1903) describes all the frauds and violence visited on migrants in process; E. Corsi, *In the Shadow of Liberty* (New York, 1937), p. 38.

19. Modell and Hareven, "Urbanization and the Malleable Household", p. 470. The 'lodger evil' among immigrants also was subject to confusion about extended families and about how kinship might make household proximity more respectable no matter how remote. For example, the Dillingham Commission remarked that "many persons in few rooms is not so serious a matter when all are members of the family as when strangers are included in the household." *Dillingham Commission*, Vol. I, p. 748. So it was not the quality of life, the health hazard, but really the "moral climate" that mattered to the authorities.

20. J.S. Woodsworth, *Strangers Within Our Gates* (Toronto, 1909), pp. 217-220.

21. *Jack Canuck*, January 1, 1912, p. 14. *Saturday Night* at least sensed the relationship of this condition to sojourning (January 20, 1912), p. 2, "He is probably counting the hours to that longed for day when he too shall appear at Salerno and jingle money in his pockets."

22. *Hastings Report*, pp. 16-17. The list of families by nationalities included all groups but Anglo-Celts. The three districts chosen for analysis were St. John's Ward, the Eastern Avenue area and the Niagara Street district. All were heavily immigrant, commercial, and the last two were industrial as well. They were not however the most squalid in the city. The juxtaposition of ethnicity with social problems was quite misleading since British lower class and Canadian pathological slum neighbourhoods were not included in the study.

23. V. Greene, "The Polish American Worker to 1930: The Hunky Image in Transition", *The Polish Review*, Vol. XXI (1976), pp. 63-78. On page 65 it is pointed that even sympathetic observers of Slavic group households left the impression that "the worker still required non-group leadership to effect the necessary reforms" in immigrant life, including housing. This same view persists among students of European guestworker systems who feel that boarding or hotel accommodations "lead to a ghetto-like life and prevent any contact with the local community… (and thus) retard a positive process of learning". W.R. Bohning, "The Social and Occupational Apprenticeship of Mediterranean Migrant Workers in West Germany" in M. Livi-Bacci, ed., *The Demographic and Social Pattern of Emigration from the Southern European Countries* (Florence, 1972), p. 226. This view, like that of turn-of-the-century Toronto, assumes that integration is the only proper course for sojourners.

24. See P. Siu, "The Sojourner"; V.G. Nee and B. de B. Nee, *Longtime Californ': A Documentary Study of an American Chinatown* (New York, 1973) Chap. II "The Bachelor Society"; R.F. Harney, "Men Without Women: Italian Migrants in Canada, 1885-1930", in Betty Boyd Caroli, Lydio Tomasi and R.F. Harney (eds.), *The Italian Immigrant Woman in North America* (Toronto: 1978), pp.79-101.

25. Traditions among South Slavs like the *zadruga* and *drustvo* and the role of wives in running *czarda* in Hungary obviously made adaptation to being a boarding house mistress easier for female immigrants from those groups.

For the Italians, M.H. Ets, *Rosa: The Life of an Italian Immigrant* (Minnesota, 1970); and the story of Rosa Mondavi in A. Pellegrini's *Americans by Choice* (New York, 1956), pp. 138-147, demonstrate the almost involuntary economic performance of immigrant wives. See J. Scott and L. Tilly, "Women's Work and the Family in 19th Century Europe", *Comparative Studies in Society and History* (Jan. 17, 1975); C. Golab, "The Impact of the Industrial Experience on the Immigrant Family: The Huddled Masses Reconsidered", *Immigrants in Industrial America 1850-1920*, Richard Erlich, ed., (University Press of Virginia: September 1977); and V.Y. McLaughlin, *Family and Community: Italian Immigrants in Buffalo 1880-1930* (Cornell University Press, 1977).

26. The study of ethnicity would profit from more awareness of issues in the study of the formation of nationality and growth of national feeling. For example, see A. Smith, *Theories of Nationalism* (London, 1971); and K. Deutsch, *Nationalism and Social Communication* (MIT, 1953). Both suggest that the scale of fellow-feeling is a function of the economic and social network which proves most useful.

27. Oscar Handlin, *Boston's Immigrants* (Harvard, 1941), p. 101.

28. Rudolph Vecoli, "Contadini in Chicago", pp. 408-411.

29. See for example, G. Prpic, *The Croatian Immigrants in America* (New York, 1971); M. Byington, *Homestead: The Households of a Mill Town* (Pittsburgh, 1910); T. Bell, *Out of This Furnace* (Pittsburgh, 1976); L. Adamic, *From Many Lands* (New York, 1939); and Vazsonyi, "The Star Boarders".

30. T. Kessner, *The Golden Door. Italian and Jewish Immigrant Mobility in New York City, 1880-1915* (New York, 1976), p. 100.

31. For the uses of *miszisz*, see Vazsonyi "The Star Boarder"; C. Panunzio, *The Soul of the Immigrant*, shows the typical Italian use of "padrone" to describe the head of the establishment; "Bordo" and "bordante" ("bordisti") are terms discussed by Amy Bernardy in *Italia randagia attraverso gli Stati Uniti* (Turin, 1914), pp. 88-122. Louise Tilly's thesis on the formation of the Milan working class, 1881-1911, shows the use of the proper Italian *convivenza* to describe urban boarding of newcomers there (Toronto: History Department, 1972), R.F. Harney, Director, p. 291. The uses of family terms like auntie, nonna, uncle, and daughter to reduce tension and define roles is mentioned in most oral testimony.

32. John Kosa, *Land of Choice: The Hungarians in Canada* (Toronto, 1957), p. 31.

33. J. MacDonald and L. MacDonald, "Chain Migration, Ethnic Neighbourhood Formation and Social Networks", in C. Tilly, ed., *An Urban World* (Boston, 1974), p. 231. This, like most sources, concentrates on the importance of sheltered work for Latin immigrant women rather than on the entrepreneurial role of family.

34. J. Marlyn, *Under the Ribs of Death* (Toronto, 1971), pp. 19-22, presents a convincing picture of the ambivalence of the children of boarding house

keepers toward their role in the extended household. Lithuanian and Polish landlords in Chicago often rented out the better units to tenants but lived in the worst rooms themselves to minimize costs: see Victor Greene, *For God and Country: The Rise of the Polish and Lithuanian Ethnic Consciousness in America, 1860-1910* (Madison, 1975), p. 53.

35. *Hastings Report*, pp. 8, 14.

36. E. Rossi, "Delle Condizioni del Canada respetto all'immigrazione italiana", *Bollettino dell' Emigrazione #4*, Anno 1903. Although the economics of boarding usually is described in terms of the boarding-boss or family with boarders profit, it must be remembered that the sojourner clientele made the system work. It was they, maximizing their savings to meet old world needs, who accepted crowded conditions and minimal service. A convincing local example can be found in R. Wilson, *A Retrospective: A Short Review of the Steps taken in Sanitation to transform the Town of Muddy York into the Queen City of the West* (Toronto, 1934), p. 32, which describes a three-room cottage with twenty Italian boarders thus: "They were all jolly good natured fellows and were highly amused at the visit of the health inspector and his inquiries as translated by the boss..." – hardly the atmosphere of white slavery and padronism. In the Canadian case, a special service offered by the ethnic boarding system was credit for room and board over the long winter months of unemployment. Nick Lombardi speaks from the perspective of the boarding house keeper: "We had a couple, not because we needed them, but because they were good friends and they wanted to stay with us. We all used to eat together. And if they didn't have any money, daddy and mom never used to worry. They knew they'd pay off the debt in the summer." (Taped interview, the Multicultural History Society of Ontario, June 1, 1976). His friend, Paul Lorenzo, remembers the situation from the sojourner's view: "We used to live over where they put the new Mount Sinai hospital, near Mt. Carmel church on McCaul Street, in an Italian boarding house – $2.50 a month. There were about 8 or 10 boarders in the house. In the winter time, we can't pay the rent – we have no money. You must wait for summer to return so you can go out and work again and pay your debts... And when you'd go to the store you had to sign a book since you had no money. And my father kept his own book too, so that he would never be cheated." (Taped interview, The Multicultural History Society of Ontario.)

37. This story was gathered by John Bodnar and Carl Oblinger of the Pennsylvania Museum of Man and will appear in a forthcoming oral history volume. P. Roberts, *The New Immigration* (New York, 1914), p. 131. The sick, wounded, and unemployed threw off the three shift bed rotation and were often evicted. Gina Petroff (Taped Interview, Oct. 12, 1976) tells the story of a man known as Nick Coca Cola. "Anyway he been sleeping on the third floor. Not working. He never get up two days, just sleep and stay there day and night, and the name is Nick... There's Depression and nobody give work to you. So anyway they kept him for a little while over... and then they kicked him out." (Unless otherwise cited, all oral testimony is from the collection of the Multicultural History Society of Ontario.)

38. See Vazsonyi, "Traces of Cicisbeism"; and A. Bernardy "Da una relazione de Amy Bernardy sull'emigrazione delle donne e fanciulli italiani negli Stati Uniti", *Bollettino dell' Emigrazione* (1909).

39. "Nanni Volpe", in G. Verga, *The She Wolf and Other Stories* (Berkeley, 1958), p. 160.

40. "The Boarding House", from *The New Pioneer* in V. Wertsman, *The Romanians in America, 1748-1974* (Dobbs Ferry, 1975), p. 62.

41. *Jack Canuck*, Vol. 1, No. 14 (January, 1912); T. Hiramatso (Taped interview).

42. Mary Caruso (Taped interview, Dec. 7, 1976). Her grandfather, a hurdy-gurdy man, left the boarding enterprise completely to his wife.

43. Michael Guzei (Taped interview, Slovak, Barr).

44. John Krar (Taped interview, Donau-Schwaben #260, Frei); *Dillingham Commission*, Abstracts, Vol. I, pp. 422-552. "Many variations upon this arrangement are met with, but some form of it constitutes the method of living usually followed by *recent immigrant households*" (read, sojourners).

45. V. Wertsman, *The Romanians*, p. 63.

46. Stoyan Christowe, *This Is My Country* (New York, 1938). The leader of a "group household" although he depended on a coterie of elders or kin, exercised control.

47. P. Roberts, *The New Immigration*, p. 124.

48. R. Breton, "Institutional Completeness of Ethnic Communities and the Personal Relations of Immigrants", *American Journal of Sociology*, Vol. 70 (September, 1964), pp. 193-205. Anna Kaprielian (Jan. 24, 1978 Armenian) – same sense of the completeness of a sojourning institution comes out of this conversation. "He had a house. The first floor was a coffee shop and library. People would go there and play backgammon, cards, read books (whoever could read). Armenians would congregate there. Everyone would tell his story, talk about his family. They'd write letters..."

49. For those who believe that the sojourning attitude shapes a migrant's relations with North America, studies about occupational mobility and acculturation should reflect the intensity of the migrant's desire to insert himself as much as it does North American conditions. The contrasting of Jewish settlers and Italian sojourners as to rates of occupational mobility without reference to their frame of mind and attitude about staying in the United States becomes silly. See Betty B. Caroli, "Italian Settlement in American Cities", in H.S. Nelli, ed., *The U.S. and Italy: Proceedings of the 9th Annual Conference of the AIHA* (Washington, 1976), pp. 156-158.

50. For example where would a man who sold balloons at Toronto parades, who also was chief money lender in the Italian community, a man who lost his arm in an abattoir accident but made a comfortable living escorting brides back and forth from Macedonia, and all the informal keepers of boarding establishments fit in the gross measures of mobility and status such as

S. Thernstrom's *The Other Bostonians* (Cambridge, 1973). Some synthesis of oral testimony and quantitative methods would greatly enhance the value of urban studies.

51. Conversation with Dr. Juliana Puskas, Toronto, January 25, 1978. In 1977 Dr. Puskas spent the year visiting Hungarian committees in the U.S. and Canada.

52. H. Lopata, *Polish American Status Competition in an Ethnic Community* (New York, 1976), pp. 608 and 19-20 gives a clear sociological view of ethnicity as a historical process, in which the *okolica*, the physical and psychic unit of group identity, changes in North America.

53. Upton Sinclair, *The Jungle* (New York, 1965), first edition 1906, p. 32.

54. P. Bertoia (Taped interview, Friulian, March 1, 1978). Ethnic identities among sojourners were nowhere near as hard-edged as prejudice and the ethnic groups' own retrospective falsification now make them appear. Finns, Swedes and Finn Swedes who lived near quarries on Cape Ann in Massachusetts changed ethnic loyalty with boarding houses. See P. Parsons and P. Anastas, *When Gloucester Was Gloucester: Toward an Oral History of the City* (Gloucester, 1973), p. 21.

55. John Carnovale (Taped interview, Italian, the Multicultural History Society of Ontario.)

56. F. Tomev (Taped interview, Macedonian, December, 1977). In a given boarding house, there would be all "pro-Bulgarian" or all patriarchist Macedonians and men from the same village would not board together if their politics differed. The sources of this rising ethnic consciousness lay in local, neighbourhood developments which affect all immigrants, even the most articulate. See Victor Greene, *For God and Country: The Rise of Polish and Lithuanian Ethnic Consciousness in America, 1860-1910*, p. 5.

57. H. Isaacs, *Idols of the Tribe* (New York, 1975), p. 43.

58. H.N. Brailsford, *Macedonia – Its Races and Their Future* (London, 1906), p. 102. "Is your village Greek, I asked him, or Bulgarian. Well, he replied, it is Bulgarian now but four years ago it was Greek... The Bulgarians heard of this and they came and made us an offer. They said they would give us a priest who would live in the village, and a teacher to whom we need pay nothing. Well sir, ours is a poor village, and so of course we became Bulgarian." For all peasant migrant groups, ethnicity was far more local and malleable than we have assumed.

59. M. Pei, *What's In a Word* (New York, 1968), p. 52

A CASE STUDY OF PADRONISM:
MONTREAL'S KING OF ITALIAN LABOUR*

❧

*O*N *23 JANUARY 1904, MORE THAN 2,000 ITALIAN LABOURERS PARADED through* the streets of Montreal. They were there to fête Antonio Cordasco, steamship agent, *banchista* and director of a labour bureau. Two foremen presented him with a crown "in a shape not unlike that worn by the King of Italy". The crown was later displayed in a glass case along with a souvenir sheet containing eleven columns of Italian names and entitled "In Memory of the Great Parade of January, 1904, in honour of Signor Antonio Cordasco, proclaimed King of the Workers." During February, *caposquadri* and *sub-bossi* organized a banquet for Cordasco. Invitations to the banquet bore a seal suspiciously like the Royal Crest of Italy, and Cordasco's kept newspaper, the *Corriere del Canada*, reported the occasion in detail.[1]

Four months later, in June and July 1904, the "King of Italian Labour" was under investigation by the Deputy Minister of Labour, about to be the centre of a Royal Commission inquiry into fraudulent business practices, and excoriated by officials of the Italian Immigrant Aid Society. What emerges from the reports, testimony and newspaper accounts about the activity of Cordasco and his competitors in Montreal is not just the picture of an exploitive and dishonest broker but a man truly in between – willing enough to put his boot into those beneath him, such as the greenhorns who depended upon him for jobs, but also forced to tug his forelock and to anticipate the wishes of the English-speaking businessmen and employers whom he served. It was these men upon whom the labour agent depended in his delicate task of wedding North American capitalist needs to seasonal labour. Cordasco's career and the public assault upon him affords us a rare entry into the world of the *padrone*, the exploitive Italian brokers who were stock – but little understood – villains in the drama of immigration.[2]

Antonio Cordasco, the protagonist of our story, appears in the end as

* This article reprinted with permission from *Labour/Le Travailleur*, vol. 4, 1979, pp. 57-84.

a nearly perfect Italian parody of the "negro king", that peculiarly ugly phenomenon of an ethnic or colonial puppet who serves those who really control the society and the economy.[3] In 1904, Cordasco's stupidity and avarice combined with circumstance – a late thaw, high unemployment in the United States, and pressure from the Montreal Italian Immigrant Aid Society and his chief competitor, Alberto Dini – to expose him to public scrutiny. He proved to be a man whose new crown rested uneasily; he had to threaten and cajole his *sub-bossi*, placate his capitalist overlords, hide from irate workers and scheme to destroy competitors who aspired to his throne. Moreover, he carried on a complex foreign policy with *padroni* in other cities and with steamship and emigration agents in Italy and on Italy's borders. Cordasco stood astride a free enterprise system that brought Italian migrant labour into contact with North American job opportunity. His power lay in his control of the communications network between labour and capital, and that was not an easy position from which to carve an empire. Like the "negro king", he had neither the affection of his people, the migrant Italian labourers, nor the trust of his Wasp masters, but he served them both as intermediary and spared them both from dealing directly with the mysterious other.

The commerce of migration which Cordasco had ridden to power had grown up in the late nineteenth century. Canadian conditions were particularly suitable for the development of a seasonal guest worker system. The need for manual labour at remote northern work sites, the attitudes of Canadian big business and of European village labourers, the climate, the difficulty of transportation and the xenophobic immigration policy of the government, all meant that only a sojourning work force could reconcile the Dominion's needs and the target migrants' self-interest.[4] The three necessary components to such a system of seasonal migrant labour were the capitalist employer, the European worker and the intermediaries and brokers who controlled the recruitment, transportation and organization of the labour pool for the employers. All involved saw an advantage in the system. For the Canadian employer – particularly the labour intensive industries such as the railways, the mines and the smelting interests – there was constant need for a docile and mobile work force, a force free from the taint of unionism and willing to be shipped to remote northern sites, a work force which tolerated exploitation at those sites in order to make ready cash, and which required no maintenance on the part of the employer during the long winter months.

Although the Canadian government preferred northwest European immigrants, the large employers of unskilled labour preferred south and east Europeans. They could be relied upon to feel alien in the new land, not to jump track, not to wish to farm and to be transient or sojourning in their frame of mind. This made them a much more reliable work force than the Swedes, Finns, English, Germans and others whom the government favoured as settlers.[5] That is why employers circumvented Canadian government policy and used steamship agents in Europe and *padroni* in Canada to draw to the country labourers who were not seen as fit stock for permanent settlement in Canada, and why conflict between industry and government profited the *padrone* system. For example, the Commissioner of Immigration in Winnipeg could report to Ottawa that large numbers of undesirable migrants had appeared in the area at the behest of the railways:

> I receive from time to time reports from Officer McGovern that there they have been passing through his hands large numbers of Italians from Boston, Massachusetts, hired under contract by the Canadian Pacific Railway to work for that company in Canada... I think it is my duty to call your attention to this fact that these people are well-known to be quite worthless as settlers and having ruined to large extent the prosperity of Boston, Mass., it seems to me unfortunate that this class of immigration should be brought in by the railways for any kind of work at all except to work in the mines. I do not know what steps can be taken to prevent it, as no one seems disposed to set the alien labour law in motion. But whether they come from the United States or not, I feel this class of emigration will not do our country any good. The blame for them coming here undoubtedly will be placed upon the Department of Immigration, although that department has nothing whatever to do with them and they have been brought here solely at the insistence of the railway company.[6]

The government was perfectly correct in its assumption that the Italian labourers did not want to settle. For the workers, the advantage of this system was that they could operate as target migrants. They had come to North America without their families, not in order to settle, but to earn enough money to change their condition of life in the old country. Their image or myth of Canada, if they had one, was of a very hostile and frozen land whose people were not well disposed toward south Europeans or toward young foreign bachelors.[7] The system usually enabled them to reach Canadian job sites for the short work season without undue delay or hardship. A single season's campaign enabled them to save money to send home; and, by staying several seasons, they could make a nest-egg so that they might never come back again.

However, because of the necessity of arriving with the thaw in time for work and leaving before the St. Lawrence froze, or because of dishonest exploitation, target migrants were often trapped for many seasons, their savings dissipated by *padroni*-run boardinghouses, saloons and provisioners.

For the intermediaries, of course, the system itself was the source of their income. Without a constant flow of labour, without being able to pose for both the village labourer and the North American capitalist as the only one who could bring the two together to mutual benefit, the steamship agent and the *padrone* had no function. In the Canadian situation, they were helped by the problems of national boundaries, the new rigour of Italian laws, the competition between steamship companies and the worker's lack of knowledge of the northern target. The North American employers maintained an almost willful ignorance of the work force. This made it easier for the intermediaries to manipulate the labour supply and to tie job brokerage to the network of migration which ran all the way from the remote towns of Italy to the remote towns of northern Ontario and British Columbia.

As Italian laws against foreign recruitment of labour grew more stringent, the town of Chiasso on the Swiss-Italian border became the centre of the illicit recruitment and flow of Italian workers to North America.[8] Unravelling the *vincolismo* of sham immigration societies, travel agencies, steamship companies, and *padroni* who controlled the flow is beyond the scope of this paper, but it is significant that a major role in this unholy commerce was taken by King Cordasco. Two simple points need to be made. First, in the so-called *commercio di carne umana* there was as much competition in earning the right to transport human cattle to the slaughter yards of North American industry as there was in running the North American holding pens. For every *padrone* in Montreal or Boston, there were one or two steamship sub-agents in a town like Chiasso or in the interior of Italy. These agents earned their way by the *senseria* paid for each migrant recruited for steamship passage, and although the more responsible or clever among the sub-agents cared whether those they sent to America found work – because their reputations as agents depended on it – they were naturally not as sensitive to the fluctuations in the demand for labour as the North American *padroni* had to be. This made the sub-agents a sometimes unreliable part of the network for those who faced the more delicate task of maintaining a balance between the labour force and the employer in North America. One agent for Beaver Lines even boasted to the Canadian authorities that in a given year he had recruited more than 6,000 passengers from Italy, Syrians and Germans and as many more as anybody might request.[9]

It was Marcus Braun, a special inspector *en mission*, who drew the most complete portrait of the Chiasso way station on the *via commerciale*. Braun, by his own account, travelled 25,000 miles by rail and 600 by "special conveyances" through Germany, Austria-Hungary, Russia, Rumania, Switzerland, Italy and France in order to study the flow of emigrants to North America. Braun considered Chiasso the most dishonest and dangerous entrepot for the travellers. "I have the honour", he wrote, "to report that whatever I saw prior to my arrival at Chiasso with reference to shady emigration was nothing in comparison to what I saw and learned while travelling in Italy and the south of France."[10]

Ludwig, as agent for Beaver Lines, Corecco and Brivio for the Compagnie générale transatlantique, and Jauch and Pellegrini for North German Lloyd's, competed for the trade in clandestine, illegal and unfit emigrants. Their clientele came as much from the southern provinces as from the Veneto. In fact, Braun added that Chiasso was one of the chief transfer points for migrants from the Balkans and the Levant also. The agents and companies mentioned, and a myriad of lesser ones, were far less careful with their human merchandise than were the steamship companies.[11]

With the possible exception of Beaver Lines and Canadian Pacific, the steamship companies sinned, if crass free enterprise was a sin in those days, by omission. They took little responsibility for the recruiting methods of sub-agents, worrying or reacting only when blatant abuses threatened to bring government inquiries.[12] So the attitudes of the great carriers paralleled those of North American big business toward its *padroni* employees.

When Braun visited Chiasso, Ludwig had clearly been earning his bounties from the steamship companies. He was under indictment in Italy, where he was considered a predator. He had paid over 20,000 Swiss francs in fines and then jumped bail. The amounts of money that he forfeited show the magnitude of his business. Ludwig and his agents shifted from preparing unfit immigrants to the United States by the "Canadian back door" to helping seasonal migrants reach the channel ports.[13] Braun reported in 1903 that recruiters of contract labour "laugh at the measures adopted against the transportation of their people, for the reason that they have the labourers instructed so well as not to entertain any fear of their deportation and the cost, etc. connected therewith."[14] So Ludwig's success in recruiting or processing young migrants for Cordasco and Dini contributed to the glut of labour in the city and to King Cordasco's crisis.

A distressing aspect of this commerce of migration appeared when some of the very people who had been appointed to local committees to protect immigrants throughout Italy from unscrupulous steamship agents became themselves sub-agents.[15] Sub-agents – the men whom both the steamship agent and *padrone* employed to reach the potential migrant in the back country – should not be depicted as wandering flim-flam men who preyed on bumpkins at country fairs, pilgrimages and feast days. They were often the local notables and officials. In the old country towns of emigration as in the North American ethnic neighbourhoods, middle-class brokers were not a criminal conspiracy but an involved web of profit, speculation and convenience. Braun's official account made note of this:

> A large number of reputable persons such as priests, school-teachers, postmasters and county notaries are directly connected with certain agents representing these steamship companies, and that they advise and instruct the emigrants how to procure steamship tickets, passports and all other things necessary for their travel, for all of which they receive a commission from agents employing them.

In at least one instance, immigrants were found to be travelling with a local *notabile* who had with him blank passports stamped with the municipal seal of his district. The government, under pressure from the press, issued a circular to those on their way to Canada:

> The government therefore makes known that the immigrants must be very particular to inform themselves beforehand of that country. It is necessary to remember that the climate there is most severe and that the winter is long, almost six months…the means of transport and communication are scarce and difficult. For unattached emigrants from rural districts who go out with the view of getting work there is no possibility of employment in Canada…it should help therefore to dissuade from emigration to Canada those who aren't provided with the necessary capital.[16]

Such a circular might dampen some prospective immigrants, but it drove others into the clandestine system. It implied that only through the networks of the steamship agents could one possibly hope for any kind of worthwhile *campagne* in Canada, and that Canada could only serve as a land of short-term or seasonal target migration not as a land of permanent settlement. Contrast the government's solemn warning with the sort of letter Cordasco wrote to his Italian contacts, such as Antonio Paretti in Udine:

> If you have any passengers you can send them without any fear. I am able to give them immediate work, the salary will be a $1.50 a day. Besides that they will get a return ticket from me to the locality,

they can board themselves or get board as they like. The work will last long and the payment is sure. Each man gets a contract in Italian containing the clear conditions under which they have work and which specifies the length of time and salary. In one word, there will be no tricks or schemes.[17]

Before we try describing the *padroni's* activities in Montreal – using Cordasco and also his competitor, Alberto Dini, as models – we have to explain the rapidity of Cordasco's rise to power athwart the lines of communication. The new king of Italian labour does not really seem to have been intelligent enough to control the situation, but the decision made by Canadian Pacific Railway to place the mantle of sole agent on Cordasco meant a small time hustler grew into a large *padrone* broker, mainly because of his felicitous relationship with one major employer and particularly with the railway's chief hiring agent, George Burns. It was Burns who made Cordasco into his "negro king". Burns operated out of an office in Windsor Station in Montreal called the Special Services Department of the Canadian Pacific Railway. Despite that euphemism, its main function was the hiring of docile foreign labour, especially Italians, Galicians and Chinese for the railway's summer work.

Burns had made up his mind during the 1901 strike that Cordasco offered him the easiest and surest means of maintaining an available labour pool in Montreal. The agent admitted as much on the stand during the Royal Commission hearings in 1904:

> What means do you take in order to obtain his extra Italian labour? Answer: I have engaged that labour entirely through Italian labour agents. Can you mention the names of these agents you have employed? During the past three years, since the summer of 1901, I have dealt almost exclusively through Cordasco. Previous to that I had several others engaged, such as Mr. Dini, two gentlemen by the name of Schenker, and possibly one or two more. But since 1901 you have dealt exclusively with Mr. Cordasco? Yes, I have Your Honour. Was that the year you had the strike? It was. And Cordasco got in touch with you during that year? I think the first business I had with Cordasco was in 1901. In connection with the strike? In connection with supplying Italians to take the place of track men who went on strike.[18]

Cordasco, working for the Canadian Pacific Railway, and Alberto Dini, on behalf of the Grand Trunk Railway, had to negotiate with the agents in Switzerland who were the immediate recruiters of manpower. A letter to Dini from the firm of Corecco and Brivio in Bodio, Switzerland, reveals the means by which North American labour agents and European steamship agents formed their alliances. The Swiss firm, in a covert relationship with both Frederick Ludwig in Chiasso and with Beaver Steamship Lines, and possibly even with Canadian Pacific Lines, masqueraded as representatives of something called "Società Anonima di Emigrazione 'La Svizzera' as well as other agencies of emigration in Switzerland which have legally been constituted."

In fact, Corecco and Brivio had tried to monopolize the Chiasso Connection and the commerce of migration there. The letter to Dini in 1904 suggested the advantages of a full alliance:

> You do not ignore that a brother of Mr. Schenker, one of those who has opened an office in Montreal for the exchange of money in order to compete with you, has lately opened an office in Chiasso, Switzerland and gets passengers from Italy through the help of Schenker who is in Montreal. The latter sends to his brother in Chiasso notices and orders for the shipment of men and the brother reads the notices to the passengers mentioning the ships they are to go by. Having acknowledged this action on the part of Schenker we took the liberty of addressing ourselves to you in order to advise you and inform you thereof and to ask if it would be possible for you to do something for us in the matter.[19]

So the steamship agents and immigration agents in Italy or on the Italian borders who needed to protect their bounties sought allies among the *padroni* while the latter sought safe suppliers of labour. In 1903, only one season after he had gained his lucrative hold over the Canadian Pacific labour supply, Cordasco wrote to Frederick Ludwig:

> By the same mail I am sending you a package of my business cards. I ask you to hand them to the passengers or better to the labourers that you will send directly to me…. To satisfy the Italians better here I have opened a banking office of which I send a circular to you from which you can see that I can do all that they request. Awaiting for some shipment and to hear from you soon. Yours truly, A. Cordasco.[20]

Cordasco apparently demonstrated both naïveté and lack of finesse in the letter to Ludwig. That gentleman, a smoother, tougher exploiter, wrote back to him within a month. Addressing himself to "Mr. Cordask", he explained that he had not answered "the letter immediately because I wanted to get some information about you." From the tone of the letter, Ludwig felt he had the upper hand in dealing with a *padrone arrivato* like

Cordasco. He informed "Mr. Cordask" that he would "try him out and send passengers to him and see if he acts as an honest man and then he will give his address to most of the migrants going to Montreal." He added, "What I especially recommend to you is not to change your address every moment like a wandering merchant. On your envelope the address is 441 St. James Street and on your business card it is 375, now which of the two is the right address?" Ludwig went on to remark that he had done business with Dini for years and had found him a capable and good business associate. "Mr. Cordask" finally is warned, "We shall see then if you will work with the same conscience and punctuality."

Communication with those in the Old World who put labour on the *via commerciale*, steamship agents, immigration agents and local notables was sometimes testy to say the least. We find Cordasco complaining to a man from Udine who had sent him men who were stone cutters not labourers. The stone cutters had expected work as skilled masons or in quarries, but Cordasco claimed that he had distinctly warned the men before they left the old country that everyone should understand that the railway work available in Canada was for labourers, not artisans. A number of these men refused to go to British Columbia to work; they claimed that they were promised free passage on the railway, skilled work and better wages than those offered them when they arrived in Canada.[21] Caught amidst the promises of the agents in the old country, his own hyperbole in the pages of the *Corriere del Canada*, the parsimonious approach to migrant labour of Canadian big business and worker demands, Cordasco's role as a go-between sometimes reduced itself to lying to all parties involved, while walking a very difficult tightrope.

It was only the *padrone* who could find himself in great difficulty if he didn't regularly satisfy the aspirations of the migrant labourers. Cordasco was clearly the man in between and, though he survived the crisis of 1904 and the public scrutiny of his practices that came with the Royal Commission, he only did so because he received the support of his employer, the Canadian Pacific Railway and because, in the long run, the migrants who were both consumers and commodities in the trade continued to accept the *padrone* system.

Cordasco himself sometimes sensed that he was a man dangling between forces which could manipulate him. There is a painful and a plaintive quality in a letter to a contact in Udine expressing his annoyance at the demands made upon him by workers: "I am not responsible for the extremely cold season that prevents the companies from starting work". The labour practices for which he was being criticized in 1904 had begun in 1901; they had begun with the approval of the Canadian Pacific Railway. Cordasco described to the commissioners the situation in that year when three officials of the railway came to him, saying they wanted labourers and asking if he had any Italian labour to supply to the Canadian Pacific. At the beginning he could find only 400 or 500 men, and the company offered him no fee or salary, probably because they assumed that Cordasco himself would charge the labourers as would a regular employment agency. However, when the strike began later in 1901, they offered to pay him a dollar a man, and with that as an incentive, Cordasco rounded up about 2,000 men from throughout North America:

> I picked up what I could get in Canada and when I could get no more here I wrote for some. Question: Where? Answer: I think I wrote to New York. Question: Nowhere else? Answer: I wrote to Boston but did not get any there. Question: Anywhere else? Answer: That is all. I wrote to New York, Boston and Portland. Question: Did you send any men down there to look for men? Answer: I think so. Question: How many did you send over to the States during that time? Answer: Let me see, I sent four or five, perhaps six. Question: They went to different parts of the States? Answer: I sent them to Boston. I remember I sent men to Philadelphia and to Boston, that has just come to my mind.[22]

Cordasco had learned in 1901 how to tap the labour force in the "Little Italies" of the eastern United States. The chance to earn a dollar a head must have been too much to resist, and it did not occur to him that, with his exclusive rights as the CPR's agent, he might reach a point where he would register more men than he could find work for. He devised a system in which each winter he registered both workers and foremen in a work book with his agency, charging a dollar a piece for workers and more for foremen, and assuring them that they would receive work in the spring from the railway contractors on the basis of their place on that list. What appeared to be a simple and sensible registration system, however, turned out to be a form of bounty not unlike that charged by the steamship agents. By over-inscribing workers and then failing to cope with a late thaw and the possibility that there would be less work than expected, Cordasco brought himself and his monarchy to the brink of economic and personal ruin in spring 1904.

In many ways the crisis in padronism was atypical because the *padrone's* profit and power, his relationship to the local "Little Italy", was based on a system far more complex than that of simply collecting bounty. The *intermediarismo* that he practised extended both into many aspects of Italian life in Canada and, as we have seen, along the communications network between European labour and North American industry. Cordasco's activities conveniently divide into those which, remembering our analogy to monarchy, we might call his foreign policy – and perhaps like the "negro king", his foreign policy was ultimately controlled by his colonial masters, Montreal's Anglo-Celtic businessmen – and his domestic policy, his organization and control of Italian labour in Canada. By extension, he helped to shape the Italian community itself.

Cordasco's foreign policy had the Chiasso Connection as its linchpin but it also included his relations with the various *padroni* and labour agents in the American "Little Italies" and his relations with the major steamship companies. The official report of the Royal Commission listed some of the methods Cordasco used to make contact with the labour supply in Europe. The investigators admitted that they could infer from the correspondence a conspiracy to mislead workers. Mackenzie King, the chief investigator, had remarked that "there is no business relation existing between himself (Cordasco) and these agents, but I think there can be no doubt as to their acting in direct accordance with an understood arrangement which he has with them.[23] King's remark has a resonance similar to that of American investigators at a later time who became convinced that the Mafia existed because they could not find evidence of it.

The nature of the *padrone* connection, the nature of *vincolismo* led North American investigators like Mackenzie King and Marcus Braun to hint suspiciously of crime, when, in fact, padronism was a business – albeit the business of pre-industrial men – that they were catching a glimpse of. The agents may have seemed *strozzini* to those outside the ethnic group, but a system of honour existed among them that depended on hand shakes, ascriptive encounters, kinship, mutual trust and respect. In every major city the leading labour bureaus and *padroni* had a shared interest in controlling and regulating their relations with one another, so that too many new competitors, upstart foremen who had learned a bit of English, could not successfully compete.

The memoranda of understanding and letters of agreement that passed between Cordasco and his peers were callous documents reflecting the tenor of the commerce in human flesh. But steamship agents and labour agents of every ethnic background dealt with migrants thus, and the line between the clever use of the free enterprise system and fraud is more discernible to us now than it was then. Also, it is obvious, from the testimony of Mr. Mortimer Waller, that business practices did not change much as one crossed ethnic lines.

Question: Is there anything else you would like to state in connection with this investigation Mr. Waller? Answer: No sir, I do not think myself that Englishmen should have as fair a chance of supplying this Italian labour as the Italians themselves. Question: You think that an Englishman should have as good a chance to supply this labour? Answer: Yes. Question: You think that English-men have not that chance? Answer: No sir. Question: Why? Answer: The companies like the CPR will not go to anybody but Italians for the men.[24]

Mr. Waller had the same system of registering labourers as Cordasco, and charged approximately the same commission for unskilled workers and foremen.

Both Dini and Cordasco readily acknowledged on the witness stand their contacts with men in Chiasso like Ludwig and, a little less readily, their arrangements with the major labour agents in the United States. In 1901, Cordasco had made contact with Bianco Stabili and Company and Torchia and Company in Boston's North End. Through Boston and through Portland he was able to bring men up on the Boston and Maine and on other railways, moving them into the Canadian labour system. He also had contacts in Providence and Fall River. In some sense, while these men made Cordasco powerful by helping him find experienced labourers in the American "Little Italies", he established their power by making them successful brokers of labour in those cities. The railway company would, at Cordasco's prompting, supply free passes for those coming to work; it could deny those passes, or it could allow part payment of passage, affording the Montreal *padrone* a subtle, but effective, device for manipulating the numbers and skills of the local labour supply. Since most of the labourers were target migrants committed to making as much cash for as short a stretch of work as possible, the calculation of travel costs proved very important.

In 1904, Cordasco may have tried to use this device as a safety valve once he saw that too many workers were arriving in Montreal. For ex-ample, in a letter to Angelo de Santis, a labour agent in Buffalo, the *padrone* reminded him that "the railway fare from Buffalo to Montreal has to be paid by the men, a free pass from Buffalo being given in July and August only, but then the season is short and the earnings little."[25] Cordasco apparently miscalculated the impact of the recession in the United States on Italian sojourners. In bad years like 1903, men were more than willing to accept the loss of income which paying their own passage to Montreal entailed.

When we first encountered Cordasco at his mock coronation, we were watching a media event. The parade and banquet took up most of a special issue of the *Corriere del Canada* and that special issue was printed and sent to many Italian towns. With touching modesty and some *campanilismo* Cordasco himself claimed that he never sent any newspapers abroad except to his own village. But it seems obvious from the testimony of trapped migrants to the Commission, that issues of *Corriere del Canada* were used as an advertising device to encourage labour to come to Canada from throughout Italy. For example, a witness from Reggio Calabria said that he had seen many circulars and newspapers, and that, at about the same time, a man had come to his village with packets of Cordasco's business card. Cordasco had also sent business cards to Ludwig and to almost everybody who addressed inquiries to him. Although hardly grounds upon which to base a charge of conspiracy to defraud, the flow of business cards back and forth seems a fitting image for describing the network that existed between *padroni* and emigration agents. It served the steamship agent in Italy well to be able to give the migrant Cordasco's card and to direct him to Cordasco, as if the *padrone* were but a runner for the steamship agent himself, and it obviously served Cordasco to have the fish directed into his net as they came toward Montreal. Braun had noticed that business cards were the *lettres de cachet* of the commerce of migration. "Most emigrants are in possession of cards of all kinds of boardinghouses, emigrant agencies and "homes" of all nationalities in all the cities of the United States. I attach here one of said cards of which thousands can be obtained daily..." An intermediary's card could stand as a free enterprise alternative to the passports and legal documents inaccessible to so many migrants of humble background.

Both Cordasco and Dini were evasive in their testimony about their use of newspaper advertising. Dini's advertisements were mostly printed in *La Patria Italiana* and Cordasco's in the aforementioned *Corriere del Canada*. These newspapers may have existed as more than advertising devices for the *padroni* – Dini and Cordasco were careful not to claim any direct relationship to the papers, and each paper had an editor who tried to be independent and to create an Italian cultural *ambiente* in Montreal – but several curious letters bring the editors' independence into question. For example, Cordasco wrote to Luigi Scarrone, a newspaperman in Toronto, describing himself "as the capitalist administrator of the *Corriere del Canada*". Cordasco asked Scarrone, as a favour, to write an article about the *padroni*, since he could not do it himself, because "if I should place this before the readers they will say that I sing my own praise or that I order others to praise me. So you can, (and I thank you for that) send articles on the work and solidity of the Canadian Pacific Railway but do not tell the readers that I belong to this newspaper."[26]

The *padrone* was an ethnic entrepreneur involved in many businesses. In his testimony, Dini told the judge, "I have got an employment office, banker is name known to Italians." Earlier in his testimony, he had also pointed out that he was the steamship agent for North German Lloyd's Line, Hamburg-American Anchor Line and two Italian lines, including La Veloce. Cordasco in turn had extracted a promise from Mr. Burns of the CPR when he helped find strike breakers in 1901, that the CPR would help him become the agent for their steamship line, for the Compagnie générale transatlantique and for several others. Like Dini, he referred to himself as a banker and his newspaper announcement to the labourers in 1904 began:

> To the army of the pick and shovel Italian labourers, bosses do not show a double face, do not be false but only one. Be true. Have a soldier's courage, apply to the elegant and solid Italian bank of Antonio Cordasco, if you do not want to weep over your misfortunes in the spring when the shipments of men will begin.[27]

Both men described themselves as bankers, perhaps as steamship agents and employment agents, but would not have used the word *padrone*. They specialized in performing as brokers between labour and capital, as transmitters of remittances and pre-paid tickets and as steamship agents, while engaging, because of the migrants' dependence on them, in many other businesses.

Cordasco's banking, for example, included lending money to foremen so that they could pay the registration fee of a dollar a head for their work gangs. Often the faith of the workers in the *banchista* was touchingly naïve. A 1903 letter reads, "We the undersigned, signed with a cross mark because we cannot write or read, both of us, we authorize Mr. A. Cordasco to draw our wages for work done in the month of October last, 1903. And we both authorize the Canadian Pacific Railway Company to pay over our wages to Mr. Cordasco at 375 St. James Street." Cordasco himself understood the complex nature of his *intermediarismo*. An advertisement appearing in *La Patria Italiana* showed a rather charming, if dangerous and old-fashioned, sense of the word *patronato*: "If you want to be respected and protected either on the work or in case of accident or other annoyances which may be easily met, apply personally or address letters or telegrams to Antonio Cordasco."[28] It was protection that the *padrone* offered, protection against undue delay, protection against fraud by others, protection against all the dangers of an unknown world, of a world where the labourer could not cope for himself because of lack of education, lack of language skills and lack of time to stand and fight when his cash supply was threatened.

Mr. Skinner, Mr. Burns' assistant, showed a certain sympathy for Cordasco, for the *padrone* who had to deal with what Skinner seemed to see as the child-like qualities of the labourers:

> He has lots of trouble. He keeps an office with a waiting room, and they are the resorts where these people spend all winter. They come to smoke, he keeps all sorts of conveniences for them.[29]

In a strange way, the chief power of the intermediary, just as in the old country, lay in his literacy. Cordasco's clerk on the witness stand mentioned writing over 87 letters a month. When Dini was pressed as to what he actually did when people came to him seeking work, he answered, "I write to several contractors, to employers, to Grand Trunk if they want labourers and if they want them I'll ship them quickly." He was asked how many contractors he represented and replied, ten or twenty. "When the contractors want labourers, they have my address, they write or telegraph me, if I have any Italians to send them." So it was their ability to correspond and to communicate with the American employer which made *padroni* powerful. They played a role no different from that played by the bourgeoisie of the small towns of the Italian south and northeast, a role in which literacy was a form of capital and the basis of the brokerage system itself. Men who would have been brokers between the well-born and the peasantry or between government and peasantry in Europe, found themselves brokers between sojourners and English-speaking employers.[30]

There is no doubt that Cordasco made a profit from both the employer and labourer. That was only fitting since he served both groups. The amount of the profit, however, was outrageous by any standard. At one point, it became clear from the testimony that Cordasco was buying from his own supplier near Windsor Station, and supplying most of the canned anchovies and bread for labourers at different Canadian Pacific sites across northern Ontario. He made 150% profit on a can of sardines, the bread was often moldy and he clearly made a high profit on it as well. In one season he cleared $3800 as a provisioner. The figure of a dollar a head for registration of men pales in comparison. Cordasco obviously was not only profiteering but down-right grasping. The foremen who came to the stand to testify against him pointed out that they had been forced to raise the money for the banquet that had been held in his honour, and that some of that money had also mysteriously disappeared into Cordasco's pocket.[31]

If the investigators had understood the system a little better, had understood the degree to which the foremen and labourers were also consumers, they would have noticed that the anger of those who came to the stand was not over the fact that they had to pay tribute to Cordasco, or that they had to register seasonally for work with him, but that he had not found jobs for them or for their gangs that year. The foremen particularly, since they too were men in between, were galled by the fact that they had promised their gangs work, that they had often raised the dollar a head for Cordasco from their gangs, and perhaps the possibility of exercising their own petty tyranny and corruption over the work force. One foreman, Michele Tisi, was pressed on the witness stand about the fact that he had paid ten dollars to be foreman of a gang of 100 men and that each of the men had paid two dollars. He admitted paying that, but felt that he had no grievance against Cordasco. He answered simply, "They went to work. I'm not complaining about that."[32]

It has always seemed illogical to speak about a large scale broker like Cordasco controlling thousands of men through ties of paesanism, kinship or even through shared ethnicity. In 1903, the CPR hired over 3500 Italians. Cordasco could not have known them all. They came from all over Italy, from the Veneto to Sicily; few, if any, were his *paesani*, let alone his friends and relatives. It was the sub-bossi who organized and controlled the work gangs. Sometimes those gangs were made up of *paesani* but not always. The testimony of the *capisquadra* partially explains one aspect of the padrone's power. One foreman, Salvatore Mollo, in his testimony pointed out to the Commission that his "men don't know him [Cordasco] at all. They know me. When I went there to his bank he would not hear me." Another foreman, Pompeo Bianco, claimed to know all of his gang of 104 men brought from the United States, except for perhaps 12.[33]

Loyalty to the bosses was functional; it had to do with their ability to operate as secondary intermediaries, in this instance between the men and Cordasco, but usually between the men and the section bosses of the CPR. If that loyalty was sometimes based on regional allegiances, such as the whole gang and the boss being Calabrese or being Venetian, it was still not synonymous with paesanism.

From the ranks of these foremen, as well as from other small entrepreneurs, individuals came forth to try to compete with Dini and Cordasco in the lucrative trade in migrants. If Cordasco was the *generone* then these were the *generetti* nipping at his heels. Whatever the true basis of loyalty between *sub-bossi* and gangs, Cordasco was able to control thousands of men from his

Montreal office without going into the field; it could depend not just on his own immediate employees but on the *sub-bossi* as vassals.

The veil did lift enough for us to see how the *padrone* ultimately depended on his Anglo-Saxon master, the employer of labourers. Cordasco saw Burns or his assistant Skinner almost daily. No doubt the lines of communication between him and Burns were closer than between most *padroni* who served a more varied clientele, but Dini's relation with the various contractors and with the Grand Trunk Railway seems to have been as intense. Much of Cordasco's power over his Italian migrant labourer clientele derived from his right to advertise himself as the only acting agent for the CPR. Although he maintained some independence from Burns and the CPR by being able to pose as the most efficient intermediary for the gathering of Italian labour, his position vis-à-vis the company was not strong. It could withdraw its patronage at any time and turn to his potential competitors or directly to his *capisquadra*.

On the stand, Burns admitted readily that he had given Cordasco a monopoly: "You have always stated that Mr. Cordasco was labour agent for the CPR. Answer: I have said that he was sole agent to hire Italians." From the phrasing, one senses that Burns really did find the ways of the migrant Italians mysterious and needed Cordasco's help. He remarked of Cordasco's runners, "these men have connections down there [the States] and they pick out forces of men, pay a lot of expenses, railway fare and two or three dollars a day."[34] He had been so impressed by Cordasco's energy and ingenuity in finding strike breakers in 1901 that he remained committed to him through the 1904 crisis.

Burns contributed directly to the expansion of Cordasco's role from that of a minor employment agent into a *banchista*. The commerce of migration led inevitably to a variety of entrepreneurial possibilities and the CPR's agent gave his blessing:

> The way it came about was this. He only had a regular office and was doing a large business but he had no steamship agencies. And of course when these Italians come back from work most of them have a good deal of money which they want to send over of their relatives and friends, some for their wives and children and they buy these steamship pre-paid tickets. Cordasco is desirous of getting a line of these tickets on the different steamship agencies. And he came to me about the matter and I told him he could easily get agencies if he made the proper representation to the agents that were in New York. Question: You recommended him? Answer: I took some steps to get these agencies for him.[35]

So from his castle in Windsor Station, George Burns protected his vassal from both do-gooders and the competition of lesser brokers, because the railway found the *padrone* system efficient and flexible. A delegation from the Italian Immigration Aid Society had approached Burns offering to provide him with Italian labourers directly from Italy through the good offices of the Italian government. Burns replied to them,

> I have taken up the question of the employment of labour with the proper authorities, and have to advise you that it is not the intention of this company to change the arrangements of the employment of Italian immigrant labour, which have been in effect during the past few years. Our present system has given entire satisfaction so far and I therefore regret I shall be unable to place direct with your Society any specific order for any number of men.[36]

Cordasco's sway over Italian migrant labour had the approval of the company. For example, at the famous banquet in the *padrone's* honour, most of the foremen in attendance were impressed by the presence of the chief superintendent of the CPR's Vancouver division. After all, that gentleman would be hiring 5,000 or 6,000 Italians during the coming spring, and he seemed to be there honouring his friend Cordasco.

In 1904, company support, even though it showed the limits of Cordasco's independence, enabled him to thwart attacks upon his monopoly. That support came in at least four ways. First, at no point in their testimony did Skinner or Burns speak explicitly enough to compromise Cordasco. Second, they maintained throughout his exclusive right to hire Italians for the railway rather than turning to aspiring *sub-bossi*. Third, they had refused to order manpower from Alberto Dini, Cordasco's main competitor. Fourth, Burns did his best to discredit or ignore the Italian Immigrant Aid Society.

With his overlords to protect him, Cordasco's lines of communication to Ludwig in Chiasso, to Stabili in Boston and to other lesser *padroni* in Portland, Providence and Fall River, and agents in New York and Buffalo were secure. Cordasco seemed as safe as a *padrone* could be. To raise money for the banquet in his honour he warned any man who hesitated to donate five dollars to the cause that he would publish his photograph upside down on the souvenir sheet. The real threat was that "anyone who refused to pay will go out of my office", that is, would be eliminated from the hiring register. In an address to labourers printed in *La Patria Italiana* Cordasco flaunted his monopoly:

If you do not want to weep over your misfortune in the spring when the shipment of men will begin you will do business with me. Do not believe that with your dollar you will be able to get work like your comrades who have been faithful. Those who had signed the book earlier. We will inspect our books and money orders and our passage ticket books and those who will not have their names in them will in their despair tear out their hair and will call Mr. Cordasco, Lordship Don Antonio, 'Let me go to work'. 'No, never', will be answered to them. 'Go to those to whom you have sent your money away....' Forewarned is a forearmed man.[37]

Despite this unintentional parody of Christ's monopoly over salvation Cordasco could not stifle all the competition. The same entrepreneurial spirit that brought so many of the migrants to North America led a certain number of men to see in Cordasco or Dini models for action. One could almost say that an infernal spirit of capitalism had begun to inject itself into his feudal system. Foremen, *sub-bossi* and *capisquadra* who had been in America for a number of seasons – especially if they spoke English well – must have seen advantage in eliminating Cordasco as intermediary even if they did not aspire to a brokerage status for themselves. The *sub-bossi* were, much like the *generetti* of the post-risorgimento, at once in a feudal and capitalist relationship with the *padrone*. The *sub-bossi* gave Cordasco his power; he gave them theirs. Each could claim to provide work to those below them. If one of the *generetti* tried to by-pass Cordasco and deal directly with the employer, Cordasco could only hope that the employer would not take advantage of the situation to undermine him.

As we have seen, George Burns of the CPR did not take advantage of the situation. He found it easier to have one reliable *padrone* and to turn a blind eye to his corruption and unfair exactions. By 1904, with the help of the company, Cordasco had defeated non-Italian suppliers of labour and had excluded Dini from the CPR system, while he himself cut into Dini's commerce with the Grand Trunk Railway. From the *padrone's* correspondence, we can see how he used Burns and the sub-contractors' fear of anarchy in the supply system to thwart emerging competitors. Cordasco went so far at one point as to write a letter to Boston interfering in the recruitment of labourers there, and in the competition between the Bianco Stabili Company and Torchia and Company. He warned Messieurs Torchia that there was no point in recruiting people for the CPR in British Columbia because he, Cordasco, was the sole agent for that railway and he would only order manpower through Stabili. He ended his letter thus, "No shipment of men will be recognized but those made through Stabili and Company."[38]

Despite the bravado of that letter, Cordasco pestered Burns with complaints about incidents in which sub-contractors along the right-of-way hired workers through Italian foremen rather than deal through Burns and Cordasco. Over the years, as Italian officials like Viola and Moroni had noted, more target migrants became stranded in towns along the railway right-of-way, especially in the North.[39] Since migrants wintered in close proximity to their foremen, it became possible for a contractor to hire a gang without referring back to Montreal. Consequently, some of Cordasco's monopoly over the labour pool needed for the interior of the country was threatened, and he turned, apparently in righteous indignation, to Burns for help. For example, Cordasco wrote to complain about an interpreter named George Patrie, alias Gaetano La Patria, alias De Patrick, warning Burns that Patrie had lied in promising seasoned workers to one of the sub-contractors. According to the *padrone*, Patrie could not supply experienced railway hands, only boys and greenhorns. In another letter, he notified Burns that Mr. Paul Christopher, an Italian foreman, had hired out a crew of 25 Italians who had not passed through Cordasco's system. Christopher's men had received a free railway pass to the job site which Cordasco considered a breach of faith on the part of the company.[40] We cannot be sure that Cordasco received satisfaction after these protests, but it is clear that Burns preferred to work through him and that Burns agreed with Cordasco that a centralized system was the most effective one for the railway to maintain.

The greatest challenge to Cordasco's pre-eminence in the commerce of migration arose from the changing attitude toward protecting labourers in Italy. If it was Montreal civic authorities who precipitated the Royal Commission inquiry into Italian migrant workers, it was the city's Italian Immigrant Aid Society, acting for the new Commissariat of Emigration in Rome, which tried to pounce upon the unfortunate situation in order to destroy the *padrone* system, or at least to discredit Antonio Cordasco.[41] The Society, even though it had existed as a local private organization for a number of years, was incorporated under Canadian law only during winter 1902. Its leadership was a compound of Italian government officials, local professionals of Italian descent and the *notabili* from among older Italian settlers of Montreal. Among the Society's officers were Honoré Catelli, director of the city's largest pasta manufactury, and – unfortunately for the Society's image – Alberto Dini,

Cordasco's principal rival as Italian banker, travel agent and employment broker.

From the outset, the Society did not seem as intent upon solving the problems that arose from clandestine Italian migration to Canada as it did upon usurping Cordasco from his position in the network. Long before the Royal Commission hearings, the Society had tried unsuccessfully to undermine the Canadian Pacific Railway's support for Cordasco. Special agent Burns admitted on the stand that he had been informed of a number of incidents in which the Society accused the *padrone* of cheating workers. A letter to Burns' immediate superior in 1903 hinted darkly that Cordasco was hoodwinking the railway, implying that Burns was in collusion with him. The letter came from the Society's offices:

> We suppose it never came to your knowledge that certain people, possibly authorized to deal with your company, engaged Italian labourers to work on your roads, only on payment of a commission of $3.00 each, and refused to engage those who cannot afford to pay such commission.... We wish to stop an abuse of charging $3.00 each or more to poor men, whose children are perhaps starving.[42]

For his part, Cordasco never treated the Society as other than a rival intermediary and labour brokerage. Dini's presence on the group's board of directors lent some credence to Cordasco's claim that there was no ethical difference between the services he rendered, or the fees he charged to sojourners, and those that the Society wished to substitute. Cordasco, with characteristically clumsy malice, tried to discredit the Society as well. In winter 1903-1904, he had written to the editor of an Italian newspaper on Mulberry Street in New York City. Paying him for advertising space, the Montreal *padrone* added, "please make an article speaking about the negligence of this Consul and the Italian Immigrant Aid Society."[43] And, even though he had written earlier to the CPR agent to warn him that the best labourers were being siphoned off by other companies, Cordasco reacted to the first public outcry against the number of Italian migrants loitering in Montreal in spring 1904, by telling Burns that it was the Society who had, by providing shelter and sending notices about agricultural possibilities in Canada to Italy, caused the embarrassing glut of greenhorns in the labour pool:

> Sure will be disgraceful [sic] for these poor emigrants with the old ones which they put up here all winter, and Italian Consul with his Society are to be blamed and they should be crushed to peace [sic].[44]

Because of Dini's presence on the Society's board, Cordasco and his lawyers were able to deflect the struggle away from the point that the Italian government would have preferred, that is, that regulation (and *patronato*) should replace exploitation and the *padrone* system. However honest the practices of Dini and his companions, he was a *banchista* and a rival broker; his presence on the board of directors brought the Society's integrity, or at least its good sense, into question. At a board meeting, Dini had protested against disbursing Society funds to help indigent Italian workers; he suggested that most of the migrants were feigning destitution in order to stay on the dole. It is not clear if Dini, like Cordasco, found himself competing with the Society as a moneylender during winter 1903-1904, but it is certain that the Society's officials directed immigrants to Dini's "bank" when they had remittance or exchange questions.[45] At any rate, the Society could not transcend the free enterprise values of its members or of the economy around them, which is why in the end, as we have noted, President Catelli had agreed with the Commissioners that the troubles of the spring of 1904 really rested with the simple statement that "business was business".

Candori, the Secretary of the Society, boasted from the witness stand that the Society had drawn to Canada a better class of Italian workers from the Veneto, "picked men, and any railway company would be glad to have these men because they are strong and even good looking."[46] Both the Society and Canadian immigration authorities tended to use words like "class" and "type", when in fact they meant race. The Society's intervention against the *padroni* was ineffective because it misunderstood the temper of Canadian officialdom, and even more the distinction between the government's desire to find agriculturalists for the prairies and the desire of the major employers of unskilled labour to find men who would not settle down. In a letter to the CPR authorities, the Society boasted that they would bring over men who, after working on the railway, would settle on the land and "make industrious Canadian citizens."[47] Such a promise pleased neither those who preferred the workers to think like sojourners nor those who preferred to people the prairies with northwest European stock. A line from the Society's bulletin – "Look at the splendid results that the Italian agriculturists have had in South America, and especially in Argentina. Why should you not have the same result in Canada?" – must have elicited the answering shudder that Canada was a protestant, northerly, British colony, not a potential Argentina.[48]

In the end, the Commission was unwilling to attack directly the major companies involved in employing Italian sojourners, and those companies refused to desert their intermediaries, so the *padrone* system came through the 1904 crisis unscathed. There is little evidence for the claim that more honest brokers began to complete successfully with the chief *padroni* after 1904, even though a limit was placed on how much a labour bureau could charge to register a worker.[49] Neither Cordasco's nor Dini's power declined after the hearings, and both passed quickly from being *padroni* to *notabili*, their prominence measured by stained glass windows in parish churches and by their presence on Montreal Italian civil committees.

The employers such as the Canadian Pacific Railway section bosses had the means to resist revolt. When Italians at Crows Nest Pass in British Columbia refused $1.50 a day, they were simply dismissed and the local labour agent began "filling orders with Galicians from the North."[50] On the other hand, Cordasco had no protection from the caprice or anger of Italian workers; he faced physical attack and verbal abuse. If men he gathered were dismissed or left a job site disgruntled, he could only plead for patience from *sub-bossi* or for patronage from other employers. So the consumer power of the migrants – before they were acclimatized or turned to North American unionism – when it was exercised, it was against the *padrone*, not the employer. In this, as in every aspect of the system, a *padrone* like Cordasco was the man in between. Not only did he face the anger of workmen and treason from his vassals, but he ran the risk of being seen as an unreliable broker by big business because he supplied troublesome men.

Cordasco then was probably a nasty man and certainly did not deserve the excess of profits he exacted from the migrant labour force, but he did, except perhaps in spring 1904, do his job. The historical literature has too often assumed that the male sojourners of the 1890s and 1900s were helpless victims of the system, potential settlers held in thrall by the *padroni* and condemned to exploitation and to transience by his machinations. At least in the Canadian case, that was simply not so.

The sojourners accepted the *padrone* because they reckoned that he provided them the best alternative in their search for cash; their commitment to the system, like their avoidance of unionism or agricultural work, reflected their desire to return home as quickly as possible with cash and with as little North American encumbrance as possible. When an official of the Commissariat asked Italian labourers in the Niagara Peninsula why they hadn't taken up some of the rich farm lands in that region, the answer was simple: "We have to think about our families in Italy."[51] In 1900, the Canadian Consul in Montreal had reported that of all the trapped migrants interviewed there, none had come to Canada to settle. Agricultural work did not bring in the cash which was the goal of the sojourning family member. Some measure both of the *padrone's* successful delivery of services and of the frame of mind of the Italian Canadian labour force, can be found in the fact that Canadian remittances to Italy were the highest per unit for any part of *Italia oltremare* as late as 1908.[52]

Dini testified honestly and simply at one point to the Royal Commission. When pressed to admit that it was the extraordinary competition between agents like himself and Cordasco which had led to so many migrants arriving in Montreal that spring, he remarked that that was not so. It was easy enough, he said, to understand why men who earned the equivalent of 25 cents a day in their home towns might come to a land where they could make $1.50 a day and twice that much if they became foremen. All of the Commissioners who investigated Canadian conditions later on for the Canadian government concurred on one point: sojourners were content with their margin of saving and profit. They complained of the cold, of unsanitary and unsafe conditions, and sometimes of a *padrone's* dishonesty, but, for example, in 1910 Viola found men in the mines at Cobalt saving a dollar a day. Foremen, according to Moroni, made as much as $3.50 a day – ten times the daily wages in southern Italy, and reason enough, if not justification, for Cordasco's surcharge when registering *capisquadra* in 1903 and 1904.[53]

Attolico, in 1912, met a Calabrese youth in the bush "at a little station four hours away from Lake Superior."[54] The youngster complained to him about missing his village but he had wintered over in a bunkhouse because he did not want to go to Port Arthur and spend his salary on *madamigelle*. The boy had already sent 350 lire – the equivalent of a half year's wages – to his mother back in his home town and had been in Canada less than three months when Attolico encountered him. He did not mind the deprivation but he kept repeating that, while there were many other Calabrese about, he was the only one from Mammole and had no one for company but God. Since the young Calabrese section hand worked for the Canadian Pacific Railway, he was mistaken if he thought the deity was his only companion. The latter might have heard his prayers, but it was Cordasco or one of his successors who had found him his job, remitted his money to his mother, delivered her letters to him, would handle pre-paid tickets for kinfolk or for his passage home later on. It was a *padrone*, not God and not the free flow of labour to capital, who had brought a man from the hills of Calabria to the northern Ontario bush.

Protest against the *padrone* system came more often from social workers, labour dealers and nativists than it did from the consumers, the migrant labourers. Historians have rather superciliously assumed that that is because the sojourners knew no better or had no choice, but in fact, the system ended when the consumer no longer found it satisfactory. Padronism was callous, exploitive and often dishonest, but it fulfilled a function for those migrants who chose to come to America, not as permanent immigrants, but in search of cash to improve their condition in the old country. To understand padronism properly and to give all parts of the system – employer, intermediary and labourer consumer – their due, we must see it as part of the commerce of migration not as a form of ethnic crime.

Notes

1. The chief source for this essay is the *Royal Commission Appointed to Inquire into the Immigration of Italian Labourers to Montreal and the alleged Fraudulent Practices of Employment Agencies* (Ottawa 1905). The Commission produced a 41 page report and 170 pages of testimony. The Commission's report is generally marred as a source by an undercurrent of nativism, ignorance of Italian ways, and a view of free enterprise as part the divine plan. Henceforth cited as *Royal Commission 1904*.

2. The word *padrone* does not appear in the testimony. Mackenzie King, chief investigator for the Dept. of Labour and future Prime Minister of Canada, probably knew the word and its connotations from his American experience. I have used the word throughout the paper as a convenient label for the chief intermediaries, but do so on the understanding that the reader has a wary and sophisticated approach to its use. I have dealt more historiographically with the *padrone* in North America in an earlier article. See R.F. Harney, "The Padrone and the Immigrant, *Canadian Review of American Studies*, 5(1974), 101-118.

3. The expression was popularized in Canada by André Laurendeau (1912-1968), the editor of Montreal's *Le Devoir*. Laurendeau claimed that Quebec was governed by *les rois nègres* – the equivalent of those puppet rulers in Africa through whom the British authorities found it convenient to wield power. The expression in English probably would have the strength of "nigger king" not "negro king".

4. See Joan M. Nelson, *Temporary versus Permanent Cityward Migration: Causes and Consequences* (Cambridge, Mass. 1976) and R.F. Harney, "Men without Women: Italian Migrants in Canada, 1885-1930" in B. Caroli, L. Tomasi and R.F. Harney, eds., *The Italian Immigrant Woman in North America* (Toronto 1978), pp. 79-101.

5. On government immigration policy, see M. Timlin, "Canada's Immigration Policy, 1896-1910", *Canadian Journal of Economics and Political Science*, 26 (1963). For popular attitudes toward the immigrant labourers, see E. Bradwin, *The Bunkhouse Man* (New York 1928) and J.S. Woodsworth, *Strangers Within our Gates* (Toronto 1909). The latter was significant enough to have a *Bollettino* of the Italian Commissariat of Emigration devoted to reviewing its ideas and impact. "Gli stranieri nel Canada guidicati da un Canadese" (*recensione*) in *Bollettino* #19 (1909). See also D.H. Avery, *Canadian Immigration Policy and the Alien Question, 1896-1919. The Anglo-Canadian Perspective*, Ph.D. Thesis, University of Western Ontario, 1973.

6. Letter from Commissioner of Immigration (Winnipeg) to James Smart, Deputy Minister of the Interior (Ottawa) 27 August 1901, *Immigration Branch Papers* RG76, Vol. 129, File 28885 part I, Public Archives of Canada. This file will be cited henceforth as *Immigration Branch 1901*.

7. There was apparently little knowledge of Canada in Italy before the mass migration of the 1900s. The only available study of Canada in Italy seems to have been E. Cavalieri, "Il Dominion del Canada. Appunti di Viaggio" which appeared first in serial form in 1887 in *Nuova Antologia* 43(4), 700-747, 44(6), 319-353, 44(8), 665-692. As late as 1914, a vademecum for immigrants, the *Calendario per gli emigrati* (Milan 1914) of the Società Umanitaria of Milan, although it had accurate descriptions of many parts of the world, showed Niagara Falls on its map of Canada but not the industrial city of Toronto.

8. For the debate over emigration in Italy and the evolution of Italian laws about protection of emigrants, see Manzotti, *La Polemica sull'emigrazione nell'Italia unita* (Milan 1969), R.F. Foerster, *The Italian Emigration of Our Times* (Harvard 1918).

9. Letter of Luigi Gramatica, General Agent (Genoa) to W.T. Preston (London) 7 January 1902 in *Immigration Branch 1901*, File 28885.

10. Braun's report, supporting documents and miscellaneous related correspondence are in the National Archives in Washington. *Immigration Subject Correspondence* RG85, File 52320/47 (1903-1904), Immigration and Naturalization, Dept. of Justice. Henceforth cited as *Braun Report 1903*.

11. By the turn-of-the-century, legislation in the countries of immigration made the transport companies responsible for return passage of those refused admission. For a model that could be applied to the study of transportation companies and sub-agents on the Italian borders, see Berit Brattne and Sune Akerman, "The Importance of the Transport Sector for Mass Emigration" in H. Runblom and Hans Norman, eds., *From Sweden to America. A History of the Migration* (Uppsala 1976). For the conflict between local agents and the great carriers in Italy, see G. Dore, *La Democrazia italiana e l'emigrazione in America* (Brescia 1964), 72-98.

12. See the attempts by the other agencies to censure Jauch and Pellegrini for their practices at Chiasso. The latter firm caused press and government concern about the Chiasso connection by preparing clandestine immigrants too carelessly. *Braun Report 1903*.

13. *Braun Report 1903* RG85, File 52320/47 contains a number of transcripts of deportation proceedings held at Ellis Island in 1903. All of the cases involved older migrants, usually physically unfit, ticketed through to Montreal. Most of the migrants seem to be planning to stay in New York area if admitted. According to Watchorn and to Rossi, the reverse device, entering the United States after being ticketed to Halifax and Montreal, was equally prevalent.

14. Letter from Knoepfelmacher to Braun, 31 May 1903, *Braun Report 1903* describes the preparation of migrants by the agencies in order to fool border authorities.

15. *Immigration Branch 1901*. "Suspect Emigration" dispatch from Chiasso to *Corriere della Sera*, 18 March 1901; *Braun Report 1903*.

16. Government circular quoted in above dispatch.

17. Cordasco letter to Antonio Paretti, La Veloce agent in Udine (1 March 1904) *Royal Commission 1904,* 80.

18. Testimony of G. Burns, *Royal Commission 1904,* 41.

19. Letter from Corecco and Brivio to A. Dini (7 May 1904) *Royal Commission 1904,* 50.

20. Correspondence between Cordasco and Ludwig (October 1903) *Royal Commission 1904,* 82.

21. Letter from Cordasco to Antonio Paretti (26 April 1904) *Royal Commission 1904,*82.

22. Testimony of Cordasco, *Royal Commission 1904,* 74.

23. Report in *Labour Gazette* (June 1906), 1350.

24. Testimony of Mortimer Waller, *Royal Commission 1904,* 48. Waller incidentally charged $2. to register labourers for work and $5. for foremen.

25. Letter from Cordasco to de Santis (10 February 1904), *Royal Commission 1904,* 130.

26. Letter from Cordasco to L.P. Scarrone (9 February 1904), *Royal Commission 1904,* 103.

27. Notice in *La Patria Italiana, Royal Commission 1904,* 106.

28. *La Patria Italiana* (20 February 1904), *Royal Commission 1904,* 107.

29. Testimony of CPR agent Skinner, *Royal Commission 1904,* 26.

30. See R.F. Harney, "The Commerce of Migration", *Canadian Ethnic Studies,* 9(1977), 42-53; on the concept of the *borghesia mediatrice.* See G. Dore, *La Democrazia italiana e l'emigrazione in America* (Brescia 1964).

31. Testimony of Pompeo Bianco, foreman, *Royal Commission 1904,* 163.

32. Testimony of Michele Tisi, foreman, *Royal Commission 1904,* 33.

33. Testimony of Salvatore Mollo, foreman, *Royal Commission 1904,* 34; testimony of Pompeo Bianco, foreman, *Royal Commission 1904,* 29.

34. Testimony of Burns, *Royal Commission 1904,* 61. It is important to note that Burns stressed that Cordasco was sole agent for Italian labour; he had in that sense an ethnic monopoly but not a franchise for hiring all track crews. As Burns pointed out (52), Italian labour had a specific purpose – "The Italians on our line are used to replace these men who have been employed earlier in the season on contracts, and to whom at this time of year, July and August, when the harvest starts, the farmer offers high wages and they jump their jobs, and the work is left behind, and we have to rely on anything we can get."

35. Testimony of Burns, *Royal Commission 1904,* 41.

36. Letter from Burns to C. Mariotti, Secretary of the Italian Immigration Aid Society (16 March 1903) *Royal Commission 1904*, 3.

37. *La Patria Italiana*, advertisement (20 February 1904), *Royal Commission 1904*, 106.

38. Letter from Cordasco to M. Torchia & Co. (12 March 1904), *Royal Commission 1904*, 89.

39. M. Zaslow, *The Opening of the Canadian North, 1870-1914* (Toronto 1971). The author estimates that over 25% of Ontario's Italian population in the 1900s was in the North. The figure would be much higher in the summer. For a discussion of the problem of the census, the thaw, and migrant Italian labour see R.F. Harney, "Chiaroscuro: Italians in Toronto, 1885-1915", *Italian Americana*, 1 (Spring 1975), 148-149.

40. Cordasco's letters of complaint to Burns, *Royal Commission 1904*, 141-143.

41. With the passage of new legislation on immigration in Italy during 1901, the Society had changed from a private Montreal charitable agency to an adjunct of the Italian consulate funded by the Italian government. Its papers of incorporation listed as the Society's purpose: "1. the assisting of Italian Immigrants to reach Canada; 2. assisting Italians to obtain employment; 3. assisting Italian immigrants to obtain land for settlement...; 4. assisting Italian immigrants in every possible way; 5. enabling persons in Canada in want of labourers, artisans or servants to get from Italy desirable citizens." (Incorporation 10 November 1902).

42. Letter from Italian Immigration Aid Society to D. McNicoll, General Manager Canadian Pacific Railway (26 March 1903), *Royal Commission 1904*, 73.

43. Letter from Cordasco to V. Capparelli, editor of *L'Operari* (28 January 1904), *Royal Commission 1904*, 139.

44. Letter from Cordasco to Burns (10 May 1904), *Royal Commission 1904*, 57.

45. Testimony of Candori, secretary of the Society, *Royal Commission 1904*, 18.

46. Testimony of Candori, Society secretary, *Royal Commission 1904*, 13.

47. Letter from Mariotti to McNicoll, *Royal Commission 1904*, 13.

48. The phrase about Argentina was contained in one of the Society's bulletins, *Royal Commission 1904*, 15. Block settlement in the Canadian West did resemble the Argentine experience, but Italians were not encouraged by the authorities. The Minister of the Interior himself wrote to an aide that "no steps are to be taken to assist or encourage Italian immigration to Canada..." *Sifton papers*, quoted in D. Avery, "Canadian Immigration Policy and the Foreign Navvy, 1874-1914", *Historical Papers* (1972), 135-156. The Italian consul in Montreal reported in 1901 that not a single Italian migrant interviewed in the city wished to settle. All were sojourners or seasonal labourers looking for ready cash, *Immigration Branch 1901*, File 28885. "As a matter of fact Mr. Solimbergo [the consul] found out that out of all Italian emigrants who were already in Canada, not one thought it of any use to become

a colonial." "Emigration of Italian peasants to Canada", enquiry of *Corriere della Sera* (June 1901), typescript translation of newspaper article.

49. See A. Spada, *Italians in Canada*, 89. The Commission recommended finally that Montreal pass a by-law, like Toronto's, which required licensing for labour bureaux and a scale of fees for registering workers for employment. *Labour Gazette* (June 1905), 1348. Cordasco in the end, made restitution to registered workers who got no work under $3,000 and resumed his business without using a registration fee system. As we have seen that was not the chief source of his income and power anyway.

50. Letter from Burns to Cordasco, *Royal Commission 1904*, 113. Burns also informed the Italian Immigration Aid Society of this matter.

51. B. Attolico, "L'agricoltura e l'immigrazione nell'Canada" in the *Bollettino* #5 (Anno 1912) Commissariat of Emigration, Rome 547.

52. See *Revista di Emigrazione* Anno 1:6 (August 1908). On a basis of amount per remittance, the figures were: Canada 221 lire, Argentina 194, U.S.A. 185, Brazil 168. 64% went to the South of Italy and the vast majority of remittances to Italy from Canada came through the postal savings system.

53. Moroni, "Le condizioni attuali", 49.

54. B. Attolico, "Sui campi di lavoro della nuova ferrovia transcontinentale canadese" in the *Bollettino* #1 (Anno 1913) Commissariat of Emigration, Rome, 7.

THE IMMIGRANT
CITY*

─────────── ❦ ───────────

*I*T MIGHT BE USEFUL TO LOOK AT CANADIAN IMMIGRANT CITIES SUCH AS TORONTO and Montreal as lying along the same spectrum as those cities which don't work because they lack inter-ethnic harmony, or because their ruling old stock have failed to encourage adequate circulation of elites, have resorted to coercion as their cultural hegemony has lost its power to control themselves.

The great cities of the world are the products of the flow of labour to capital, the mass migration of workers from countryside to city, often across political and cultural boundaries. The flow goes on everywhere and always. Today in the Arab Emirates of the Persian Gulf, the primary work force is drawn from Korea and the Philippines. At the turn of the century, more than 60 percent of the population of Buenos Aires could trace its origins to Italy; in towns in the heart of the Amazonian jungles are the descendants of Barbadians who went there to build a railway. East Indian miners from Fiji live and work in the Canadian Far North, and towns on the Canadian prairies are peopled by farmers from the great Eurasian plains who cling to vestiges of the culture their ancestors had a century, a continent and an ocean away. As Rome fills with immigrants from Asia and Africa, and as many of the guest workers who came from the Mediterranean and Levantine peripheries in the 1960s chagrin the ethnocentric societies of Western Europe by showing signs they intend to stay, the numbers of Italians, Greeks and Portuguese migrating eastward from Canada are greater than those coming westward, suggesting that a *de facto* guest worker system has existed in Canadian cities as well.

If the coming and going of peoples to form or inform cities is the way of the world, it is, by its very dynamic, a disruptive force and a source of tension. What cultural price should a newcomer have to pay to function in the city that is the target of his migration project? Should labour

───────────────────

* This article reprinted with permission from *Vice Versa*, no. 24, 1988, pp. 4-6.

migrants and refugees, drawn or driven from their homeland, be expected to negotiate identity similarly? If we employ sophistries about the difference between integration and assimilation, have we done more than paper over the psychological costs that come with having a language, folkways and *mores* of the home or ethnic enclave different from those of the hegemonic forces in a city? Doesn't illiteracy or diglossia in the host language make the migrant exploitable and cause distortions in the urban economy that affect everyone? Doesn't a sojourning or ghettoized mentality retard democratic political participation and thwart efforts at equality before the law and of access to services? Are all such questions just a preamble to "blaming the victim?"

The ancient Romans recognized the unease that exists in the polyglot city between valuing the old and the new, between stability and change. They mediated the problem through the minor deities, Penates and Lares to whom Italo Calvino has given voice:

> The true essence of [the city] is the subject of endless debate. The Penates believe they are [the city's] soul, even if they arrived last year; and they believe they take [the city] with them when they emigrate. The Lares consider the Penates temporary guests, importunate, intrusive; the real [city] is theirs, which gives form to all it contains, [the city] that was there before all these upstarts and that will remain when all have gone away.

Today, almost every major city in the world has ethnic variety and, with it, dichotomies between those long in the land and newcomers. To a remarkable extent, Canadian intellectuals and urban historians practice a species of "exceptionalism" in which they accept a dichotomy between their cities and the cities of the world, between the solvable problems of immigration and polyethnicity in their cities and the seemingly intractable communal strife of cities elsewhere in the world. In the worst moments of the September crisis in 1970, no image of Beirut, Belfast, Algiers or Johannesburg was offered in the texts of the Anglophone discourse and few, if any, in the Francophone, nor would such analogies have found wide acceptance from readers except for the few in Quebec who would read them through the texts of Third World discourse. It is even less likely that parallels to Detroit, Watts, or Cleveland would have occurred to anyone. In a sense the idea of the city as contested terrain fits ill with Canadian stereotypes about the land as a "peaceable kingdom". If such a way of thinking was not applied to conflict between two indigenous communal elements in Montreal, it was even farther from the thinking about encounter between old stock and immigrant, between White and Asian and Black or Native in the history of other Canadian cities such as Toronto, Winnipeg, or Vancouver. This is so, despite the fact that mass migration and a class-based urban hegemony that often corresponded to an ethnically defined hierarchy prevailed in Toronto, Montreal and most metropoles.

THE CITY AS PEOPLE

The Canadian city then emerges from the pages of most of our history books with an image – often reinforced by comparisons with the urban violence in the Babylon immediately to the south – of peaceful homogeneity. Generally, one would have to look elsewhere than in the pages of Canadian histories over the last decade to find the city imagined in terms of a polyphony of voices, a hierarchy of discourses affecting one another, a contested terrain among ethnic groups – let alone in the extreme form, suggested by Mike Royko's description of Chicago as "a collection of ethnic villages" together in the same encampment.

There may be reason for caution in using such models and imagery for Canadian cities that simply were, before World War Two, more ethnically homogeneous than American ones and merit to the argument that, in this instance as in some others, applying American social science to Canadian situations does damage. However, that same argument is clearly not good enough when it refers to the smaller industrial cities and resource towns which, from the 1890s on, were home or base camp to large numbers of immigrants.

The absence of *ethnies* and ethnics in the story of our cities may be part of a more general problem of urban studies suggested by James Scobie's lament that reams of research "on urban services, such as paving, parks, sewage, police, lighting and garbage disposal, on the location, regulation and expanse of industry, on education, public health" have been produced about cities, but little is written about the people of the city. Of course, increasing study of urban elites and decision-making is one answer to Scobie's call to historians to people the landscape of urban history, as are sophisticated mobility studies and approaching the city in terms of class struggle. But given the immigrant character of so much of the Canadian workforce in the twentieth century, it is surprising that the process by which those immigrants alter the *ambience* and physical appearance of the city, do or do not form *ethnies*, affect the workplace as well as patterns of leisure, change the local relations of labour to capital, of city politician to constituency, goes largely unstudied.

Descriptions of two cities from Italo Calvino's *Invisible Cities* have helped me to think about what may have shaped the sort of canon revealed by the texts, both present and absent, in *Forging a Consensus*:

> It is the mood of the beholders which give the city of Zemrude its form. If you go by whistling, your nose atilt behind the whistle, you will know it from below: window sills, flapping curtains, fountains. If you walk along banging your head, your nails dug into the palms of your hands, your gaze will be held on the ground, in the gutters, the manhole covers, the fish scales, wastepaper. You cannot say that one aspect of the city is truer than the other. Despina can be reached in two ways: by ship or by camel. The city displays one face to the traveller arriving overland and a different one to him who arrives by sea.

Calvino's words should remind us of the obvious: that the city encountered at any given moment by immigrants is not the city encountered by intellectual observers long in the land, that the insertion of most alien newcomers into urban economies has more to do with the gutters and manhole covers than with fountains and flapping curtains, and that – and I admit that this may be putting too fine an edge on my gloss of Calvino's parables – urban historians are most often native to the North American city or its hinterland and, in approaching by camel rather than by ship, may fail to perceive some of the conflict and competition that those who literally or figuratively struggle up from the docks see.

Recently Werner Sollors, in his study of ethnic literature in the United States, *Beyond Ethnicity. Consent and Descent in American Culture*, described Eugène Sue's *Les Mystères de Paris* as a work helping "to create the [modern] image of the city as a swarming mass of signals, dense, obscure, undecipherable". One would have to read Mordecai Richler on Montreal or Michael Ondaatje's novel of pre-World War Two Toronto, *In the Skin of the Lion*, rather than our history books, to find a sense of the Canadian city as being a rich and multi-layered semiotic text. In 1960 Kevin Lynch described the city as something akin to a literary text, a landscape which was intelligible to those with the literacy to read it. In the mid-1970s, Steven Marcus's studies of the Victorian city as his *Engels, Manchester and the Working Class* followed this rich vein of research farther.

The city as text

The insights of these urbanists from different disciplines coincided with the emerging "new ethnography" which called for a recognition of the fact that a polyphony of authentic voices and valid or plausible narrative emplotments existed in every inter-ethnic encounter. Despite the fact that historians have now begun to appreciate the many and varied mental maps, psychic worlds and individual or familial migration projects which propel the city's residents about in their diverse trajectories, the full pluralist import of combining this knowledge with advances in semiotics and anthropology has not been felt yet by Canadian ethnic and urban studies. The narratives of the hegemonic *elites* and the reading of the city as text by the old stock remain privileged. Nonetheless, the Canadian city is (and was) "a swarming mass of signals", a semiotic text and conflict – no matter how muted or mediated by coalition politics, mutual avoidance and patterns inducing public order and civility – has to be the inevitable result of the cultural differences each reader brings to the text. For what each reader brings to his reading of the city comes from the other texts which inform him or her, and at no time in the city's history were the texts of a single discourse shared by all the populace. At the very least, the existence of an immigrant press and ethnic neighbourhoods made such homogeneity of information supply impossible.

Migrants in Canadian cities until after World War Two, and perhaps then as well, were seen as threatening when they gathered in enclaves. As *Missionary Outlook* observed in 1910:

> Every large city on this continent has its fourfold problem of the slum, the saloons, the foreign colonies and the districts of vice. The foreign colony may not be properly called a slum, but it represents a community that is about to become an important factor in our social life and will become a menace in our civilization unless it learns to assimilate the moral and religious ideals and the standards of citizenship.

It is unclear whether Canada's current multiculturalist ethos and policies have changed our views on "foreign colonies" as menaces to our city. Certainly the lexical monstrosity now emerging in government documents, "multicultural group", suggests not a respect for the "double consciousness" of ethnics or the right to cultural retention of immigrants but rather a peculiarly sanitized, dependent form of hyphenated Canadianism.

What is most sad is that these *ethnies* generated by the politics of multiculturalism may keep scholars from ever looking more closely at the dynamics through which migrant pre-selection, entry status in the city economy and ethnicization are an historical process, one that could be understood far more richly if studied on a global level, freed of the now smug "exceptionalism" of multiculturalism.

For if few of Toronto's or Montreal's neighbourhoods could qualify in the Marxist sense as "internal colonies", societies "within a society based on racial, linguistic and marked cultural differences of social class", and subject to control by "the dominant classes and institutions of the metropolis", yet the concept of internal colonies is at least as useful a model as images of homogeneity or rapid assimilation. It reminds us to look at the ethnic community as a separate place, to think of its interior life and not just its boundaries. It reminds us of what Walter Firey observed studying Boston's neighbourhoods many years ago: a neighbourhood is at one and the same time part of the city hierarchy and system and a "little homeland", a spatial corollary to a set of values, of networks, of ways of thinking and being, of ethos.

This more complex and notional sense of the neighbourhood then as an *ambiance*, a psychic world for the immigrants and their children and perhaps their children's children, with its moving mix of ethnocultures, part-cultures and pressures to change the *mores* and folkways, produced by encounter with the North American situation, is a world we must come to know. The new emphasis on history from the "bottom up", along with ethnohistory's interest in analysis of culture and society, invites us to move beyond the study of the external and quantifiable to the more deeply textured and nuanced study of *mentalités*, perceptions in encounter and conflicts, strategies for adjustment or persistence in relation to the changing real condition of being immigrant and for coping with a changing personal or group sense of ethnos. The task of ethnohistory should be the difficult one suggested in the phrase of Jacobo Timmerman, "to penetrate the affective world of the other". To do that, we need to look at the immigrant and ethnic neighbourhoods of the city without assuming we comprehend the intent of each person's migration project, the intensity of their ethnic networks or of their loyalties to ethnoculture.

Information and insight into all these ideas are accessible to us if we combine the little used sources generated from inside the community, such as club and church records and ethnic newspapers and print ephemera, with a more extensive and systematic use of oral testimony. The city might then have the sort of history Lawrence Levine describes as "the attempt to present and understand the thought of people who though quite articulate in their own lifetimes, have been rendered inarticulate by scholars who devoted too much of their attention to less recalcitrant subjects". Levine's thought parallels almost exactly that of the social anthropologist Clifford Geertz who writes: "At base, thinking is a public activity. Its natural habitat is the house yard, the market place and the town square."

Any "city walker" can see the places where ethnocultural thinking as a public activity goes on. In backyards, corner stores, factories, restaurants and halls, adult immigrants review the text – written, oral and semiotic – of the *ethnie* and the circumambient society. In playgrounds and in school rooms, their children negotiate their ethnic and social identities. The "town square" is usually the space and shop around a place of worship on weekends. From these places, they go forth to deal with the larger city as "contested terrain", to make their way in migration, trying not to offend the Lares.

THE CITY AS CONTESTED TERRAIN

In the 1930s, Walter Benjamin's *A Berlin Chronicle,* presaged the urban geographer literature of mental maps, psychic worlds and nodal points. The language he used to describe the superimposing of life histories and life chances on the city scape suggests that he also understood the role of *meprison* and conflict in the relationship of activity to space:

> I have long, indeed for years, played with the idea of setting out the sphere of life – bios – graphically on a map. First I envisaged an ordinary map. But now I would incline to a general staff's map of a city centre, if such a thing existed. Doubtless it does not because of ignorance of the theatre of future wars.

Borrowing Benjamin's idea of *bios* on a map, we can trace the quotidian occasions of competition, misstepping and mutual incomprehension in a polyethnic city. According to Benjamin, the wandering *bio* crossed "thresholds of class" and "frontiers not only social but topographical" in its "intercourse with the city's streets." If we view the *bio*, not in class terms, but as an atom from the nucleus of the *ethnie*, we can move with him or her across a cityspace mapping ethnocultural conflict and the potential for it. One general feature of our map will be a diffuse hostility that immigrants or members of minorities feel directed at them by the old stock, or at least those groups longer in the city. That hostility, where it exists, derives from a sense of displacement which feeds on the visible evidence of ethnic residential and occupational succession and of changing land use and rapid urbanization.

We need to look at some of the sources and theatres of potential inter-ethnic conflict and competition that appear when the city is seen as "contested terrain", and that provide heuristic texts for the speakers in the ethnocultural discourse. The phrase "contested terrain" is borrowed from studies about the struggle between management and labour in the workplace where social class and economic power are the "sense makers" of daily encounter. Without trying to displace class as a central feature of the modern urban encounter, historians of immigration and ethnicity, especially those sensitive to the complex interplay of class and culture in ethnically or racially segmented labour markets, need to examine more closely the role of ethnic identity and ethnoculture as "sense makers" of daily life. In Montreal and Toronto, ethnic recognition defined encounter in many categories, and the "hidden injuries" of ethnicity were at least as ubiquitous as those of class. (Of course, because of the "entry status" of most migrants, ethno-class niching and stereotyping, the two sorts of injuries were usually inextricably tied together.) National origin, language manner, or appearance were as salient features as social class in such encounters. Each actor's personal attributes transmitted direct references to texts, written, spoken and semiotic, about ethnic groups, or maybe the texts defined the individual's attributes. For then as now the personal identity of each individual in an encounter was in a complex relationship with the existence, or the perception of the existence, of a collectivity with whom he or she was identified by others, or an *ethnie* with whom he or she identified. Characteristics attributed to a whole ethnic group seem always to be invoked in articulating irritation or hostility to a single member of the group.

When we think of contemporary cities such as Belfast, Beirut, Johannesburg and Detroit which stand at the far end of the spectrum that runs from inter-ethnic peace to open communal strife, it is easy enough to comprehend that it matters how one *ethnie* sees another or defines appropriate citycraft. The lessons drawn from reading the city as text by those in Soweto or in the Falls Road are clearly not compatible with the way the urban *elites*, or occupying power, behave and expect or force others to behave. Life chances on either side of the Green Line in Beirut or either side of the ghetto walls in Detroit are so different that they represent not different neighbourhoods but alien worlds. It might be useful to look at Canadian immigrant cities such as Toronto and Montreal as lying along the same spectrum as those cities which "don't work" because they lack inter-ethnic harmony, or because their ruling old stock have failed to encourage adequate circulation of *elites*, have resorted to coercion as their cultural hegemony has lost its power to control themselves.

If we did look at the city in this more open and global manner, we would, I believe, begin to understand our urban reality in terms of what is right and what is wrong, what works and what does not, what scars us in an inhumane or undemocratic way and what holds out false hope to newcomers.

III

THE
POLITICS OF
ETHNIC RELATIONS

E PLURIBUS UNUM:
LOUIS ADAMIC AND THE
MEANING OF ETHNIC HISTORY*

*A*MONG THE MOST PROLIFIC AND POPULAR *A*MERICAN WRITERS OF THE *1930*S AND
1940s was a Slovene immigrant, Louis Adamic. His career as journalist,
amateur historian and public philosopher seemed to represent all the
good that could come for the United States and for immigrants when the
ethos of Americanization prevailed and rapid acculturation was the norm.
Adamic had come to America in 1913, at the age of fifteen, from his home
in the Habsburg Monarchy. He learned English quickly in New York City
night schools and enlisted in the American army during World War One.
Shortly after the war, he began a career as a journalist on the west coast.
His native Slovene language was almost forgotten, and his English language prowess was such that H.L. Mencken accepted one of his stories
for the *American Mercury.* Adamic went on to write pieces for *Harper's,*
the *Nation* and the *Saturday Review of Literature.* His 1931 book, *Dynamite: The Story of Class Violence in America,* established him as an important radical democratic voice. He continued on the fringes of the New
Deal Left, remaining a critic of socialism and Marxism, despite his later
support of Tito.

By the time of his death in 1951, Adamic had influenced American
opinion about ethnicity, pluralism and democracy as well as about the
Jugoslav question. His publications, including translations into nine languages, ran to over 570 titles. Among them were *The Native's Return,* his
1934 account of his first trip back to Slovenia, which became a book-of-
the-month-club selection, and *My America,* which appeared in 1938 and
went through ten English-language printings. With the coming of World
War II, Adamic directed most of his energy to the Common Council for

* This article appeared in the *Journal of Ethnic Studies,* Spring 1986, vol. 14, no.
  1, pp. 29-46.

American Unity and its journal, *Common Ground*, while continuing to develop his plans as general editor for a multi-volume history of American ethnic groups – a series prefigured in his own *From Many Lands* (1939) and *A Nation of Nations* (1944).

Since Adamic had supported the cause of Tito and communism in Jugoslavia and had consistently championed the common man and radical democracy, his reputation in the United States in the dark years of McCarthyism was challenged. Church-going Slovenes in America and red-baiting Americans denounced him and his work. (Almost as mindlessly, modern Slovene scholars have made of him a cult figure.) Despite such partisan hostilities about some of his attitudes, no one, I assumed, could doubt that Adamic had laid the groundwork for the postwar "ethnic revival". In popular and populist form, he had announced the agenda for the ethnic and immigration studies of the 1960s and 1970s.

Recently I had reason to wonder whether my easy assumptions about Louis Adamic, his influence on my parents, me, on a whole generation especially of ethnic Americans were well-founded. In an opening aside that reflects, I think, more their ignorance of American ethnocultural history than it does Adamic's marginality, the editors of the new *Harvard Encyclopedia of American Ethnic Groups* remark that they were well along in their effort, before they became aware that Adamic had planned an encyclopedia and a series of volumes on ethnicity some forty years ago. I find this admission a bit startling especially if it comes from the *Encyclopedia's* consulting editor Oscar Handlin.[1] However, it has caused me to think about Adamic's place in ethnic studies. I looked for reference to him first in the body of that new encyclopedia. Philip Gleason's theme essay on American identity and Americanization mentions him in connection with his editing of the periodical *Common Ground*. He is not cited by Michael Novak in his entry "Pluralism: a Humanist Perspective" – perhaps Adamic was too humanist and not enough pluralist. In his article on Slovenes, Rudolph Susel treats Adamic fairly but sparely. One sentence identifies him; another refers to his ties with the Roosevelt White House and to the Slovene-American National Council (SANS) and the partisan cause in Yugoslavia. A third sentence begins "While Louis Adamic who soon outgrew the confines of the Slovene community."

Was it possible that Adamic outgrew his own ethnocommunity to influence and to forge a bond – at once ethnic, American, sentimentally democratic and wartime patriotic – with readers like my parents (themselves not Slovene, but children of immigrants from four nations), but that he had not got beyond ethnicity and popular journalism enough to have impact on ethnic and immigration studies in our universities? The suspicion that this was so grew when I read the judgment on Adamic written in 1948 by Edward Saveth in his *American Historians and European Immigrants, 1875-1925*. Saveth dismissed Adamic as one who "repeats the stock arguments of the ethnic jingoists" and worse yet did it "before an audience broader than the filiopietists ever reached."[2] My parents were part of that audience; my boyish enthusiasm for *A Native's Return, My Native Land, From Many Lands* and a *Nation of Nations* would be explained by the professional historian as a young ethnic feeding on the hallucinogenic pap of Adamic's wartime falsification of American history. For my mother, Adamic counted as part of an ill-defined little band – always quoted at me – that included Saroyan, Steinbeck and Frank Capra, the film-maker. These men were among the prophets of the non-ideological but anti-fascist American common man.

I don't think my parents knew much about Adamic's project to create a multi-volumed history of American ethnicity, and they did not read *Common Ground*. His books were the non-fiction part of a celebration of the role of immigrants and their children in the American war effort. *Two Way Passage* (1941), *What's Your Name* (1942) and *A Nation of Nations* (1944) were, in my house anyway, companion pieces of those multi-ethnic patrols, familiar in fiction from *The Naked and the Dead* and *A Walk in the Sun*, where each man's name ended in – ski or – ino or – stein. Adamic, remember, was being read in little Massachusetts cities, where squares and streets were being rededicated to some fallen Greek, Italian, Polish or Lebanese American non-commissioned officer with a wonder-fully, proudly American, unpronounceable name. Each of them, as we saw it and as Adamic hinted, had received baptism of desire and baptism of blood by walking bravely into the new melting pot – the burning tank turret, the flaming cockpit, the exploding warship.

Rereading Adamic over the last six months for this conference has not been pleasant. It brings confusion about too many things learned at home, once believed, and lost with the 1960s. It raises questions of how much of humanity the professional historian leaves behind to be profes-sional and whether one can ever properly evaluate other times. The whole exercise is fraught with anachronism and the cheap tricks of ret-rospective falsification – one example. I can marvel at Adamic's brave and precocious decision to list Negro slave revolts as important components in Black American history and in the American revolutionary tradition itself.[3] If I can approve of that, do I have a right to be appalled when he happily recounts how a Black woman – right here at the St. Paul's Inter-national Festival in 1941 – reconciled herself to her roots and joined the parade of nationalities in her "mammy clothes"?

There are risks beyond scolding and indulging in anachronism. The application of a social scientific critique to the work of someone like Adamic is unfair. To demand consistency of a man who so believed in the integral relationship of thought and deed, of the compatibility of diversity and unity that he could be described as a late Mazzinian, is to measure a minor prophet by the constricted standards of the academy. The pretense of distance, the need for neutrality – virtues of the university historian – would have seemed cowardly devices to Adamic. He was, after all, the man who wrote that "tolerance is largely intolerance grown subtle, polite, distant and beyond reach, where no one can deal with it". He would have known intuitively what claims to academic impartiality were worth in the field of American ethnic history.

Adamic did choose though to write ethnic history, to use history as an instrumentality to overcome what he saw to be the malaise of America. So his history must be judged by the discipline's standards. For him history was a heuristic device, the means by which America would come to know its true self and its role in humanity; it was never merely a record of the past but more a medium to be captured by those who believed in an open, democratic and multi-ethnic America from those who held a more narrowly Anglo-conformist or meaner view of the nation's history and potentialities. Much of his energy in the decade from 1938 to 1948 was taken up in this effort to correct America's image of herself through the re-writing of her history. In this paper, I will discuss briefly the malaise as Adamic saw it; the philosophical, one might say national mythic solution he sought for that malaise, and how he intended to use his revisionist history to create a new myth of America. Finally I will look for a moment at the way in which he viewed and wrote multicultural history.

What started with the publication of *My America* (1938), really with the article "Thirty Million New Americans" in *Harpers* magazine in October 1934 and went on through his "Plymouth Rock and Ellis Island" publishing projects and editorship of the journal *Common Ground*, had begun as a response to the depression and the coarsening of relations among peoples in Europe and America, though later it turned into a subspecies of America's total war effort. By the time Adamic wrote *What's Your Name* and *A Nation of Nations*, his work and the work of the Common Council for American Unity became confused with contrived attempts at national fusion and maintaining the morale of the ethnic populace during World War Two. But Adamic's massive *pensiero ed azione* grew from deeper roots than the war emergency and remained greater in spirit than the wartime propaganda with which it became entwined.

In the public lecture entitled "Plymouth Rock and Ellis Island"[4]

Adamic described the evil he was confronting: "At the risk of oversimplification", he wrote "this backlash and the Depression have been effective in increasing prejudice and intolerance, and in driving – more or less – the various elements back upon their own resources as groups.... This thing is spreading. It is noticeable in the halls of Congress. It creeps into the speeches of professional patriots." Adamic was reacting to an increase of nativism and anti-Semitism, the activities of the KKK and unemployment as it exacerbated ethnic differences. The mood of the nation reinforced ghetto walls, increased the old stock's fear of the alien and crippled America to serve humanity in need. He believed that mood was fed by an overemphasis on the nation's Anglo-Saxon origins in popular writing, the press, theatre and movies. "In spite of the presence here of about 50,000,000 new immigrant people, not a few old stock Americans go on believing they are on the inside track of a pattern of civilization and culture which was fixed long ago, once and for all", he wrote. In the face of the prevailing mood, the immigrant and minority member and his children reacted with "mutual fear, defensiveness, indecision, fretting and withdrawal." Adamic concluded that a proper understanding of America's past and her contemporary makeup would come from what he called "an intellectual – emotional synthesis of old and new America; of the Mayflower and the steerage...of the Liberty Bell and the Statue of Liberty. The Old American Dream needs to be interlaced with the immigrants' emotions as they saw the Statue of Liberty. The two must be made one story."[5]

If the "two" were made "one story", he reasoned, then the immigrants would react to America with "affirmative intelligence, passion and will", and the old stock would recognize that "American Civilization...is not Anglo-Saxon or Germanic or Slavic or Latin or Oriental or African. It is American, something which from the beginning has been shaped and woven and blended and grown from all our population groups." They would know that "the share any one element has had in its building is not sufficiently unmixed with other shares to overshadow the contribution of any other element",[6] and knowing that would be enriched by seeing America not as their patrimony threatened but as "a teeming nation of nations".

One can be daunted by Adamic's naive sense that the truth makes whole, and that prejudice is merely the product of ignorance as when he wrote in the *Two Way Passage*, "And it would be simply great if old-stock Americans also knew about Mazzei, Pulaski, Haym Slomun, von Steuben, Schurz and other such "foreigners". It would free many of prejudice and intolerance toward their fellow Americans."[7] Yet one can admire his total commitment between 1938 and 1948 to ending that ignorance. "This", he wrote in 1939, " – roughly – is my task as a writer now and I hope that it soon will become the task of other writers, educators and historians."

What Adamic set out to do was to document the multi-ethnic quality of the American past and later the ethnic contribution to the war effort so that no one again would dare treat the non-"old stock" as foreigners. He seems to have believed that evidence of the reality of multi-ethnicity, broadcast throughout the nation, would create an ethos of cultural pluralism. The war years may have caused him to emphasize unity over diversity, and so the outer limits of his pluralism are frayed. There are also some problems of language and perspective that trouble me about Adamic's approach to democratic pluralism as civic philosophy, and to the study of a multi-ethnic past as foundation for that philosophy. His approach to ending prejudice depended on a species of pluralism of origin, the celebration of the heritages of the many peoples who have contributed to America. He offered no formula beyond the historical obscurity of *E pluribus unum* for a pluralism of destination and therefore assumed eventual amalgam or a melting pot. Of course Adamic would not have denied this, he used neither the words ethnicity nor pluralism but rather juxtaposed his "Americanism" which would reach "not only the aliens, the recent immigrants, but everybody, all of us, immigrants and old stock Americans…white and coloured"[8] an Americanism in which we will all be "able to achieve a subjective identification with the country and face its problems"[9] to the forced Americanizing and re-ghettoizing of peoples.[10]

The Irish say that volubility is a form of silence. Adamic wrote and spoke so much and so often on his favourite theme of diversity within unity that the formula's meaning became obscure. We can say that he rejected what Milton Gordon would later label Anglo-conformity; for example, he wrote in *From Many Lands*, "in the past there has been entirely too much giving up, too much melting away and shattering of the various culture values of the new groups", and he believed that the "central educational and cultural effort should be not toward uniformity and conformity…but toward accepting, welcoming and exploiting diversity."[11] Programs for rapid acculturation created an "Americanized foreigner" who became "a cultural zero paying lip service to the U.S., which satisfied the Americanizers."[12] In fact, it brought "the uniformity which usually means what is left of you after you have been under pressure to change and you have yielded."[13] Adamic wanted more and less than the Americanizers. In *From Many Lands*, he had waxed Crèvecoeurean about the new immigrants. They told him tales of "how tears filled their eyes, how they wanted to fall on their knees, how they lifted their children to see the goddess (Statue of Liberty)." These immigrants he said, "were American before they landed." [14] From such men and women, he wrote, "a new type of human being is evolving in America, an amalgam of many strains and cultures. It will not be an Anglo-Saxon type, nor Polish, nor German, nor Bulgarian. *It will be an American.* And the Americans of the future will have names derived from many nations. They will not be particularly English, Scottish, Polish, German or Czech. They will be American." [15] That statement might well be found in Israel Zangwill's *Melting Pot*, for its lack of pluralism of destination is almost breathtaking.

Even the diversity that Adamic invited – the celebration of our many pasts so that each man's claim on American identity would be equal, contained a veiled melting pot logic. For he wrote:

> inviting diversity, being interested in it, will tend to produce unity in a democratic country; ...will operate against the concentration-camp like foreign sections and ghettoes and restricted residential districts, and will encourage movement and dispersal.

In fact, Adamic added:

> inviting diversity brings out the basic sameness of people, just as the opposite results only in more and sharper differences. It breaks down both the superiorities and inferiorities which are equally bad....[16]

This view confirms a definition of pluralism, which puzzled me, by Adamic's contemporary, the sociologist Clyde Kiser. He wrote that, "cultural pluralism...recognized the ethnic diversity of our population and *takes cognizance of the time element in processes of assimilation.*" [17] So accepting diversity was a good thing not because our various backgrounds were important in themselves, rather they are, Adamic wrote, "important and valuable *only* as material for our future American culture." [18] This sort of pluralism was good because all of us – particularly the young – "would begin to make new integrations on the basis of individuality rather than on race, religion, or national background." [19] In a vivid description of this process, one that would, by the way, irk ethnic revivalists now who accuse public agencies of trivializing the issue by reducing multiculturalism to "fascists dancing in their church basements" and "pizza and pysanky days", Adamic described the St.Paul International Festival of 1941. First he provided a long description of the ethnic food available, and then:

In one of the corridors after the show on the same evening I chanced upon a score of young men dancing the Virginia reel. One was a Mexican, most of the others were American-born sons of Scandinavian, Italian, German, Ukrainian, Armenian, and Greek and Chinese immigrants, all wearing the costumes of their parents old countries. The spirit of the occasion had led them spontaneously to accept one another.[20]

Adamic's elixir for America's ailment – whether we see it as pluralist or assimilating – was above all based on seeking to erase the slights done other ethnic groups by the old stock, or Anglo-Saxon, hegemony over the pages of our history books. "This Americanization", for that is what he called it, "should be a great educational movement built, roughly, out of the cognizance of a number of facts, conducted on several fronts...." Chief of these facts was that the United States was "racially, socially, culturally, religiously, spiritually, a human extension not alone of the British Isles, the Netherlands, France, Germany, Ireland and Africa, as it was in the late 1700s but all of Europe, of the West Indies and Mexico, of parts of Asia."[21] Moreover, the American Way itself was a cosmopolitan accomplishment:

> The Anglo-Saxon Americans worked out the practical basis of the political and cultural setup of the U.S. with the ideological aid...of Plato and Shakespeare, and also of the 13th century Scholastic philosophers who were Spaniards, Italians, and Frenchmen; of Rousseau, another Frenchman, of the Old Testament, a Jewish book, and of Jesus Christ, a Jew, and...with the tangible help and on the assistance of the Irish and German elements that were here early in the career of the country and had within them powerful urges toward liberty.[22]

The front that this "Americanizing" would take place on was the writing of history. American history would cease to be the monopoly record of any single people. Through the rephrasing of our history, Adamic felt that the Americanized immigrant – "a man deprived of his own history, with no inner continuity" – would "from the Atlantic to the Pacific, from the Canadian to the Mexican border" whether he was "Swedish American, Russian, German, Italian, Irish, Negro, French, Spanish, Oriental, Czech and double check American would feel themselves at home in the history of America."[23]

For Adamic the word history had two meanings. On the one hand, it was the "methodical record of public events", on the other, "the course of human affairs".[24] Since he felt that, in the course of human affairs, "the coming of peoples to this continent, voluntary or in chains, (was) at the very heart of their historical process."[25] Adamic saw the two meanings of the word history as being at variance in the late 1930s:

> American history as it is written is not the same as American history as it happened. For three hundred years, the record and the process have grown farther apart.... The record written into the standard textbooks portrays the U.S.A. as white Protestant Anglo-Saxon country with a WASP civilization patched here and there with pieces of alien civilization.[26]

The history writing that existed was nothing but Emerson's "shallow village tale" or a "fog" that obscured the American truth. The two meanings of history would be aligned, according to Adamic, when "immigration might cease to be a footnote on page 137 and become a main subject in the text, so that each group would be seen as a necessary and integral thread and would receive proper stress...."[27]

Rewritten history he felt would bring changes in the contemporary cultural atmosphere and relationship of ethnoclasses. Adamic set out then both to rewrite American history and to become a catalyst for the systematic revision of history by others. "There was", he wrote, "an enormous mass of American history...suppressed" and he added, "the word [suppressed] wasn't quite what I meant."[28] Counteracting this "suppression" required a plan. The Project as Adamic defined it had begun with the public lecture "Plymouth Rock and Ellis Island". In it he invited listeners or readers to send for what he called the Broadside – a questionnaire, seven pages in length, with a special supplement for Negroes. The questionnaire was well titled Broadside since it was as much composed of harangues and leading questions as of requests for information. It included questions for new immigrants and a section for the old stock, questions about prejudice encountered, the immigrant experience, ethnic family victory over adversity and attitudes towards America's prospects. I have no knowledge of how widely the Broadside was distributed (he wished to send out hundreds of thousands) or how much response Adamic received, but he always acknowledged in his later books that much of his material had come to him by this means.

By the 1940s, Adamic had written chapters about thirteen different ethnic and immigrant groups in America and was planning pieces on on twenty-eight more. He considered as part of what he variously referred to as the Plymouth Rock and Ellis Island or the "nation of nations" project his volumes – *From Many Lands* (1940), *Two Way Passage* (1941), *What's*

Your Name (1942), *A Nation of Nations* (1944). He planned a fifth volume for after the war to be entitled *Plymouth Rock and Ellis Island*. Adamic saw these five volumes as a popular introduction to the real task of striking an ethnic balance in American history as record. He wrote chapters on each ethnic group; he believed entire books on each one should be written. After negotiating, in the early 1940s, with both Harpers and J.B. Lippincott, he agreed to be general editor for the latter of a series to be called *The Peoples of America*. By 1945, ten of twenty proposed volumes in the series had been commissioned (including those on Indians, Mexicans, the English, Irish, Blacks, Hungarians, Norwegians, Japanese, Italians and Armenians). Many of the prospective authors were distinguished and interesting choices, such as Carey McWilliams, Francis Winwar and Joseph Dineen.

At the same time that he initiated these history writing Projects, Adamic became the moving spirit behind the Common Council for American Unity and first editor of its journal *Common Ground*. If the Common Council was on the one hand a wartime expedient to maintain the morale of what Mencken called the "assistant Americans" it was also an ambitious program for the preservation, research and public awareness of ethnocultural history and records. In fact, I know of no program, including those of the Immigrant History Research Center of the University of Minnesota or the Balch Institute in the United States or at the Multicultural History Society of Ontario, that was not recommended first by Adamic in his manifesto dealing with ethnic (read American) studies in the first issue of *Common Ground*. He proposed, among other things, the creation of ethnic archives, field studies, the stimulation of doctoral work in ethnic and immigration studies, co-operation with foreign language historical societies, publications and exhibits about ethnic groups, curricular programs for teachers, educational work with radio and the movies, and finally – point twenty-one of his proposal – "an ethnic and racial encyclopedia or handbook of the American People."[29] The end of the war and Adamic's own political difficulties caused the Project to atrophy. His dream of giving the other ethnic groups their place in American history became simply a great scheme abandoned.

Adamic's impact on the writing of ethnic history was blunted also by his filiopietism and the lack of rigour in his methodology. Problems arose from his insistence that history serve so many contemporary social needs. If knowledge of one's American heritage was therapeutic – building belongingness and ending *atimia* (ethnic self-disesteem) among the new immigrants – and if such knowledge led the old stock to understand that the non-British were not sudden intruders in the land, then he reasoned claims on longevity in the land should be stressed to the limits of credibility. It was easier to explore and celebrate America's pluralism of origin even into the remotest mists than it was to explain the exact contribution of the many strands. In the process, Adamic should have heeded Charles Francis Adams' warning to a fellow Yankee historian guilty of enthusiasms approaching chauvinism. Adams wrote, "in the treatment of doubtful historical points there are fewer things which need to be more carefully guarded against than patriotism or filial piety."[30]

It would be easy enough to make fun of the excesses, the steeple-chase for priority in the land, into which Adamic stumbled and upon which the value of his work faltered. In *A Nation of Nations*, Adamic seems to have wished to help each of the thirteen ethnic groups discussed to overtake the Mayflower and pass her. He described the old stock as "resting on their own sense of priority",[31] and he should have laughed at claims to status based on time in the land. Instead, he competed, repeating without critical comment as outlandish a set of claims as advanced by any "ethnic jingoist" on behalf of a given group. Adamic's cast of characters and stage set included St. Brendan and the Old Irish text which referred to America as Irland it Mikla (Greater Ireland); Leif Erikson and the Norse settlements in Massachusetts in 1,000 A.D.; the Pole Jan Z. Kolma who reached America seventeen years before Columbus. Both the Jewish and the Greek claims on Columbus as a countryman along with the traditional Genovese one; the Ragusan fleet which left for America in 1540 to mix with the natives and become the Croatan Indians; the Teuton who accompanied Leif Erikson and the Hessians who were among the Huguenots slaughtered in Spanish Florida in the 1500s. There were also, the inevitable Armenians, Polanders and Venetians starting the labour movement at Jamestown in the early 1600s. Adamic's hopeful search for each ethnic group's American Adam must have heightened his credulity, so that without a trace of chauvinism or ethnocentrism he gave wide public exposure to claims of a kind which discredit ethnic studies. Such claims continue to plague ethnic studies and retard the interest of serious social scientists in the field.

For the point, of course, is not whether any particular ancestral claims to being first in the land have historical merit, nor, as we can deduce from Charles Francis Adams warning to Palfrey, that filiopietist excesses are a monopoly of the new immigrants. The question is rather why Adamic, who knew better, whose very formulation reconciling the Americans of Plymouth Rock with those of Ellis Island showed that he did, fell into this unfortunate and vaguely pathological game of American ancestor hunting, a game, after all, played on an old stock field by WASP rules.

Adamic had seen the issue more clearly in 1938 when he began the Project:

> They are different from the old stock Americans. Their Old world heritage is not England, but Poland, or Italy or Bohemia or Armenia or the Balkans etc. *And the beginning of their vital American background as groups is not the glorified Mayflower but the as yet unglorified immigrant steerage*; not Plymouth Rock or Jamestown, but Castle Garden or Ellis Island or the International Bridge or the Mexican or Canadian border.[32]

I can only speculate that the urge to filiopietism and the popular value placed on having roots in colonial America overcame Adamic. The war years made it especially necessary to claim antique ties of loyalty with America, political respectability, and to mute praise for, or loyalty to old country heritages. Moreover, his tendency to distribute the Broadside through certain kinds of ethnic organizations – for example, he sent questionnaires to all those listed in an Italian Who's Who which was a sure-fire way of soliciting filiopietist and Italian chauvinist response in the 1930s – skewed his findings.

Then too the therapeutic burden that Adamic placed on history as record, its need to cause "a sense of what psychiatrists call belongingness, which is considered necessary for a full, balanced development of character and personality, and for one's effectiveness in a creative way within a culture",[33] led him down dangerous paths. A good example of the eliding in his thought of therapy, heritage and descent group attachments appears in *Two Way Passage*, where his efforts to console a young man caught between his American and Italian identities leads to a totally fatuous exchange. The child had been abused by nativist classmates and was uncertain whether he should defend Italy and fascism or abjure all connection with his surname identity. Adamic's solution displayed his typical use of pluralism of origin and filiopietism to encourage individual pride of heritage but preclude pluralism of destination. He tells the boy:

> the fact that you are Italian American has nothing to do with Mussolini. The fact that you are Americans of Italian descent is much more likely to mean that your ideals are those of Garibaldi and Mazzei.

The boy's ignorance of Mazzei and of his role in American history was seen by Adamic as the reason for his confusion of identity:

Mazzei was part of the highest American tradition, and I think Italian Americans ought to know about him. It would make it easier for them to become more completely integrated with America. They would see that they are part of American history.[34]

So although Adamic's goal – pluralist or not – was laudable, the value of knowledge of heritage became confused, in his writings, with implicit or stated descent group characteristics or propensities and with the affirmation of a questionable dichotomy[35] between an early and elite immigration and a later wretched, unskilled mass immigration, a dichotomy which was the antithesis, I think, of what Adamic really believed about America, but one that he espoused occasionally because of his encounters with filiopietists, many of whom were simply heritage-mongers or seekers of pedigree.

Thus no one was safe from his terrible need to make significant and respectable the ethnic past. He recounted in a tone approaching elation Duke Ellington's genealogy, descended from the first twenty blacks who came to Jamestown, and he described the many first slaves who "had belonged to the foremost clans in their tribes, a few were headmen and princes."[36] Even in *Dynamite*,[37] he had slipped into this corruption, describing the first labour activists from Europe as "not the underdog element, but rather the elite, the intelligentsia of immigration." That was a fitting descriptive counterpart to the way in which he described his countrymen in *Laughing in the Jungle* or "The Bohunks" article:

> for the most part, simple peasants who lacked any definite nationalistic consciousness, and who, next to tilling the earth and fishing, were interested only in fighting, love and verse-making, drinking, dancing, singing, strumming the *gusle* or *tamburice*, and last but not least, keeping on the good side of Yahweh. They thought of themselves as fighters, lovers, poets, dancers, singers, and children of the Almighty before it occurred to them that they were also members of definite national and political groups. They were very proud of their endurance at hard physical labor, their productive powers (their women were used to very frequent child-bearing), their singing voices, and their ability to carry liquour like men.[38]

His emphasis on genealogy and illustrious roots in the land suggested not a reconciliation of Plymouth Rock and Ellis Island but an embarrassed immigrant replication of the dichotomies of origin, status and time in the land within each group.

Moreover, his descriptions of ethnic groups, fond and sympathetic as they always were, took the leap to stereotyping and to thoughtless attributions of group characteristics. In *Dynamite*, he described Molly Maguire activities as being the product of "the intense, Irish temperament"[39] and his careless discussion of ethnic group characteristics, see for example, his discussion of the quality of *sisu* among the Finns, makes a thoughtful reader uncomfortable. He wrote describing the American character:

> Spice all this with the flavour of cynicism and humanitarianism from the Jews, sex and sophistication from the French, and sentimentality and love of comfort from the old fashioned Germans.[40]

Adamic had begun to do more than rewrite American history; he was peopling it with his own cast of stock players. Even his paeans to unity in diversity reflected some unthought out problems about attributing groups' characteristics to individuals. He described the St. Paul's festival as a chance for the "diverse elements to discover one another's racial, national, cultural and spiritual values, talents, instincts and other attributes which they brought over from the old countries."[41] Such remarks may seem harmless until the adjectives are put with the nouns and specified.

The trouble, of course, was the scale and purpose of Adamic's history writing. Unlike the many ethnic jingoists, there is no evidence that his search for great men in each ethnic group carried the implication that "all individuals born within the group have all the biological potentialities for genius."[42] In fact Adamic, understood environment and choice as they affected characteristics. He told immigrants that "one should seek all the good elements out of one's background and then…hang onto them."[43]

In his heart Adamic knew that filiopietism and the search for first settlers was irrelevant and elitist. His chapters on each ethnic group became uneasy patchworks of descriptions of heroic or talented, if often obscure, early immigrants, unsubstantiated episodes and tributes to the mass of immigrant workers in industrializing America after 1880. I like to think that he was more comfortable describing the contribution to America of the old Slovene who said, "Just the shell of me was returning to Carniola. The actual me, my strength and youth, was staying in America in those bridges and skyscrapers,"[44] or writing about the American baptism of blood and desire of Lieutenant-Commander Milton Pavlic, killed in action at Guadalcanal, than when he tentatively whimpered that "judging by their names…a handful of Slovenian soldiers served in George Washington's forces."[45]

Beyond the wartime emergency and the heuristic necessity to edify and heal, Adamic's writing of ethnic history fell short for another and basic reason. He neither wished that ethnic groups persist as corporate entities in America nor believed that they did so in any healthful way. If they did, as in the case of the Negroes or of the clusters of "Bohunks" or Italians beyond the immigrant generation, it was to him a sign of pathology. Either the promise of America was being thwarted by prejudice, or the group itself was obtusely clinging to vanished values and emblems of identity. Adamic, after all, had described ethnic neighbourhoods as "concentration-camp like foreign sections" and warned against the mentality which caused "new groups to withdraw into national or group pride or egoism."[46]

His was a celebration of pluralism of origin; he could not conceive of pluralism of destination in America. He moralized rather than theorized about the nature of neighbourhoods and enclaves, of ethnic persistence; and he showed little interest in the texture, networks, sub-culture and socio-economy of ethnic groups.

In his history writing and elsewhere, Adamic's thought reflected the unsolved tension without which *E pluribus unum* becomes a cheap slogan. In *From Many Lands* he wrote that, "in the past there has been entirely too much giving up, too much melting away and shattering of the cultural values of the new groups. There is still too much of that to the detriment of individuals and of America.[47] Five years later – one might say a world war later – he wrote in the Preface to *A Nation of Nations* "at the same time there is more getting-together among Americans than ever before, more acceptance of people on the basis of their personal qualities regardless of background. This is especially true of the men in the service. There is nothing like being together in a foxhole, a bomber or a submarine."[48]

One can easily recognize the new pluralists (ethnic revivalists), according to Harold Isaac's *Idols of the Tribe*; they are those who say that the melting pot "was used by the wicked Wasps of the old Northeast to boil away all the rich pure stuff of non-Waspness and cook up a great thin mess of pasty second class Waspness, which then became the essence of the common American culture."[49] Adamic would not be among such thinkers. Adamic, I believe, would tell the children of immigrants and the grandchildren of Black slaves to take their share of American history away from the old stock and to make an American culture that represented all. It was, he would say, not the pot, but the uneven way it burned and melted – too many old stock, new immigrants and Blacks clung to the sides. He wrote in the Broadside that began his great Project:

I don't like the phrase 'Melting Pot' but since it is popularly used, let me say that I want to dig into the 'Pot'. I suspect that some of the stuff in it is rather cold and some so hot it is burning holes in it, at the same time that it probably holds great spiritual and cultural resources now largely neglected and wasted but still available to be developed into enhancements of a positive democracy in the U.S.[50]

John Higham has written, perhaps too categorically, that "the democracy of integration is an equality of individuals; pluralist democracy is an equality of groups."[51] Adamic sought to impose the latter on our national historical myths in order to insure the former.

The editors of the new *Harvard Encyclopedia of American Ethnic Groups* end their brief description of Adamic's Project and of their lack of indebtedness to it by citing his wistful opinion that his Project would be done – somehow. They conclude: "the job has been done somehow."[52] If they really believe that they have done the job Adamic the historian and public philosopher set out to do, the renovation of America's very sense of herself, then they are as blind to his true purpose as are the new ethnicity's partisans.

Notes

1. *Harvard Encyclopedia of American Ethnic Groups*, ed. S. Thernstrom, (Cambridge, 1980), p. v.

2. Edward N. Saveth, *American History and European Immigrants 1875-1925*, (New York, 1948) pp. 216-217. *Universa E. Kardelja v Ljubljam Louis Adamic Simpozii/Symposium,* Lyublyana, 1981, contains a number of articles in English. The best biography of Adamic is Henry Christian, *Louis Adamic: Immigrant and American Liberal*, Ph.D. dissertation, Brown University, 1967.

3. On Black history, see Louis Adamic, *A Nation of Nations*, (New York, 1945); see also his "The St. Paul Festival of Nations" *Common Ground* I:4 (Summer, 1941) p. 109.

4. He gave the lecture with some variations to a large number of audiences. All references in this paper are to the version printed in Louis Adamic, *From Many Lands* (New York, 1940) pp. 291-301.

5. *From Many Lands*, p. 299.

6. Louis Adamic "American History as a Record and a Process" *Common Ground* VIII: 4 (Summer 1948) p. 22; see also the Preface to *A Nation of Nations*, p. 6.

7. Louis Adamic, *Two Way Passage* (New York, 1941) p. 154.

8. Louis Adamic, "This Crisis Is an Opportunity" *Common Ground* 1:1 (Autumn 1940) p. 64.

9. *From Many Lands*, p. 299.

10. Adamic's reactions to his own experience of forced Americanization can be found in his *Laughing in the Jungle: The Autobiography of an Immigrant in America* (New York, 1932) p. 23; on ethnic resistance to narrow Americanization, see *Two Way Passage*, p. 88.

11. *From Many Lands*, p. 301 and "This Crisis Is an Opportunity" p. 65.

12. *Two Way Passage*, p. 61.

13. *Two Way Passage*, p. 77.

14. *From Many Lands*, p. 298.

15. Louis Adamic, *What's Your Name?* (New York, 1942) p. 144.

16. *From Many Lands*, p. 299.

17. Clyde Kiser "Cultural Pluralism" *Annuals of the American Academy of Political and Social Sciences* (Philadelphia, 1949) v. 262, p. 129.

18. *From Many Lands*, p. 301.

19. "American History As a Record and a Process" p. 23.

20. "The St. Paul Festival of Nations", p. 105.

21. "This Crisis Is an Opportunity", p. 64 and *Two Way Passage*, p. 15.

22. "This Crisis Is an Opportunity", pp. 65-66.

23. *Two Way Passage*, p. 61. This view should be contrasted with his more negative view of his countrymen's 'cultural baggage' when they arrived. See Louis Adamic, "The Bohunks" *American Mercury* XIV: 55 (July 1928) pp. 318-324 and especially *Laughing In the Jungle*, p. 108.

24. "American History As a Record and a Process", p. 20.

25. *A Nation of Nations*, p. 9.

26. "American History As a Record and a Process", p. 21.

27. *A Nation of Nations*, pp. 4-5.

28. *A Nation of Nations*, p. 3. "The size and amount of historical fact which have been omitted from the record is tremendous", he wrote in "American History as a Record and a Process" (p. 22).

29. The Project was presented to the public in detail in "This Crisis Is an Opportunity", *Common Ground's* first issue (1:1 Autumn, 1940) pp. 69-71.

30. Charles Francis Adams quoted in E. Saveth, *American Historians and European Immigrants*, p. 202.

31. Adamic describes there thus in "The St. Paul Festival of Nations", p. 106. The examples of filiopietism in "Mayflower" which follow are drawn from the relevant chapters in *A Nation of Nations*.

32. *From Many Lands*, p. 296.

33. *From Many Lands*, p. 296.

34. *Two Way Passage*, p. 154.

35. There is evidence in Adamic's own career as an immigrant to suggest that he had early accepted this dichotomy. Certainly his articles on "The Bohunks", his response to the editor of *Contempo* about ethnic working class readership (see *Contempo, A Review of Ideas and Personalities* I:2 (June 1931) Chapel Hill, p. 3, and some of the incidents rather spitefully recounted in I. Molek, *Slovena Immigrant History, 1900-1950* (Dover, Delaware, 1979) show a tendency to *atimia* and an effort to distance himself from the stereotype of the Slovene immigrant.

36. *A Nation of Nations*, p. 195.

37. Louis Adamic, *Dynamite: The Story of Class Violence in America*, (New York, 1931) p. 42.

38. *Laughing In the Jungle*, p. 108.

39. *Dynamite*, p. 19.

40. *A Nation of Nations*, p. 112.

41. "The St. Paul Festival of Nations", p. 106.

42. See David Rodnick "Group Frustrations in Connecticut" *American Journal of Sociology*, XLVll: 2 (September 1941) pp. 159-166.

43. *From Many Lands,* p. 300.

44. Louis Adamic "An Immigrant's America" in M.B. McLellean and A.V. DeBonis (eds.) *Within Our Gates: Selections on Tolerance and the Foreign Born of Today* (New York, 1940), p. 50.

45. *A Nation of Nations*, p. 195.

46. *From Many Lands*, p. 296, 299; *What's Your Name,* p. 94; *Laughing In the Jungle*, p. 10.

47. *From Many Lands,* p. 301.

48. *A Nation of Nations*, p. 5. Adamic seemed uncertain about how much the immigrant should give up of his culture when embracing Americanness. His reproduction and comments on Oscar Hammerstein's parody of *Old Man River* done for the Writers' War Board (see *A Nation of Nations*, pp. 362-364) and his various essays on retention or changing of foreign names (see especially "Names" *Common Ground* lll: 1 (Autumn 1942) pp. 21-26), imply the need for an internalizing of forced Americanization by "right thinking" immigrants.

49. Harold Isaac, *Idols of the Tribe*, (New York, 1975) p. 310.

50. *From Many Lands*, p. 303.

51. John Higham, "Integration versus Pluralism: Another American Dilemma" *Center Magazine*, (October/November 1974), pp. 67-68.

52. S. Thernstrom, *Harvard Encyclopedia*, p. v.

PHOTOGRAPHS

FINN FORUM '79

An international conference on the history of Finnish immigration to North America

To be held at
The Ontario Institute for Studies in Education
252 Bloor Street West
Toronto, Ontario

November 1 - 3, 1979

Sponsored by
The Multicultural History Society of Ontario
in conjunction with
The Ontario Institute for Studies in Education, Toronto,
and the
Institute for Migration, Turku, Finland

Paula Groenberg, with the Ontario Minister of Culture and Recreation, Reuben Baetz, and Robert F. Harney, November 1979, transfer of Ukrainian National Federation Archives to the Multicultural History Society of Ontario.

THE STATE
THE STATE OF THE ART
THE STATE OF THE ART
OF THE ART
OF THE ART

a conference on
ethnic and immigration studies
in North America

to be held at
St. Michael's College
University of Toronto
81 St. Mary Street, Toronto, Ontario
May 28–31, 1980

sponsored by The Multicultural History Society of Ontario

Massimo Scala and Robert F. Harney, "Salute to Italy," 2 April – 11 May 1980.
Photo courtesy of Lovello, Toronto, Ontario.

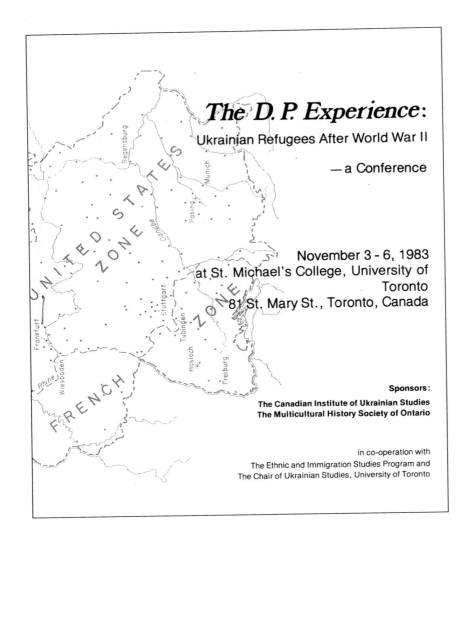

The D. P. Experience:

Ukrainian Refugees After World War II

— a Conference

November 3 - 6, 1983
at St. Michael's College, University of
Toronto
81 St. Mary St., Toronto, Canada

Sponsors:

The Canadian Institute of Ukrainian Studies
The Multicultural History Society of Ontario

in co-operation with
The Ethnic and Immigration Studies Program and
The Chair of Ukrainian Studies, University of Toronto

Robert F. Harney, Raymond Breton, and Lilly Breton.

Jung G. Kim, Robert F. Harney, and Harold Troper.

Robert F. Harney

Franc Sturino, John Zucchi, and Robert F. Harney, *Piazza del Popolo*, Rome 1984, Canadian Academic Centre in Italy Conference, "Writing About the Italian Immigrant Experience in Canada."

Stan Zybala, Robert F. Harney, and Benedykt Heydenkorn at booklaunch for "Poles in Ontario," special issue of *Polyphony: The Bulletin of the Multicultural History Society of Ontario*, vol. 6 no. 2 (Fall/Winter 1984).

IMMIGRATION
AND ETHNICITY
IN ONTARIO
An Exploration in
Women's History

LIPTONS TEA

May 8-10, 1985

at University of Toronto, St. Michael's College
121 St. Joseph St., Toronto

Conference Sponsors:
Multicultural History Society of Ontario
Ethnic and Immigration Studies Program (University of Toronto)

THE WARD

Adrian Papanek and Judy Young, Multiculturalism Directorate, Jean Burnet, Chief Executive Officer of the Society, and Robert F. Harney, December 1986, tenth anniversary of the Multicultural History Society of Ontario, greetings and congratulations from the Secretary of State of Canada, the Honourable David Crombie.

Robert F. Harney, Liu Xian Zhao, Executive Vice-Director-General of the Chinese Centre for Studies of Ethnic Issues, and Wu Jinguang, Chinese Foreign Affairs and Member, Chinese Academic Committee on Nationalities in the World, Toronto, December 1988.

Robert F. Harney, Villa Colombo, Toronto, 21 May 1989, Order of the Sons of Italy, acceptance speech for the transfer of the Order's Ontario archival collection to the Multicultural History Society of Ontario.

UNDOING THE RISORGIMENTO:
EMIGRANTS FROM ITALY
AND THE POLITICS OF REGIONALISM *

"I was seized by a strong desire to tell you of my valley, of my folks, of my native town. I love my valley and my folks as myself. I know their soul which is my soul."

BARTOLOMEO VANZETTI *(from death row, 1926)*[1]

*T*HE ROLE THAT CAMPANILISMO AND REGIONALISM HAVE PLAYED IN THE LIVES OF Italian emigrants is referred to so often in popular discourse and scholarship on both sides of the Atlantic that it has achieved iconic status in the canon of migration studies. The *contadino* immigrant is portrayed as the ultimate xenophobe, one who believes that anyone who comes from beyond his *paese* is a potentially dangerous stranger. After travelling extensively in the United States and Canada at the turn of the century, Adolfo Rossi, an official of the Commissariat of Emigration, described the immigrant's state of mind and sense of identity.

> In them is a profound and tenacious tie (*vincolo*) to family, in their hearts, after their affection for their own family comes their attachment to their village; so that after their relatives they are most attached to their fellow villagers (*compaesani*), then their relatives' friends, then those from their region (*comprovinciale*). At that point begin the strangers, l'indifferente, the men whom the south Italian instinctively distrusts.[2]

Such a view of the immigrant usually appears as the interpretive base for any description of the welter of *paese* clubs, chains of migration, sub-neighbourhoods, and networks of opportunity based on *paesani*, as well

---

* This text was prepared in 1987 for a proposed volume entitled *Immigrant History of Molisani*. Another version of this text will appear in *Italy-Canada-Research: Canadian Studies,* Vol. 2, Library, a special issue of the *Annali Accademici Canadesi* (Ottawa, forthcoming), edited by Dr. Matteo Sanfilippo.

as of the "fractionalism" that thwarted priests, consuls, ethnic politicians, and businessmen become *prominenti,* who sought to organize a coherent *ethnie* among the migrants.

Beginning a quarter of a century ago with Rudolph Vecoli's influential article "Contadini in Chicago: A Critique of the Uprooted," scholars of the Italian Americans began to graft their picture of the Italian migrant onto the sacred texts of American immigration such as M.L. Hansen's *Atlantic Migrations* and O. Handlin's *The Uprooted.*[3] At first glance, the string of studies inspired by Vecoli's article – his sub-title was an overt riposte to Handlin's Pulitzer Prize-winning work – such as H. Nelli's *The Italians in Chicago,* J. Briggs' *An Italian Passage,* and D. Cinel's *From Italy to San Francisco,* modified and seemed to invalidate the themes of uprooting, of undergoing a sea change, of hungering to be American, of mobility and acculturation that had formed the American canon. Although Nelli failed to see beyond the genetic cohort of "Southerners," the other authors (I should add parenthetically, followed bravely in Canada by Harney, Ramirez, Zucchi and Sturino) revelled in demonstrating the "rootedness" of the Italian migrants, dwelling on their *campanilismo,* the economic advantage they derived from paesanism, their sojourning mentality, their "double consciousness," i.e., active interest and concern for the *terra natale* (a sufficiently vague geographical term no matter how evocative to spare one from explaining the difference between paesanism, regionalism, and patriotism). Affirming the image of the first North American Little Italies as places "of a thousand trifling provincial and local animosities," where the idea of *paesani,* although a *"fecondo creatrice di nuclei coloniali,* defeated every attempt at thinking on a larger scale, of renewing or changing the moral [and political] atmosphere,"[4] the historians demonstrated that most migrants from Italy were definitely not "uprooted" from their primary loyalties.

Most also agreed that not just Americanization, but ethnicization took place. Within a generation, the institutional life and rhetoric of the migrants, often when they were on the very threshold of acculturation and assimilation, moved from campanilism and regionalism toward a pan-Italian and Italian American sensibility. From a vantage point looking across three generations of Italian Americans, scholars could see the objective conditions in North America – geographical proximity to migrants from many parts of Italy, Italian "national" parishes, shared encounters with prejudice, competition against other ethnic groups for a "piece of the [political and economic] pie" and for reputation, the relentless assault on the migrant audience by the nationalist preachments of *prominenti*, consuls, and some clergy, ironically combined with a decline of real knowledge of Italy and a rise of nostalgia – that had conspired to encourage the development of a sort of Italian national consciousness among the immigrants. Drawing upon these North American realities, different historians have pointed out different causes for the decline of *campanilismo* and regionalism, and the growth of national feeling, a sense of shared ethnicity, to use the jargon of North American social science, among the immigrants and their Italian-American descendants.

Some saw bigotry and exploitation – or, if one emphasized the degree to which Italian Americans were petty capitalist *contadini* rather than permanent proletariat, of barriers to mobility – as playing a major role in forging an Italian identity among the migrants. For example, Vecoli ascribed the tendency of Italians on Minnesota's Iron Range "to remain within their group" as partly a matter of choice, but also as "a reaction to ostracism by the dominant Anglo-Scandinavian element." He added that "one consequence of this exclusion was that the Italians gradually came to recognize that their common identity as a nationality group was more important than regional differences, and that only through unity could they challenge the entrenched WASPs." Others saw the decline of particularism, ethnicization, and the rise of Italian-American national consciousness as a product of the rhetoric of World War I, and of the Fascist propaganda efforts to *italianizzare* the immigrants. Cinel characterized the mental journey that San Francisco's Italians made in a century thus: "They started out with *campanilismo* and ended with Americanization." With chapters entitled "Italian Regionalism in San Francisco," and "From Regionalism to Nationalism," Cinel left no doubt that he accepted a model of identity negotiation which began with paesanism, moved to regionalism, then to *Italianità*, and then to the Italian American ethnic group, or to fuller acculturation and assimilation.[5] Although few Italian-American scholars have shown sufficient distance to study the matter, yet it is clear that a renewed nationalism or ethnicism, with accompanying jeremiads about the consequences of the lack of ethnic cohesion, has also been nurtured by the "status anxiety" of the 1960s and 1970s which led some Italian Americans to embrace the "new ethnicity" in the face of WASP hegemony and Black mobilization.

In Canada, John Zucchi's work has illustrated the dynamics of paesanism and emergent nationalism among Italian immigrants before World War II, in more detail, and with more subtlety than has the American literature on the subject. According to him, the new realities that the earliest migrants to Toronto faced, such as the need to create a national parish and common business interests, to expand mutual aid insurance pools, to find suitable marriage partners from a given *paese*, and to share neighbourhood with migrants from many regions, all fostered a continuum in which loyalty to *paesani* was not xenophobic campanilism, but rather a necessary building block toward a sense of *Italianità*. Zucchi concluded that "loyalty to the hometown group therefore did not preclude loyalty to the larger Italian population of the city.... It was through the hometown that the immigrant began to identify with an Italian community in the city." Zucchi has gone on to demonstrate the "nationalizing" role played by various elites within the pre-Second World War Toronto Italian collectivity. Reinforcing the theme of ethnicization, i.e., that the migrants from the Italian peninsula became Italian, or were forged into an Italian ethnic group in North America, are thoughtful studies on parallel ethnic groups, such as F.M. Padilla's recent work on the development of a shared Latino consciousness among Mexicans and Puerto Ricans in Chicago.[6]

What is striking about all these accounts of prewar Italian immigrants in the United States and Canada, is how closely they resemble the "exceptionalist" myths of earlier American historiography that they claim to subvert. In the end, the Italian-American literature enriches the canon with ancillary texts and without changing its essence. Certainly the image of the "uprooted" peasant is modified by accounts of migration chains, paesanism, and sojourning mentalities. Certainly Handlin's Crèvecoeur-ean assertion that migrants crossed the sea looking to escape oppressive European ways, and landed on the shore anxious to become American, is modified by the ethnicization thesis and the idea that immigrants developed Italian national feeling even as they acculturated to North America. Such revelations are only exegesis to the canon's original texts which claim that immigrants arrived as "men of their village" and ended as Americans whether Anglo-conformists, products of the melting pot, or partisans of the "new ethnicity."[7] In all these texts, the American vector toward the future is confirmed; migrants come from an identity of origin and move – after a period of felt and ascribed hyphenated ethnonational identity – toward their American identity of destiny. That odyssey of sentiment is viewed as in lockstep with objective social reality, especially geographical and economic mobility, and acquisition, through experience or education, of the mainstream culture.[8]

The diachronic form the American canon takes leads to historicism. Put simply, since the story of immigration and ethnicity is seen exclusively as part of a national drama of becoming or failing to become the America of the dream, any synchronic sense that conditions and sentiments change in the homeland, that the natural patterns of immigrant pre-selection change, that the post-industrial world's sense of *paese* and *madrepatria* varies, that the political culture and social ideas and conditions of the homeland continuously intrude and shape immigrant identity, becomes irrelevant. It is true that some American studies have dealt with the impact of World War I patriotism, of Fascism, and of the war years on Italian-American identity, and one A. DeConde's *Half Bitter, Half Sweet* is, if not a synchronic study of Italy and Italian Americans, at least an effort to deal systematically with "double consciousness among immigrants from Italy in the United States." However, the idea of studying the immigrants and their American children as sharing a continuing history with their country of origin, and with those they define as part of their global diaspora living in other target countries, the idea of viewing political and cultural change in the old country as an integral part of immigrant history, of listening to the dialogue between immigrants and their homeland, would seem to contravene orthodoxy and lie outside the canon.

It would be a silly and visceral anti-Americanism to argue that the exporting of "exceptionalist" myths about immigration is the fault of the thoughtful scholars, who tried to create the most elegant models for explaining Italian-American immigrant history, only to be incorporated in those myths. Nonetheless those who study the Italian experience outside of the United States, especially the new and larger phenomenon of post World War II migration, need to comprehend how the mass migration of the turn of the century became mythopoeic in American thought.[9] It is a mistake, for example, for historians of postwar Canada, Australia, and even the United States to assume the applicability of the scriptural account of the prewar migrant's sentimental journey from particularism to Italian national feeling, and then to assume the assimilation and/or the "new ethnicity" which dominates the American canon. At least, we cannot do so without testing it against the contemporaneous reality.

In the same year, 1964, that the appearance of Vecoli's "Contadini in Chicago" signalled the beginning of rigorous study of the place of Italians in American immigration myths, I began teaching the history of Italy and of immigration at the University of Toronto. Since then, the American literature has informed much of my work and that of some of my students. The idea of immigration history as a vector of progress from localism through ethnonationalism to acculturation served admirably as a way of describing prewar Toronto Italians who were, after all, merely an outrigger of the flow of labour to capital that went on so massively in the United States. However, I have become increasingly uneasy about applying diachronic ideas with their emphasis on ethnicization fading into acculturation – and their untidy dependence on concepts like "ethnic rediscoverers," the "need for roots," and the "third generation return" to account for anomalous instances of renewed ethnicism – to postwar global migration, and to the Italian collectivity in greater Toronto specifically. Too many things have changed in the world for a model that fits the 1900s in the United States to explain the choices which immigrants make in Canada in the 1980s.

Before mentioning some of those changes and suggesting how they may affect interpretation of the immigrant's world, I wish to describe the nature and magnitude of the Toronto-Italian collectivity, one of the largest and most vibrant outside of Italy and one, unlike American Little Italies, dominated by immigrants rather than North American-born ethnics. (Indeed the very magnitude of Toronto Italia may skew my interpretation. Perhaps what I am about to describe could only happen in so large a collectivity.) About six out of every ten Canadians of Italian descent live in southern Ontario, four of ten live in Metropolitan Toronto. Between 1951 and 1981, the population of Toronto has doubled from a little over a million people to its current two and a half million. The source of that growth is revealed by the fact that in the 1981 census, 43% of the city's population was listed as foreign born and that, after immigrants from the United Kingdom, the largest group of newcomers were from Italy. While the city's population has doubled in those thirty years, the Italian descent group has grown almost tenfold, from under 30,000 to well over 300,000. The immigrants come from all regions of Italy with the largest contingents, probably in descending numbers, from Calabria, Abruzzi and Molise, Friuli and Treviso, Lazio, Puglia and Lucania. This new concentration of Italians, generally in one broad corridor of settlement throughout the west end of the city – with a second predominantly Sicilian and Foggian collectivity in the east end – has an *ambiente* and "ethnic institutional completeness," an immediacy of ties to both the Italian state and "high tradition," as well as to hundreds of sending *paesi*, unmatched anywhere in the world. According to the 1971 census, the Italians of Toronto were 54% immigrants and 28% the children of immigrants. Only 17% were the children of the Canadian-born. Over 50% of the migrants had come to Toronto in one great wave between 1951 and 1961. In 1971 only 6% of the group had both parents in North America. The Italian-born continue even now to outnumber the Canadian-born, especially among adults. It is significant though that some of the leadership is passing from the prewar *prominenti,* and those who came as young adult workers, to those who came as dependent children after World War II.[10]

No discussion of the magnitude of the Italian immigrant collectivity in greater Toronto can possibly impart a sense of its variety, and of the mercurial pace at which the psychology of ethnolinguistics, associational life, loyalties, culture, and identities move. Toronto, after all, has as many Italians as Florence, drawn from many more parts of the peninsula and freed, some might say confused, by the conditions of being migrant and of having exchanged the yoke of one hegemony for another. That should be kept in mind when one judges the influence of consuls speaking of a *colonia*, of National Congress of Italian Canadians (NCIC) officials who refer to the community, or of young Italian-Canadian politicians who invoke a bloc vote. To paraphrase D'Azeglio, Toronto Italia may exist "ma bisogna ancora fare gli italo-canadesi."

In fact, it seems to me that Toronto Italia defies the definitions imposed upon it by those seeking hegemony over it, in the same way that its present and its future cannot be contained within the simple model borrowed from prewar American experience. For me, looking at the history of Toronto Italia as an episode without predetermined vector, analyzing synchronically the sentiment, behaviour and political, and cultural choices made here as part of a *fenomeno coinvolto* that ties together immigrants in Toronto, returnees, and people left behind in the *paesi,* and migrants from those *paesi* in colonies around the world, is a necessary antidote to North American clichés about immigrant history and ethnic group life as well as to the tendency to accept as reality the definitions of community preferred by competing "agents of articulation" and contenders for hegemony over the immigrants. I am convinced that a more deeply textured narrative of the immigrant collectivity's history is possible. We need to learn from literary criticism, especially discourse theory and social anthropology, in particular the Geertzean idea that one can find a nexus of significance, and a cultural narrative through "thick description" of communal occasions in order to comprehend Italian-Canadian history in process. We need to be open to the possibility that 1) changes in the migrants themselves; 2) changes in Italian political culture; 3) the slow growth of a pluralist alternative to assimilation in the receiving countries; and 4) the revolution of transportation, communication, leisure and interlocked service economies in the Atlantic world, make it unlikely that postwar migrant settlement history will repeat that of the 1900s.[11]

Obviously I could spend much time delineating the nature of change in each of the categories mentioned above. The new migrants to Canada, unlike their Umbertine great grandparents who had rarely participated in the political process, are the products of first a unified, then a fascistized

Italy, and finally of the clientele systems or ideological patterns of mass democracy. A century-long migration tradition informed their choice of migration targets and defined their migration projects. Although many have come from the less developed regions of the country, the *paesi* they left behind were not isolated, but rather the vital labour supply periphery of a fully industrialized Europe, with all that implies in terms of their knowledge of job opportunities throughout the world and their levels of expectation. Return migration, annual seasonal return, return for specific ritual occasions, sending Canadian-born children on visits to Italy are, along with marriages and new household creation, a central pre-occupation in Toronto Italia. The reasons for this are many and inter-twined. They include the availability of low cost, rapid, and comfortable transportation; the comparative well-being of the *paesi* – itself a by-product of successful migration strategies – ; the social safety nets of the modern Italian state; the constant coming and going of migrants within the European labour market; decisions in the *paesi* to encourage mondialization (*apaeseamento*); and the neo-capitalist system's fostering of both tourism and periodic leisure time for workers.

If the migrant's sense of the consequences of the act of migration have changed, so, slowly has the receiving society's sense of who the migrants are. The existence of guestworker systems that discourage permanent settlement and assimilation, provide both Italian migrants and Canadian and Italian authorities with models of behaviour that under-mine the view that the prewar American experience will repeat itself here. Although most of the objective conditions which draw immigrants toward acculturation – or at least toward formation of a sense of self and group in keeping with their real condition – pertain in Canada, there are new conditions as well. The declared policy of multiculturalism, state support for heritage language teaching, the pandering of political parties to the ethnic groups as potential bloc voters, encourage a sense of ethni-city and group persistence. The multicultural policy, especially seems to imply penalties for any group of migrants who do not mobilize, form an *ethnie,* and show sufficient ethnoversion to impress the host society and the government with their political potential.[12] That is one reason why an observer can detect a tone of voice, a sense of competitive performance, among those who call for an active and coherent Italian-Canadian *ethnie,* very reminiscent of the Risorgimento intellectuals' embarrassed laments about the Italian peninsula's disunity, the low national consciousness of the people, and the national failure to be a great power in the mid-nineteenth century. If the Jewish and Japanese ethnic groups can build magnificent cultural centres or homes for their elderly, if Ukrainian Canadians can exercise so much political influence, why can't Italian Canadians? Or, shouldn't we?[13] So far, the forces favouring ethnicization, followed by acculturation, would seem to be dominant, especially when one adds to the formula the impact of an English-speaking host culture little inclined to make regional distinctions about Italians. Indeed, as Ontario becomes more multiracial, there have been occasions when representatives of visible minorities refer to all the white populace, including Italian Canadians, as Anglo-Saxons.

Among the most interesting juridical, political, and sentimental changes affecting the postwar Italian emigration is the emergence of regional government as a force in the lives of migrants overseas. When the 20 regional juntas, promised in the Republican Constitution of 1948, finally came into being in 1970, many might have agreed with the assessment that saw the creation of the regions as a cynical effort by the mass parties, denied power at the centre to build their clientelist systems on the periphery. A few analysts were acute enough, even then,[14] to see that while part of the populace would fret over another level of government as bringing "more taxes, more political officials, and more bureaucrats to harass the citizenry," others would understand the "concrete benefit to determinate individuals which more government can provide." Few could have predicted the special helix of mutual need that seems to be emerging between regional politicians and those from the region overseas, or how the combination of tourism and well-heeled *rientrati* may become for regions what remittances once were for *paese*.

Since the emergence of regional governments in Italy, immigrants overseas or in western Europe have been offered an alternative rally of loyalty and way of seeing themselves, to that of citizens of a unitary nation, or to the particularist view of themselves as *paesani*. The complex needs of politicians and intelligentsia in Italy to find status, employment and justification through regionalism, meshes nicely with the need of immigrants or their children to identify with an area and population less obscure than the hometown, and less impersonal than the nation state. Regional authorities find in the tourist and trade possibilities of increased ties with emigrants, a financial resource which should more than compensate for the decline of remittances which comes naturally with the maturing of a migration cohort overseas. In the nostalgia for "home" and search for "roots" which often signal the completion of the migration process, many immigrants are a natural audience for regionalist texts in the ethnic discourse. They can imagine themselves as fellow members of a regionalist community, and since all communities larger than a village must be based on imagination rather than face to face contact, such an imagined community, with the proper nurturing, can grow in relevance.

Although it tries to ally itself with, and use efforts at mondialization (*apaeseamento*) also underway in Italy and in the *colonie*, this new political regionalism is different from traditional forms of *paesano* loyalty as expressed in the idea of *campanilismo*. Political regionalism battens on the technological and psychological forces which make mondialization possible, especially the flow of people and news back and forth, and the proliferation of "little magazines" and newspapers among the *paesani*, but its agenda and its goals are not about the small towns of emigration.[15]

In the remainder of this discussion, I wish to look at three topics in order to comprehend the appeal of regionalism for some "agents of articulation" and a portion of their audience within the *ethnie*, and to encourage closer study of the daily conversation and discourse that goes on there. The three topics are: 1) the nature of the discourse within the *ethnie* – who are the speakers, what are the texts, and who are the readers of texts (as well as where, and what are the fora, within which the discourse takes place); 2) what is the special appeal of regionalism to emigrants from Italy in southern Ontario now; and 3) a case study of the forging – I use the word with the mischievous double meaning that Yeats intended when describing the rise of Sinn Fein in Ireland – of a region-alist "national identity," in this case among the so-called "Molisani" in Toronto.

To begin to hear the discourse and the daily discussion in the *ethnie*, we need to abandon definitions of ethnicity, or nationality based on descent rather than consent. Ethnicity is a North American process; it is a continual negotiation of identity within a context of the concentric circles of loyalty and patriotism toward family, friends, town, region, country of emigration, as well as nascent loyalties to new friends, neigh-bourhoods, cities, and country of immigration. Ethnocultural com-munities or *ethnies*, only to a certain extent, are the logical consequences of immigration, settlement, and diglossia. They emerge first as natural shelters from the violent forces of prejudice, exploitation, and accultu-ration that surround migrants and their children. Ethnic groups in the end, unlike immigrant collectivities, are made, not born; they are arti-fices, quasi-polities within which clergy, politicians, notables, middle class brokers and entrepreneurs, visiting old country intellectuals, consuls, and government officials from the sending countries, and organic intelligentsia of the Left and Right struggle to attain hegemony over the emergent ethnocommunity's discourse. The immigrant often lives in a whirl of conflicting or mutually unintelligible written, spoken, and semiotic texts which guide him in his choices of loyalty, identification with group, and intensity of ethnoversion. The existence of the ethnic group is, to paraphrase Renan, "a plebiscite of all the people, every day." The fluidity of ethnicity is reflected in the situational way in which people respond to the questions posed in a polyethnic society like Canada, questions such as "Who are you? Where are you from? What language do you speak?" Questions which, of course, deserve and receive different responses when they are posed in English, Italian, or dialect. It is this situationalism that gives ethnicity a historical life, and makes the borrowing of earlier historiographies problematic."[16]

The question posed in the title, "When is an Italian Canadian?," reflects the migrant's changing situational sense of primary membership, a sense described by labels such as Italian, Italian Canadian, Italo-Canadese, Calabrese, Consentino, Canabrese, and new Canadian. This variety of adjectives is the inheritance of the struggle within the discourse, the hierarchy of discourse in the city, the clutter, the misreading, and the slippage which characterize a group of people who possess so much freedom of choice, leisure, and access to mass com-munications; a group of people who, in the same month, may have to access their relationship to a fund-raising effort encouraged by the Italian embassy to build a museum in honour of Marconi, the quasi-regal visit of the president of the Abruzzi region to Toronto, the visit of the president of the Italian Republic – Prime Minister Mulroney of Canada breaking bread with both presidents, the *feste* of several hometown saints. The catalogue can seem endless and the ink, air time, sermons as well as the gossip in the little storefront *paese* clubs dedicated to such events, excessive. In fact, it seems unlikely that any regnant ideology could be imposed on the people who live in Toronto Italia. Until recently three regimes of truth, which I characterize as the colonial, the proletarian, and the "coming Canadian" have dominated the interpretation of who the immigrants are, or who they are supposed to think they are.

In the first view, the migrants are seen as Italians in danger of losing their *Italianità* in Canada – or as an embarrassment to the ethnonational intelligentsia because they have never been carriers of Italy's urban "great tradition." With variations, Italian officials posted to Toronto see the *colonia* that way, while those in the various party-based parts of the *patronato*, such as FILEF and ACLI, often describe immigrants as *lavoratori italiani emigrati all'estero*. In this view, there is little sense that immigration is permanent or that primary political loyalty might shift to Canada. There is also a tendency, reflected in the recent legislation on *comitati consolari* to see the collectivity as a *colonia* or community to be directed from Rome, and to view *paese*-based or regional clubs as quaint, or perhaps as a source of advisors, courtiers or, agents for combatting fractionalism, or lethargy and indifference in the collectivity.

Texts in the discourse have location as well as audience. As Toronto Italia moves northwestward, the consulate remains in the older downtown. In Toronto, as in Montreal, the Istituto per la cultura italiana is located near the premier university, not in the community. That is not mere accident, for as one official put it: "If I bring in a major Italian theatre company, for instance, it would be wrong to drag everyone to some building on the city's periphery." One can hear echoes of older Italian struggles between urban and rural culture in such remarks.[17] Clearly the texts about group identity and culture one would hear or read at the Istituto or the consulate, define the *ethnie* differently from those present on a given cultural or social evening at the Famee Furlane, or the community-run Villa Colombo rest home and Columbus Centre; and as Luciani has pointed out, not only the texts but the medium would be very different in the dozens of *paese* clubs and "soccer-supporter" cafe/billiard parlors where "one speaks only the dialect of the region with linguistic variations which characterized such and such a village." For an ethno-culture to exist, it has to be embedded in a coherent sub-society.[18] Toronto Italians can hardly be said to have such a basis.

Of course, the effort to make Italian national identity the primary loyalty of the immigrants receives powerful boosts from the same sorts of events and crisis which cause patriotic surges in the homeland. It is a truism that when nationalist texts can be grafted onto latent patriotism or *amour propre*, fractionalism declines. The response to slurs directed at the community, especially those that trade in the mafia mystique, and to moments like a World Cup soccer victory leave no doubt that the collectivity always has latent pan-Italian national feeling. Thus, community response to earthquakes in Italy transcends regionalism. At the time of the Friulan earthquakes in the mid 1970s, journalists in the community marvelled that "tutti gli italiani si sentono fratelli," and that they had moved "fuori di ogni barriera regionale."[19]

In the second view the immigrants are seen, not in ethnonational terms or as sojourning guestworkers, but in a Canadian socio-economic context. They are peasants turned labour migrants, faced with the difficulties of insertion into an industrial economy, victimized either by bigotry and capitalist exploitation or by their own diglossia, in need of political mobilization to protect themselves. That mobilization of course should, in this view, be under the aegis of a Canadian labourers' party such as the NDP. The problem for these speakers in the discouse is that while their texts had great relevance for the first generation of migrants, and for those who are the continuing victims of the migration process and Canadian industrialism, it seems to appeal less and less to that large segment of the immigrant cohort who came as labourers in the 1950s and 1960s, and who have participated successfully in the Ontario boom, and satisfied many of the very petty capitalist impulses which inspired their original decision to migrate. Another part of the organic intelligentsia competing for hegemony, and to impose their texts on the *ethnie*, is the clergy. Depending on their own background, length of time in the land or pastoral sense, priests in the collectivity adhere variously to the view of their parishioners as exploited labour migrants, *paesani* in need of the religious and local cultural *ambiente* of their towns of origin, or Italians who face the loss of their culture from the onslaught of secular media, a Protestant or religiously indifferent host, and an Irish Roman Catholic hierarchy.

Finally there is the view of the Italian immigrants which sees them as hesitant new Canadians, as people in search of economic improvement, opportunity for their children, and as people about to be swept into the Canadian mainstream by mobility and acculturation. The maintenance of aspects of a *via vecchia*, of *paese* clubs, of close-knit neighbourhoods, of the Italian language or of various dialects are, in this view, which is mainly held by Canadian "caretakers," barriers to full participation in Canadian life, or at best, ingredients for symbolic differentiation and folkloric celebration of heritage through which "multiculturals" – the lexical monstrosity often preferred now in public circles to the use of the word "ethnics" – contribute to the Canadian mosaic.

The truth is that, if ethnicity is processual and situational, a negotiation of every day, then all of these "regimes of truth" claiming to define the migrants have their moments of relevance or explanatory power. A fourth "regime of truth," which is how the migrants see themselves in relation to their act of migration and to the various speakers and texts competing to tell them who they are, emerges from an attempt at a more demotic intellectual history of the *ethnie*, that is intellectual history as the history of the immigrants and their children thinking. That fourth "regime of truth" has an increasingly regional idiom.[20] Michael Kenny's study of Spanish migrants abroad offers a view of the relationship between ethnonational texts and regionalism that usefully suggests the competition of speakers and hierarchies of discourses inherent in shaping an *ethnie*: "Regionalism is artificially preserved and indeed exaggerated abroad by a kind of mouth-to-mouth network of mutual aid and celebration of "little traditions." Over this transplanted regionalism, Kenny describes a superficially grafted "great tradition" and nationalism which, he believes, is "arbitrarily univeralized into ethnonational holidays and group causes."[21]

I believe the case can be made that such a grafting of the "great tradition" and nationalism – despite committees to celebrate Columbus Day, to put Caboto on a stamp, and to build a Marconi museum, and despite less symbolic efforts to manipulate migrants as potential voters in Italian or Canadian elections, or to emulate the more ethnoverted communities of refugees from eastern Europe in demanding group recognition and a "piece of the pie" in terms of appointive offices – generally fails in Toronto Italia. There is, in effect, the same lack of a true *azione sui contadini* that characterized the Risorgimento and made of it a *rivoluzione passiva* incapable of revolutionizing the sentiments of the mass of the people.

The absence of this central mobilization into an ethnic community bothers those who involve themselves in the discourse at the level of ethnonationalism. Thus, an influential newspaper editor, significantly one of the few educated Milanese in the migration, called as early as 1959 for a "piccolo parlamento di una grande communità" which could "give the Italian-Canadian community a center, a direction, a program."[22] In such a context, manifestations of regionalism are only tolerated if they can be translated into a confederal basis for ethnonationalism. At the first meeting of the Circolo Calabrese in 1956, the president called for the club to expand its activities "to the advantage of all Calabresi residents in Toronto." An influential businessman who played an intermediary role with the host society interrupted from the floor to endorse the work of the club and to suggest that: "it would be more desirable if all the activities of various regional clubs *confluiscono* into the activities of a bigger and all encompassing *circolo italiano*." Two decades later, the need to break through regionalism to develop an ethnonation was described in much the same way: "The community," wrote a journalist, "lives like an island, or perhaps an archipelago formed by many little islands: the Sicilians, the Calabresi, the Abruzzesi and Friuliani and so on...." He went on to observe that "*paese* or regional clubs are important and no one wants to diminish them but in the nature of things they do not help the community show a common face to outsiders...."[23]

"A common face to outsiders," the ethnonationalist's plea for solidarity at the expense of factionalism can seem harmless to some and has the ring of an unthinking parody of Italian nationalism from Crispi to World War II to others, but it has left room for the emergence of regionalism, no longer seen as crippling or irrelevant in the new world context. As a new "regime of truth," regionalism sees the immigrant squarely as a man of a region, nurtured by a regional government, an active member of a regionally-based club or federation in Canada, tied to a confederation of such clubs throughout the diaspora. Such a man may be Canadian in citizenship, replete with latent patriotism for Italy, but regionalist in his sense of fellow feeling, his networks of acquaintance, his culture, and his dialect (which may, in this view, be a mark not of ignorance of the *lingua dantesca,* but rather possession of a nascent national language). In some synchronic sense, such a man is not a migrant from Italy, not merely *un paesano,* but a part of Molise, or Calabria, or Friuli *nel mondo.* The idea of being primarily identified as from a region and the ideology of having to act on the existence of that idea are different stages in consciousness and mobilization.[24] Thus, being an emigrant from near Cosenza in Calabria can be variously read as being a Rendese, a Cosentino, a Calabrese, or an Italian. Increasingly the texts – written, oral and semiotic – that cause some of the migrant readers to describe themselves in regional terms grow in appeal.

In Toronto, one especially powerful, and in many ways misleading, semiotic text available to those from the regions created in 1970 is the success and coherence of the migrants from Friuli. (The group's experience is misleading because Friuli as a region has had autonomy since the 1940s, has an ancient sense of being a nation, and its migrants in Toronto have often had the advantage of having the right physical characteristics to please the sensibilities of a racialist north European host society.) With their separate hall (fogolar), distinct language,[25] economic success, relative endogamy, and their ability to be Friulian, Canadian and yet exercise group power within the Italian-Canadian entity, the *Friuliani* trigger what a leading analyst of modern European ethnonationalisms, Walker Connor, labels "the demonstration effect" among submerged peoples.[26] "If they can persist or assert themselves as a people, we can and should too."

To understand how regionalism may be affecting the ethnicization of Italian Canadians and subverting some of the texts of Italian officials and the nationalist intelligentsia on the one hand, and of the *paese* associations on the other; we need to look more closely at how an ethnic group is made, what lies beyond the adjective *Italian* in the Canadian census, and the assertions of the leadership that a mobilized ethnic group or ethnocommunity, as opposed to a simple collectivity of migrants, exists. I suspect that regionalism among the immigrants works like a virus or "worm" lurking in a computer program, either flaring up to dominate the discourse or slowly changing the agenda. It does this by subtly altering the texts of true *campanilismo*, and intruding into the various fora (clubs, *circoli*, weddings, picnics, etc.) where *paesani* gather. At the same time, it insinuates itself through the party structure of the *patronato* and through regionalist participation in the official and semi-offical *giro di propaganda*, into the Italian government's work with the *lavoratori emigrati all'estero e i figli*. The number of regional delegations, politicians, and entities paying visits to Toronto in the last three years seems to grow exponentially. In the last year or so, I have attended, or have been invited to attend Abruzzese, Molisan, Friulan, Calabrian, Sicilian, Trentine, and Puglian affairs where the machinery of the regional government was apparent. In a city that lacks large numbers of immigrants from urban northern and central Italy, the numerically strong contingent from the Abruzzi have often appeared to represent mainstream *Italianità*. That perhaps obscures the fact that for many years the regional government of the Abruzzi has been the most active in Toronto.

"Agents of articulation" for the regional governments are busy creating what the historian, David Potter has called the "two psychological bases" of nationalism: "the feeling of common culture and the feeling of common interest."[27] One sees the changing emphasis in the discourse everywhere. It can be a telephone call from a speechwriter, unwilling to identify himself, in search of a line from a regional poet suitable for a Canadian politician or the president of a regional club, to quote in a banquet speech. The proliferation of new publications such as *Il Laghetto dei serresi nel mondo* or *Guzzura: Mensile d'informazione dei Santonofresi nel Mondo*, and the even more significant efforts to "regionalize" such *paese*-based discourse with new magazines such as *Dimensioni Calabro-Canadesi, Cisiliute* and *Molise*. Other magazines or newspapers such as *Cisiliute, L'Eco d'Abruzzo*, and *Giornale di Sicilia* play some of the same roles for Friulians, Abruzzese, and Sicilians respectively. All such publications encourage a view of the region as a shared homeland, an "imagined community."[28] Along with efforts to suggest that the *paesi* should be allied in regional efforts, such publications introduce the extension of some of the values of comradery felt about *paesani* toward *comprovinciali*, as well as toward those from one's own region. In this, of course, they reinforce some of the North American realities of proximity, smaller numbers, mobility, and recycled regional barriers of bigotry that had already begun to conflate family into *quasi-parenti*, into *paesani*, into fellow Calabresi, Molisani, and occasionally into *Italiani* as well.

Content analysis of texts such as those in the magazines and newspapers mentioned above would show that they also contribute to the other base of nationalism that Potter refers to, that is community of interest. Advertisements in such publications give a sense of the range and power of the regional descent group in Canada; imply the advantages of business networks and patron/client relations based on regional fellow-feeling, and the fact that people from the same region "understand each other and speak the same language," and show that successful immigrants are unembarrassed by their regional ties. In fact, dialect-speaking can move from a reason for exclusion from the "high tradition" to a diacritical mark allowing membership in the new and more comfortable world of the region. Recreation, accessible culture, *intermediarismo*, work opportunities, and clientelism can go on within an *ambiente* more familiar to most immigrants than that offered by Canada or by those representing official Italy and its culture. Not just *anomie* and a growing sense of alienation from the more massive and impersonal world of the state or the ethnonation, but also a species of resentment, of the periphery getting even with the core, is at work. Certainly it is not surprising that some migrants who feel they have been told repeatedly that they speak a crude dialect, and that they come from the margins of Italy's urban cultural mainstream, can enjoy being described as the heirs of *Magna Graecia,* or as speaking Italian with Sannitic influences rather than with the dialect of Campobasso. Such filiopieties are no truer and no more ignoble than the texts of the speakers of the "high tradition" who imply that the individual talents of Dante, Galileo, or Columbus are national traits, or of the Italian-Canadian speakers who see in Marconi or Caboto a more illustrious ancestor than their immediate ones.[29]

I would like to conclude with a foray into social anthropology about emergent Molisan regionalism in Canada. (I think one could do this for Calabria or Friuli as easily, but I find the Molisan case more charming and whimsical.) To help "defamiliarize" the texts and cultural artifacts further, I will describe the phenomenon as the rise of Molisan national feeling, or nationalism. Although I suspect that Azoreans, Basques, Bretons, Croats, Frisians, Friulians, Ladinos, Macedonians, Scots, Slovaks, Welsh – maybe even Genovese – will all have nation states of their own before *Molisani* do. I see no way to predict that such a thing could never happen. As Ernest Gellner puts its, too cynically to be sure, "Nationalism is not the awakening of nations to self-consciousness: it invents nations where they do not exist." An historian has to believe it possible that the modern unity of the Italian peninsula may prove episodic, that the unitary state is merely a long Mazzinian or Savoyard detour from Cattanean or neo-Guelf ideas.[30] Perhaps we should even take heed of the Jamaican dub poet who defines the national language as the dialect the army and bureaucracy speak. And if one insists that *Molisani* are not potentially another people but merely variant Italians, Walker Conner points out:

> one of the oddities of our period (in large part a response to the quality and quantity of communications networks) is that as the cultures of various groups are becoming more resemblant of one another, the saliency of feelings of ethnic distinction is also growing. What would seem to be involved here, then, is not the degree of cultural similarity. It is psychological and not cultural assimilation with which we are dealing ....[31]

The two cultural artifacts that I will draw on are a Molisan-Canadian banquet that took place in Toronto last year, and the international symposium on Molise that took place at Campobasso last summer. I also wish to discuss two texts, one is the new newspaper, *Molise*, the periodical of the Associazione Molisani Canadesi, and the other is the two-volume cookbook, *La Cucina Molisana* which appeared in 1986. Clifford Geertz defines a cultural artifact – "whether suttee among Balinese or baseball in America as analogous to a dream or a Freudian slip.... If properly addressed, it will tell an important story about the collective mental life of the people among whom it is found."[32] Banquets staged for one pretext or another are pervasive among migrants from Italy abroad; they are just such a cultural artifact.

I am not clear about the relationships that exist between the tentatives of the Molisan regional government and the efforts of some migrants from the Molise in Toronto to raise regionalist consciousness through the creation of a Federazione Associazioni Molisani Canadesi. It is one of those subjects that requires more synchronic study, or perhaps like all nationalist movements, its origins are shrouded in mystery. In 1986 the announcement of the creation of ARMA (Associazione Regionale Molisani d'America) appeared in Italian North American newspapers.[33] The bellicose sounding association was created, according to the newspaper, to "break the grip of the enemy that has kept us silent for centuries: *accidia*, the natural ally of isolation and solitude." The newspaper added that ARMA would be a constituent part of l'Associazione Molisani nel Mondo. Such a cultural entity, the reader was told, existed for nearly all the other regions of Italy.

It is impossible to know the exact number of migrants from Molise who have entered Canada since World War II, especially since they were statistically lumped with those coming from the Abruzzi. The figure is probably close to 25,000. It would be even more difficult to determine how many of that number saw themselves primarily as *Molisani* rather than as first men and women of their *paese* or province such as Casacalenda or Campobassan, or even Abruzzese or Italian. If "words provide clues to attitudinal states," then the infrequent use, indeed absence, of the substantive noun *Molisani* in any Toronto Italian publication until the 1960s should suggest that there was no primary loyalty to region among the immigrants, or at least remind us of Apter's point mentioned earlier that being from a place and feeling the need to act on that fact of birth ideologically are two different things, a point akin to the usual sequence preferred in nationalism studies: that people progress from nationality to national feeling to nationalism.[34]

What is common to the regionalist banquets and the International Symposium on Molise in the summer of 1987 is an effort, either conscious or unconscious, to assert the existence of a people called the *Molisani*, who have common traits, common past, and common destiny. The symposium was intended to be, and I am sure it was, scholarly. (So, of course, were the many congresses of Italian scientists held throughout the 1840s that preached Italian nationalism under the very noses of the Habsburg overlords.) The blurb for the symposium calls for scholarship, but a normative and filiopietist note does creep in, "Both the successes and failures of the emigrants will be noted: needless to say, attention will center on some *Molisani* and their progeny who did enormously well as measured by any standard, and who achieved fame and recognition."[35] Moreover, the symposium is clearly seen as a vehicle for helping *Molisani* in the world see themselves as *Molisani*, learn about their fellow-regionalists in other migration target cities, and recognize the commitment of the region, or regional government, to drawing them into its own species of mondialization, "Consequently the ties between Molise and America are like the bonds that a mother feels for her children who have gone off into the world and have not been heard from for a long time." The migrants and their children are to be transformed from *paesani* dispersed in search of work opportunities to *Molisani* in diaspora, with all that term implies for shared destiny and eventual reunion. Thus, while a number of sessions in the symposium are entitled *Molisani* this and that, or in such and such a city, only one has the name of a *paese* in the title. At the same conference, the designated *vate*, or Molisan national poet/prophet, in this case the novelist Giosue Rimanelli, significantly teaching "in exile" in America, played a central role in the program.

The banquets of the *Molisani* in Canada provide more semiotic texts than written ones. A popular priest from the region says grace and is seen to bless the regional tentative. Caterer and hall are managed or owned by a *Molisani*, giving special meaning to Potter's idea of common interest as one of the bases of nationalism. The presence of displays of Molisan food, industrial and folk art products such as Colavita oil and La Molisana pasta suggest a commerce of regionalism. At least one *piatto* in the catered meal is duly described as a Molisan food specialty and a sign of regional/national genius. The presence of politicians from the Regional junta, leaders of clubs made up of *paesani* from the many Molisan towns of emigration to Toronto, and of mayors of various *paesi* on the *giro di propaganda* of town mondialization promise that things will get worse after the meal. They will be introduced at length and will speak, usually at great length, about the ties that bind and that survive the Atlantic crossing. What Eric Hobsbawm calls the "invention of tradition" is in the air. Whatever form it takes, one can be sure that it will begin with antiquity, with a time when the Sannitic tribes were the cultural or political equals of Rome. It will include reference to recently discovered traces of a past greatness. (Unfortunately the *Molisani* have not yet found or invented anything to match what the *bronzini* of Riace do for Calabrian national price.) If the official speeches are in Italian, almost all other conversations go on in dialect or English. One feels a certain tension between the *paese* leaders and the regional politicians and speakers. The officers of each *paese* club are introduced; young people in the distinctive costume of various provinces or towns are paraded through the room to rounds of applause. For the regionalist agenda to work well, the various *paesi*, especially those with large contingents must be portrayed as *tessere* within the regional mosaic, part of the glory of Molise. There is no question that those who attend the banquet leave with a heightened sense of being *Molisani* together.

For an awakening nation, no text is innocent. A good example of that is the two-volume cookbook, *La Cucina Molisana,* published at just about the time ARMA was formed. Beyond setting the boundaries of the "imagined community" through the compilation of a large number of recipes defining a distinctly Molisan cuisine, the cookbook is overtly "nation-building." "The identity and existence of Molise," write the cookbook's authors, "has been left in question because of the long isolation and the relative recency of regional autonomy." The authors conclude that, not just isolation and economic backwardness, but "the fragile and intermittent nature of cultural discourse, the not always adequate promotional efforts of public institutions, have left in the shadows for a long time, relevant moments in regional history that would have been able to sustain attention and respect for the name Molise."[36] In one such sentence from the cookbook, we have seen perfectly parodied Fanon's statement that "while politicians situate their actions in daily life, men of culture take their stand in history," as well as an affirmation of the old Mazzinian adage that revolution can only follow insurrection, that is that only after the mechanisms of the state are in the hands of nationalists can the people be educated to their national identity.

The nation-building role, intended and incidental, of the new Federazione Associazioni Molisani Canadesi publication, *Molise*, is even more manifold.[37] The advertisements of businessmen and professionals of Molisan descent, lists of Molisan *paese* clubs and all their officers, lists of candidates of Molisan descent (*candidati molisani*) for Canadian public office, lists of the members of the regional government and mayors of towns in Molise dominate the pages of the paper. The lead headline in boldface reads "Convegno communità molisana in Canada e Molise." That same *communità molisana* is described in an advertisement as *numerosa e laboriosa*. There is as well a two page socio-economic profile of Molise containing a large map of the region/nation. A list of titles of books held in the new Federazione's library also suggests that malleability of history and how the new regionalist texts have proliferated. The books include a multi-volume set of *Il Molise dalle origini ai nostri giorni* and other books on the region's history. (Of course there is no way of knowing from the newspaper list whether the library is talismanic or a true resource.)

The attempt to equate regionalism with nationalism may seem far-fetched, but it should at least reinforce the notion that ethnicity and nationality are a negotiation, a response by readers to texts, an artifice by speakers and leaders seeking to impose their own view of the world as a hegemonic idea on others. Regionalism – admittedly most often in the context of the continuum from family and town to the Italian nation – seems to be taking increasing hold over Toronto's immigrants from the Italian peninsula. Recently Roberto Perin has raised questions about the nature of old world cultural persistence among immigrants, a central and vague tenet in Canadian multiculturalism, questions that show he understands that ethnicity is process not inheritance, and that the tension that exists between speakers for the "high tradition" and, those who carry for the culture of Italy's small towns is a form of hegemonic struggle between factions of intelligentsia.[38] "What is to be retained," he asks, "the culture of the metropolis or that of the immigrants?" The politics of regionalism suggests the question need not be put so badly. The strategies of regional government, the inadequate or half-hearted efforts at an *azione sui contadini* by the officials of the central government and the organic intelligentsia of the "high tradition," and the psychological needs of *paesani* in transition to the Canadian middle classes, may combine to make his question moot. Regional man will create, or retain, a space between the cultural dictates of the core, and the fractured, and the folkloric "little tradition" of the *paese*/periphery. In a poem about Calabria, Pasolini, himself a man of the periphery who felt himself culturally oppressed by the core, saw the matter apocalyptically, "They will obliterate Rome/ and upon its ruins/they will sow the seed / of ancient history."

Notes

1. Letter of Bartolomeo Vanzetti to Mrs. Russell (18 September 1926), in M.D. Frankfurter and G. Jackson, eds., *The Letters of Sacco and Vanzetti* (New York, 1956).

2. A. Rossi, "Per la tutela degli Italiani negli Stati Uniti" in *Bollettino dell'Emigrazione*, no. 16 (Rome, 1904), pp. 20-21.

3. M.L. Hansen, *The Atlantic Migration* (New York, 1961); O. Handlin, *The Uprooted* (New York, 1951); and a good attempt to describe the development of the canon is M. Passi, and *Mandarins and Immigrants: The Irony of Ethnic Studies in America Since Turner* (Ann Arbor, Mich., 1972). For the logic of its origins, see E. Saveth, *American Historians and European Immigrants, 1875-1925* (New York, 1948). The Italian-American responses and additions include R. Vecoli, "Contadini in Chicago: A Critique of the Uprooted," in *Journal of American History,* XII (1964); H. Nelli, *The Italians in Chicago, 1880-1930: A Study in Ethnic Mobility* (New York, 1970); J. Briggs, *An Italian Passage* (Yale, 1978); and D. Cinel, *From Italy to San Francisco: The Immigrant Experience* (Stanford, 1982). Some newer studies that have a more sophisticated approach to the migrant vector and suggest the canon may be changing are Wm. O. Douglass, *Emigration in a South Italian Town: An Anthropological History* (Rutgers, 1984); D. Gabaccia, *From Sicily to Elizabeth St. Housing and Social Change Among Italian Immigrants, 1880-1930* (Albany, New York, 1984); and G. Mormino and G. Pozzetta, *The Immigrant World of Ybor City: Italians and Their Latin Neighbors in Tampa, 1885-1985* (Illinois, 1987).

4. C. Panunzio, *The Soul of the Immigrant* (New York, 1921), pp. 78-79; and A. Bernardy, *America Vissuta* (Rome, 1912), p. 323.

5. R. Vecoli, "Italians on Minnesota's Iron Range," in R. Vecoli, ed., *Italian Immigration in Rural and Small Town America* (1987), p. 186; and R.F. Harney, "Toronto's Little Italy, 1885-1945," in R.F. Harney and J.V. Scarpaci, eds., *Little Italies in North America* (Toronto, 1981), pp. 52-58.

6. J. Zucchi, "Italian Hometown Settlements and the Development of an Italian Community in Toronto, 1875-1935," in R.F. Harney, ed., *Gathering Place: Peoples and Neighbourhoods of Toronto, 1834-1945* (Toronto, 1985), p. 140. See also J. Zucchi, *Italians in Toronto: The Development of a National Identity* (Montreal, Kingston, 1988); and F.M. Padilla, *Latino Ethnic Consciousness: The Case of Mexican Americans and Puerto Ricans in Chicago* (Notre-Dame, 1985).

7. For example, Handlin's chapter 7, "In Fellow Feeling," from *The Uprooted*, actually predicts almost everything that is contained in the newer ethnicization and overcoming of parochialism thesis, but perhaps treats the subject too much as an episodic breathing space rather than a processual stage that can be prolonged indefinitely by circumstances.

8. This is not the place to analyze the literature of the "new ethnicity" in the United States. In general, however, lamenting the deprivation of culture of origin as the price of acculturation, leads only to a normative rather than a factual questioning of the validity of the vector that is central to the canon.

9. Only a very few volumes by American historians try to combine into a single narrative and analysis, the history of prewar and postwar, of white and non-white immigration. See. D. Reimers, *Still The Golden Door: the Third World Comes to America* (New York, 1985); and T. Archdeacon, *Becoming American: an Ethnic History* (New York, London, 1983).

10. C. Jansen and L. LaCavera. *Fact Book on Italian Canadians* (Toronto, 1981).

11. C. Geertz, "Thick Description: Toward an Interpretive Theory of Culture," in *The Interpretation of Culture: Selected Essays* (New York, 1973).

12. R.F. Harney, "'So Great A Heritage As Ours' Immigration and the Survival of the Canadian Polity," in *Daedalus,* CXVII, 4 (Cambridge, MA, 1988), pp. 63-87.

13. An early indication of the impact of competition on *ethnie*-formation can be found in O. Bressan, *Non Dateci Lenticchie: Esperienze, Commenti, Prospettive di Vita Italo-Canadese* (Toronto, 1958), who urges his fellow migrants to emulate the Chinese and Jews of Toronto in building an ethnocommunity.

14. The reality is more complex. Five special border regions had received autonomy at the time the Republican constitution was promulgated in 1948. The remaining 15 (Abruzzi and Molise were made separate entities in 1963) held their first regional elections in 1970. See N. Kogan, "Impact of the New Italian Regional Governments on the Structure of Power within the Parties," in *Comparative Politics,* IV (Chicago, 1975), pp. 393-94; and P. Allum and G. Amyot, "Regionalism in Italy: Old Wine in New Bottles," in *Parliamentary Affairs* XXIV, 1 (London, 1970), pp. 53-78.

15. A good description of the continuum of loyalty from the local to the provincial to the regional, and how the terms of that continuum can be manipulated through vague usages such as *terra natale,* can be found in R. Berdahl, "New Thoughts on German Nationalism," in the *American Historical Review,* no. 77 (Washington, D.C., 1972), pp. 65-80.

16. It is for this reason that I have borrowed the title of this essay from an anthropological study of minorities in the Balkans, M. Schein, "When Is an Ethnic Group: Ecology and Class Structure in Northern Greece," in *Ethnology,* XIV, 1 (Pittsburgh, 1975), p. 83 in particular.

17. U. Kareda, "The Not So Dolce Vita of Francesca Valente," in *Toronto Life,* V (Toronto, 1987), p. 10.

18. G. Luciani, "Les Immigrants d'origine italienne au Canada anglophone," in *Annales de l'Université de Savoie* (1983), p. 73.

19. An editorial by S. Tagliavini in *Corriere Canadese* 11-12 May 1976, p. 1. The recriminations and accusations of fraud, inefficiency, and egomania that

seem invariably to follow these Italian-Canadian efforts should be analyzed. Certain "hidden injuries of class" among men who started as humble labour migrants together, and different success rates, as well as revived regional hostilities, seem to inspire such post-mortems.

20. See L. Levine, *Black Culture and Black Consciousness: Afro-American Folkthought from Slavery to Freedom* (New York, 1977), p. iv.

21. M. Kenny, "Which Spain? The Conservation of Regionalism among Spanish Emigrants and Exiles," in *Iberian Studies,* XXII (Newcastle, 1976), p. 47.

22. See editorial by A. Scotti in *Corriere Canadese,* 14 November 1984.

23. On the Circolo Calabrese, see *Corriere Canadese,* 26 October 1956, p. 14; and for the journalist's remarks, see *Corriere Canadese,* 11 May 1979, editorial entitled, "Columbus Centre: un voto per il futuro della communità".

24. D. Apter, *The Politics of Modernization* (Chicago, 1965), p. 314.

25. A few years ago there was a serious debate in *Cisiliute* among the Zovins Furlans (Friulian youth) as to whether the Italian hegemonic language would wither away among them in the New World to be replaced by English and French as well as their own Friulian language.

26. W. Connor, "Ethnonationalism in the First World: The Present in Historical Perspective," in M. Esman, ed., *Ethnic Conflict in the Western World* (Cornell, 1977), pp. 22-23.

27. D. Potter, "The Historians' Use of Nationalism and Vice-Versa," in *American Historical Review,* no. 67 (New York, 1961-62), p. 937.

28. B. Anderson, *Imagined Community: Reflections on the Origin and Spread of Nationalism* (London, 1983).

29. For more on this phenomenon, see D. Rodnick, "Group Frustration in Connecticut," in *American Journal of Sociology,* XLVII, 2 (Chicago, 1941), pp. 159-60.

30. G. Carbone, "The Long Detour: Italy's Search for Unity," in F. Cox et al. eds., *Studies in Modern European History in Honor of F.C. Palm* (New York, 1956), pp. 49-80.

31. Connor, "Ethnonationalism in the First World," p. 29.

32. See P. Robinson's review of C. Geertz, *Local Knowledge: Further Essays in Interpretive Anthropology* (New York, 1983) in the *New York Times Book Review,* 25 September (New York, 1983), p. 11.

33. "Angolo del Molise," in *La Gazzetta del Niagara e di Hamilton,* no 3, 3-4 (Hamilton, 1986), p. 31.

34. C. Hayes, *Nationalism: A Religion* (New York, 1960).

35. For an attempt to do a content-analysis study of the adjectives that accompany a given ethnic or regional identity such as *Molisano,* see D. Knobel, *Paddy and the Republic: Ethnicity and Nationality in Antebellum*

America (Wesleyan, 1986). For the ways in which regionalism resembles or becomes ethnicity, see J.S. Reed, *One South: An Ethnic Approach to Regional Culture* (Baton Rouge, 1982).

36. A.M. Lombardi and R. Mastropaolo, *La Cucina Molisana*, two volumes (Campobasso, 1986), pp. 11-16.

37. *Molise: Periodico a cura della Federazione Associazioni Molisani Canadesi,* I: 1 (1986).

38. R. Perin, "The Immigrant: Actor or Outcast," introduction to R. Perin and F. Sturino, eds., *Arrangiarsi* (Montreal, 1989). If there are choices to be made in "making a future from our past" as the Ontario government's Heritage Branch puts it, the role of speakers in the discourse, or organic intelligentsia, will be crucial. No studies such as W. Beer's excellent analysis of Basques and Bretons entitled, "The Social Class of Ethnic Activists in Contemporary France," in Esman, ed., *Ethnic Conflict*; or even J. Higham, ed., *Ethnic Leadership in America* (Baltimore, 1978) have been done about Italian Canadians.

"SO GREAT A HERITAGE AS OURS"
IMMIGRATION AND THE SURVIVAL
OF THE CANADIAN POLITY*

---

*I*N 1947 PRIME MINISTER MACKENZIE KING CALLED FOR A REVIVAL OF THE MASS immigration to Canada that had been curtailed during the depression and World War II. "The objective of Canada's immigration policy", he wrote, "must be to enlarge the population of the country. It would be dangerous for a small population to attempt to hold so great a heritage as ours."[1]

At the time of Mackenzie King's pronouncement, 50 percent of Canada's 12 million people claimed descent from the British Isles and 30 percent from France. Seen regionally, the homogeneity of the population was even more striking. In Ontario, the most populous province, three out of four residents could trace their origins to the United Kingdom or Ireland. In Toronto 80 percent were of British descent. At the same time, 90 percent of the country's Francophones were in Quebec and the adjoining French corridors of northern Ontario and northern New Brunswick.

The policy that Mackenzie King initiated has changed the face of Canada. In the four decades since the end of World War II, the country's population has more than doubled. Over 5.5 million of Canada's 26 million people are immigrants. They and their children have settled heavily in Canada's largest cities. Since the war, many of the immigrants have been non-British and non-French, and since the late 1960s, non-European. They represent not only an expanding urban work force but also an enormous and highly visible increase in the country's cultural diversity. Today the effects of forty years of mass immigration, tensions between Francophones and Anglophones, the unresolved issue of the rights of the indigenous people, the disruptive pseudoethnogenesis lurking in the regionalism of the West and the Maritimes, and the

---

* This article reprinted with permission from *Daedalus*, issue entitled, "In Search of Canada," vol. 117, no. 4, 1988.

traditional fear of absorption by the United States interact to make survival of the Canadian polity a recurring theme in public discourse.

Conversations about Canadian politics, society and culture, if not saccharine accounts of the joys of multiculturalism, are full of complaint about the divisive nature of certain policies; they seem to begin and end as a "lament for a slain chieftain", the postcolonial dream of a unified, perhaps dualist, Canadian nation felled by the intrigue or ambitions of warring clans – the "French", the "ethnics", the "westerners", the "Anglo-Celts". Of course, maintaining a viable political state and achieving a successful (i.e., integrative) nationalism as an ideology and an identity for those who live within that state are two different issues, but they rarely appear so in Canada. Questions about cultural diversity, population, and government policy combine as a single national obsession, a state of affairs that can be characterized as a polity in search of a nation.

"In a state of affairs", writes the philosopher Wittgenstein, "objects fit into one another like the links of a chain. In a state of affairs objects stand in a determinate relationship to one another." Both Canada's "state of affairs" and the debates born of differing perceptions of it are best understood against the backdrop of complex, unexpected ways in which the aspirations of the Francophones, the effects of mass immigration, and the imperatives of the Anglophone hegemony have since World War II interplayed with the drive to ensure the state's survival.

Immigration policy has always reflected a dialectic between the desired population increase and the impact of immigration on Canadian ways or on the racial and ethnocultural composition of the country. In the 1890s, when the energetic minister of the interior of the day, Clifford Sifton, initiated a policy of peopling "Canada's empty prairies" through an aggressive recruitment of settlers and the importation of migrant labor to build the railroad and industrial infrastructure, preference was shown for British and American settlers or for other "good" (i.e., northwest European) stock. The realities of the British and Scottish economy and of anti-immigrant recruitment laws in Germany meant that Sifton had to find his largest bloc of settlers not in the United Kingdom or Nordic Europe, but in the Slavs of the Austro-Hungarian Empire. With remarkable resilience, the minister came to see the "stalwart [Slavic] peasant in a sheepskin coat, born on the soil, whose forefathers have been farmers for ten generations, with a stout wife and a half-dozen children" as "good quality" for the task of defending the prairie from American incursion.[2]

Five purposes of Canadian immigration policy, appearing under changing flags of convenience and employing different idioms, have remained relatively constant over the century from the 1890s to the present. Canada has needed immigrants to:

1. Occupy the country in sufficient numbers to discourage the expansionary tendencies of the American colossus.
2. Protect the Pacific Rim from heavy Asian immigration.
3. Create economies of scale and a rational East-West axis for an independent polity and a viable economy.
4. Maintain a British hegemony by combating separatism, whether in its Prairie Métis and Indian form of the last century or in its Quebecian form in this one, and to counter the *revanche des berceaux* of the *Canadiens* against the British conquest.
5. Foster the image of Canada as a new place of opportunity, a country of potential greatness, and "a land of second chance", characterized by the fairness of British institutions and now by the civility of state-sponsored democratic pluralism in the form of official multiculturalism.

The idea of using immigrants as part of a strategy to ensure the state's survival and to create a nation from former French and British colonies has two corollaries – first, a preoccupation with the country's "absorptive power", and second, a sense that the migration phenomenon exists to serve the host country, not the migrants, and that not only the flow of immigration but its sources and character are matters that Canadian authorities can and should manipulate. In 1909 J.S. Woodsworth warned his countrymen that all Canada's other problems "dwindle into insignificance before the one great commanding, overwhelming problem of immigration." Woodsworth, a well-known evangelist and later one of the founders of the Co-operative Commonwealth Federation (the forerunner of the New Democratic Party), went on to state, under the heading "Racial Effects", that the mass migration Sifton had encouraged would have its impact on Canadians: "Canada will not remain Canadian", he wrote.[3]

Mackenzie King's views on what peoples might best serve Canada's need to expand its populace, without causing a "fundamental alteration in the character" of the country, remained remarkably consistent over his long and influential career. Barely a decade after Sifton had encouraged mass migration from the Continent, King, as a deputy minister of labor, advocated keeping out those "belonging to nationalities unlikely to assimilate and who consequently prevent the building up of a united nation of people of similar customs and ideals." His preferred list included American, British, French, Belgian, Dutch, Swiss, German, Scandinavian and Icelandic settlers.[4] If the argument was not always made overtly from racialist premises about north European stock having more proclivity to orderly society and free parliamentary institutions, such premises, along with those about the compatibility of Northwest Europeans – in terms of complexion, mores and religion – lay behind the assumption that migrants from the countries King mentioned were the most easily assimilated.

Another prime minister, R. B. Bennett, expressed this way of thinking succinctly in the 1930s: "The people [Continental Europeans] have made excellent settlers…but it cannot be that we must draw upon them to shape our civilization. We must still maintain that measure of British civilization which enables us to assimilate these people to British institutions rather than assimilate our civilization to theirs…."[5]

King himself observed in his May 1947 statement that, "it is of the utmost importance to relate immigration to absorptive capacity" and added his well-known line that "the people of Canada do not wish to make a fundamental alteration in the character of their population through mass immigration."

Within five years of King's statement, an article in *Maclean's*, one of Canada's most influential magazines, suggested that something was awry with the new mass immigration. In an article entitled "What Kind of Canadians Are We Getting?" the alarm was sounded: "The British share of immigration to Canada has been drying up. Until 1924 it was 62 per cent. By 1948 it was down to 38 per cent. Now it's 17 per cent. Meanwhile the proportion of immigrants from continental Europe has climbed from an inconsequential 20 per cent to more than 75 per cent." A former commissioner of immigration for the Canadian Pacific Railway was quoted as saying that a "slow but certain change in the racial composition of the Canadian people is inevitable unless the trend is arrested."[6] The process begun by King ran afoul of the old dialectic.

Over time, the use of language has become more circumspect. "Founding nations" replaces "founding races" as a label for the French and British. Immigrants are categorized by their assimilability or place within a multicultural mosaic rather than in terms of their "stock". Interethnic and interracial antagonism are given the pseudodistance of social science. Immigrants of certain groups are not undesirable because of their distance from the racial and cultural core but because of the impact they may have on those already in Canada, those "somewhat nervous about rapid ethnic change." As the report of the Canadian Immigration and Population Study had it in 1975, people were "concerned about the consequences for national identity that might follow significant change in the ethnic composition of the population."[7]

By the 1980s, Canada was caught between a potential for zero population growth early in the next century and the prospect of continuing policies that seemed to promise a "fundamental alteration" of her populace, her cultural ways and her public ethos and justification of nationhood. The central objective of Canada's immigration policy had always been the growth of Canada through the importation of foreign labor and talent. The policy's secondary purposes had to do with the disposition of the displaced and the allied after World War II, and with the imperatives of the Cold War and then of good citizenship in the United States and the Commonwealth, especially concerning refugees and the struggle for human rights and against racism. In effect, Canada's current search for a principle of collective national identity can be traced to the impact of the postwar decision to grow through immigration, and the ways that an immigration policy escapes the state's control to become an instrument of migration strategies. Canada's state of affairs today derives from what John Stuart Mill once described to Henry George as:

> two of the most difficult and embarrassing questions of political morality – the extent and limits of the rights of those who have first taken possession of the unoccupied portion of the earth's surface to exclude the remainder of mankind from inhabiting it, and the means which can be legitimately used by the more improved branches of the human species to protect themselves from being hurtfully encroached upon by those of a lower grade of civilization.[8]

When Mackenzie King and the Senate of Canada spoke to the need for a new age of mass migration policy in the late 1940s, they did so impelled by two traditions of Canadian immigration policy. First, the Canadian population needed to grow in order to defend the space it had inherited from the colonial period. Second, an expanding population was necessary for the development of a healthy economy. King had noted in his diary that all the cabinet was agreed "that in the long range view, Canada would certainly need to have a large population if she hoped to hold the country for herself against the ambitions of other countries and build her strength." Among his colleagues there were some who believed that Canada faced the possibility of a postwar economic boom that would lead her to her postcolonial destiny as a great power. That boom would be thwarted by an absence of manpower.

By 1947, representatives of Canadian industries such as mining, agriculture and forestry had approached the government for help in finding new sources of cheap and pliable workers. Australia had already begun to tap the Continent's displaced peoples for migrants, and Canada would be remiss if she did not follow suit. When King made his views public in May, he spoke of Canada bringing over immigrants at a rate that would be compatible with the country's absorptive powers. Although the surface of his remarks dealt with this issue of absorption in terms of economics, full employment and industrial expansion, the usual subtext about finding suitable ethnic and racial stock that would be assimilable broke through the text, especially in the explicit call for exclusion of Asian immigrants. It is clear that his colleagues and the Opposition were aware of the subtext since he was asked immediately in the House of Commons whether he had begun negotiations with the governments of the United Kingdom, France and the Netherlands about recruiting immigrants there officially.

By appeasing anti-Asian racism in western Canada (King made his remarks in the same year that the new Canadian Citizenship Act finally gave Asians the vote in British Columbia) and paying lip service to an ancillary flow of French-speaking immigrants ("born in France" was given equal footing as a category of admission with "British subject"), the government freed itself to act. In the aftermath of the war, there seemed to be pools of prospective immigrants from Europe who could fulfill long-range demographic needs while nicely satisfying, or at least not antagonizing, the constituencies in Canada. Within the atmosphere of the Allies' goodwill, thousands of veterans of the Polish army in exile began arriving in Canada after 1946. The specific terms of payment for their ship's passage, even with the not entirely altruistic help of the British government in dispersing them through the Empire, often led to a period of what amounted to indenture in the Canadian North or in specific industries in need of workers. Canadian Jews and Ukrainians lobbied the government to help their kinsmen who had either survived death camps or were in displaced-person (DP) camps. Such lobbies would prove that in a democracy, existing groups must be heard, but immigration officials were often more interested in developing systematic recruitment in Holland, Scandinavia and the United Kingdom.[9]

The four forces shaping recruitment choice, then, were: (1) the racialist or cultural assumptions of officials and many politicians, (2) the ethnic lobbies in Canada, (3) the availability of potential migrants of certain nationalities because of wartime and aftermath displacement, and (4) the voracious hunger of Canadian heavy industry for workers who could stand up under strenuous, dangerous and dirty work done in remote and unhealthy places. The competition among these four forces distorted the population policy King initiated. In the collective memory of the immigrants of the 1950s and 1960s, being able to show an immigration inspector calloused hands and a body ready for hard work is remembered as a more essential rite of passage than questions about ethnicity or wartime politics.

At first the DPs provided ideal, almost chattel labor. Moreover, their recruitment satisfied that order goal of Canadian policy, the maintenance of a reputation for high moral purpose among the community of nations and the image of generosity of spirit in providing access to a land of second chance. Bulk labor schemes worked out with the International Relief Organization soon brought large numbers of Balts and other East Europeans to join the displaced Poles. The discourse's subtext, that immigrants should not only fit into the economy but also into the ethnic and racial needs of the country, continued to break through the surface. Of the first thousand women recruited from the DP camps as domestic servants, the recruiters in the field were reminded that "Protestant girls are preferred, possibly Estonians and of the best type available."[10] Only a year after the war, a Canadian Institute of Public Opinion poll showed 49 percent of Canadians against Jewish immigration as opposed to only 34 percent who would have barred Germans.[11] Race clearly mattered more than politics for most Canadians when it came to an immigrant's credentials. However, the Canadian Jewish Congress sought more vigorous screening of those who had fought with the Axis, and the Association of United Ukrainian Canadians had to remind the government that it should give priority to those immigrants who had fought against Nazi Germany and her satellites, if it wished to pay honor to the Canadian war dead.[12]

Elements in the primary sector of the economy – mining, timbering, railway work, industrial agriculture such as sugar beet production – some of which had used POWs as labor during the war, were in great need of manpower. Many industries also saw the chance to keep native-born labor off balance and to dilute the power of unions. The representatives of these industries shared King's view that coming to Canada was not "a fundamental human right" but a "privilege" that desperate men would acknowledge by being grateful and compliant in the workplace. An official of one of Canada's largest sugar companies described how his firm could use the Polish army veterans. They "could be quartered in the existing [POW] camps…. These camps could be operated successfully in a manner similar to the former camps but with much less expense and organization since no guards would be needed."[13] In the 1950s, at least 80 percent of the immigrants who were Poles, Ukrainians, Balts, Dutch, Germans and British had Ontario and Quebec as their targets. They were accompanied, after the lifting of the Enemy Alien Act, which had excluded citizens of Axis countries from Canada, by a growing stream of Italians, and then by Portuguese and Greek immigrants. Over two decades, Ontario's population of 4.5 million was swelled by another half million immigrants.

Efforts to control the flow of migrants once in Canada and to define areas of settlement were difficult in its context of democracy and free enterprise. Although most mining and railway towns in the North had prewar enclaves of East Europeans, the arrival of large numbers of Polish veterans, displaced Lithuanians, Slovaks, Croats, Ukrainians, Donau-Schwabs and other German peoples revivified the ethnic collectivities – often, however, with misunderstanding and conflict between the Left and the Right, and the old and the new immigrants. At the same time, many migrants, after an initial stay in the smaller work sites, moved on to Montreal or the megalopolis of the Golden Horseshoe in southern Ontario. Others joined one of Canada's oldest and strongest migration patterns by seeking entry to the United States. Dutch and German settlers were distributed more evenly by occupation and geography across Ontario and the West. The country received the new immigrants with mixed feelings; the DPs were anti-Communist (usually committed to capitalism) and had a higher percentage of educated people among them than earlier waves of immigrants. Many, especially among the Dutch and the Balts, were of the Nordic physical type idealized in Anglophone-Canadian culture. In this respect they were welcome, but the signs of ethnic persistence they showed from the beginning were less so.

By the late 1950s, the numbers of immigrants from northeastern Europe, which the DPs represented, had begun to dwindle, but Canada's need for manpower had not. The coming of Italians in large numbers and the urban pattern of their settlement brought tension between the demographic and the racial goals of the immigration policy. The matter was rarely couched in language quite so bald. Both the lessons of World War II and the United Nations Charter caused civilized nations to give up talk of the right stock. Sentiment changed more slowly, and issues such as sponsored versus independent migration, assimilability and enclaving, and the appropriateness of recruiting more actively in the British mother country were the media within which the Italian question was studied. Ontario had had since the turn of the century its own immigration and colonization department. In keeping with that province's reputation as a loyal outpost of the British Empire, the department focused on recruiting immigrants from the United Kingdom, but it saw in the Dutch and Scandinavians appropriate surrogates. In 1947 Ontario's premier, George

Drew, began a successful effort to airlift 10,000 British immigrants directly to Toronto.[14] As late as 1964, Ontario's deputy director of immigration toured northern Europe in search of settlers who presumably might counterbalance the heavy flow of Southern Europeans.

That tour took place about five years after the moment, startling to some Canadian authorities, when Italians, who had been listed as "nonpreferred stock" in prewar immigration department documents, surpassed the British in numbers entering Canada in a year. The Italian flow, although partly induced by renewal of earlier chain migration, had been, in the main, a flow of labor to capital, of migrant drawn to crude workplace. The subtext about their suitability as new Canadians and assimilability was always present. As the Italians, along with the Portuguese and the Greeks, became the engine of the rapid urbanization of much of southern Ontario, their visibility changed. Massive ethnic enclaves in the city were not the same quaint, impoverished Little Italy clinging to the sides of a smelter, mine, or railway yard. Given the traditional assumption that immigration policy was an aspect of population policy and that regulatory manipulation could fix rates of flow that went awry, it is instructive and a fillip to the anarchist to note how completely the Italian immigrants defeated the Canadian "gatekeepers" between 1947 and 1967.

The Immigration Act of 1952 was intended to secure the type of immigrants that Canada's political leadership had sought shortly after World War II. In the discretionary powers accorded the minister and bureaucrats under the act, the imperatives of the subtext on suitability of stock became text but were couched in a manner that would not insult the U.N. Charter. An immigrant could be prohibited from entering Canada for reason of nationality, geographic origin, peculiarity of custom, unsuitability of climate, and probable inability to "become readily assimilated." A 1952 *Maclean's* piece railed at "Ottawa's zealous publicity men" who were obscuring the impact on the Canadian future that emerges from an honest analysis of the "characteristics, moral fiber, skills and racial composition of the hundreds of thousands of immigrants" then passing through reception centers. The article added that the people in public relations "don't tell you that our most adaptable class of immigrants, the Briton, is an ever declining proportion of our total immigration."[15]

The 1952 act, then, reflected the view of much of the Anglophone host society. In 1956 an influential series of articles in the *Globe and Mail* described the virtue of some German, Dutch and Estonian immigrants. Nonetheless, it added that "people from the British Isles are more rapidly accepted than those from European countries."[16] Although Barbadian

Canadians successfully challenged the systematic exclusion of Blacks as unassimilable and unsuitable for reasons of climate[17] and even though southern European migrant laborers, with the Italians as bellwethers, shattered Canada's dream of keeping the population northwest European, attempts to control the flow of immigrants from certain backgrounds continued until the late 1960s. A spate of press accounts about illegal Chinese immigration schemes was followed in May of 1960 by concerted Royal Canadian Mounted Police raids on all of Canada's major Chinatowns in search of incriminating evidence. Whatever else the raids signaled, they showed the government still to "be on guard" for White Canada against a change in its "fundamental character."[18]

The impact of the new mass migration has been especially unsettling for Ontario. In the forty years since the war, the population has gone from 3 out of 4 to less than 3 out of 6 residents of British descent. (It should be added that such figures beg the question of whether using the census category "British" and the political term WASP, which mask traditional Celtic-English divisions and the generational distance between new immigrants from Brixton and the Midlands and the old stock, are of any value. They lump together people of such diverse cultures and backgrounds.) A polity that had about 100,000 foreign-born in 1951 had more than 2 million two decades later.

The impact of mass immigration on Quebec was even more unsettling, although it was less a matter of numbers than of the fact and image of non-French-speaking strangers massing in Montreal and the French-Canadian interpretation of that invasion. Between 1946 and 1971, 3.5 million immigrants arrived in Canada. Only about 15 percent of the newcomers settled in Quebec, but fewer than 5 percent of those who did were Francophones. Although many of the educated DPs and Italian and Portuguese migrant laborers who reached Montreal could function in French, they seemed to identify with the Anglophone culture and with Canada as a polity rather than with *francophonie* and Quebec. Quebec's nationalist view, and perhaps the French-Canadian view generally, was that "le ministre de l'Immigration a introduit le cheval de Troie au Canada français" in order to pierce "une muraille imprenable".[19]

Since the number of immigrants coming from France between 1946 and 1986 was not only less than the number coming from the United Kingdom but also less than the contingents of Italians, Portuguese, Greeks, West Indians, Poles, Germans, and those from Hong Kong and the Indian subcontinent, *la survivance* of the *Canadien* required higher fertility rates among French Canadians and an ability and a willingness to acculturate immigrants. By the 1980s, the *Québécois* birth rate was among the lowest in Canada; a combination of turning inward to Quebec rather than a pan-French-Canadian strategy and the assimilation by law, if necessary of all immigrants in the province, recommended itself. Immigrants arriving in Quebec usually had little idea or interest in the fact that they were entering a cultural and political battle zone. The gallicization of Montreal and the defeat of the Anglophone hegemony were the front, and it was not a place for noncombatants.

English as a language had higher status than any other in Canada, in North America and in the world, and since their strategies required a primary interest in mobility, the immigrants saw the acquisition and use of standard English as crucial. Learning French might help one get work on the telephone exchange or the police force and might be necessary to a small shopkeeper, but it did not open the door to greater North American opportunity. Moreover, the nationalism, not to say racism, of the *Québécois* enabled the immigrants to claim with some justification (although the same point could certainly have been made about Montreal's Anglophones of British descent) that the fault lay with the Francophones themselves, "who, as xenophobes, were not inclined to accept the immigrants and who would claim that those same immigrants could neither speak nor learn French correctly."[20]

Something of a self-confirming hypothesis existed on both sides. In 1962-1963, 25 percent of the Italian immigrant children were in the French-speaking school system; by 1971-1972 the figure was 10 percent. More than that, it is probably true, as some scholars have pointed out, that the initiation price for acculturation into Anglophonie is acquiring a certain disdain for "the French fact" and for speaking French in Canada.

Since the perception and reality of the urban Italian communities as potential centers of political power were a major element later in making the "third force" of non-British, non-French descent more than a Prairie-based Slavic movement and in contributing to the assertion of a public policy of multiculturalism, one can say that the failure of the immigration authorities to maintain a flow "consistent with the country's ability to absorb" had serious consequences for the forging of the Canadian nation. One should add that the image of Montreal's Italian immigrants of the 1950s and 1960s choosing Anglophonie in preference to assimilation to a sister Latin culture, especially since many prewar Italians had become gallicized, played a significant role in Quebec's separatism as well. It is not as if the authorities did not attempt to manipulate Italian immigration from the beginning. There is even some suggestion that Canada's doors opened to Italians in the late 1940s, not just because of the pressures for family reunification and labor needs but because of the NATO allies' fear that Italy's population problems would improve the chances of the Communist party coming to power there. Canadian officials showed the traditional concern for cutting a good figure among their senior allies. As a dispatch from the Canadian Department of External Affairs had it, "Any increase in emigration to Canada would be of practical help to Italy in tackling her greatest problem. It would also be a small, but distinctly Canadian, contribution to strengthening the present democratic 'western' government...."[21]

Canada had always preferred northern to southern Italian immigrants. That preference was couched in terms of skills and adaptability by the 1950s, but steeped in assumptions about the "Germanic" roots of the Friulians and other northerners and the Mediterranean ways of the southerners. Some authorities felt that opening recruiting stations south of Milan would not "draw the best class of immigrant." As sociologists have shown about Italian migration to Australia, in the struggle between "the manifest function of bureaucracy" and the "latent function of informal networks", the latter – family strategies, chain and serial migration and ethnic group networks of assistance – are always faster, more resilient and smarter than government agencies.[22] As a result, Italians, predominantly from the South, appeared for more than a decade among the top five arriving groups in Canada.

The government estimated with a note of terror that every Italian male laborer who entered Canada in the 1950s was responsible for forty-nine other Italian immigrants. When efforts were made to manipulate the regulations in order to slow the Italian flow, restrictive definitions of who could be sponsored, previously applied only to the Chinese, were tried. "I doubt if we could get away with it but one step worth considering might well be to announce that 50% of the total Unemployment Insurance Commissions claims in the Toronto area...are Italians", wrote a deputy minister of citizenship and immigration in 1960, but he knew better: "We must not make the mistake again of letting the story get abroad that anything we may be attempting is designed to cut down Italian immigration."[23] The immigrants had become political clientele, and the conditions for mass immigration to turn to polyethnicity, and for polyethnicity to lead to multicultural politics, had emerged.

There are a number of ways to tell the story of how the visible polyethnicity that accompanied postwar immigration intruded on the exigencies of French-English relations and of how that intrusion led, in the late 1960s and early 1970s, to a revolution of policy and rhetoric, if not of sentiment. As the charter groups sought to define the new Canadian nationhood in terms of bilingualism and biculturalism, a third force emerged demanding multiculturalism rather than biculturalism. Canadians as "the other North Americans" needed an identity that would no longer be subordinate to the British metropole, that would dampen the appeal of separatism in Quebec, and that would continue to sustain political, social and cultural values assumed to be distinct from those of the United States. The Royal Commission on Bilingualism and Biculturalism, established in the early 1960s, had as its main task the search for that new identity and for an amicable and more equal sharing of power and culture by the two "founding races". The commission was "state intervention to restructure the symbolic order" in Canada.[24] The French-British dualism that had in the past been seen as a tale of mutual antagonism, of exploitation and inequality, as an impediment to the emergence of the Canadian, would now be refurbished as a national virtue.

Along with it came revival of the old saw that *la survivance* of the *Canadien* was a key element in the survival of the Canadian in the face of the American urge to continental imperium and vice versa. Any assessment of recent Canadian history has to include the sense of surprise, sadness and anger felt by the mainstream when its effort to build national independence on dualism (in the form of an official bilingualism and biculturalism) foundered on the ethnocentrism of some Anglophones, the extremism of some Quebec separatists, and an unanticipated demand on the part of those claiming to represent a "third element", or "third force". These were the one-quarter to one-third of the population who were of neither French nor British descent and who wanted to share power and help formulate the country's culture.

Some explanations of the events of the late 1960s and early 1970s may seem more cynical than others, and some have more explanatory power and appeal for one set of players than another, but all have the sort of truth described by the Indian from James Bay who told a Quebec judge that he could not swear to tell the truth but only what he knew. One can view the public policy of multiculturalism that has emerged since 1971 in four different ways – as:

1. A product of the postwar convergence of arriving nationalist DP intellectuals – Poles, Balts and Ukrainians especially – and a failure of the will to assimilate on the part of Anglo-Canadian officials.

2. An innovative and altruistic civic philosophy of democratic pluralism to replace loyalty to the British Empire as a legitimizing principle for the Canadian state.

3. A device used by Anglophones to minimize the uniqueness of the French minority in Canada.

4. A tactic of venal politicians to find a medium of exchange and thus a way of controlling new ethnic and immigrant voting blocs.

Whichever narrative proves most elegant, they all include the same three mythic protagonists: the British (sometimes and not exactly synonymously identified as the Anglophones or Anglo-Celts), the French (sometimes and again not synonymously described as *Canadiens*, Francophones, and *Québécois*), and the "other ethnic groups." Moreover, there is in all of the accounts a sense of the intrusion of the ethnic groups into an antique struggle between the real Canadians/*Canadiens*.

For, although some of the spokesmen for the settlers of the Prairies, especially the Ukrainians, spoke as if they were a third founding nation, in the belief, one assumes, that as the first to break the prairie sod, they met the white man's definition of proprietorship through exploitation and settlement, and although later Ukrainian immigrants spoke as if traces of the failed Hapsburg monarchy had crossed the sea with them; no one until the 1960s thought of Canadian history except in terms of the titanic contest between the British and the French. Both saw immigrants and Canadians of other backgrounds as potential Anglophones and, to paraphrase H.L. Mencken, as "assistant Canadians" brought in to counterbalance *la revanche des berceaux*. They romanticized the presence of the Prairie isolates such as Mennonites, Hutterites, Icelandics and Galicians. One participant in the second Canadian Conference on Multiculturalism in 1976 recalled the way in which a more diffuse pluralism had always been used to combat dualism: "Ukrainians, Germans and others could provide a kind of counterweight to the French Canadians". Faced with claims and complaints from the French, the English of western Canada could come back with "What about the Ukrainians?" He added, perhaps giving away too much about the caretaker's reasons for supporting multiculturalism, "More broadly and generally, the tension when two social groups compete within a polity seems likely to be reduced insofar as there are a number of groups."[25]

The 1960s saw the transformation of polyethnicity from a social consequence of recent immigration to its assertion as a permanent feature of the Canadian political landscape. Polyethnicity evolved along with multiculturalism, an idea en route to an ideology fashioned from the rhetoric of ethnocultural impresarios huckstering for the folkloric and visiting British royalty, searching for a way to describe the colorfulness of the colonies (no doubt after countless onslaughts by Cree, Blackfoot and Ukrainians in full ethnic battle dress, herded by red-tunicked guardians of "the Canadian way"). The speed with which the newcomers, in alliance with some older Prairie ethnic elements, managed to become players in the shaping of the new Canada, is evident in the last-minute addition to the mandate of the royal commission of a study of the third element. The study is summed up in the fourth volume of the commission's report, entitled *The Contribution of the Other Ethnic Groups*. This title seems less startling when one thinks about the rapid concentration in urban enclaves of the new immigrants: 84 percent of the Greeks, 82 percent of the Chinese and 75 percent of the Italians are in cities of more than 500,000 inhabitants. Also important were the revitalization of some ethnic groups engendered by the arrival of large numbers of their countrymen (already mobilized by nationalist sentiment), and the salience that the issues of ethnocultural rights and ethnic identity acquired in Canadian public discourse because of the separatist movement in Quebec. Among the immigrants and the spokesmen for the third element there was a natural uneasiness that "a deal was being cut without them." As the noted Canadian sociologist Raymond Breton has observed, "the name of the Royal Commission [on Bilingualism and Biculturalism] itself was a symbol generating status anxiety [for the third element] as were several other themes permeating the debate: founding peoples, charter groups, the two nation society."[26] Many immigrant intellectuals also lived with a misunderstanding – reinforced by the fact that they first encountered and understood Canada through the medium of the Anglophone hegemony or the ethnoverted discourse of their own kind – of Quebec as an *ethnie* overreaching itself rather than as a suppressed nation engaged in a "quiet revolution", or, in the case of the fanatical few, an insurrection.

Several other factors contributed to the rapidity with which immigrants regrouped and underwent the sort of ethnicization that led them to participate aggressively in the debate about Canadian identity under way in the 1960s and 1970s. Some of the groups arriving – especially the Polish army veterans, the Baltic DPs, and the Ukrainians (veterans of war or labor camps) – saw themselves as "saving remnants" of their people, as nuclei of nations in exile. In all cases, they were peoples who, through long stretches of their history, had had to sustain their national identities without having at their disposal the machinery of nation-states of their own. The democratic structure of Canada and the uncertainty of the Canadian host society and government in responding to the tactics of group persistence of the ethnonationalists, encouraged the building of ethnies. It is fair to add that among the same DPs and among immigrants form other parts of continental Europe, there were many who advocated democratic pluralism, or multiculturalism, not as a device to facilitate the maintenance of the nation in exile or to forge ethnic groups, but rather as a humane and civil form of nationhood to replace the very ethnonationalism they saw as a cause of World War II.

Distortions and ambiguities in the way Canadians think and talk about ethnicity also have contributed to the impact of the immigrants, and of the third force generally. Politicians and the public have confused the fact of polyethnicity with the idea of multiculturalism, and the latter term has generally been used to apply to both.[27] Leaders have generally preferred to think of those they represent as ethnic groups rather than immigrant groups, since *immigrant* conjures up the thresholds of acculturation while *ethnic* implies a permanent quality of otherness. However, as we shall see, the penumbra of the Greek meaning of *ethnos* persists in English, so that to be called ethnic in Canada is to be called less, as in "ethnic writer", and marginal, as in "ethnic enclave". The word *ethnic* has, from the beginning, raised the conundrum of whether multiculturalism is "for all Canadians", including "the founding nations", or just for "ethnic Canadians". Avoiding the term leads to lexical monstrosities such as "the multilingual press" and references to "multicultural groups" or "we multiculturals". The increasing diversity of the population was further magnified by the workings of the Canadian census, which until recently required everyone to list patrilinear ethnic origin and rejected "Canadian" or "American" as answers except for Amerindians. This official definition and measurement of ethnic group membership, maintained at the insistence of French Canada (which saw in it a way to assert the size of the *Canadien* nation by descent, since the more subtle calibration by mother tongue and home language showed great attrition outside Quebec and the adjoining corridors of northern Ontario and New Brunswick), also served ethnic and immigrant leaders well. They could ignore the workings of acculturation and the question of intensity of participation and feeling within the group. At the very least, reference to the census abetted those who played the numbers game; it also encouraged the impression that phalanxes of like-minded immigrants and ethnics were massing behind their leaders, an image bound to frighten or fascinate elected politicians.

Within a year of the great commission struck by Lester Pearson to "inquire into and report upon the existing state of bilingualism and biculturalism in Canada and to recommend what steps should be taken to develop the Canadian confederation on the basis of an equal partnership between the two founding races", a Ukrainian-Canadian senator from the Prairies – Paul Yuzyk – rose to give his maiden speech in the Senate. The speech was entitled "Canada: A Multicultural Nation", and Yuzyk used the occasion to denounce biculturalism as a misunderstanding of Canadian reality, which, he said, had "changed from paramountly British and French...to multicultural."[28] He went on to speak of the third element, to which one-third of Canada's people belonged according to the census data the senator produced. It was one of the first of years of "arguments from the census" to define the Canadian future, a phenomenon that in Canada has always carried the uncomfortable implication that everyone must have a tribe to belong to, that ethnic identity is stamped at birth and is neither volitional nor processual, and that census group and interest group are synonymous. "Do you know", wrote another ethnic leader, "that the 5,764,075 so-called 'others' outnumber the entire population of seven provinces, the Atlantic and Prairie provinces combined...and that the 1,317,200 German Canadians are more numerous than the total population of provinces such as Saskatchewan, Manitoba and Nova Scotia", that there are "more Ukrainians [in Canada] than people in Newfoundland?"[29]

Since the spokesmen for the third element rejected the idea of a separate *Canadien* nation, they tended to see the argument over dualism and the commission's bilingual and bicultural mandate as one about power, not history. In this view, ethnic numbers, density, intensity and perhaps even hints of societal strife were the strategies by which the *Québécois*, if not the *Canadiens* of other provinces, had forced the British to negotiate. As an exasperated Ukrainian leader put it, "Is it necessary for all these people to establish their own ethnocultural enclaves before their cultural and linguistic aspirations are truly respected and encouraged?" In their speechmaking, the politicians who have advocated multiculturalism have flexed the muscles of the third force as if they were their own. From the beginning, then, the politicians have confused (usually purposely) immigrant first-settlement areas with permanent ethnic enclaves, and immigrant sentiments of "fellow-feeling", as well as the reality of diglossia, with a sense of ethnic community, group maintenance of boundaries and shared destiny in Canada. With the French Canadians, some of the ethnoreligious groups of the Prairies, and the Ukrainians as models, the idea of ethnic persistence rather than inevitable Anglo conformism could be brandished as both a norm and an ethos to be pursued, even if statistics on language loss and intermarriage over generations suggest that only extreme geographical and religious isolation has slowed the rates of assimilation.

One of the best and most influential examples of the rhetorical uses of immigration statistics to promote both uniethnic persistence and multiculturalism came from Ontario's minister of citizenship in 1972:

> No other part of the globe, no other country can claim a more culturally diversified society than we have here in this province.... But does everyone really grasp that Ontario has more Canadians of German origin than Bonn, more of Italian origin than Florence, more Canadians of Greek origin than Sparta? That we have in our midst, 54 ethnocultural groups, speaking a total of 72 languages...? Just 100 years ago the Canadian identity was moulded in the crucible of nationalism; it is now being tempered, tempered by the dynamics of multiculturalism.
>
> One effect of the postwar boom in third element immigration has been to bolster ethnocultural groups, some of which have been here through four generations. The government has welcomed and encouraged this immigration. We have recognized and helped to foster all our constituent cultural communities. Is it then any wonder that these communities have heightened expectations in many areas?[30]

The commissioners and researchers preparing *The Contribution of the Other Ethnic Groups*, Book IV of the royal commission report, were by the late 1960s operating on vanished premises. On the one hand, a new *Québécois* identity, based on a geographically, demographically, and institutionally compact and self-contained nation in one province, was rising to challenge the diffuse legal and linguistic ideal of a Francophone-Anglophone partnership stretching form sea to sea. On the other hand, few spokesmen for the third element – ethnic leaders as opposed to caretakers in support of multiculturalism – were content with this volume. Its authors observed that: (1) it should be "noted immediately that while the terms of reference deal with questions of those of ethnic origin other than British or French, they do so in relation to the basic problem of bilingualism and biculturalism from which they are inseparable"; (2) "that acculturation is inevitable in a multi-ethnic country like Canada"; and (3) that "multiculturalism within a bilingual framework can work, if it is interpreted as it is intended – that is, as encouraging those members of ethnic groups who want to do so to maintain a proud sense of the contribution of their own group to Canadian society.... If it is interpreted in a second way – as enabling various peoples to transfer foreign cultures and languages as living wholes into a new place and time – multiculturalism is doomed."[31]

Book IV, then, was the first modern public recognition of the possibility of group cultural rights for minorities and of limits for Anglo conformity and gallicization. The volume clearly set the limits of acceptable diversity as well. The commission envisaged study and celebration of pluralistic origin, and expressed a willingness to tolerate, even to encourage, the maintenance of ethnocultures, especially for immigrants and their children. Neither political nor linguistic pluralism would be possible, however, and the issue of what amounts of public money and what sort of public programs would be directed toward the support of ethnies remained ill defined enough to offend all three players – the British, the French and the third element.

Looking back now through some of the havoc and bad feelings about ethnic politics and population policy, to the 1970 convergence of "apprehended insurrection" of the Front de libération du Québec, through the declaration of a multicultural policy by Prime Minister Pierre Elliott Trudeau and the reaction of Anglophones to what many saw as the country "coming unraveled", it is helpful to borrow from the thought of the Italian Marxist anthropologist Ernesto De Martino. He said that groups despairing for the survival of their ways are not likely to feel much generosity of spirit toward the cultural rights of others.[32] In 1970 the two founding nations, the Prairie ethnic blocs, and the new immigrant ethnies all thought their pieces of the pie and the survival of their cultures were threatened. The sense of impending cultural and demographic doom affects the Anglophones because of everything from Quebec separatism to the ravishes of American cultural imperialism; the sense of survival that has always informed Quebec nationalism is nothing but a prolonged struggle against the apocalypse, the disappearance of the French language and culture from the continent.

It is easy to see how the arrival of masses of non-French immigrants to their chief city, Montreal, and the apparent anglicization of those newcomers could signal both the impotence of their nation and its imminent destruction. As political scientist Karl Deutsch has observed, the condition of being immigrant is always apocalyptic in that each generation must make reflective and ideological efforts to counter the effects of acculturation and slippage.[33] The rhetoric as well as the behavior of all groups toward one another, since the uncertainty of the late 1960s, reflects the scars of those times as much as or more than it does the putative cultural arrogance of one group or another.

Only with this point in mind can one make sense of how shrill the debate over immigration and multiculturalism can become. Certainly the policies and programs the government initiated after Trudeau announced the government's response to Book IV in October of 1971 were not so far ranging, expensive, or intrusive as to fire up the opponents of multiculturalism. "We believe", the prime minister said, "that cultural pluralism is the very essence of Canadian identity. Every ethnic group has the right to preserve and develop its own culture and values within the Canadian context. To say we have two official languages is not to say we have two official cultures, and no particular culture is more 'official' than another. A policy of multiculturalism must be a policy for all Canadians." Between Trudeau's pronouncement – his first and last parliamentary utterance on the issue – and the Multicultural Act, Bill C-93, brought before the House of Commons in Ottawa late in 1987, there has been no enabling legislation of any kind about multiculturalism or ethnic group rights.

Since 1973, there has been a multiculturalism directorate within the Department of the Secretary of State. Through grants to scholars, the arts and ethnocommunity organizations, the directorate seeks to carry out the three chief goals of multiculturalism: (1) to help maintain ethnic group life and culture, (2) to foster cross-cultural understanding, and (3) to integrate immigrants through teaching the two official languages. These goals hardly promise balkanization, and the granting structure does not approach the resources available to mainstream cultural activities through the Canada Council and other agencies.

One might suppose that the ethnic and immigrant clientele would lead the hue and cry against the limited and perfunctory implementation of multiculturalism. To a certain extent, it has. Despite the truth of the remark that the "concerns of the non-British, non-French segment of the society were not primarily with cultural maintenance" and were instead with "status anxiety – fear of being defined as second class citizens",[34] immigrant and ethnic leaders, even on advisory bodies carefully selected by the government, have protested the degree to which the integrative aspects of multiculturalism have been advanced over programs to sustain their own cultures. These programs, which they see as the government's obligation, are modeled on the federal programs that provide funding to prepare and pay teachers of French outside Quebec. The report of the very first Canadian Consultative Council on Multiculturalism (CCCM) has as its paramount concern the relationship between language retention and the preservation and future development of the ethnic group:

> Without language, cultural pluralism (or to use the contemporary term, multiculturalism) emerges as truncated multiculturalism, confined to such aspects as folk dancing, native costumes, special

foods, embroidery, instrumental music or even folk songs with words which few can understand or are encouraged to learn.[35]

While Canadian teachers ran "pizza and pysanky" days and educators met to complain that "all too often such organizations [ethnic clubs and halls] plan extensively for the enrichment and enhancement of their own images and unique purpose without appropriate acknowledgement of all other group", the politicized ethnic clientele of the government's multicultural policies saw only trivialization of their ethnocultures. The federally funded community cultural centers and multicultural centers that were to implement these policies were, according to the CCCM, more "compatible with the melting pot concept" than with pluralism. In 1977, the Ukrainian Canadian Committee made its dissent clear:

> Any attempt to develop and maintain the various cultures simultaneously as distinct yet intermixed together in a multicultural centre is a contradiction, as it leads to one blend or mass....[36]

Perhaps the two charter groups would have thought the demands of "the ethnics" excessive under any circumstances, but the strong, though rarely garish, funding programs and the accompanying "ethnicking" for votes clearly fueled the conflict. There were dark mutterings of not dispensing government funds to help "keep ex-fascists dancing in their church cellars." A guest editor in *Maclean's* described English Canada as being "in danger of having its old, familiar British North American culture half bludgeoned to death by the cast iron balalaikas of multiculturalism", while the helpless Canadian taxpayer watches as "in the name of 'heritage' programs, he pays for Polish and Swahili Canadians to be taught in Polish and Swahili in the supposedly all-Canadian public school."[37]

Multiculturalism as a policy was denounced for many of the same reasons assimilationists have always objected to the maintenance of ethnicity. It would breed "double consciousness" – loyalty to more than one country; it would contribute to turning immigrant quarters into permanent ethnic ghettos; it would slow the process of overcoming the ignorance of English and French that made the immigrants exploitable. Part of most ethnic heritages is a traditional enmity for some other group. Was the Canadian government intending to contribute to that problem by funding ethnocultural organizations? Among the English-speaking, hostility to multiculturalism ran from the viscerally xenophobic to well-reasoned preference for a laissez-faire approach to liberal meritocracy and an abhorrence of state intervention in the issue of group status, even if a hierarchy of privilege based on ethnicity and class was obvious in the economy. Sometimes, of course, the viscerally xenophobic and the apparently reasonable became confused with one another. "You and me and our children have enough to do with the basic problem of hyphenated Canadianism, that is the French and English duality, without enshrining the whole world's diversity within our history and our borders", a well-known journalist and legislator told the Canadian Conference on Multiculturalism, and many well-intentioned Canadians of every ethnic background agreed with him.[38]

The need to involve newcomers and to inject multiculturalism into the effort to encourage the growth of a new postcolonial Canada seemed initially to confuse many mainstream intellectuals, Anglo-Celt in origin or not. Although embracing multiculturalism as an alternative to the hateful melting pot practiced to the south should have worked as well as paeans to dualism as a basis for a unique history, the mainstream often reacted defensively and a bit meanly. Some, for example, whittled away at the authenticity of the figures that gave "the others" one-third of the population.[39] Failing that, the Anglo-Canadians tended to speak of themselves in the 1970s as a "vanishing breed", to add hastily how nice their ethnic cleaning ladies were, and to point out that anti-British feeling, or the myth of British bigotry in Canada, was too negative a thing upon which to build the new multicultural Canada. The report of the Commission on Canadian Studies, issued seven years after Trudeau had declared the multicultural policy, was entitled *To Know Ourselves*. It contained only one reference to any ethnic group: "The remarkable Celtic contribution to the life of this country for example has received little attention. The British or Anglo-Canadian heritage is in danger of being ignored by scholars who fail to perceive that it, too, is part of the Canadian mosaic."[40]

The French-Canadian response to the declaration of the policy was, if anything, more ferocious and more consistent. Although in the last several years Francophones in the Prairie Provinces and Ontario have cooperated to gain heritage language rights, no sympathy, to say the least, existed among Francophones for multiculturalism during the 1960s and 1970s. The *Canadiens* who resided outside Quebec saw themselves orphaned by the *Québécois*, who increasingly turned to strategies of seizing control in their own province, or *indépendantisme*. Despite government promises of protection under the Official Languages Act, they also saw multiculturalism as a device directed against them. As a French-Canadian prelate and scholar from Nova Scotia put it, quoting a *Le Droit* editorial, "We cannot help but see this as an insidious and steady shift away from biculturalism toward a crushing of *francophonie's* special needs under the political weight of multiculture...."[41] The response from Quebec nationalists like René Lévesque was less civil and circumspect: "Multiculturalism, really is folklore. It is a 'red herring'. The notion was devised to obscure 'the Quebec business', to give an impression that we are all ethnics and do not have to worry about special status for Quebec."[42]

It could be argued that the emergence of the multicultural policy was a godsend for Quebec separatism. It offered proof that the thousands of new immigrants who had come to Montreal since World War II were not prepared to become Francophones; it seemed to promise that bilingualism on a national scale would fail and thus confirmed the Quebec nationalist view that only a core of unilingual Francophones could guarantee the future of the French culture in Canada. On the other hand, the French-Canadian reaction guaranteed that most immigrants would see support for multiculturalism as their only refuge from cultural genocide and the English language as their only avenue of socioeconomic mobility. Two headlines in an Italian newspaper in Toronto reflect the tone of the relationship between the immigrants and the advocates of the new Quebec in the 1970s: "E Assurdo Dover Studiare Il Francese" ("It is absurd to be made to study French") and "I Franco-Canadesi Vogliono Francesizzare Gli Italiani Del Quebec" ("The French Canadians want to gallicize the Italians of Quebec").

Two French-Canadian intellectuals, one a professor at the Université de Montréal and the other Quebec's ministre d'Etat au Développement culturel, expressed the Francophone view of the policy most forcefully. The first, Guy Rocher, had his remarks read to a federal conference on multiculturalism.[43] Rocher saw the policy as a continuation by other means of an Anglophone campaign to define the French Canadians as first among the minorities rather than as a second nation within the Canadian polity. He pointed out that without biculturalism, the French language would function within bilingualism as merely an administrative and a government language. Multilingualism would, he believed, eventually appear to be the logical corollary of multiculturalism and then the uniqueness of the French existing in Canada would be lost. "At a time when 90 percent of the ethnic minorities of Quebec are opting for the English language and the Anglophone culture", he wrote, "thereby constituting one of the most serious threats both politically and culturally to the Francophone community of Quebec, the federal government has undertaken to define Canada as a multicultural nation."

A year later the minister, Camille Laurin, lectured the Canadian Ethnic Studies Association meeting in Quebec City, on the difference between an *ethnie* and a *nation*. An *ethnie* "renvoie à un ensemble de caractéristiques et de traditions dont l'existence ou la persistance peuvent se vérifier au niveau des individus et des familles." A *nation*, however, is "une société globale, une société complète, qui possède ses caractéristiques propres en tant que société, qui a son propre mode d'organisation et de fonctionnement, qui a sa propre continuité historique, une tradition juridique et politique et enfin un territoire bien identifié." Laurin went on to point out that all nations had the right to make their mother tongues official languages and to expect minorities to learn those languages. Those who "immigrated to a fully formed nation should not expect 'to modify the character and structures' of their adopted land" but should rather "accept the nation and share its destiny."[44]

While the larger Canadian state has groped toward a public policy of pluralism, Quebec has sought to acculturate its immigrants. Once French Canada saw immigration as a threatening program of the federal government and immigrants as allies of "les héritiers des conquérants", but because of the decline of the French-Canadian birth rate and the nationalists' and separatists' dreams of nation building, Quebec now sees immigration as a way to draw and assimilate newcomers. This is especially so since natalization programs to encourage Quebec women to have more children seem unsuccessful. Provincial legislation in Quebec has clearly been an instrument to use the state to ensure *survivance*, but the terms of such laws have as their target the immigrants, not merely the vestiges of the Anglophone hegemony. Loi 63 (1969), "pour promouvoir la langue française au Québec", was directed toward ensuring the use of French in the workplace; Loi 22 (1974), "sur la langue officielle", had as its purpose forcing non-Anglophone immigrant children to attend the French language school system; Loi 101 (1977), "Charte de la langue française", required the use of French in all domains of social life – public administration, justice, commerce, small business. Its purpose was to make Quebec unilingually French. Although less than 100,000 of the 250,000 immigrants to Quebec spoke French on arrival, the success achieved in gallicizing the instruments of the provincial government seems to have made Quebec society more confident in its dealings with immigrants of every kind. It is not so much that 25,000 Haitians present less challenge to assimilation than the Italians and Portuguese who preceded them but rather, I believe, that great psychological gain has accompanied the rise and success of *indépendantisme* in Quebec, even among those who see it only as a tactic for improving French-Canadian fortunes within confederation. Seeing itself as a colonized majority in its own land, with a small colonialist elite to neutralize and immigrants to acculturate through state mechanisms, rather than as part of a shrinking minority in a vast land, Quebec can act out of confidence that it will survive rather than fear that it will die.

Despite the hostility and cynicism of much of the intelligentsia, which speaks for those born to or acculturated to one of the charter groups, and despite the limited definition of multiculturalism as an instrument of "gentle canadianization" held by educators and caretakers, the idea has become a political system and an ideology for many. Ambiguities about what *multiculturalism* should mean, what constitutes an *ethnie*, and how this policy affects individuals' negotiation of identity, remain and may even facilitate the exchange between the government and its clientele, the citizens. The Canadian mosaic, the rainbow, polyphony and the symphony orchestra have all been tried as images, and the first governor general of non-British and non-French descent – Edward Schreyer – spoke of Canada as a cathedral. In his installation speech, he quoted Sir Wilfrid Laurier, who at the turn of the century had called for a Canada on the model of a Gothic cathedral of granite, oak and marble: "It is the image of the nation I wish to see Canada become. For here, I want the granite to remain the granite, the oak to remain the oak, the marble to remain the marble."[45]

The politicians and the intelligentsia have proven more adept at using metaphors for multiculturalism than at drafting legislation and programs to encourage the emergence of a public ethos of pluralism, that both the charter groups and the other ethnic groups could share. In response to the programs of Ottawa and the provinces, an ethnic clientele has grown up that politicians and civil servants try to manipulate. It is easy enough to see the political exchange between the two sides, but it is difficult to see in the exchange more than symbolic gestures and partisan politics. Of the four elements of the policy – integration, the right to cultural retention, cross-cultural understanding and equality of access and opportunity – the ethnic (at least the white) clientele is most interested in the parts of programs that help ethnic groups persist. They wish to see as corollaries access to the mainstream through acquisition of the official languages, the sort of intercultural understanding that affords each group a good status and a distinct identity in Canadian life, and an end to bigotry and discrimination. Most spokesmen and leaders, however, begin from the premise that the numerical and institutional strength of the *ethnie* and the coherence of its political mobilization are the prerequisites for gaining the government's attention.

The government, in turn, has an interest in dealing with a limited number of effective leaders from well-organized ethnic blocs. The multiculturalism sector of the federal government runs a program to organize advocacy for newer, less demanding, or more fractious ethnic collectivities. One astute social scientist has observed that the associational structures of most Canadian ethnic groups have so many personnel who represent the "organic intelligentsia" of state-sponsored multiculturalism, and depend so heavily on government grants to operate, that they cannot be considered independent spokesmen for ethnic feeling any longer.[46] Those who are uncomfortable with the low status of the adjective ethnic now favor the term multicultural, as in "multicultural group" or "multiculturals". To the extent that ethnic groups become the creations of government rather than representations of the natural sentiment of those of the descent group, this usage, which seems a semantic monstrosity at first, may be sound usage.

The most ambiguous aspect of multicultural politics, and one that makes the policy and ethos suspect to many, can be summed up in a few unanswered questions: what is the relationship between negotiating one's personal ethnic identity and dealing with the politics of the *ethnie's* status? What is the ethnic interest (which the *Québécois* might call *un projet social ou national*) of an immigrant *ethnie*? In other words, what do immigrants or ethnics want, and does the existence of organized ethnic leadership and a multicultural policy provide what they want? How can government recognize the ethnic group except through funding ethnocultural activities and associations? Recognition of ethnies has received an especially bourgeois and hierarchical spin and reminds one of the quips by the great Italian Marxist thinker, Antonio Gramsci, that in the exercise of hegemony in a parliamentary context, "corruption or fraud stand midway between consensus and force." Since 1972, advisory councils composed of ethnic representatives, always appointed rather than elected, have recommended that "persons of various ethnocultural backgrounds" be named to boards or hired by a great variety of government agencies.

In 1976 the minister responsible for multiculturalism, John Munro, reacted to criticisms of the policy by denying that it was "a cheap political bone" thrown to the so-called professional ethnics. The policy, he said, was for all Canadians. It was not an English plot to subvert official bilingualism and to dilute the French voice in Canada. Nor was it tokenism or a smokescreen to make the imposition of bilingualism on the third element easier.[47] Despite such disclaimers, largesse for ethnic organizations and activities, whether doled out by Liberals or Progressive Conservatives, whether handled by federal or provincial civil servants, has often had a distinctly partisan appearance and the scent of the patronage pork barrel. The policy has always been linked to the idea that particular parties can control the votes of particular immigrant or ethnic groups by forms of patronage bestowed in the "legal tender" of the day – magistracies, commission seats and so forth – on the notables from each collectivity. Prominent politicians make visits to the *ethnie's* central institutions and pay at least lip service to the *ethnie's* concerns that arise from "double consciousness" (its interest in the homeland of origin and the foreign policy objectives that go with that interest). Especially significant in the exchange between government and the displaced peoples has been public anti-Sovietism and support for the "captive nations", in some ways a less expensive price for politicians to pay than honest responses to later demands for a piece of the pie in Canada.

It is unclear what underlies the apparent convention in Canada that the interests, standing and *amour propre* of the *ethnie* coincide with the personal negotiation of status and identity by certain ethnoverted individuals. Collective status and personal mobility come together in the form of the parceling out of an appropriate number of appointive offices. An elaborate list of sinecures, honorifics and appointments has become the medium of exchange between the ethnic groups and the political parties and bureaucracies. There are as well the inevitable new plaques and parks named after notables and ethnonational heroes to compete with older Anglo-Celtic filial pieties.

These activities are accompanied by grants for community-based historical research and ceremonial ethnonational toponymic changes as well. In the belief that history is infinitely malleable to the civic purpose, the government makes funds available for the rewriting of the national history of Canada, with the third element in. Although such programs provided some leaven to the peculiarly ethnocentric and elitist national historiography, their chief result often seems to be an intellectual steeplechase to prove longevity in the land, rather like the "Mayflowerism" that once characterized ethnic history societies in the United States.

The Canadian party system, as well as the colonial inheritance of competent and intrusive public administration, led to a species of ethnic "wardheeling" in which the entire ethnic group rather than that of a single political constituency was seen as a source of votes in return for attention, jobs and favors. Such ethnicking was highly visible for several reasons.[48] For one thing, until very recently, the third element was underrepresented among both civil servants and elected politicians: "Although these groups comprised a quarter of the population by ethnic origin in the early 1960s, they elected only 4.4% of new members of the House of Commons and controlled an even smaller proportion of Cabinet positions."[49]

As a result, the exchange of everything from money for a new ethnic hall or old-age home to funds to teach "ancestral" or "heritage" languages for bloc votes – as portrayed in the media – had a quality of capturing charter group politicians and ethnic leaders *in flagrantis*. Generally the problem is less the local candidate's ethnicity or networks of influence with the ethnic groups in his riding, than the party's relationship with each group on a national scale. If the local politician delivers grants and honors with fanfare, it is the quieter funding of ethnic persistence through civil services controlled by one party or another that can affect political choice. John Kenneth Galbraith, with a disarming ethnocentric fall from grace to absolve his Scots-Canadian kinsmen, has observed the game of ethnic politics where groups are "solicited, by oratory, unconvincing efforts at identification and inspired banality."[50]

Galbraith and others who criticize politicians for mongering for ethnic votes miss an essential point, usually because they hold too simple a view of the ethnics and the dynamics of maintaining an *ethnie*. At the level of symbolic politics and the forging of the instruments that enable ethnic leaders to promote ethnogenesis and then ethnicization of the immigrants (that is, to mobilize them politically toward group objectives), there is very little gullibility and a perfect understanding of the exchange of gifts. (Anyone who has spent two decades, as I have, watching politicians struggle to say a few words in the heritage language and promising funds for new wings on ethnic halls, as if the money came out of their own pockets rather than the taxpayers', while ethnic leaders lead rounds of applause as proxies for future votes they cannot deliver, learns not to gag on his pasta or cabbage rolls and gains a new understanding of the "social contract" in a pluralist society.) There are in Ontario, Manitoba and Alberta politicians who are legendary for the number of ethnic groups with which they claim blood ties. One is described derisively by those among whom he "ethnicks" as claiming descent from all the peoples whose homelands touch the Vistula, the Danube and the Dnieper.

If the claims of politicians on the multicultural stump are suspect, so are the claims of leaders and spokesmen who say they represent coherent ethnies but are more often self-appointed or government-designated than elected. Of course, opponents of the multicultural policy make much of how unrepresentative ethnic leaders are and of what a corrupting and trivializing effect ethnicking has on issue-oriented politics. A more accurate critique of multiculturalism would be that the policy may serve to perpetuate the hegemony of the British as the elite of Canada. By encouraging political loyalties on lines that cut across class and by rewarding leaders and spokesmen whose concerns are ethnoverted rather than class oriented, multiculturalism softens issues of immigrant exploitation and representation and removes them from the frame of the flow of labor to capital. A 1973 study found members of ethnic groups more concerned with problems of cultural and linguistic retention than with inequality of opportunity and prejudice in the job place.[51] It is unlikely that a survey of members of visible minorities who arrived in Canada after the impact of the relaxing of racialist immigration restrictions in the 1970s would have similar results.

At the same time, equality of access to services, the struggle against bigotry in the host society, and the guarantees of social mobility are added to the multicultural texts. Most of these issues have no intrinsic relationship to group life, and all of them have objectives that could be met by enforceable legislation. These additions may serve both hegemony and the participants in the ethnic discouse who use the idiom of culture rather than that of law, power and class to define the immigrants' situation.

The problem with a pluralism based on assumptions about ethnic persistence among immigrants is simply that ethnicity is more and less than a biological given or census fact. It is processual. Canada may tolerate or promote ethnies, but, as Camille Laurin warned, they are not nations. Immigrants and their children negotiate their own identities, and the texts of the ethnoverted leadership are but one level of discourse among many. Without renewal through continual heavy migration and without a territorial base, with porous boundaries and the lure of the mainstream culture, with a public school system and intermarriage, the question becomes less whether intermediaries and leaders represent ethnies and more whether the *ethnie* is merely an epiphenomenon of immigration that will disappear unless regularly funded institutions of ethnic maintenance are legislated. Recently a Ukrainian Canadian observed rather bitterly that he and others had deluded themselves. He had come to realize that the Prairie Ukrainians were the only ethnic group in the third element. The rest were postwar immigrants facing rapid generational slippage and loss of ethnoculture.[52] An informal count of the leadership of most groups as well as of those who serve on the various multicultural advisory boards shows a majority to be foreign-born.

Measuring the differentials among the census categories "ethnic origin", "mother tongue" and "home language" suggests that, despite the declared policy of multiculturalism, the optimistic or obfuscating claims of ethnic spokesmen, and the presence of extensive heritage language programs, immigrants to Canada and their children are acculturating rapidly. "Linguicide", the label that advocates who believe multiculturalism will be credible only if multilingualism is possible, seems inevitable under current conditions. To the extent that a subculture needs a subsociety in which to embed itself, only geographical, cultural and institutional isolation could preserve language. The prevailing situation is diglossia – immigrants speaking English as a second language, with all the limits that implies, and at the same time slowly losing their mother tongues. Their children speak English as a first language at school and on the street and are either bilingual or unable to speak their parents' language.

The leading ethnolinguist, Joshua Fishman, has noted that within three generations the language of the street usually becomes the language of the cradle. Only about half of those who describe themselves as Italian Canadians use Italian as their home language. That number is even less than the number of foreign-born in the group. In the 1971 census, only 71,000 Poles spoke Polish at home regularly, although 135,000 claimed Polish as their mother tongue and over 315,000 as their ethnic origin. For the Dutch in Canada, a group for whom assimilation is considerably easier, the figures are 36,000 speaking Dutch at home out of 425,000. The majority of these speakers of Dutch live in fairly isolated rural settings or have religious ties that are strongly ethnoverted. Since it is the Ukrainians who have led the way for the third element and who have made the most concerted effort to join various of their immigrant cohorts in a single "nation in exile", one would expect language retention to be high. Only about half the census group lists Ukrainian as its mother tongue, and only about a third speaks Ukrainian regularly in the home.

There are, of course, bases of ethnic identity, if not of ethnoculture, other than retention of the mother tongue. Generally, however, Canadian ethnic spokesmen, dismissive of what they view as decultured third- and fourth-generation ethnic identity in the United States, emphasize language as the cement of community. (I am aware of ethnic hockey and basketball teams that have collapsed, not for want of athletes of the descent group but because speaking the heritage language was a requirement for making the team.) Studies of the intensity of associational life and commitment to the discourse of ethnoculture are rare, and sophisticated ones are even rarer. A study of the National Congress of Italian Canadians a few years ago showed only about 30 percent of Canadians of Italian descent active in any ethnic institution except the parish.[53] It is such results that cause ethnic leaders to hesitate before analyzing the *ethnie* publicly.

Ethnic leaders have reason then to seek means as quickly as possible to turn living immigrant ethnocultures into ethnies with institutions that can aid group persistence through future generations, even if immigration ceases. The texts that they produce for discourse with both the immigrant community and the government more and more emphasize this Canadian rather than the old-country side of their double consciousness.

Canada's new Constitution, born of the British juridical and political tradition, is a document about individual rather than group rights. Such an approach to rights and freedoms fits ill with political pluralism. One result has been to add group rights to the document; such an attempt is the Meech Lake Accord, which recognizes Quebec as a "distinct society". The result for ethnic leadership has been disappointment that there are no justiciable multicultural rights in the Charter of Rights and Freedoms. Article 27 speaks of multiculturalism as a quality of Canadian life and promises that all other articles of the Charter will be interpreted in a manner consistent with multiculturalism. It is, then, an affirmation of multicultural ideals but not a statement of ethnic rights or multicultural obligations. No ethnies will be "distinct societies". *Canadien* spokesmen and those of the aboriginal peoples, Indian or Inuit, can write and speak of pluralism of destination, of the right to public funding to create institutions of otherness as part of a permanent status within Canadian confederation. It is not at all unusual or destructive of consensus in the political discourse for such leaders to describe policies that encourage acculturation and assimilation into Anglophone Canada as cultural genocide. Very few Canadians would, however, tolerate expressions of a similar kind about the rights of ethnic groups.

After the new Charter of Rights failed to address ethnic group persistence directly, many hoped that Bill C-93, the Multicultural Act, brought before Parliament in 1987, would offer redress. The bill is also long on affirmation of the polyethnic Canadian reality and the value of a multicultural ethos but short on enforceable programs. Affirming multiculturalism while legislating first bilingualism and then Quebec's right to a "separate way" in Canada puts the government's view of the rights of immigrant and ethnic minorities in perspective. As always, however, the lack of shared definitions of the boundary and content of multiculturalism as well as uncertainty about the nature and life cycle of group ethnicity itself, has been as much an impediment to the development of a public policy as its ideological enemies have been. There is disagreement about whether a minister of multiculturalism would ghettoize those he served, whether a commissioner of multiculturalism could work as effectively as the commissioner of official language has functioned in enforcing bilingualism. Could such a public servant enforce sensitivity toward ethnic cultures and a fair distribution of jobs without appearing to be tainted with a species of pluralist McCarthyism? Should the mainstream be multiculturalized rather than vice versa? In other words, should the secretary of state for multiculturalism or the minister of culture and communications take over all funding for the arts, control of the CBC, and allocations for research?[54]

Is this then "the way the world ends, not with a bang but a whimper?" Without the possibility of enforcement through either the Charter or the Act, this would be a multiculturalism that would amount to no more than the modest statement made in 1969 in Book IV of the Royal Commission about "encouraging those members of ethnic groups who want to do so to maintain a proud sense of the contribution of their own group to Canadian society...." Both ethnic and panethnic associational spokesmen have suggested tactics for funding ethnic group persistence, from annual group maintenance grants to tithing. One suggestion is that each Canadian taxpayer could assign 1 percent of his or her taxes to an ethnic umbrella organization, presumably one of his or her choice, not one determined by the census. The possibility of extending tax credits of the kind allowed for charitable donations to gifts given to ethnic associations has also received consideration. The vexing questions of how much this would cost the community and whether the mainstream is obligated to support alternative cultures arise. Politicians usually prefer not to look at them directly.

For those who speak for ethnies formed from the DP experience or from a history of Prairie isolation as well as for the immigrant Italian *ethnie*, numbers are crucial. Even since Senator Yuzyk raised the census artifact of ethnic origin to forge the third element, both individual ethnic groups and the third element have depended on the threat of bloc votes and the moral suasion of rights by magnitude to press their case. A guest editorial in response to the proposed new Multiculturalism Act recently appeared in the *Ottawa Citizen*. It represents a genre of texts going back to remarks by John Yaremko, Ontario's first minister of citizenship and culture, to Heritage Ontario in 1972, a provincially sponsored forum on multiculturalism. Yaremko assumed, or chose to assume, that census identity and personal ethnocultural sentiment are synonymous, that polyethnicity automatically engenders multiculturalism: "According to the 1986 census, 38% of the Canadian population have origins other than British or French. Cultural diversity is not a fringe factor as was the case at the time of Confederation."[55]

It is in this context that one must understand the politics of census taking in Canada. Changes in census categories that allow the recording of multiple identities and alternatives to a patrilineal definition of ethnic origin, and that make the reporting of ethnic origin voluntary, threaten to strip the generals of their field forces. According to the Assistant Statistician of Canada, more and more people "simply refuse to report origins no matter how we attempt to phrase the question. They steadfastly insist that they are Canadian...."[56] The census, he added, "is a questionnaire which is completed by the respondent, and the respondent's perception is what determines what the respondent will answer." Such a democratic and volitional approach to ethnic identity can hardly be faulted, but it causes major problems for those who use ethnic origins as an instrument of political power. The assistant statistician went on to observe that his office had many requests for information from ethnic associations. He also showed some of the wisdom that comes from long experience with the ethnic numbers game:

> A related problem stems from what we might call old world conflicts, in which rival groups will object to the inclusion of each other in the census counts. For example, spokespersons for the Armenian community might object to any associations in the enumeration with Turks. Spokespersons for the Greek community may insist that Macedonians not be counted separately, but be included in the count of Greeks, and spokespersons for the Macedonian community will demand exactly the opposite. There will be complaints that the Irish are included with the British in the summary tables...

For all the concern with ethnic origin statistics and the maintenance of ethnies, there seems remarkably little information about how the public policy affects the quality of life in other than cultural or psychological terms. If immigrants have prospered or remained niched at the bottom of the economy, what role, if any, has the polity had in bringing about such results? It is forty years since the new mass migration began and over twenty years since John Porter published *The Vertical Mosaic*,[57] a study of ethnicity, stratification and social mobility. His book has proven to be the antitext to the multicultural canon and a vade mecum for those who believe that liberal principles of individualism and meritocracy along with benign (i.e., unbigoted) forms of assimilationism are the only fair and effective policies for an immigrant nation.

Porter contended that Canada's charter groups had remained in terms of wealth, power and status in a relatively unchanged relationship to the other ethnic groups. He used indices of disproportionate representation in various occupations and strata to show the British group's hegemony and dominance of elite positions in business and other professions, politics and cultural life. He attributed this dominance more to longevity of residence, networks of influence, and the low "entry status" of many non-British immigrants rather than to systematic racialism operating against Southern Europeans and other minorities. For Porter, a policy of multiculturalism risked enshrining inequality and low social-class niching for certain ethnic groups. After showing that Porter overemphasized the lack of change to fit his central thesis, his followers, both sympathetic and hostile have attempted to test his views on the increasingly polyethnic Canadian reality.[58] Thus a 1975 study, using measurements similar to those Porter used in the 1960s, found that although the non-British and non-French components in the higher levels of management and the professions had gone from 1 percent to 5 percent, and although French-Canadian access to the elite had grown a bit, the control of elite categories by the British had only declined from 92 percent to 86 percent in a country in which they made up about 50 percent of the population. A study in Toronto at about the same time showed "significant inequality of income opportunity among immigrant men". The kind of choices available to Canadians, with the exception of the Jews, fairly well paralleled earlier immigration department information about what was possible for preferred and nonpreferred stocks: opportunity was best for the English and decreased to less and less for the Jews, the Italians, the Slavs, the Greeks, the Portuguese, the Asians and the Blacks, in that order.[59]

Such attempts to relate ethnicity to stratification and social mobility are fraught with risky inferences. The numbers game may be the only way the third element can maintain political clout, but it is not a sufficiently sophisticated way to measure immigrants' life choices, levels of satisfaction, or intensity of ethnic identity. It is clear that Porter and others underestimated the strength of parallel pyramids of opportunity. In the face of the barriers of discrimination and denial of access to mainstream economies and elites, alternate strategies do develop. It is clear that both the Jews and the Italians have prospered from such parallel economic structures or from concentration in occupations less attractive to charter group elites, such as the construction industry and retail or wholesale commerce. Other ethnic groups have found similar, if less profitable, niching in the food services industries and control of airport limousines. New generations of professionals from the children of these immigrant groups find their clientele within the niche but begin to circulate in the larger society and economy as well.

However, among continental European immigrants, especially those from southern Europe, there remains a mixed sense of place in Canada. Books with titles like *Don't Feed Us on Lentils* and *Bastards of the Nation* remind us that immigration has been painful and that the first purpose of all Canadian immigration policy has been to find the manpower the country needs. For all the talk of seeking skilled immigrants, the policy continues to mean, in the words of the most recent annual report of the minister of immigration, finding people to "accept jobs at distant and remote locations" and to "take jobs that are not accepted by residents".[60] The least unionized, lowest-paid and most unpleasant urban work in Canada is done by immigrants, especially immigrant women. Latin Americans, Middle Easterners, Asians and East Africans now do what Slavs did in the 1950s, Italians in the 1960s, and Portuguese and Greeks in the 1970s. No number of individual immigrant or ethnic success stories, either heralded by multicultural or ethnic flacks, or splattered across the country's slick magazines with innuendos about organized crime, fraud and swindling, can obscure the low entry status of most non-British immigrants to Canada. What immigrants have added to the civility and vibrance of Canada's cities, especially as shopkeepers and restaurateurs, testifies to a presence that has enriched the whole economy.

Almost fifty years after the mass migration of the non-British and the non-French began to intrude into the struggle for *Canadien survivance* and for the survival of the Canadian polity, the situation remains inchoate. It is inchoate in Wittgenstein's sense that the determinate relations between subjects and the nature of objects themselves seem only now to be forming. French-Canadian *survivance*, despite recent successful tests in the Prairie Provinces of the Charter's guarantee of French language rights, is now condensed into the concept of Quebec as a distinct society or the dream of an independent Quebec. *English Canadian* has increasingly become a linguistic rather than an ethnic or a sentimental designation as the third element has been acculturating and the distance from British roots for all Canadians growing. As a corollary, despite the Charter, the pending Multiculturalism Act and highly differentiated ethnic and panethnic organizations, there are many signs that ethnicity is proving itself an epiphenomenon of several postmigrant generations rather than a basis for permanent communal differences.

Meanwhile, the external threat to the polity takes two forms. Candian fertility rates and those of white immigrants are below replacement level. Canada faces zero growth and, to sustain itself, will have to turn to races and ethnic groups that Mackenzie King, not to say other Canadians, might not welcome. The second external threat to the Canada that King would have recognized comes from attempts to create a North American free-trade zone.

The current public discourse about Canada's state of affairs reminds one of the advice of German Marxist philosopher Walter Benjamin, that the only way to understand the times one lives in is to try to catch "the dialectic at a standstill" by observing the contradictions and choices available to men and women in a "present without resolution". Benjamin went on to suggest the writing of a book made up solely of quotations to fulfill this purpose.[61] I will end with something of the sort.

The Saskatchewan Multicultural Association believes that it has found a "determinate relation" of significance: "If free trade in multiculturalism means adopting the concept of the melting pot rather than cultural pluralism, then multicultural organizations must oppose free trade." Importing the myth of the melting pot, it adds, "would be a far more significant threat to multiculturalism than the Meech Lake Accord." Meanwhile, that accord, with both its promise of special status for Quebec and its implication that such a status might include separate Quebec policies on immigration and the maintenance of ethnic groups, leads to a chorus of protest from the third element. The Canadian Jewish Congress and the National Congress of Italian Canadians denounce the idea. Some Prairie Ukrainian leaders offer a smug "I told you so" and dream dreams of a strategy for Alberta like that of Quebec that would create a regional Ukrainian-English bilingualism.[62] They can point to some stunning facts: that the number of bilingual Canadians has not risen much from the 15 percent it was when the Official Languages Act came into force a decade ago; that in 1986 Statistics Canada reported under 5 percent for Ontario and under 3 percent for British Columbia of non-Francophone children in French immersion programs; that Quebec nationalists also view a national bilingual policy with suspicion, as a "Trojan horse"; and that more often than not, bilingual Francophones outside Quebec become unilingual Anglophones, usually within a generation.

The effects of Meech Lake are apparent already. The accord establishes the idea that Canada is a dual society, but it does not oblige the English-speaking provinces to increase their bilingualism. A recent revolt of Tory backbenchers, mainly from the West, is attempting to thwart efforts to reconcile the new Charter of Rights with the Official Languages Act. In 1988 the premier of Ontario rejected a call to make Ontario officially bilingual. The call came from a Franco-Ontarian association, which speaks for the province's 500,000 Francophones, orphaned by the Quebec nationalist strategy and the Meech Lake Accord. At about the same time they were making their appeal, a witness before the Parliamentary Standing Committee on Multiculturalism, meeting in Toronto, told the legislators that:

> multiculturalism is totally meaningless without multilingualism. The equity envisioned in the act is not possible in our Canadian school communities, unless the languages of the children in the community are used.... Song and dance is not enough.[63]

In April 1987 Keith Spicer, a former commissioner of official languages and the influential editor of the *Ottawa Citizen*, spoke out. He saw the matter starkly:

> The final question runs deeper – isn't the time coming to stop making a religion of mosaics altogether and to start fostering a national spirit we can all identify with? With constant intermarriage, for how many generations more must an English- or Ukrainian-Canadian revere his presumed roots?[64]

Only a naif would ask why Spicer did not add French Canadians to his list; that would be to step outside the limits of legitimate discourse. He went on to accuse the government of "making a virtue of a weakness, a glory of a hindrance to nationhood; we pay people to have foreign roots."

One wonders if those engaged in the Canadian discourse about identity and policy now are ready for the next intrusion. With Canadian fertility rates unable to sustain growth, with the natural decline of immigration from Europe because of similar birth rates there, new Canadians will increasingly come from the Third World. This trend began in 1968 with the end of racialism in immigration legislation.[65] In that year 65 percent of the immigrants to Canada came from Europe. By 1984 the figure was down to 24 percent. The Asian share of immigration rose in that same period from 12 percent to 50. In 1961 no Asian country was among the top sending countries; by 1984 five out of ten were. Caribbean and Central American immigration has also risen rapidly since the yearly 1970s. Those who deal with the dialectic between the need for numbers and the desire to maintain the "right stock" are at work again.

A demographer for the Department of National Health and Welfare recently told the Parliamentary Standing Committee on Multiculturalism about the demographic situation of Canada. He reminded them of the decline of European fertility and went on to describe the impact on immigration of "lumpy events" such as the reversion of Hong Kong to China in the near future. One cannot think of the possibility of other lumpy events, in Johannesburg, Belfast, the Punjab, Sri Lanka and the West

Bank, which could change the pools of potential new Canadians. Would large numbers from any of these places, labeled refugee or DP, start the same problems that began in Canada after World War II? How would their coming affect multiculturalism and bilingualism?

If this has been a darkling portrait of Canada's population policies, it should be balanced against some thoughts about the quality of life amid what amounts to a pluralism of pluralisms. Practical acceptance of polyethnicity and the presence of free and fair institutions make daily life in Canada rich, safe and hopeful. The economy inclines to meritocracy and free flow despite the hold of old elites upon it and the aspirations of those who believe in corporate rights and freedoms to control part of it. It works for most immigrants, although not without the economic struggle and scarring that accompany insertion into a strange, and often hostile, social and cultural environment. It clearly does not work for the native people and some of the native-born poor, who lack the networks and the strategies that the newcomers have developed to carve out patterns of survival and mobility. If Canada can be saved from the full realization of anyone's dream of multiculturalism – that of the ethnic leaders, the "caretakers" or the politicians – we will continue to live in a civil polity between balkanization and assimilation, between petty nationalism and laissez-faire continentalism, between a begrudging, ungenerous dualism and a separated Quebec. Robert Louis Stevenson once remarked that the "pleasure was in the traveling, not the getting there." For Canada, survival lies in the traveling toward an identity, and we will all be better served if that traveling itself remains our identity.

Notes

1. The text of King's statement appears in *Hansard, House of Commons Debates*, 1 May 1947, 2644-47. It is reproduced as Appendix A of the *Report of the Canadian Immmigration and Population Study (CIPS): The Immigration Program* (Ottawa: Information Canada, 1947). There is no general history of Canadian immigration policy and immigrants. For the postwar period, see D.C. Corbett, *Canada's Immigration Policy* (Toronto: Canadian Institute of International Affairs, University of Toronto, 1957); F. Hawkins, *Canada and Immigration: Public Policy and Public Concern* (Montreal: McGill Queen's University Press, 1972); and R. Whitaker, *Double Standard: The Secret History of Canadian Immigration* (Toronto: Lester & Orpen Dennys, 1987).

2. For studies of the earlier mass immigration see D. Avery, *'Dangerous Foreigners': European Immigrant Workers and Labour Radicalism in Canada, 1896-1932* (Toronto: McClelland and Stewart, 1979); R.C. Brown and R. Cook, *Canada, 1896-1921: A Nation Transformed* (Toronto: McClelland and Stewart, 1974).

3. J.S. Woodsworth, *Strangers Within Our Gates; or, Coming Canadians* (Toronto: F.C. Stephenson, 1909), 162.

4. See King's 1910 report, as quoted in *The Immigration Program*, 9.

5. Quoted in J.S. Frideres, "British Canadian Attitudes toward Minority Ethnic Groups in Canada", in *Attitudes Toward Minority Groups in Canada – Ethnicity*, no. 5 (Toronto: Prentice-Hall, 1978). See also H. Palmer, "Reluctant Hosts: Anglo-Canadian Views of Multiculturalism in the Twentieth Century" in *Multiculturalism as State Policy*, conference report of the Second Biennial Conference of Canadian Consultative Council on Multiculturalism (Ottawa: Ministry of Supply, 1976), 81-118.

6. F. Bosworth, "What Kind of Canadians Are We Getting?" *Maclean's* (15 February 1952): 17.

7. *Demography and Immigration in Canada: Challenge and Opportunity* (Ottawa: Employment and Immigration Canada, November 1987): 18-20.

8. John Stuart Mill to Henry George in October 1869, quoted in R. Takaki, *Iron Cages: Race and Culture in Nineteenth Century America* (New York, Knopf, distributed by Rando, 1979), 245.

9. I. Abella and H. Troper, *None Is Too Many: Canada and the Jews of Europe, 1933-1948* (Toronto: Lester & Orpen Dennys, 1982), chap. 8.

10. M. Danys, *DP, Lithuanian Immigration to Canada after the Second World War* (Toronto: Multicultural History Society of Ontario, 1986), 134.

11. N. Tienhaara, *Canadian View on Immigration and Population: An Analysis of Postwar Gallup Polls* (Ottawa: Department of Manpower and Immigration, 1974), 59.

12. Brief of Association of United Ukrainian Canadians on immigration submitted to the Senate, 5 June 1947, 149, reprinted in *Anglo-American Perspectives on the Ukrainian Question, 1938-1951*, ed. B.S. Kordan and L. Luciuk (Kingston, Ontario: Limestone Press, 1987).

13. Quoted in M. Danys, *DP,* 84.

14. F. Hawkins, *Canada and Immigration*, 201-2.

15. F. Bosworth, "What Kind of Canadians Are We Getting?"

16. "Gateway to a New Life", *Globe and Mail*, 12 September 1956, 7.

17. D.C. Corbett, *Canada's Immigration Policy*, 52-53.

18. E. Wickberg, ed., *From China to Canada, A History of the Chinese Communities in Canada* (Toronto: McClelland and Stewart, 1982), 214-15.

19. R. Morin, *L'Immigration au Canada* (Montreal: Editions de l'Action nationale, 1966), introduction.

20. N.E. Assimopoulos and J.E. Humblet, "Les Immigrés et la question nationale: étude comparative des sociétés québécoise et wallonne", in *Studi emigrazione/Etudes migrations* 24 (86) (June 1987): 155-86.

21. Dispatch to the Department of External Affairs (Ottawa), 8 March 1949, in RG 76, pt. 10, Public Archives of Canada, as quoted in F. Sturino, "Post-World War II Canadian Immigration Policy toward Italians", *Polyphony: Bulletin of the Multicultural History Society of Ontario* 7 (2) (Fall/Winter 1985): 68. See also R.F. Harney, "Italophobia: An English-speaking Malady?" in *Studi emigrazione/Etudes migrations* 22 (77) (March 1985): 6-43.

22. See J.S. Macdonald and L. Macdonald, "Italian Migration to Australia, Manifest Functions of Bureaucracy versus Latent Function of Informal Networks", *Journal of Social History* (Spring 1967): 254.

23. "Investigation of Settlement Arrangements", *Immigrants from Italy Agenda Item* 2(1961), RG 26, vol. 128, Public Archives of Canada.

24. See R. Breton, "The Production and Allocation of Symbolic Resources: An Analysis of the Linguistic and Ethnocultural Fields in Canada", in *Ethnic Canada, Identities and Inequalities*, ed. L. Driedger (Toronto: Copp Clark Pitman, 1987), 44-64.

25. N. Keyfitz, "How the Descendants of English-Speakers See the Speakers of Other Languages and Their Descendants", in *Second Canadian Conference on Multiculturalism Conference Report* (Ottawa: Minister of State, Multiculturalism, 1976), 69.

26. R. Breton, "The Production and Allocation of Symbolic Resources", 55.

27. E. Kallen, "Multiculturalism: Ideology, Policy and Reality", *Journal of Canadian Studies/Revue d'études canadiennes* 17(1) (Spring 1982):51-63.

28. Senator Paul Yuzyk, *For a Better Canada* (Toronto: Ukrainian National Association, 1973). "Canada, A Multicultural Nation" was delivered in the Senate on 3 March 1964.

29. M. Lupul, "Canada's Options in Time of Political Crisis and Their Implications for Multiculturalism", in *Ukrainian Canadians, Multiculturalism, and Separatism: An Assessment* (Edmonton: Canadian Institute of Ukrainian Studies, 1978), 160.

30. Heritage Ontario, *Report* (Toronto: Government of Ontario, 2 June 1972).

31. Book IV: *The Cultural Contribution of the Other Ethnic Groups*, report of the Royal Commission on Bilingualism and Biculturalism (Ottawa: The Queen's Printer, 1969), 4-5. These are remarks of one of the chief authors of the report. See J. Burnet, "The Policy of Multiculturalism within a Bilingual Framework: An Interpretation", in *The Education of Immigrant Children*, ed. A. Wolfgang (Toronto: Ontario Institute for Studies in Education, 1975).

32. E. De Martino, *La fine del mondo* (Turin: Einaudi, 1978).

33. K. Deutsch, *Nationalism and Social Communication, An Inquiry into the Foundation of Nationality* (Cambridge: MIT Press, 1953).

34. R. Breton, "The Production and Allocation of Symbolic Resources", 58.

35. *Report of the First Conference of the Canadian Consultative Council on Multiculturalism* (Ottawa: Minister of State, Multiculturalism, 1972), 4-5, 18-20.

36. "UCC Slams Multicultural Centres", *Ukrainian Echo* 1 (1) (April 1977): 2.

37. L. Zolf, "Mulling Over Multiculturalism", *Maclean's* (14 April 1980): 6.

38. D. Fisher, presentations in *Multiculturalism as State Policy* (Ottawa: Minister of State, Multiculturalism, 1976), 15.

39. For a discussion of these matters, see J. Burnet, "Myths and Multiculturalism", *Canadian Journal of Education* 4(4) (1979): 43-58.

40. *The Symons Report*, an abridged version of vols. 1, 2 of *To Know Ourselves: The Report of the Commission on Canadian Studies* (Toronto: Association of Universities and Colleges of Canada, 1978), 60.

41. Rev. Léger Comeau, "Multiculturalism – A Francophone Viewpoint", in *Second Canadian Conference on Multiculturalism Conference Report* (Ottawa: Minister of State, Multiculturalism, 1976), 27.

42. R. Lévesque, "Education in a Changing Society, A View from Quebec", in *Canadian Schools and Canadian Identity*, ed. A. Chaiton and N. McDonald (Toronto: Gage Educational Publishing, 1977).

43. G. Rocher, "Multiculturalism: The Doubts of a Francophone" in *Second Canadian Conference on Multiculturalism Conference Report* (Ottawa: Minister of State, Multiculturalism, 1976), 47-53.

44. C. Laurin, "Le Sort des minorités ethniques dans un Québec indépendant", in *Frontières ethniques en devenir*, ed. D. Juteau Lee (Ottawa: Editions de l'Université d'Ottawa, 1979).

45. See the imagery of Yuzyk's 1964 speech. Governor General Schreyer quoted Laurier in his address at his installation, Ottawa, 22 January 1979.

46. D. Stasiulis, "The Political Structuring of Ethnic Community Action: A Reformulation", *Canadian Ethnic Studies* 12(3) (1980):18.

47. Address by the Honorable John Munro, minister responsible for multiculturalism, in *Multiculturalism as State Policy*.

48. "Now I have had experience as a politician, and I recognize the temptation of what I used to call 'ethnicking' in John Diefenbaker's day..." D. Fisher, presentation in *Multiculturalism as State Policy*, 17. "Today's official multiculturalism leads to the worst of demagogueries: for example, John Diefenbaker promising to liberate the Ukraine, and all this for a handful of Ukrainian Canadian seats; Joe Clark moving embassies for a fingerful of Jewish seats..." L. Zolf, "How Multiculturalism Corrupts", *Maclean's* (15 November 1982): 21.

49. D. Stasiulis, "Cultural Boundaries and the Cohesion of Canada" in R. Rosandric, ed., *Cultural Pluralism and Cultural Identity, The Experience of Canada, Finland and Yugoslavia*, final report of the UNESCO Joint Study on Cultural Development in Countries Containing Different National and/or Ethnic Groups (Paris: UNESCO, 1985), 79.

50. J.K. Galbraith, *A Life in Our Times: Memoirs* (New York: Houghton-Mifflin, 1981), 1.

51. Study by K.G. O'Bryan, J. Reitz and O. Kuplowska published as *Non-Official Languages: A Study in Canadian Multiculturalism* (Ottawa: Multiculturalism Directorate, 1976), cited in D. Stasiulis, "Cultural Boundaries and the Cohesion of Canada", 78.

52. M.R. Lupul, "The Tragedy of Canada's White Ethnics: A Constitutional Postmortem", *Journal of Ukrainian Studies,* 7 (Spring 1982):5-7.

53. *Italian Canadians: A Cross Section, a National Survey of Italian Canadian Communities* (Ottawa: Congress of Italian Canadians, 1978). It is only fair to add that it took some courage to publish the report and that the research was flawed and the statistical base insufficient. Its result does, however, dovetail with many other informal indicators of low ethnoversion in terms of participation, except world-cup soccer and family and *paese* rites of passage.

54. J. H. Grey et al., *Multiculturalism and the Charter: A Legal Perspective* (Agincourt, Ontario: Carswell, 1987); for the debate about the act and what it should include, see especially *Multiculturalism, Building the Canadian Mosaic*, report of the Standing Committee on Multiculturalism, House of Commons, no. 5, June 1987, in *Minutes of Proceedings and Evidence of the Standing Committee on Multiculturalism* (Ottawa: The Queen's Printer, 1987); see other criticisms of the proposed act in *Ethno-Canada, The Newsletter of the Canadian Ethnocultural Council* (Ottawa, Winter 1988), a special issue on the Multiculturalism Bill C-93.

55. L.A. Cardozo, "In Defense of the Federal Government's Multicultural Policy", in "Guest Column", *The Ottawa Citizen*, 19 January 1988, C-1. The columnist is the executive director of the Canadian Ethnocultural Council, an organization that receives large annual grants from the Multiculturalism Sector within the Secretary of State.

56. Testimony of a demographer for the Department of National Health and Welfare and of the Assistant Archivist of Canada before the Standing Committee on Multiculturalism, *Minutes of the Proceedings and Evidence of the Standing Committee on Multiculturalism*, House of Commons, no. 13, February 1988 (Ottawa: The Queen's Printer, 1988), 23.

57. J. Porter, *The Vertical Mosaic: An Analysis of Social Class and Power in Canada* (Toronto: University of Toronto Press, 1965).

58. The most important correctives and confirmations of the truth of Porter's general points are G. Darroch, "Another Look at Ethnicity, Stratification, and Social Mobility in Canada", *Canadian Journal of Sociology* 4(1979):1-25; W. Clement, *The Canadian Corporate Elite, An Analysis of Economic Power* (Toronto: McClelland and Stewart, 1975); and various investigations by J. Reitz, conveniently synthesized in his book *The Survival of Ethnic Groups in Canada* (Toronto: McGraw-Hill Ryerson, 1980). In a lighter vein, Peter Newman's book *The Canadian Establishment* (Toronto: McClelland and Stewart, 1976) confirms Porter's view.

59. J. Goldlust and A. Richmond, "A Multivariate Analysis of the Economic Adaptation of Immigrants in Toronto", mimeograph, Institute for Behavioral Research, York University, 1973.

60. *Annual Report to Parliament on Future Immigration Levels* (Ottawa: Employment and Immigration Canada, 1987).

61. W. Benjamin, *Reflections, Essays, Aphorisms, Autobiographical Writings* (New York: Schocken, 1986).

62. *Saskatchewan Multicultural Magazine* 6 (3) (Fall 1987): 1; *La Voce del Congress* (February 1988), open letter from National Council of Italian Canadians presidents to the prime minister expressing misgivings about the Meech Lake Accord; "Meech threatens rights, Jewish group says", *Toronto Star*, 24 February 1988, A2; "Peterson rejects demand for official bilingualism", *Toronto Star*, 18 February 1988.

63. Remarks of representative of Ontario Coalition for Language Rights in *Minutes of Proceeding and Evidence of the Standing Committee on Multiculturalism*, House of Commons Issue, no. 11 (December 1987).

64. *The Hamilton Spectator*, 15 April 1987, A7.

65. *Canadian Ethnic Studies/Etudes ethniques au Canada*, special issue: *The Green Paper on Immigration* 7 (1) (1975). See especially P. Cappon, "The Green Paper: Immigration as a Tool of Profit", and G. Singh Paul, "The Green Paper and Third World Immigrants, A Subjective Analysis."

POEMS

BLUEBERRIES

It took the better half of a day
to reach the woods and piggery
up beyond the Lynn road
blueberrying with Capt.
He knew the route, the sun,
prickly shrubs and soggy spots.
He knew the granite outcroppings
beneath the berry bushes
the snakes nesting there –
garter, milk, and copperhead.
He overturned the stones with sticks
making startled humus steam
and baby snakes wriggle
like green tendrils at low tide
of shorewall seaweed.

Beyond the ledge was the piggery fence.
Sows and swill, the farmer's share
of Salem's scavenger economy.
The sun made us giddy, the brambles stung
we dreamed Capt.'s tales of bears and lynx,
and so a grunting sow, a piglet's squeal,
a towhee rustling through the leaves
made the stooping berrypickers freeze.
My sister and I believed in bears
in Salem's woods.
The old man's stories made us surer,
gave circumstance and color to the dream.
The fear we knew to be untrue,
for what they didn't convert,
the Puritans drove away or slew,
and that included beasts as well as men.

Then to show our own descent,
our links in time and space to them.
We threw the little snakes by handfuls
as morsels for the hungry sows
propitiating bears and
exorcizing woods.
Making the ledge
forever safe for blueberrying.

MANHATTAN WIND

Once five years ago a wind
off the Verazzano straits
abated for me, or perhaps it
only parted for us,
near Battery Park.
Derelicts stood up and grinned
and brokers paused.
Ferry-bound commuters
leaned into the Park,
and the woman at my side became
all women, a sign
of the good ways of god.
Then the gale closed in again,
tearing eyes and blurring vision.

That same Manhattan wind
sixty city blocks dirtier
now whips at the skirts of
prostitutes on the corners
at the south edge of the Park.
It ripples through the bazaar wares
that deep black Haitians hawk
along the avenues
as it slips past the too white legs
of the hustlers.
And everyone on the island is whore in the wind
and virgin in the calm.

BICOASTAL MUSING

There's a feel to a day I've never felt here.
a breeze that once – in memory or dream –
caressed down on a young boy's cheek.
Touch of the wavy scilla or sea anemone
come ashore as shiver of delight.
Braille signal of a foghorn unsounded
in Salem's morning sun.

The Prairie starts at Schenectady,
all alluvial soil and manifest destiny.
The seabreeze stops east of there.
And its western mate beats softly on the Sierra's face.
Between them lies the vast cemetary
where those born to the sea imagine
phantom winds upon their cheeks.

Coming North

Once in St. Paul
by the Amtrak station
in a stand of dry sumac
I heard them sing
"Old Sam Peabody"
Rebel badinage rather
than melody,
a charivari for America

Now strangling on the shibboleth
"O sweet Canada"
slatey juncoes leap the
borderline.
Picking nervously at the moraine,
they send stray sounds of
a migrant lullaby
ubi panis, ibi patria.

I've never found again
that Salem sun
which slanted into
my child's alley
turning old brick lambent
and small boy's thoughts
to swimming off

Forest River rocks
Perhaps my eyes have grown weaker
for leaving the coast
It is wrong to
criticize spring
for being better than winter
but not so good
as springs gone
forever

How lugubrious
that old men watch their
passing
by tenderly
evoking their children selves
I'll welcome this spring sun
with Ch'en Yu Yi
and try to pretend it isn't
shade.

who could not capture
birds in his spring garden
with a net of prosody

My books are always forthcoming
I'm seriously short on plot
I enjoy the agony of writing
while suburbanly free from want

Next to my bed
various Yiddische tagebuchs
or an Armeno-American letter-writer
to teach me the pain
of ancestry
to lift me over the
supermarkets and lawns
to people who had a plot

I need to be seized
by an Amazon lady
who'll ply me with
Bushmill's and praise
Who'll make me write
as her love slave
prose on the ways of our days

She'll free me from being effete
from a sense of a lack
of effect
They'll hail me as a
late bloomer
(or is it a Daedalus)
and buy me the villa in Antibes

In Kyoto they spare one
vacuity
while hunting the narrative thread
Give me a language
of ideograms
with being and feeling for plot
with mountains and streams
as stories
with black on white paper
beautiful
no matter how banal the thought

EUROPE - SPRING 1984
with images too concrete and precise for prosody

H Block is Ireland's Auschwitz
cries a limerick cement wall
to the dirty train passing
A fact without lilt, a slogan without rhyme
Sad shadow of graffiti on the Gianicolo
Palestina libera
and Carabinieri guard a synagogue
with flack jackets for Christian armour
Buttiamo al mare
le basi americane
posters in Trastevere promise
Silkwood or a Baez concert
Irlanda libera
and bones found near Armagh
may be those of British intelligence officer
says the Irish Countrymen
winner of four blues at Oxford
for rowing, then Grenadiers, a mother in Devon
Died like a soldier say the provos
who tortured him
a terrible beauty, the troubles, poetry that rhymes
and graffiti that doesn't
H Block is Ireland's Auschwitz
and the comitato anonimo per la
controinformazione rules the land.

In the piazza San Silvestro
a Carabiniere on a motorcycle
pulls over the #75 autobus
and yells poetastro discende
I am under arrest for lack of ideology
I have been denounced by the stray cats
in the ruins of the Roman baths.
They heard me laughing over pasta at La Carbonara
They heard me misquote Gramsci or Togliatti or Il Duce
I am trivializing straniero born beyond the limes
indifferent to culture, an exploiting borghese

a cultureless Nordamericano, an oriundo d'Italia
turned barbarian, by my silence confederate
of Greek colonels, strangeloves, and cowboys.
I will not be killed but rehabilitated by a
thousand potent slogans daubed across the ochre
walls of a vanished Empire.
Israele assassino
autonomia proletaria
Kissinger ha ucciso, no more, no more, ma piu pasta asciutta per piacere.

In the Crowsnest Pass

We came up through Spokane
the first time
A section boss, Irish
name of Fafferty
had used Italians before
he gave us work
better than Dukhobors or
Romanians he said
That's if you get the right type
northerners
men who've laid track before
in Turkey, Russia, Tunisia
State of Washington or Oregon

We knew it would be cold but
but most made enough in summer
to head for Italy in fall
Some stayed on
for the work at the smelter
That's how Joe Agnone died
the flange snapped and he
flew like a diver
from the top of the dam

The Cristoforo Colombo should
have buried him
we had the box made anyway
there must be a cortege,
the soci agreed
Flowers even in winter and marching
with tricolore and black cocards
Agnone wouldn't be disgraced
The box of course was empty
The wife in Abruzzi wanted his
body back
we couldn't help
Our medico dei soci, a doctor
an educated man
wrote to her how Joe loved

the Rockies
and wished his body there
We followed the empty box
to our camposanto
just a coulee with an entrance cross
Someone said Joe was floating
subterraneanly in the streams
through the mountains,
down the Columbia
to the Adriatico
He would get home
but it would have been warmer to die in steerage

OLD TIMERS

(in Italian Anziani or I
Vecchi) (or only outsiders can admire the
via vecchia)

Un vecchio, an old muck farmer, withering
among his vegetables
Un anziana, someone's nonna, tats lace
with arthritic, automatic hands
Me ne frego for the via vecchia!
Huddled in famiglia or ethnos, finding
solace in a certainty of seasons,
Pulverized by their fathers' ovine adages
so that they fertilize the vines and
compost the barnyards.
Io non sono di loro, I am not one
of them, not content to ripen and
fall, or turn to burnt umbrian clay
for the mason's trowel.

NEW HAVEN LOCAL

A whine
to signal a man
trying to speak
over the sound of heavy machinery
Some mills
asbestos shingles
on tenements
flashing by, the modern replicas
the Sound's
elemental coast

Local tickets please
to maintain rusty nails
cut through marsh
and redbrick mausoleums
of Yankee brass mills fueled with
Bohunk and Sicilian bones
America's charcoal slow burnt
first across the sea

Hard to celebrate
Bridgeport sacrificed
in two wars
immigrants killed in battle
on the home front, someone else's,
to make Darien safe for
manhattans and shingles new cut
and brass objects.

Two men only I've seen
move like that
One was Milosz at the
doorway
of a victorian library
of admiring Poles
The other Percy Humphreys
cornet in hand
outside Preservation Hall
One was small and pale
and Slav
The other graceful and fat
and Black
Each man suppressed a sigh
seeing their public
As if to say father why dost thou
grant the burden
of making me able to sing
to my people
In the room they take on
cruci-calm
They are not the singers
just vehicles of
the song.

Bibliography

BOOKS:

Robert F. Harney, ed. *Gathering Place: Peoples and Neighbourhoods of Toronto.* Toronto: Multicultural History Society of Ontario, 1985. 220pp.

Robert F. Harney. *Dalla Frontiera alle Little Italies: Gli Italiani in Canada 1800-1945.* Rome: Bonacci, 1984. 313pp. (Winner of the Francesco Bressani Prize, 1986)

Robert F. Harney and Vincenza Scarpaci, eds. *Little Italies in North America.* Toronto: Multicultural History Society of Ontario, 1981. 210pp.

Robert F. Harney, Betty Boyd Caroli and Lydio Tomasi, eds. *The Italian Immigrant Woman in North America.* Toronto: Multicultural History Society of Ontario, 1978. 386pp.

Robert F. Harney and Harold Troper. *Immigrants: Portrait of the Urban Experience.* Toronto: Van Nostrand, 1975. 212pp. (Winner of the Toronto Book Award)

OCCASIONAL PAPERS:

Italians in North America. Toronto: Multicultural History Society of Ontario, 1982. 47pp.

Toronto: Canada's New Cosmopolite. Toronto: Multicultural History Society of Ontario, 1981. 22pp.

Italians in Canada. Toronto: Multicultural History Society of Ontario, 1978. 27pp.

Oral Testimony and Ethnic Studies. Toronto: Multicultural History Society of Ontario, 1978. 14pp.

ARTICLES:

"Preface." *In Portugese Migration in Global Perspective.* Edited by David Higgs. Toronto: Multicultural History Society of Ontario, 1990. pp. ix-x.

"Caboto and Other Italian-Canadian Parentela." In *Arrangiarsi: The Italian Immigration Experience in Canada.* Edited by R. Perin and F. Sturino. Montreal: Guernica, 1989. pp. 37-61.

"The Immigrant City." In *Vice Versa. Magazine transculturel,* (Montreal), no. 24 (Spring 1988), pp. 4-6.

"The Italian Immigration and the Frontiers of Western Civilization." In *The Italian Immigrant Experience.* Edited by J. Potestio and A. Pucci. Thunder Bay, Ontario: CIHA, 1988. pp. 1-28.

"Se si dovesse scrivere una storia di Toronto Italia del dopoguerra." In Ministero degli Affari Esteri, ed., Atti del Convegno, *Le societa in transizione: italiani e italomaericani negli anni ottanta.* Rome: Ministero degli Affari Esteri, 1988. pp. 376-402.

"The Palmetto and the Maple Leaf: Patterns of Canadian Migration to Florida." In *Shades of the Sunbelt: Essays on Ethnicity, Race, and the Urban South.* Edited by R.M. Miller and G.E. Pozzetta. Connecticut: Greenwood Press, 1988. pp. 21-40. (Also University of Tennessee paperback)

"Political Discourse and Toronto's Slavic Ethnies." In *Multiethnic Studies in Uppsala: Essays presented in Honour of Sven Gustavsson*. Edited by I. Svanberg and M. Tyden. Uppsala, Sweden: Uppsala University, 1988. pp. 31-46.

"'So Great A Heritage as Ours' Immigration and the Survival of the Canadian Polity." In *Daedalus. Journal of the American Academy of Arts and Sciences* (Cambridge, MA), vol. 117, no. 4 (Fall 1988), "In Search of Canada," pp. 51-97.

"Karaim — an afterward." In *Les Karaites en Europe*. By S. Sisman. Uppsala, Sweden: Centre of Multiethnic Research, 1987.

"E Pluribus Unum: Louis Adamic and the Meaning of Ethnic History." In *Journal of Ethnic Studies* (Spring 1986). It also appeared in Polish in the journal of the Polonian Institute of the University of Krakow.

"Preface." In *The Finnish Baker's Daughters*. By Aili Grönlund Schneider. Toronto: Multicultural History Society of Ontario, 1986. pp. 9-10.

"Preface." In *Looking into My Sister's Eyes: an Exploration in Women's History*. Edited by Jean Burnet. Toronto: Multicultural History Society of Ontario, 1986. pp. ix-x.

"Ethnicity and Neighbourhoods." In *Gathering Place: Peoples and Neighbourhoods of Toronto, 1834-1945* (1985), pp. 5-24.

"Italophobia: English-speaking Malady." In *Studi Emigrazione (Brescia, Morcelliana)*, vol. XXII, no. 77 (1985), pp. 6-44.

"Entwined Fortunes: Multiculturalism and Ethnic Studies in Canada." *Siirtolaisuus - Migration*, vol. 3 (1984), pp. 68-94. Special decennium issue of the quarterly of the Institute of Migration Studies - Turku, Finland.

"Suspicion of Italo-Americans has Deep Historical Roots." *Baltimore Sun* (Section D: Perspective), 26 August 1984, p. 1. Reprinted in *Justice, Bulletin of the Sons of Italy* (Winter 1984); and also reprinted in *Notizie della Stella: Bulletin of the American Italian Historical Association*, vol. VIII, no. 4 (1984).

"Ethnic Archival and Library Materials in Canada: Problems of Bibliographic Control and Preservation." *Ethnic Forum (Kent, Ohio)*, vol. 2 (Fall 1982), pp. 3-31.

"Franco-Americans and Ethnic Studies: Notes on a Mill Town." In *The Quebec and Acadian Diaspora in North America*. Edited by Raymond Breton and Pierre Savard. Toronto: Multicultural History Society of Ontario, 1982. pp.77-88.

"General Editor's Preface." In *The Gordon C. Eby Diaries, 1911-13: Chronicle of a Mennonite Farmer*. Edited by James Nyce. Toronto: Multicultural History Society of Ontario, 1982. p. 3.

"Preface." In *The Quebec and Acadian Diaspora in North America*. Edited by Raymond Breton and Pierre Savard. Toronto: Multicultural History Society of Ontario, 1982. pp. vii-xi.

"Preface." In *The Finnish Diaspora I: Canada, South America, Africa, Australia and Sweden*. Edited by Michael G. Karni. Toronto: Multicultural History Society of Ontario, 1981. pp. ix-x.

"Preface." In *Finnish Diaspora II: United States*. Edited by Michael G. Karni. Toronto: Multicultural History Society of Ontario, 1981. pp. vii-viii.

"Toronto's Little Italy, 1885-1945." In *Little Italies in North America*. Edited by Robert F. Harney and J. Vincenza Scarpaci. Toronto: Multicultural History Society of Ontario, 1981. pp. 41-62.

"Unique Features of Fraternal Records." In *Records of Ethnic Fraternal Benefit Associations in the United States: Essays and Inventories*. St. Paul, Minnesota: Immigration History Research Center, 1981. pp. 15-24.

"The Padrone System and Sojourners in the Canadian North 1885-1920." In *Pane e Lavoro: the Italian American Working Class*. Edited by George Pozzetta. Toronto: Multicultural History Society of Ontario, 1980. pp. 119-37.

"Ethnic Heritages and Multicultural Futures." In *Ethnic Heritages and Horizons: An Expanding Awareness*. By the Ethnic Affairs Committee of Baltimore, 1979. p. 15.

"The Italian Community in Toronto." In *Two Nations, Many Cultures*. Edited by Jean L. Elliott. Toronto: Prentice-Hall, 1979. pp. 220-36.

"Italians in Canada." In *The Culture of Italy, Medieval to Modern*. Edited by S.B. Chandler and J.A. Molinaro. Toronto: Griffin House, 1979. Also published as an occasional paper by the Multicultural History Society of Ontario, 1978.

"Montreal's King of Italian Labour: a Case Study of Padronism." In *Labour/Le Travailleur: Journal of Canadian Labour Studies* (St. John's, Nfld.), vol. 4 (1979), pp. 57-84.

"Uomini Senza Donne: Emigrati Italiani in Canada, 1885-1930." In *Nordamericana: Canadiana. Storia E Storiografia Canadese,* vol. 5 (1979), pp. 67-96.

"Boarding and Belonging." In *Urban History Review* (Toronto), vol. 2 (October 1978), pp. 8-37. Reprinted in *The Canadian City: Essays in Social and Urban History*. Edited by A. Artibise and G. Stelter. 2nd rev. ed. Ottawa: Carleton University Press, 1984.

"Introduction." In *Urban History Review* (Ottawa), vol. 2 (October 1978), pp. 3-7. By Robert F. Harney and Harold Troper.

"Men Without Women: Italian Migrants in Canada, 1885-1930." In *The Italian Immigrant Woman in North America*. Edited by Betty Boyd Caroli, Robert F. Harney and Lydio Tomasi. Toronto: Multicultural History Society of Ontario, 1978. Reprinted in *Canadian Ethnic Studies* (Calgary), vol. XI, no. 1 (1979), pp. 29-47. Also reprinted in *Twentieth Century Canada: a Reader*. Edited by Irving Abella. Toronto: McGraw-Hill Ryerson, 1986.

"The New Canadians and Their Lives in Toronto." In *Canadian Geographic Journal* (April-May 1978), pp. 20-27.

"The Commerce of Migration." In *Canadian Ethnic Studies*, vol. 9 (1977), pp. 42-53.

"A Note on Sources in Urban and Immigrant History." In *Canadian Ethnic Studies*, vol. 9 (1977), pp. 60-76.

"From Central Asia to the Soo: the Adventure of Italian Migration." In *Mosaico* (São Paulo, March 1976), pp. 18-21.

"Frozen Wastes: the State of Italian Canadian Studies." In *Perspectives in Italian Immigration and Ethnicity*. Proceedings of the symposium held at Casa Italiana, Columbia University, 1976. Edited by S.M. Tomasi. New York: Center for Migration Studies, 1977.

"The Italian Experience in America." In *A Handbook for Teachers of Italian*. Edited by Anthony Mollica. American Association of Teachers of Italian, 1976, pp. 219-41.

"The Italians." In *Canadian Family Tree*. New edition Ottawa, 1976.

"Ambiente and Social Class in North American Little Italies." *Canadian Review of Studies in Nationalism* (Charlottetown, P.E.I.), vol. 2 (1975), pp. 208-24.

"Chiaroscuro: Italians in Toronto, 1885-1915." In *Italian Americana* (Buffalo, New York), vol. I (Spring 1975), pp. 143- 67.

"The Padrone and the Immigrant." *Canadian Review of American Studies* (Toronto), vol. 5 (Fall 1974), pp. 101-18.

CONTRIBUTIONS TO:

Polyphony: The Bulletin of the Multicultural History Society of Ontario.

"Introduction." *Polyphony: The Bulletin of the Multicultural History Society of Ontario*, vol. 11 (Double Issue 1989), "Heritage Languages in Ontario," pp. 1-12.

"Preface." *Polyphony: The Bulletin of the Multicultural History Society of Ontario*, vol. 10 (Double Issue 1988), "Ukrainians in Ontario," pp. 1-2.

"A History of the Multicultural History Society." *Polyphony: The Bulletin of the Multicultural History Society of Ontario*, vol. 9, no. 1 (1987), "Commemorative Issue," pp. 3-20.

"Preface." *Polyphony: The Bulletin of the Multicultural History Society of Ontario*, vol. 7, no. 2 (Fall/Winter 1986), "Italians in Ontario," pp. 1-6.

"Italophobia: an English-speaking Malady?" *Polyphony: The Bulletin of the Multicultural History Society of Ontario*, vol. 7, no. 2 (Fall/Winter 1986), "Italians in Ontario," pp. 54-59.

"How to Write a History of Postwar Toronto Italia." *Polyphony: The Bulletin of the Multicultural History Society of Ontario*, vol. 7, no. 2 (Fall/Winter 1986), "Italians in Ontario," pp. 61-65.

"Homo Ludens and Ethnicity." *Polyphony: The Bulletin of the Multicultural History Society of Ontario*, vol. 7, no. 1 (Spring/Summer 1985), "Sports and Ethnicity," pp. 1-12.

"Toronto's People." *Polyphony: The Bulletin of the Multicultural History Society of Ontario*, vol. 6, no. 1 (Spring/Summer 1984), "Toronto's People," pp. 1-14.

"Immigrant Theatre." *Polyphony: The Bulletin of the Multicultural History Society of Ontario,* vol. 5, no. 2 (Fall/Winter 1983), pp. 1-14.

"The Ethnic Press in Ontario." *Polyphony: The Bulletin of the Multicultural History Society of Ontario*, vol. 4, no. 1 (Spring/Summer 1982), pp. 3-14.

"Emigrants, the Written Word and Trust." *Polyphony: The Bulletin of the Multicultural History Society of Ontario*, vol. 3, no. 1 (Winter 1981), pp. 3-8.

"Records of the Mutual Benefit Society: a Source for Ethnocultural Studies." *Polyphony: The Bulletin of the Multicultural History Society of Ontario*, vol. 2, no. 1 (Winter 1979), pp. 5-18.

"Religion and Ethnocultural Communities." *Polyphony: The Bulletin of the Multicultural History Society of Ontario*, vol. 1, no. 2 (Summer 1978), pp. 3-10.

Printed in Canada